The term of Rebel is no certain mark of disgrace. All the great assertors of liberty, the saviors of their Country, the benefactors of mankind in all ages, have been called Rebels.

—Charles J. Fox[1]

---

[1] Charles James Fox PC (1749 – 1806) was a prominent British Whig statesman whose parliamentary career spanned thirty-eight years of the late eighteenth and early nineteenth centuries. Fox became a prominent and staunch opponent of King George III, whom he regarded as an aspiring tyrant; he supported the revolutionaries across the Atlantic, taking up the habit of dressing in the colors of George Washington's army.

The statement by Fox was in response to Lord North of the British Parliament referring to the fallen General Richard Montgomery (1738-1775) as a "rebel." Montgomery honorably served in the British Army during the French & Indian War, later retiring in New York. When the Revolutionary War broke out Montgomery sided with the American Rebels and was commissioned as a Brigadier General in the Continental Army. Montgomery was killed at the Battle of Quebec on 31 Dec 1775.

Private Joseph R. Stonebraker
Company C, First Maryland Cavalry, C. S. A.

JOSEPH R. STONEBRAKER

Company C, First Maryland Cavalry,

Maryland Line, Army of Northern Virginia

Original work published by
Wynkoop Hallenbeck Crawford Company, Printers, New York and Albany, 1899

This annotated and revised edition published by
Washington County Historical Trust, Inc., Hagerstown, Maryland, 2016

Published by
Washington County Historical Trust, Inc.
P. O. Box 2021
Hagerstown, Maryland 21702
www.washingtoncountyhistoricaltrust.org

Copyright © 2016 by Washington County Historical Trust
All rights reserved.

Original work published 1899
WCHT 2016, First Edition

ISBN 0972571515
ISBN 978-0-9725715-1-7

All rights reserved. No part of this book may be reproduced, stored in a retrieval system, or transmitted in any form by any means without prior written permission of the publisher.

Readers may submit corrections and comments by visiting
www.washingtoncountyhistoricaltrust.org

This book was produced by volunteer efforts of members of the Washington County Historical Trust. All proceeds will be invested in preservation efforts to help identify, evaluate, preserve, and revitalize the historic, archaeological, and cultural resources of Washington County, Maryland.

Printed in Washington County, Maryland.

Contents

FORWARD – WASHINGTON COUNTY HISTORICAL TRUST	7
INTRODUCTION – DENNIS E. FRYE	9
PREFACE – JOSEPH R. STONEBRAKER	13
LIST OF [ORIGINAL] ILLUSTRATIONS	14
INTRODUCTORY – GENERAL BRADLEY T. JOHNSON	17
SCHAFFER'S	21
STONEBRAKER'S	29
HAPPINESS WITHOUT CONTENTMENT	30
THE FATHER OF WATERS	33
ANTIETAM VALLEY	34
FUNKSTOWN	35
ANTIETAM CANAL COMPANY	37
RACE OF MILLERS	39
OLD ENGLISH CHAPEL	40
STRANGER THAN FICTION	41
CORK	42
ANCIENT CUSTOM	44
SCRATCH	46
MILITARY	47
HAUNTED HILL	48
OUR EASTERN HOME	49
BEAR BAIT	50
SPRING TIME	51
PIERCE AND KING	52
COW BOY	53
HARVEST TIME	54
CORN HUSKING	55
TEMPTATION	56
CHOLERA'S APPEARANCE IN AMERICA	57
JOHN BROWN	61
BRAVE BUT TOOTHLESS	66
TOW BOY	68
POLITICAL PRISONER	71
WANDERING	80
RETREAT FROM GETTYSBURG	81
BATTLE OF FUNKSTOWN	86
BORDER STATE	99
BRUTAL TREATMENT	100
OFF FOR DIXIE	103
BATTLE OF WINCHESTER	108
FISHER'S HILL	110
BATTLE OF CEDAR CREEK	116
SOLDIER	121

PETERSBURG TO APPOMATTOX	147
HIGH BRIDGE	151
THREE DESPERATE MEN.	152
A BRAVE FEDERAL OFFICER.	153
APPOMATTOX COURT HOUSE	157
LAST CHARGE AND THE LAST MAN KILLED IN THE ARMY OF NORTHERN VIRGINIA	158
A NARROW ESCAPE	164
RENDEZVOUS	166
TO THE GALLANT BAND WHO CLAIM THIS SONG	168
DISCHARGE	171
IN THE MESHES	177
RECONSTRUCTION	179
EPILOGUE	181
LEGEND OF FUNKSTOWN POEM	218
BATTLE OF FUNKS-TOWN POEM	221
INDEX	246

A Rebel of '61

Foreward

Reading the first-hand account of an average person who lived amid the swirl of momentous events can be a refreshing, even striking, experience. Rebel of '61 by Joseph R. Stonebraker and a companion volume, War Reminiscences by Angela Kirkham Davis, are designed to appeal to everyone from casual readers to history buffs looking for new insights.

Both authors were citizens of the same deeply divided small town during the Civil War, just a few miles from bloody Antietam battlefield. Violence and emotion arising from opposing sympathies throughout their rural county split their lives. Located in the border state of Maryland, within a northern continuation of the strife-torn Shenandoah Valley, they endured the presence of both Union and Confederate troops.

Although loyal to different sides, each author writes of simultaneous fear and respect for those of contrasting opinions in the surrounding community. Each perceives himself to be in a threatened minority. Each senses underlying hostility from people they encounter in their daily routine as well as from the alternating armies. Indeed, lives in exile play a role in both narratives.

We have attempted to illuminate these tales and provide context for modern readers by supplying illustrations as well as explanatory footnotes, in addition to those found with the original text. For those not familiar with 19th-century historical allusions, we have attempted definitions that should help readers better understand and enjoy the original author's text. For Civil War aficionados, we offer fresh local color such as excerpts from a newly discovered cache of the *Hagerstown Evening Globe*, the nearest newspaper of record. All in all, these volumes offer fresh insight into the Civil War period and indeed, mid-19th-century life, in a fashion that no secondary account or history book can quite match.

All proceeds beyond the expense of publication are used to encourage and promote the preservation of historic structures in Washington County, Maryland, the main setting for these books. A modest price, a meaningful cause, and a munificent read—please enjoy, as we did.

Research and footnotes by Sandra Izer, editing by Patricia Schooley, David Schooley, Merry Stinson, Jean Izer, and Dr. Steven Hatleberg, and members of the Washington County Historical Trust.

—Washington County Historical Trust

Introduction

Curiosity launched Joseph Stonebraker into the Civil War. Not the curiosity of soldiering. Nor a morbid fascination with a battlefield. Instead, the ascension of a hot-air balloon attracted the eighteen-year-old lad and, in an instant, he was pinned in a Yankee prison.

Stonebraker and his Funkstown family epitomized the uncertainties and the dangers of day-to-day life in a community trapped between North and South. The jaws of Civil War pinched Washington County, Maryland. Burdened by its borders—the Mason-Dixon Line and the Potomac River—Washington County became geographically isolated, its boundaries literally separating the Union from the Confederacy. Its unfortunate location forced the county to host the Battle of Antietam, the bloodiest single day in American history. For residents, 1,500 days of civil war ensnared Washington County's captive citizens.

This tangled web of war wreaked havoc on the Stonebraker family. As admitted Southern sympathizers, they were a minority in Washington County, predominated by Union supporters. As a result, Joseph and his family were persecuted, punished and plundered. Martial law ruled supreme in Maryland, and its tentacles stretched and squeezed virtually every aspect of existence. Trade was contained. Travel was confined. Talk was controlled. If one dared question Northern authority, consequences could be catastrophic.

Thus explains Joseph's title, Rebel of '61. The headline infers service in the Confederate army, but Joseph does not become a Southern soldier until the summer of 1864, more than three years after the war commences. For Stonebraker and his family, rebel has a deeper and more profound meaning—a mission of resistance and refusal.

"All the world knew where they [the Stonebrakers] stood as long as their tongues could wag," Joseph declared. But this unwavering commitment to Southern sentiment cost the family dearly. Three months into the war, Joseph's father was forced to resign as postmaster of Funkstown because "some of our Union friends reported us to be Rebels, and intimated that we would destroy the letters instead of mailing them." Near Christmas, 1861, the barn of Joseph's uncle was burned. The following spring, his father's C & O Canal boat—full of wheat sold to him by Virginia farmers—was seized by Union soldiers and purposely toppled over Dam Number 4, resulting in a loss of $4,500 (the average yearly income in 1860 was $300).

The first year of war had ravaged the Stonebraker family. The nearest battlefield, however, was days from Washington County and Funkstown. Then Joseph experienced his first battle…not at the battlefield, but at the balloon ascension. Young Stonebraker had traveled just a few miles to Hagerstown to witness this modern marvel, when suddenly, without provocation or warning, Union soldiers surrounded and arrested him. "Take the oath or go to jail," the bluecoats demanded. Joseph refused. Promptly incarcerated as a "political prisoner," the youngster of eighteen years eventually ended up in a horse stable at Baltimore's Fort McHenry. On three occasions, Joseph declined to take the oath of allegiance to the United States, stating "I had never committed any overt act against the Government, and thought it both unfair and unreasonable to be required to take the oath." After nearly three months in prison, Joseph swallowed his moral pride and pronounced the oath before Union authorities, although he admitted he had no intention of respecting it.

As a result of his imprisonment, Joseph missed the September 1862 Battle of Antietam in Washington County. He did witness the county's next great action, however, during the Gettysburg Campaign. On July 10, 1863, "from the garret of Mrs. Keller's house," Stonebraker watched the Battle of Funkstown. The battle narrative he shared was not his own. Instead, he cobbled together after-action Union and Confederate reports to explain the battle he observed. Although the readers may be disappointed that Stonebraker did not describe the battle in his own words—the very first battle he witnessed——in essence, he attained a credibility that many post-war writers lacked: an acknowledgment that he had no idea what was happening before him. He did know where and on whose farms the fighting was occurring, however, and his notations of local names and places identified the battlegrounds for posterity.

One year after Gettysburg, a portion of the Confederate army once again returned to Washington County. During the first week of July 1864, Jubal Early led the corps formerly commanded by Stonewall Jackson across the Potomac River near Shepherdstown, West Virginia. Much of the local population panicked, especially afraid that the Southerners had come to seize their horses. Stonebraker helped lead a team into the mountains, where he "joined quite a number of refugees who had assembled there from all parts of the County." The terror soon subsided, as General Early turned his army toward Washington, advancing closer to the Union capital than any other Confederate force. Early's expedition convinced Joseph "the time had now arrived for me to consummate a determination. . . to cast my lot with the Southern people."

The final third of Stonebraker's recollections cover his experiences as a soldier in the Confederate army. His words are crisp, and his story is dramatic. He details dates, places, and names with clarity and accuracy, indicating he likely uses a war-time diary as his principal source. His thoughts are poignant and immediate as he relives his role in the final months of the Confederacy.

Young Stonebraker chose a bad time to join the Southern army. About the same time Joseph was walking south twenty-six miles to officially become a rebel, the Union high command assigned Major General Philip H. Sheridan the task of wiping out Jubal Early's Confederate army operating in the Shenandoah Valley. When Stonebraker first joined Early's force, he linked up with his uncle, Captain A. S. Stonebraker of the 2nd Virginia Infantry, who was serving as an ordnance officer in the famous Stonewall Brigade. From his seat with the ordnance trains during the fall of 1864, Joseph witnessed three catastrophic battles—Third Winchester, Fisher's Hill, and Cedar Creek—each a smashing Union triumph. As the Confederate army in the Shenandoah Valley disintegrated, Sheridan commenced burning the mills, fields, and barns of the Valley. With Early's army practically destroyed, Joseph determined to fight on, this time in the cavalry.

For students of the Civil War, Stonebraker's experiences as a Confederate cavalryman during the war's closing months are most interesting and intriguing because his detailed accounts help fill a void—one resulting from a dearth of official reports concerning Confederate operations during this period. Stonebraker's record of movements, descriptions of engagements and his witnessing of significant events make his observations invaluable to Confederate military literature. Of particular interest is his description of the retreat from Petersburg to Appomattox and his involvement in the last stand of the Army of Northern Virginia.

Stonebraker's account during the period following Appomattox also carries importance. Joseph does not surrender at Appomattox but instead joins other Confederates in their attempt to link with a Rebel army operating in North Carolina. His travels and travails during the month following Appomattox are dramatic and suspenseful, finally ending with his surrender near Harrisonburg, Virginia, during the second week of May 1865.

Throughout the diary-like accounts of Stonebraker's cavalry experience, one theme remained constant—the depravation and destitution of the Confederate soldier. Stonebraker's narrative was replete with comments concerning lack of food. "Subsistence was our greatest trouble." "Rations for the men and forage for the horses came at irregular intervals." "My stomach had been empty so long that it ceased to feel hungry, but weak and nauseated." In addition to his own hunger, Stonebraker repeatedly commented on the lack of food for his horse. "[T]he horses are in a starving condition," he noted during the late fall of 1864. "A small party from our company stole corn during the night. I am free to confess that I felt like a thief. . . but necessity knows no law; the Government can't feed our animals, and it is steal or walk."

After the war, Joseph found life in Washington County difficult, as many in the community refused to forgive him for his Confederate service. Thus Joseph moved to Baltimore, where his uncle Captain A. S. Stonebraker resided, and he soon prospered as a banker. Baltimore became a haven for hundreds of retired Maryland Confederates. Prior to the war, Baltimore was considered a Southern city, and it proudly claimed itself as the second largest port in the South. When war erupted in April 1861, US volunteers were attacked in Baltimore, forcing the Lincoln Administration to respond with a tight-fisted martial law that drove many Southern supporters out of the city and, ultimately, out of Maryland. Hundreds of men from the Baltimore region crossed into Virginia to serve in the Confederate army, and, when the war ended, to Baltimore they returned. No doubt Joseph Stonebraker felt more comfortable in Baltimore, surrounded by Confederate veterans, than he did at his former home in Washington County.

In 1899, thirty-four years after the war had ended, Stonebraker published his Rebel of '61. Apparently he wrote his reminiscences with no intention of their publication. "I have written. . .[so] that my children may know the part I took in the War between the States, humble though it was." But former Confederate General Bradley T. Johnson, who had organized the first Maryland regiment to fight for the South, convinced Stonebraker his narrative should be published. "It is the record of the honorable service of a gallant young Marylander," General Johnson declared. Johnson was correct. Stonebraker's account of life on the border between North and South, his arrest and confinement as a political prisoner, his witness to military movements in Washington County and the Battle of Funkstown, his role and observations as an aide to an ordnance officer in the Stonewall Brigade and his life as a soldier in the Confederate cavalry make his narrative distinctly unique.

Despite his fascinating story, perhaps Stonebraker's greatest lesson—and his most powerful message—is delivered in this passage: "In those trying times, the writer's family almost suffered martyrdom because of their convictions and, strange as it may seem, the greater the persecution, the firmer the faith. So it has been in all ages and so it will continue until the end of time."

— Dennis E. Frye

Antietam Rest
Burnside's Headquarters (Sep 25 – 6 Oct 1862)

Preface

I have written these Reminiscences that my children may know the part I took in the War between the States, humble though it was.

I am not one of those who half apologize by saying, "We fought for what we believed to be right." I think we fought for what was right—self-government.

My view of the conflict was not so much to protect the right of property in the slaves as it was to maintain the great principle that the Creator was greater than the creature—the States made the Government, and not the Government made the States.

It is now more than thirty years since the conflict ended, and I have never had a regret for any part I took in the strife.

J. R. S.

Baltimore, *April 2,* 1897.

List of Illustrations

The original 1899 edition contained the thirty-nine images listed below. This annotated edition has many added images, photographs, and maps to enhance your understanding of Stonebraker's adventures.

GEN. BRADLEY T. JOHNSON.	16
LOG CABIN BUILT BY ALEX SCHAEFFER IN 1738	20
ROXBURY, JOHN SCHAFFER'S HOMESTEAD, BUILT IN 1782	22
JOHN JOHN SCHAFER AND CATHARINE, HIS ELDEST DAUGHTER	24
MOUNT MORIAH, CATHARINE RENTCH'S HOMESTEAD	25
JOS. STONEBRAKER'S HOMESTEAD, BUILT IN 1783	27
HENRY STONEBRAKER	30
ANGELICA E. STONEBRAKER	31
BIRD'S EYE VIEW OF AN ANCIENT PORTION OF FUNKSTOWN	35
ANTIETAM WOOLEN MILL, DESTROYED BY FIRE, 1834	37
BELOW THE DAM, WHERE THE IRON PIN WAS PLACED	39
SHANTY IN CORK	42
MRS. ANNIE ROSINA JOHNSON	45
OLD GRIST AND SAW MILL, AT MARSH RUN, OPERATED BY SAMUEL SHAFER	48
OLD DISTILLERY, AT MARSH RUN	49
ANTIETAM CREEK AND ISLAND	51
PICKANINNIES	55
HENRY STONEBRAKER'S FUNKSTOWN HOME, 1847	59
MICHAEL STONEBRAKER'S HOMESTEAD, BUILT IN 1804	69
SOLOMON J. KELLER, POLITICAL PRISONER, 1862	73
JOS. E. WILLIAMS, POLITICAL PRISONER, 1862	80
HAUCK'S BARN, RIGHT OF THE CONFEDERATE LINE	89
STOVER'S BARN, CENTER OF THE CONFEDERATE LINE	89
STONEBRAKER'S BARN, LEFT OF THE CONFEDERATE LINE	89

CAPTAIN A. S. STONEBRAKER, A. Q. M.	104
JOS. R. STONEBRAKER, IN CONFEDERATE UNIFORM	121
MARYLAND BATTALION ON THE WAR PATH DECEMBER, 1864, BY ALLEN C. REDWOOD*	133
WILLIAM F. WHARTON, CO C., MARYLAND BATTALION	137
WILLIE REDWOOD, CO C, MARYLAND BATTALION	141
HERMAN HEIMILLER, CO. C, MARYLAND BATTALION	159
LAST CHARGE — MARYLAND BATTALION AT APPOMATTOX, BY ALLEN C REDWOOD*	161
JOHN RIDGELY, COLOR BEARER OF THE MARYLAND BATTALION, C.S.A.	162
JOHN H. HAGER, CO. C, MARYLAND BATTALION	171
THOS. SHERVIN, CO. K, MARYLAND BATTALION	172
THOS. H. GROVE, CO. C, MARYLAND BATTALION	173
GROUP	176
MRS. MARY B STONEBRAKER	178
JUSTICE	180

*The writer wishes to call especial attention to the War scenes of this Volume on pages 133, 161, sketched by that clever artist Mr. Allen C. Redwood, who was a peerless Soldier of the Maryland Battalion, and familiar with the scenes that he has portrayed.[2]

---

2   Allen Christian Redwood and family, see footnote 341.

A Rebel of '61

Introductory

When the writer of these Reminiscences sent them to me a short time ago for my perusal of the War portion, I was so well pleased with it, that I insisted, and prevailed on him to print it.

I wanted this done, first, because it is the record of the honorable service of a gallant young Marylander, and second, because it is a graphic description of the motives which stirred the chivalry of Maryland, in that glowing epoch, and their experiences in the bivouac, and in battle, in camp and on the march.

Several diaries were kept by the boys in the ranks. I know of but one by a commissioned officer. But a pocket diary carried over the heart after a long day's fight, or a march, received the impressions of the writer, as he lay tired and hungry by the fire—impressions hot with enthusiasm and radiant with the joy of battle.

I wish more of them could be published, for they will help to do justice to the motives and the conduct of those Marylanders who left their homes to dare and die for the sake of a great principle, and to help their friends.

I repeat and reiterate and emphasize the fact that the Maryland Confederate was the most chivalric, the most sentimental, the most devoted knight that ever rode to battle, and to death, since Peter led the chivalry of Christendom to the rescue of the Holy Sepulchre.

Not twenty men in the Maryland Line had any interest in Slavery as a property interest. In fact they did not care one way or the other.

They detested the abolitionists, who for a generation had been stirring up "battle and murder and sudden death" through midnight insurrection, and arson, and rape, and had been killing Marylanders, who pursued their property into the northern States.

The murder of Kennedy and Gorsuch at Christiana in Pennsylvania,[3] where they were set upon by a mob, when in pursuit of runaway negroes, and the foray of John Brown in Virginia, had burnt a deep brand into the hearts of the boys of those days, and when the "Black Republicans" were marching into Virginia,[4] to do what John Brown failed so ignominiously to

---

[3] James Kennedy of Hagerstown, MD died as result of mob injuries he sustained on 2 Jun 1847, at Carlisle, PA while attempting to reclaim his runaway slaves. Kennedy and Howard Hollingsworth were assaulted by an angry crowd as they attempted to leave Carlisle with their slaves in the "McClintock Riots" named after Dickinson College Professor John McClintock, who was charged with inciting the riot. Three years later the passage of the Fugitive Slave Act in 1850 made it legal for slave owners to pursue escaped slaves into any state or territory in the union.

Edward Gorsuch (1798-1851), a wealthy landowner from Baltimore County, MD, was killed by a vigilante fugitive slave group on 11 Sep 1851, in Christiana, Lancaster County, PA while trying to reclaim his runaway slaves. Sometimes called the "Christiana Riot," Gorsuch's death marked the first bloodshed in resistance to the Fugitive Slave Law of 1850. Harrold, Stanley, *Border War: Fighting Over Slavery before the Civil War* (University of NC Press, 2010), 109-110, 153-154, 181-183.

[4] At the Illinois debates of 1858, Stephen Douglas read articles from a Republican party group opposing slavery expansion and the fugitive slave laws, calling them "Black Republicans." The Black Republican Party was believed by most southerners to advocate abolition and black equality.

do, they fired up, as the author of this diary shows, and with the blessing of their mothers, hot, loving and tender, they crossed the Potomac, at every point between pickets, from Oakland to Point Lookout, by the ford, and ferry, and joined their friends and neighbors.[5]

As I look back after all these years, the thing grows on me and amazes me more and more—such an outpouring of devotion and love never has been seen in all the tide of time.

The women, everywhere from Cumberland to Snow Hill, sent their sons, their brothers, their lovers, "across the river," and they had no interest in the issue, visible, tangible.[6]

There was no reason in it, except that it was right, when friends and neighbors were attacked, to run to their rescue; it was the part of duty, of manliness, of justice, of honor, and with wrenched and breaking hearts, but with nerves of steel, and faces firm and fixed, many mothers sent their first born off, in the watches of the night, to do his duty to Kin and Country.

How many tears, how many sobs, how many heart throbs, who shall dare estimate! No one can tell. And this extraordinary enthusiasm, this ardent zeal swept like an electric storm over the State. It was confined to no section and no class.

The women along Mason and Dixon's line were as enthusiastic as they were in St. Mary's, and in the humblest tenements of the eighth ward,[7] as they were around the Monument, for to the eternal honor of the Maryland Line it will be recorded, that its ranks included representatives of every historic Maryland family, which had made its mark since the landing on St. Clement's Isle on Lady's Day, 1632, through the Rebellion of 1775-1781 and the War of 1812, and that with Mexico, who marched, and rode, and slept, and fought, and died, side by side, with the sons of fathers, who swung the sledge, or drove the plane.

The Maryland Line represented the whole State, all her society from heart to circumference, and no man can ever say that any part ever shrank from duty, danger or death.

---

5   Oakland, MD is one of the westernmost towns in Maryland. Over 190 miles to the east is Point Lookout on the southern tip of St. Mary's County, MD.

6   For a second time the General is illustrating by geographical comparison the breadth of southern sympathies in Maryland. Cumberland is in Allegheny County, the far western portion of Maryland. Snow Hill is over 260 miles to the east in Worchester County, the easternmost county in Maryland fronting the Atlantic Ocean.

7   In 1796, the Governor and Council of Maryland passed the Act of Incorporation for Baltimore City and approved the division of the city into eight wards, each to contain nearly equal inhabitants. The eighth ward of Baltimore is east of downtown, overlooking the more prosperous Mount Vernon neighborhood where the Washington Monument (1829) is located. Lefurgy, William G. *Baltimore's Wards 1797-1978: A Guide, Maryland Historical Magazine, Vol. 75, No. 2*, (Baltimore, MD, Jun 1980), 145-153.

> Good Knights and true
>> As ever drew
> Their swords with Knightly Rowland,
> Or died by Sobieski's side
>> For love of martyred Poland,
> Or knelt with Cromwell's Ironsides,
>> Or sang with brave Gustavus.
> Or on the field of Austerlitz
>> Pour'd out their dying "Aves."[8]

This young country lad tells the story, how his red blood boiled, and how he left home to stand by kin, in Virginia.

I hope this publication will lead to others, as valuable, and as interesting. I ought to say that the author is typical of the Maryland Confederate in another way. Returning home to start his life work, he has now—not yet a middle-aged man—made his mark in business, and won a first place in the respect and regard of the community in which he lives.

I therefore present him as typical Maryland Confederate, one of "we few—we happy few, we band of brothers."[9]

BRADLEY T. JOHNSON[10]
The Woodlands, Amelia Court House, Va.,
May the 7th, 1898

---

8   Excerpt from *Stonewall Jackson's Grave*, by Margaret Junkin Preston (1820-1897). Pennsylvania born Mrs. Preston was the sister-in-law of Confederate General Thomas Jonathan "Stonewall" Jackson (1824-1863). She began writing and publishing poetry as early as 1856, and is sometimes referred to as the Poetess Laureate of the South. *http://www.frontierfamilies.net/family/junkin/family/D1MJ.html/.*

9   A passage from St. Crispen's Day Speech in Shakespeare's *Henry V* (1599).

10   Confederate Brigadier General Bradley Tyler Johnson (1829-1903) was born in Frederick City, MD. A graduate of Princeton in 1849, he finished his legal degree at Harvard College. When the Civil War began, Johnson organized and equipped a company at his own expense, and later took part in forming the 1st Maryland Infantry, of which he became major and subsequently colonel. Bradley declined a lieutenant colonel's commission in a Virginia regiment because of his belief that his strongest obligation was to his own state. Johnson was advanced to the rank of brigadier general in 1864. After the war, Johnson practiced law in Richmond, VA until 1879, when he moved to Baltimore, MD. After the death of his wife, he moved to Amelia, VA where he died.

This photograph first appeared in Reverend Phillip Columbus Croll's Ancient and Historic Landmarks in the Lebanon Valley (1895) *identified as the home of Alexander Schaeffer built in 1738. The cabin no longer stands. Photo from original text.*

LOG CABIN BUILT BY ALEX SCHAEFFER IN 1738

For many years the Historic Schaefferstown Association promoted this stone structure as the 1738 home of Alexander Schaeffer. Recent architectural evidence and dendrochronology of the home suggest it may have been built in the later part of the 18th century. Photo courtesy of Historic Schaefferstown, Inc. by Diane Wenger, PhD, Vice-President.

Schaffer's

In 1710 thirty-three families of Germans arrived in New York, and settled in Schoharie Valley.[11] Because of some unjust treatment by the landed proprietors, about sixty families, in a body left the State in disgust, and journeyed by way of Philadelphia, and the Susquehanna River to Pennsylvania, and located on the Tulpehocken Creek in 1723, which is now part of Lebanon County.

Among these emigrants was Johan Nicholas Schäffer, who arrived in New York in 1710, but it is not known whether he was the father of Frederick and Michael, who were on the committee, that erected the first Church that was built in Lebanon Valley in 1727.

However, there were several families of the same name, among the early settlers, along the Tulpehocken, and they were all leading lights among the community. We find in about 1738, Alexander Schaeffer, building a log cabin on the Suabian Hills, who in 1758 laid out Schaefferstown.[12]

Henry Schaeffer[13] was a captain in Colonel Greenawalt's Regiment which took a conspicuous part in the Revolutionary War.[14] He had with him a faithful body servant, and when about to engage the enemy for the first time, Hans implored the captain in the most tender manner: "Mine Herr, do not risk your life, by going into action, but let me take your place." But the roar of the musketry and the zip, zip of the bullets were so demoralizing to Hans, that he beat a hasty retreat, and took shelter behind a tree, where he was found shortly afterwards, in no frame of mind to lead a company, and no doubt thankful that the Captain had not accepted his offer.

After the War the Captain became an associate Judge, which position he held until his death, which occurred in 1806.

In 1800 we find Henry Schaeffer's name signed to a lottery ticket, No. 1547, for the sum of one hundred dollars, the proceeds to be used in "defray-

---

[11] The Schoharie Valley is a corridor that runs through Schoharie County from Schoharie to Gilboa, NY, about forty miles west of Albany. The name comes from a Mohawk Indian word meaning "floating driftwood."

[12] Tulpehocken is an Indian name meaning "land of turtles" and also the name of the creek that flows through Heidelberg Township in Lebanon County, PA. The Schaefferstown area boasts some of the most fertile farmland in Pennsylvania.

[13] **Original footnote: Alex. Schaeffer's son – Ancient Landmarks Lebanon Co., Rev. Croll.** Stonebraker is citing *Ancient and Historic Landmarks in the Lebanon Valley* by Reverend Phillip Columbus Croll (Lutheran Publication Society, Philadelphia, PA, 1895) published two years prior to *Rebel of '61*.

[14] Captain Henry Johan Heinrich Schaeffer (1749-1803) was the son of Alexander Shaeffer and Anna Engle of Heidelberg Township, Lebanon County, PA. He commanded the 8th Regiment of Colonel Philip Lorenz Greenawalt's (1725-1802) First Battalion of Lancaster County in the Revolutionary War. Greenawalt was born in Germany in 1725, came to America in 1749 and settled in Ephrata, PA. He was a farmer and hotel keeper and was commissioned a colonel in the Revolutionary War and served with Washington in many engagements. The Historical Society of Dauphin County, PA, Richards, Henry Melchior Muhlenberg, *The Pennsylvania-German in the Revolutionary War, 1775-1783*, Volume 17, (Lancaster, PA, 1908), 402.

ROXBURY, JOHN SCHAFFER'S HOMESTEAD, BUILT IN 1782.

A stone foundation ruins along Roxbury Road on the Antietam Creek is the only remaining evidence of Roxbury, the stone home and grist mill built by Stonebraker's great-grandfather John Shafer. Photo from original text.

ing the expenses of erecting the Churches lately built by the German Reformed Congregations respectively, in the borough of Lebanon, and the town of Heidelberg, in the county of Dauphin."[15]

Again we find Rev. F. D. Schaeffer, a noted divine, who was in some way connected with the first Reformed Church built in Harrisburg, but in about 1788 took up his residence in or near Carlisle, and preached stately for the Lutheran Congregation at Harrisburg.

In 1772 John Schäffer,[16] with his wife and two sons, emigrated from Lancaster County, Pennsylvania, near where Schaefferstown, now stands, to western Maryland, which was a part of Frederick County.[17]

He located on the Antietam Creek, where he secured a large tract of land, built a grist mill and distillery, and named the place Roxbury. Here he greatly added to his already large wealth, which he invested in land and slaves.[18]

He died in 1783, leaving a widow and seven children, four of them boys, which he named as follows: John John, John Henry, John George and John Leonard.[19] The records of the German Reformed Church of Schaefferstown show conclusively that he was very friendly with if not otherwise related to the founder of that town.[20]

---

15 The author's source for the lottery ticket was page 124 of *Ancient and Historic Landmarks in the Lebanon Valley* previously cited footnote 13. Lotteries in colonial America played a significant part in the financing of both private and public ventures. More than 200 lotteries were sanctioned between 1744 and 1776, and played a major role in financing roads, libraries, churches, colleges, canals, bridges, etc. Ezell, John Samuel *Fortune's Merry Wheel: the lottery in America* (Harvard University Press, 1960).

16 **Original Footnote: John, the head of the Maryland branch, always used the German umlaut over the ä instead of the diphthong æ as did the founder of Shaefferstown. †See Appendix No. 1 and No. 2.**

17 Washington County separated from Frederick County on 1 Oct 1776, becoming the first county in the new nation named for the General George Washington. The journey from Schaefferstown, PA to Washington County, MD is about 100 miles.

18 On 4 Jul 1770, John Sheffer [sic] of Frederick County, MD purchased from John Jasper two contiguous parcels of land on the east side of the Antietam Creek for £300. *Frederick County Maryland Land Records*, (hereafter cited as *FCLR*) N-229.

19 In naming their children, many 18th and early 19th century Germans gave first, a spiritual name in honor of their favorite saint that was repeated to all the children of that family of the same sex, then second, a secular name. The boys would be John Adam, John George, or Philip Peter, Philip Jacob, etc. Girls would be named Anna Barbara, Anna Margaret, or Maria Elizabeth, Maria Catharine, etc. After baptism, the children would be known as Adam, George, Peter, Jacob, Barbara, Elizabeth, and Catharine, respectively.

20 In 1899, the author could not confirm the relationship of Alexander Schaeffer, founder of

Under the old English law, John John, being the eldest male child, inherited the whole of his father's estate, but being endowed with that spirit of justice and generosity rarely found, he divided the estate into eight equal parts, gave his mother a share, and the balance he distributed among his brothers and sisters.[21]

He kept the old homestead for his share of the estate, and operated the mill and distillery, and prospered. He was noted for his integrity and kindness of heart, which brought him a large circle of friends.

His first wife was Elizabeth Hess, from where Keedysville now stands, and who died within one year after their marriage.[22] A short time after her death, he mounted his horse and rode to Schaefferstown, the place of his birth, for a short visit. While here he met, wooed and married Angelica Troutman, and with the horse that her father gave her as a bridal present, they journeyed on horseback, some two hundred miles south through the Cumberland Valley, to the groom's home. His return with a new wife, in less than a month, from the time he left home, was a great surprise to his friends.

They raised four sons and two daughters.[23] Jonathan was the hero of the family, being with the Maryland militia, when they showed their heels to the English, at the battle of Bladensburg, in 1814.[24]

He no doubt consoled himself with the thought that "he who fights and runs away, will live to fight another day."[25] However, the thought of that eventful day was a source of much mortification to his father, for the mere mention of the fact would put him in a bad humor.

His third wife was Catharine Miller, from Middleburg, Franklin County, Pennsylvania.[26] She was a great tease and often related to me the story

---

Schaefferstown, to his GGGrandfather, John Schaffer. A few years later, in 1901, A. S. Brendle published *A Brief History of Schaefferstown* (Dispatch Publishing Company, York, PA, 1901) asserting that John Schaeffer (1729-1783) was the eldest son of Alexander Schaeffer and that he had moved to Maryland in 1772.

21   John Schaffer died intestate in 1783. Under Maryland law, his estate was divided equally among his children and wife Barbara. *Washington County Maryland Land Records*, D-425 (hereafter cited as *WCLR*).

22   Elizabeth Hess was the daughter of Jacob Hess (1749-1815) and Margaret Orndorff (1750-1814). In 1768, Jacob Hess built a home and grist mill and on the bank of the Little Antietam Creek about halfway between Boonsboro and Sharpsburg. For that reason, the town that subsequently grew up around the mill was known as Centerville. After his death, Hess's property was purchased by John J. Keedy. In 1840, through the initiative of Samuel Keedy, a post office was established in the town and the name changed to Keedysville.

23   Most sources indicate the Schaffers had seven children: John, George, Henry, Leonard, Anna Maria, Catharina, and Maria Elizabeth.

24   On 24 Aug 1814 at Bladensburg, MD, 7,000 Americans faced 4,500 British. The defeat of the American forces allowed the British to capture and burn the public buildings of Washington. It has been called "the greatest disgrace ever dealt to American arms." Three Private John Shafers are listed in the Maryland Militia at the time of the battle: Stembel's 3rd Regiment, Schucht's 2nd Regiment, and Jameson's 1st Regiment. Quotation from James Sterling Young's *The Washington Community, 1800-1828* (Columbia University Press, 1966), 184.

25   According to *Morris Dictionary of Word and Phrase Origins,* the phrase is such a truism that it was likely first uttered by a weary caveman. One of the first written records of the phrase is credited to Demosthenes, the famous Greek orator and political leader. Reproached for his seeming cowardice on the battlefield, he replied: "A man who runs away may fight again." Morris, William and Mary, *Morris Dictionary of Word and Phrase Origins, Second Edition* (HarperCollins, Publishers, Inc., NY, NY), 283.

26   The couple was married 17 Jan 1809 in Washington County, MD by Reverend Rauhauser.

JOHN JOHN SCHAFER AND CATHARINE SCHAFER RENTCH, HIS ELDEST DAUGHTER.

The author's grandmother, Catharine Schafer Rentch (1795-1889), and his great-grandfather John John Schafer (1764-1861), Photo from original text.

of the battle, and when great grandfather was present, took great delight in saying, "Yes, Jonathan ran at the first fire and never stopped until he reached home," when the old gentleman would go storming out of the house.

She was an invalid for years before she died, but was a very bright woman and kept herself posted on the current events of the day, especially in politics. Being a staunch Whig, she was a great admirer of Henry Clay, and delighted in calling me a "red mouth locofoco."[27]

When the American "Know-Nothing" party made its appearance in the early fifties,[28] she was an ardent supporter of its principles, and was never better pleased than when in debate with the gentleman of the "Manor," who often called to have a friendly "set-to" with "Aunt Kitty."[29] They generally left feeling that they had met a foeman worthy of their steel.

The War of 1812 greatly inflated prices, causing an era of speculation, as all Wars usually do, when an intimate friend of his purchased the Tilghman property, and induced him to endorse a long time note for seventy-five thousand dollars, as part payment.[30]

Liquidation set in at the close of the War, and values commenced to seek their normal condition. Finally, land that had sold for one hundred and fifty dollars per acre, declined to one-half of that figure, when his friend failed to meet the note which he had endorsed as an accommodation, which gave him

---

Middleburg is a rural village on present day US Route #11, straddling the Maryland/Pennsylvania border at the village of State Line, PA. In Pennsylvania US Route #11 is also the Molly Pitcher Highway. In Maryland US Route #11 is Pennsylvania Avenue, formerly called the Middleburg Pike.

27   The Locofoco Party was a radical wing of the Democratic Party organized in New York City in 1835. Made up largely of working men and reformers, the party opposed state banks, monopolies, tariffs, and special interests. The name is derived from friction matches, known as *locofocos*, that radicals used to light candles when Democratic Party regulars tried to oust them from a Tammany Hall meeting by turning out the gas lights.

28   Also called the American Party, the Know-Nothing Party was prominent from 1853 to 1856. Originally organized as a secret society, its members professed to outsiders to be completely ignorant regarding the party. Largely composed of Protestant, native-born voters, "know nothing" policies were anti-immigrant, anti-Catholic and often employed rough electoral tactics.

29   The manor is *Conococheague Manor*, an 18,000 acre land tract originally the private property of Lord Baltimore, encompassing all of the land from Williamsport, MD east to Fairplay, MD. By the 1850s, "the manor" was a regional term for the privately owned farms and residences of that area.

30   In Apr 1814, Frisby Tilghman (1773-1847), owner of the plantation known as *Rockland* along present day Sharpsburg Pike, sold to David Cook of Lancaster County, PA 1,216 acres of land just south and east of present day Lappan's Crossroads for the amazing sum of $100,000. That same day, Tilghman recorded a mortgage with Cook for the property. John Shaffer's name does not appear in either document, so it is assumed that Shaffer privately loaned Cook the initial payment of $75,000. Shaffer's property was contiguous to the north of Cook's purchase. In December of 1821, with over $51,689 overdue, Tilghman foreclosed on Cook and repossessed the property. *WCLR, Deed Z-407, Mortgage Z-411, Deed EE-964.*

MOUNT MORIAH, CATHARINE RENTCH'S HOMESTEAD

Mount Moriah built circa 1820, photo circa 1897, from the original text. Mount Moriah was the home of the Stonebraker's maternal grandmother, Catharine Schafer Rentch, and the home where his mother, Angelica Rentch Stonebraker, was reared.

Mount Moriah still stands at the intersection of Bakersville and Spielman Roads about halfway between Downsville and Fairplay, MD. Erin Black Photography, Williamsport, MD.

Mount Moriah Church, built circa 1850, stands near the intersection of Spielman and Bakersville Roads. Today it is a private residence. Erin Black Photography, Williamsport, MD.

no end of trouble, and eventually the loss of the old homestead.[31]

He believed that the States which formed the general Government were Sovereign and Independent, and therefore was a Jeffersonian Republican–Democrat, as was all his "kith and kin," and worked and voted for the party, until after the marriage to his third wife, who influenced him to vote for Henry Clay.[32]

She, by her strong will and persuasive arguments, kept him to her way of thinking, or rather voting as she wished, up to the time of her death, which occurred a few years prior to his. He cast his last vote in 1860 for John C. Breckenridge, and died in April 1861, at the age of 97.[33]

Catharine, his eldest daughter, married John Rentch, who died early in life,[34] leaving a number of small children. She was a lovely character, the best known and most respected widow in Washington County. She was a friend to all the ministers of the Gospel, especially those of the Reformed Church, of which she was a member.

She was noted for her horsemanship, and for twenty years, could be seen almost daily, on the back of her faithful sorrel pacer Salem, named after General Putnam's horse that safely carried him down the precipice, out of the reach of the English Dragoons, while his one hundred and fifty men took to the swamp.[35]

---

31   On 11 Feb 1831, John Shaffer and wife Catharine sold the 'homestead' house and mill to his brothers: Henry, Jonathan and Leonard Shaffer, for $2,000. The 1840 US Federal Census shows John Shaffer residing next door to Jonathan Shaffer in the Boonsboro District, suggesting that John and Catharine Shaffer continued to reside at the mill homestead for at least 10 years after the sale. By 1847, John and Catharine Shaffer were living at *Mount Moriah* with Catharine Shaffer Rentch, his widowed daughter, as indicated by Stonebraker's later recollections of the fire at *Mount Moriah* and confirmed by the 1850 and 1860 US Federal Census. Catharine Miller Shaffer died in 1860 and John Shaffer in 1861 at *Mount Moriah* at age 97. *WCLR, Deed MM-1011.*

32   The Democratic-Republican Party, or Jeffersonian Republican Party, are the names used to refer to the American political party founded in the early 1790s by Thomas Jefferson and James Madison. Members typically called themselves "Republicans." It was formed to oppose the programs of the Federalist Party led by Treasury Secretary Alexander Hamilton.

33   John Cabell Breckenridge (1821-1875) of Lexington, KY was a lawyer and politician who served as a US Representative and US Senator from Kentucky. He was the 14th Vice-President of the United States (1857–1861) under President James Buchanan and, to date, the youngest vice-president in US history, inaugurated at age 36. In 1860, he unsuccessfully ran for President as one of two candidates of the fractured Democratic Party, representing Southern Democrats. He served in the Confederate Army as a general and the fifth and final Confederate Secretary of War.

34   From the *Herald of Freedom & Torch Light,* (Hagerstown, MD) 27 Apr 1814: Died on Monday the 18th intestate. After a short illness, at his residence about three miles from Hagers-town, Mr. John Rentch, in the 31st year of his age.

35   The account of Revolutionary War General Israel Putnam's (1718-1790) daring horseback

She kept a diary and rarely failed to make an entry in it each day. She lived the greater portion of her life on Ringgold Manor, near where the Mount Moriah Church now stands, and died in 1889 at the age of 94 years, and was buried in the old graveyard at Shepherdstown, West Virginia.[36]

JOS. STONEBRAKER'S HOMESTEAD, BUILT IN 1783

This stone home was the residence of the author's paternal grandfather, Joseph M. Stonebraker, and where his father, Henry Stonebraker, was born in 1815. Photo from original text.

The Stonebraker house stands today on Fairplay Road just south of Bakersville. Erin Black Photography, Williamsport, MD.

escape from the British down a steep precipice at Horseneck [West Greenwich] CT appeared in print in numerous publications of Stonebraker's time. Putnam was born in Salem Village [Danvers], MA, likely accounting for the horse's name of Salem. Tarbox, Increase Niles *Life of Israel Putnam "Old Put": Major-General in the Continental Army*, (Lockwood, Brooks, and Company, Boston, MA, 1876), 315-316. Inman, John and Robert A. West, *Columbian Lady's and Gentleman's Magazine, Volume 3* (Israel Post, NY, 1845), 139.

36   The Mount Moriah church stands today as a private residence near the intersection of Bakersville and Spielman Roads. Photograph page 26.

- *After their marriage in 1837, Henry and Angelica Rentch Stonebraker rented the Rowland farm just north of Downsville until 1840 when they moved to Missouri.*
- *Mount Moriah Church stands today as a private residence.*
- *John Rentch (1791-1822) married Catharine Shaffer (1795-1889) in 1813, and they built* Mount Moriah. *John died nine years later leaving Catharine a twenty-seven year-old widow with four young children.* Mount Moriah *stands today a private residence.*
- *Both of the stone Stonebraker homes south of Bakersville stand today as private residences.*

Stonebraker's

Stonebraker is an Anglo-Saxon name, and there is a tradition that the family originally came from Stone-henge, Wiltshire, England. Here it was that the Saxon name was anglicized. Whether the origin of the family name had any connection with that old Saxon Temple on Salisbury Plains, whose age and purpose will always remain an unfathomable mystery, is not known.[37]

The writer does not vouch for the above, but gives it for what it is worth. However, he made great efforts to trace the early history of the family, but nothing is positively known of its advent into America.[38]

Shortly before the close of the Revolutionary War, Michael Stonebraker located on the Potomac River, near where Bakersville now stands, and in 1792 became possessed of a large tract of land, where he raised four sons and four daughters.[39]

His eldest son, Joseph, the father of Henry, lived a long and honorable life, and died on his farm, adjoining the old homestead, in 1865, at the age of 83 years. His wife was Anna Landis,[40] who died in 1871, at the age of 73, and both are buried in the old graveyard at Bakersville, about one mile from their home.

The most important event of his life was after the battle of Bladensburg, when he as a soldier started for the seat of War, but when they reached Boonsboro, they learned that peace had been declared, and with joy returned to the bosom of his young wife.

---

[37] Middle English [Stonebreaker] and Middle High German [Steinbrecher/Steenbreker] both derive from an occupational name for a worker in a quarry or 'stone', and an agent derivative of breken 'to break'. The anglicization of Gerard/Garrott/Gerhart Stonebraker's name in deeds and other land transactions in Washington County would suggest the author's family was of Germanic descent.

[38] The earliest Stonebraker land transaction in Washington County, MD is on 14 Jan 1778 when Gerard Stonebraker (1742-1813) purchased three tracts of land along Beaver Creek for £500 from Samuel Lilly. Gerard/Gerhart/Garret Stonebraker was an accomplished millwright, having built at least two mills near Staunton, VA for Michael Faukler and Jerome Switzer, as evidenced by depositions of Dec 1791. *WCLR, Deed A-142* and *Deposition G-597*.

[39] Michael Stonebraker's (1759-1815) first property purchase in Washington County was 14 Apr 1792 when he purchased 161 ⅛ acres in the Bakersville area from Thomas Lesler for £725. The farm and stone house purchased by Michael Stonebraker in 1814 from Leonard Middlekauff remained in the Stonebraker family until 1867. *WCLR Deed G-736*.

[40] Joseph Stonebraker married Nancy Landis on 24 Oct 1814. Morrow, Dale (compiler) *Marriages of Washington County, Maryland, Volume 1, 1799-1830*, (Traces, Hagerstown, MD, 1979).

Happiness without Contentment

HENRY STONEBRAKER

Henry Stonebraker (1815-1877) father of the author Joseph Stonebraker. Photo from original text.

Henry Stonebraker and Angelica E. Rentch were married in November, 1837, at the bride's home at Mount Moriah, and immediately after the ceremony, in a two-horse carriage, began their bridal tour, and at the end of two days reached Baltimore.[41]

Washington's Monument was one of the city's attractions, but great was their surprise to find it located on a hill some distance from the city, the surrounding country densely covered with heavy timber.

At that time the monument had been completed about eight years and the population of Baltimore was less than 40,000 souls, and a visit to the spot at this time will show the wisdom of the location.

They settled down to the stern realities of life by leasing the Rowland farm near Downsville, Washington County, Maryland.[42]

Here they spent several very happy and prosperous years, but the conquering spirit of the Saxon was not entirely extinct in Henry, and in the spring of 1840, he took his wife and eighteen months' old baby girl,[43] and started for the great West, with bright anticipations, little dreaming of the hardships and failure that they were to encounter.

They traveled in a two-horse, covered wagon, such as was used in those days by persons emigrating West. They passed over the old National Pike that runs through Hagerstown and Cumberland, and when they reached Wheeling, Va., they embarked on a steamboat, sailing down the Ohio River to St. Louis, where they disembarked, traveling overland to Shelby County, Missouri, being more than three weeks on the road.[44]

---

41   The couple was married 30 Nov 1837. Dodd, Jordan, *Maryland Marriages, 1655-1850* (database on-line. Liahona Research, Provo, UT, 2004).

42   The Stonebrakers rented the 250-acre Isaac Rowland farm along the Old Manor Road, today the Downsville Pike. Isaac Rowland purchased the 250 acres for $11,250, 5 Apr 1832 from Marie Antionette Ringgold. *WCLR NN-148 Hagers-Town Mail*, 14 Feb 1840.

43   Henry and Angelica Stonebraker's oldest child was Anne E. Stonebraker (1838-1934). Most genealogical resources indicate the couple had a son named Daniel (1839-1850). As Stonebraker does not mention the son, it is likely the child remained in Maryland with relatives for health reasons. He died young.

44   The distance from Funkstown, MD to Shelbyville, MO is about 850 miles on interstate highways, or a fifteen hour drive. In 1840, the Stonebrakers traveled approximately 1,435 miles. From Funkstown to Wheeling along the National Road [US Rt. 40] by covered wagon is about 200 miles. The journey by steamer boat on the Ohio River from Wheeling to Cairo, IL where the Ohio River joins the Mississippi River is about 890 miles. From Cairo north on the Mississippi River to St. Louis, MO is about 195 miles. Finally, from St. Louis to Shelbyville is 150 miles.

In these days of Royal Blue and Limited Express trains,[45] one can scarcely imagine what privations the travelers suffered before reaching their destination. Even then their real labor just began. The section where they located was a typical Western spot. Land had to be cleared, house and outbuildings to be erected, all of which took time and energy to accomplish, and during this period twin baby girls were born.[46]

About this time there appeared at their home a person who had been raised in the same neighborhood in Maryland that father came from, and after much persuasion, induced him to form a co-partnership, when they erected a grist mill and distillery.[47] This party had been living West for some years, and had failed in business, and by some dishonest method, obligated the new firm for his old debts without father's knowledge or consent. This act caused father to lose everything he had—they even took the colored girl that mother had taken West as her maid.[48]

The perils and hardships of the pioneer's life were such that it nerved the women to cheerfully undertake that which would now seem to be almost improbable.

In November, 1842, mother, with three little girls, two of them were twins but eight months old, without any assistance, started on a journey to visit her parents who resided in Maryland.

The trip was a long and tedious one, and to make matters worse, the weather became so cold that the river froze over, detaining the boat some miles below Wheeling.

ANGELICA E. STONEBRAKER

Angelica E. Stonebraker (1814-1906) mother of the author Joseph Stonebraker. Photo from original text.

---

45   The Royal Blue was the B&O Railroad's flagship luxury passenger train between New York City and Washington, DC beginning in 1890. Express, or Limited Express trains make a small (limited) number of stops instead of stopping at every station.

46   The 1900 census lists the birth of Clara Amelia Stonebraker [Keller] and her twin sister Ellen, as September of 1840. Yet Stonebraker writes his sisters were born in March of 1842. *US Federal Census 1840 and 1900.*

47   As Stonebraker was not born until 1844, the information regarding the family's adventures in Missouri was undoubtedly provided by his 85 year-old mother, Angelica Stonebraker (1814-1906). This would account for the minor discrepancies in dates and the assertion that Henry Stonebraker was without fault.
Henry Stonebraker's partner was William H. Eakle, Jr. (1811-1889) the son of William H. Eakle, Sr. (1798-1851) of Funkstown. In Sep 1839, Henry Stonebraker purchased 83+ acres about 6 miles northeast of present day Shelbina along Black Creek. Together, Stonebraker and Eakle built, or purchased, a grist mill and distillery and formed the partnership of *Eakle & Stonebraker.* The 1840 census for Shelby County, MO shows 24-year old William H. Eakle living alone, very near the eight-member Henry Stonebraker household. By Oct 1841, the business had failed with significant debt. In an effort to limit his financial liability, Stonebraker filed a bond declaring his "penal sum," or limits of liability with Eakle restricted to $2,000, and sold his interest in the property and the distillery to Eakle for $100. The plan did not work. To satisfy his many creditors in Dec 1841, Stonebraker sold most of his possessions, including 11 cows, 100 hogs, 5 horses, a wagon, farming implements, assorted household furnishings, and a negro girl named Evaline. *WCLR Z-8, Shelby County MO Land Records A-611, B-571, B422, B460, B485.* Special thanks to Leon O. Kearns and the Shelby County Historical Society, Shelbina, MO.

48   Stonebraker identifies Evaline as his mother's maid, but the 1840 US Federal Census of Shelby County, MO lists Evaline as a slave.

Here they remained about ten days, hoping the river would open up, but as the weather showed no signs of moderating, she hired a sled and proceeded to Wheeling, where she secured passage on the four-horse stage coach to Hagerstown. The sympathy of her fellow travelers did much to lighten her burden, and cheer her on the way.

She remained with her friends until the following spring, when she returned to her new home over the same route, but was fortunate in having a friend of the family who was going West as a traveling companion most of the way.

Henry Stonebraker's moving to Missouri Auction. Hagers-Town Mail *(Hagerstown, MD) 14 Feb 1840.*

> **PUBLIC SALE.**
>
> WILL be offered at Public Sale, on *Wednesday the 4th day of March next*, at the residence of the subscriber, (the farm of Mr. Isaac B. Rowland,) about 4 miles from Williamsport, on the road leading from Hagerstown to Falling Waters, the following property, to wit.
>
> **7 head of Horses,**
> 20 head of CATTLE, among which are a *Teeswater* BULL, and seven MILCH COWS; 20 head of HOGS; two Wagons, one Cart, one Threshing Machine, 1 Wheat Fan, (Watkins') two pair of Grain Ladders, one Grain Rake, 1 Cutting Box, Horse Gears, Ploughs and Harrows, and other Farming Utensils.
>
> A set of first-rate Blacksmith Tools, one Sleigh and Harness, one Grindstone; a quantity of Oats and Potatoes by the bushel, Vinegar, a quantity of BACON and LARD by the pound.
>
> Also—GRAIN IN THE GROUND; with a variety of
>
> *House and Kitchen Furniture,* consisting of Beds, Bedsteads and Bedding, one Clock, one Secretary, Bureau, Cupboard, Tables and Chairs, two ten-plate Stoves, and many other articles unnecessary to mention.
>
> Sale to commence at 9 o'clock, A. M. when the terms, which will be liberal, will be made known.
>
> **HENRY STONEBRAKER.**
> February 14—3w*

32   *A Rebel of '61*

The Father of Waters

In 1845 father moved his family to LaGrange, Lewis County, a small town situated on the banks of the Mississippi River, and opened a hotel, which he kept for several years.[49]

It was here I first saw a steamboat. Fritz, an old family hand, often took me in his arms to the river bank, to see the boats pass up and down stream, and taught me the difference between a stern and side-wheel steamer.

Political parties have their strong adherents in the sparsely populated sections, as well as in the older settlements. In fact the people take more interest, and go farther to a meeting of this kind in the new, than they do in the older sections. Instead of mass-meetings, as we now have, they called them barbecues, where the whole population would gather, to hear the speeches, meet friends and have a good time.

Such a meeting took place when I was a little tacker, father taking the whole family. Some time during the day, while chasing "chip-munks," I wandered off in the woods and got lost. Two men who were riding through that section, found and took me to the meeting place, but my absence had been discovered, and a searching party was forming to look me up. It was fortunate that I was found, for had I remained in the woods all night, the wolves would have made short work of me, as the country was infested with that ferocious, and detested animal.

In April, 1847, father with his family, removed to his native State, taking the only route then traveled. One day while on the boat, some one created a panic among the passengers by reporting the vessel to be sinking. A stranger with a high silk hat took me on the upper deck. I was too young to be alarmed, but was delighted with the sight of a brush fire on the prairie. It is needless to say the report was false.

When we reached Maryland, we went to Grandmother Rentch's home for a short time. While here we had a fire that nearly proved disastrous to our six months' old baby.[50]

How plainly now I can hear the cry of fire, fire, and see old Great Grandfather Schäfer, staggering up the stairs, trembling with fear and excitement.[51]

The Champions of the Mississippi. Lithograph by Currier & Ives, NY. LOC/P&P. LC-USZC2-3743.

---

49   La Grange, MO on the Mississippi River is about fifty miles east of Henry Stonebraker's previous homestead. There is no record of Henry Stonebraker purchasing property in Lewis County, MO.
50   The baby was Stonebraker's younger brother John R. Stonebraker (1847-1921).
51   John Shaffer (1764-1861) lived with his daughter, Catharine Shaffer Rentch, at *Mount Moriah* from the mid-1840s until his death in 1861.

Antietam Valley

The Antietam Creek rises in the hills of Pennsylvania, and like a great serpent, slowly winds through one of the most beautiful valleys of Western Maryland, emptying into the Potomac River, southeast of the now historic Sharpsburg.

A more beautiful, and self-satisfying scene is nowhere to be found, as you stand in the midst of this valley, in the month of June, the air laden with the perfume of new mown hay, and fragrant blossoms, looking out upon the green waving sea, of heading wheat, or behold the vast fields of Indian corn, whose broad green blades, and yellow brown tassels, swing to and fro in September's autumn breeze. While to the West, and the East, like eternal sentinels, guarding happy rural homes, from storms and cyclones, stand the North and South Mountains, whose sides are forever enveloped in that hazy blue, of which the eye never tires, and "Black Rock," like a frowning fortress, looms up in the distance.

The stone bridge and mill at Funkstown. Photo courtesy Washington County Free Library, Hagerstown, MD.

34   *A Rebel of '61*

Funkstown

In the heart of this valley, nestling in the bend of the Antietam Creek, is the picturesque village of Funkstown, which in its early history, was known as Jerusalem Town.[52]

On the opposite side of the creek, ascending from its banks, is a timber covered ridge, fragrant with memories of the past. It was here in April, 1755, that General Braddock cut an opening in the timber through which his soldiers passed on their way to Fort Duquesne, and disaster.[53] In July, 1863, the same woods sheltered from the noon day's heat, Lee's weary, ragged, but defiant Rebels, on their retreat to the Potomac, after their defeat at Gettysburg. And a few days later, General Meade with his legions, occupied and entrenched a portion of this same ridge, while facing General Lee's army.

When in 1776 Washington County was divided from Frederick, Funk, the founder of Funkstown, conceived the idea of making it the county seat. He informed the founder of Hagerstown of his intentions, and while he planned to extend the town, west beyond the creek, selecting a beautiful site on the crest of Braddock's ridge, overlooking the ancient village of Jerusalem, for the Court House, Hager mounted his horse, rode to Annapolis and secured the prize for his own.[54]

BIRD'S EYE VIEW OF AN ANCIENT PORTION OF FUNKSTOWN

Photo from original text.

---

52   In 1762, Jacob Funk (1725-1794) increased his original 1753 land patent of 50 acres called *Good Luck* with a massive 2,000+ acre addition aptly named *Addition to Good Luck*. The addition included the 160± acres within a horseshoe bend along the Antietam Creek. Within this horseshoe he laid out a 177-lot town he called Jerusalem, designating a lot each for a church and cemetery. On 1 Jun 1768, he sold the first lot in the town to Henry Snider. Twenty-three years later in Aug of 1791, Funk sold the remaining 50 unsold lots to Henry Shafer and moved to Jefferson County, KY where he died in 1794. Jerusalem was incorporated as a municipality in 1840 under the name Funkstown. Maryland Archives *Maryland land patents YS8/220:GS1/140, BC18/435:BC19/634, WCLR L-237, L-386,* and *G-192*, Vol. 592, 61.

53   Stonebraker is erroneously assuming General Braddock's forces came through Funkstown in 1755 on his way to the disastrous Battle of Monongahela during the French & Indian War. Colonel Thomas Dunbar, leading one of General Braddock supply trains, crossed through Washington County along the old Keedysville Road south of Funkstown, then on the Conococheague Road to the supply depots at Williamsport, MD. before heading west.

54   Washington County was created from Frederick County by resolve of the Maryland Constitutional Convention of 1776. According to T. J. C. Williams in *History of Washington County, Maryland from the Earliest Settlements to the Present Time,* (Philadelphia, PA, 1906), both Jonathan Hager of Elizabeth-Town [Hagerstown], and Jacob Funk of Jerusalem [Funkstown] desired their settlement be declared the county seat. Williams asserts that Hager rode to Annapolis and convinced the Maryland Assembly to select Elizabeth-Town, yet there is no record of Hager appearing before the Maryland Convention in the fall of 1776.

The Jacob Funk house at 35 W. Baltimore Street in Funkstown on lot #165. In May of 1790 Funk sold the lot to Henry Shafer, Stonebraker's maternal great-grand uncle for £150. Funk moved to Jefferson County, KY where he died three years later. Shafer also purchased Funk's mill and 92 acres on the Antietam Creek for £2,150. The house remained in Shafer's possession for a number of years, later to be known as South's Hotel. Erin Black Photography, Williamsport, MD.

In 1790, John Henry Schäfer located in the town,[55] built a grist mill[56] and became the president of the Antietam Woolen Manufacturing Company.[57] He eventually became the owner of the enterprise, which he greatly enlarged, and in 1829, was making ingrain carpets. A few years later he made further additions, and brought from London an Englishman who put up a loom to weave Brussels carpets. He wove a number of rugs, some of the patterns—the Rose of England, and the Thistle of Scotland—were much admired.

They had a roll of Brussels carpet on the loom when the factory took fire and was destroyed in 1834—being a total loss as the insurance policy had expired a week before, and through carelessness had not been renewed.[58]

Daily about the mill were seen long lines of Conestoga wagons, drawn by six and eight horses, some unloading wheat, while others were loading flour which they carried to Baltimore and Washington markets. Railroads were unknown, and stage coaches had not yet reached that point, as Mrs. Schafer in her coach and four drove to Baltimore—a two day's journey.

---

55   On 5 May 1790, Henry Shafer (1766-1855) Stonebraker's maternal great-grand uncle, purchased lot 165 for £150, today 35 W. Baltimore Street, Funkstown, MD. The large purchase price indicates significant improvements on the property at the time of the sale. Today the 18th century stone home is known as the Jacob Funk home, and Funk is logically credited as the builder. *WCLR G-91.*

56   In addition to Jacob Funk's stone home, that same day Henry Shafer also purchased from Funk 92 acres called *Establishment*. The parcel began at "a stone standing in the edge of the mill dam," with the majority of the land on the west side of the Antietam Creek and only a small part in the town of Jerusalem. The large purchase price would indicate Shafer purchased a completed functioning mill. *WCLR G-92.*

57   In 1813, thirteen businessmen from Washington County formed the Antietam Woolen Manufacturing Company. After 1816, the business continued under the ownership of only Henry Shafer and Gerard Stonebraker, operating as the Antietam Woolen Factory. The company papers are archived at the Hagley Museum and Library in Wilmington, DE. Additionally see: Bahr, Betsy, *The Antietam Woolen Manufacturing Company: A Case Study in American Industrial Beginnings. Working Papers from the Regional Economic History Research Center*, 4 (no. 4, 1981), 27-46. Powell, Barbara M. and Michael A., *Mid-Maryland History: Conflict, Growth and Change* (The History Press, Charleston, SC, 2008), 105-111.

58   From the *Hagerstown Mail, 26* Dec 1834: Destructive Fire—On Sunday evening last, between 8 and 9 o'clock, an extensive fire was discovered to be raging in the direction of Funks-town. . . which proved to be the Woollen Factory of Messrs. George & Henry I. Shafer, in Funks-town. . . The Factory and all its contents (excepting the books, a few manufactured articles, and a small quantity of wool) were consumed. . .The value of the property destroyed is estimated at from $15,000 to $25,000, the whole of which loss falls upon the enterprising proprietors—there being no insurance.

ANTIETAM WOOLEN MILL, DESTROYED BY FIRE, 1834

Antietam Canal Company

Schäfer's energy and enterprise greatly stimulated the citizens, and it became a thriving town. About 1808 a charter was secured from the State for the Antietam Canal Company, who proposed to make the creek navigable to the Potomac River, by means of slack water.[59]

In 1812 the company built two locks, and connected the two dams by digging a canal some eight hundred feet long. The boat which was about one hundred feet long, gondola shape, sharp at both ends, without deck, was loaded with one hundred and twenty-five barrels of flour, passed safely through the canal and into the lock, but was wrecked while passing into the lower dam, and the cargo became a complete loss.

This accident so discouraged the company that the project was abandoned and Schäfer afterwards utilized the canal by building a saw and cement mill over the locks.

Photo from original text.

---

59 After the opening of the bypass canal around Great Falls in the Potomac River near Georgetown in 1802, the Potomac Company board began to plan for the expansion of the Potomac River navigation system by planning lateral canals that would feed commerce to the Potomac River. Five waterways were considered: the Shenandoah River, the Conococheague Creek, the Monocacy River, the Seneca, and the Antietam Creek. At thirty-eight-miles long and relatively unobstructed by falls or rapids, the Antietam was viewed as a "highly promising avenue for shipping the produce of this fertile country to the Potomac River navigation."
 The Maryland Assembly passed legislation in 1811 authorizing the Potomac Company to condemn lands along the Monocacy, Conococheague, and Antietam for the purpose of "making canals and locks in improving the navigation on such branches." Local farmers and millers organized and loaned the Potomac Company $20,000 plus interest to complete the task. The loan would be repaid from tolls once the project was completed. Work began on locks in the Antietam in January of 1812. Belatedly, in April of 1812, an engineer surveyed the Antietam and estimated the project would cost in excess of $90,000 to complete. The investors defaulted on their promised funds, and by March 1814 the project was shut down. Reportedly, Henry Shafer's lock at his mill at Funkstown was the only lock on the Antietam Creek to be completed. Kapsch, Robert J. *The Potomac Canal, George Washington and the Waterway West* (WV University Press, 2007), 162-171. Maryland State Archives, *Session Laws 1811, Vol. 614:239.* Guzy, Dan, *Navigation on the Upper Potomac River and its Tributaries* (Chesapeake & Ohio Canal Association, 2008).

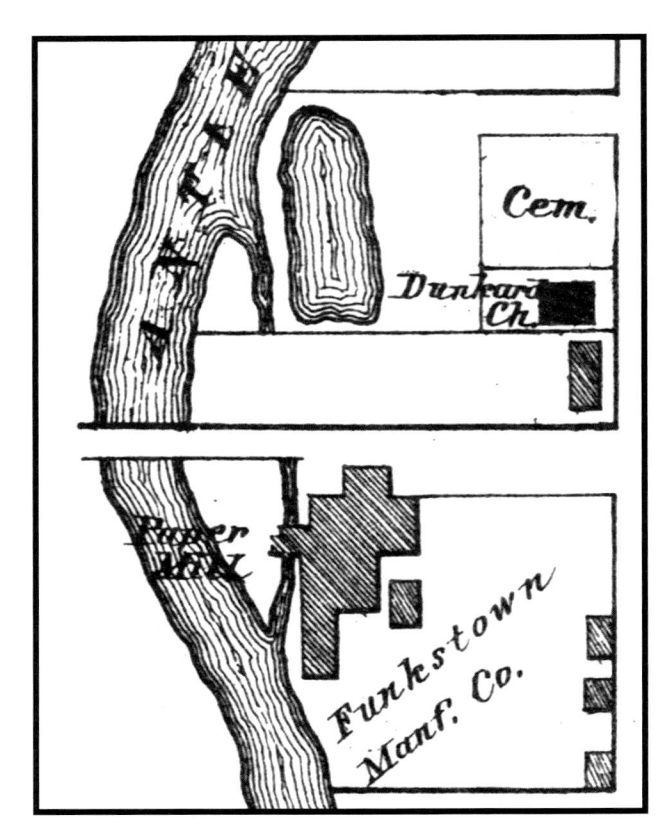

Finally Schäfer erected a large barn on Funk's Court House site, and planted an orchard on the slope below. Instead of the noisy advocate, trying to persuade twelve well meaning men, to render an unjust verdict against their neighbor, the low of the cattle in the yard, and the sound of the flail on the floor was heard.

Here, too, lived Ira Hill, the Yankee pedagogue, who, during his idle hours, wandered along the streams and through the forests, looking for relics of the Aborigines. While here he wrote "Antiquities of America Explained," in which he proves to his own satisfaction, that the American Indians descended from the Jews and Tyrians.[60]

Above: Henry Shafer abandon the canal project and built a saw and cement mill over the defunct canal lock. This enlargement of the Funkstown plat from the 1877 Illustrated Atlas of Washington County, MD shows the canal flowing beside the Funkstown Manufacturing Company.

An 1863 Edwin Forbes pencil drawing of General Meade's Army crossing the bridge at Funkstown. This drawing also shows Henry Shafer's mill and the canal as it streamed under the mill. Frank Leslie's Illustrated Newspaper, 1 Aug 1863. LOC/P&P. LC-USZ62-126961.

60   Born in Connecticut, Ira Hill (1783-1838) was a teacher in Funkstown in his last years. In his *Antiquities of America Explained,* Hill asserted that the American Indian tribes were descended from the Hebrew or the ten lost tribes. In his first book, *An Abstract of a New Theory of the Formation of the Earth*, Hill presents an equally astounding view of the formation of the earth and a memorable theory that the Dighton Rock of Berkley, MA, bore inscriptions from an expedition sent to the New World by King Solomon. In 1824, Hill proposed Congress build a ten-acre, three-dimensional garden map of the world adjacent to the US Capitol building. *Antiquities of America Explained,* (W. D. Dell, Hagerstown, MD, 1831). *An Abstract of a New Theory of the Formation of the Earth* (N. G. Maxwell, Baltimore, MD, 1823). *Ira Hill's Memorial and Remarks to Congress.* (United States, 1824).

A Rebel of '61

BELOW THE DAM, WHERE THE IRON PIN WAS PLACED

Race of Millers

For three generations the Schäfers were millers and dealt in grain, and today where ever you find a grist-mill that was built, owned or operated by one of the name, close by you will find the ruins of a distillery. The only exception being John Henry, who was a temperance man, as the following story clearly demonstrates.

There were so many mills on the Antietam Creek that they dammed up the water on each other, causing no end of disputes, and in very many cases, the courts were called upon to settle the question just how far one man could back the water on his neighbor's wheel.

John Henry had one of these protracted suits, and after the court had decided the question, the officials were present to direct where the hole should be drilled, in the rock above the dam, at the edge of the water, into which an iron pin was driven, as a water mark.[61]

After the pin had been set, a two gallon jug of whisky that some one had provided, was brought forward to celebrate the event. Of course Schäfer was expected to lead off with the first "swig." He took the jug, and held it high above his head, and let it drop on the pin with a crash, then politely tipped his hat, and bid the disappointed and muttering crowd good day.

The 1823, three-arch stone bridge over the Antietam Creek on the Old National Pike. The bridge is still in use today. Photo from original text.

---

61   In 1813, Henry Shafer (1766-1855) won his suit against Christian Boerstler (1748-1833) for damming the waters in the Antietam Creek. In addition to monetary compensation, two commissioners marked with a pin the highest level Boerstler was allowed to dam his water. Boerstler was instructed to never "raise or cause to be raised the water in his said Dam higher or above a particular mark made upon a rock by the said Henry Shäfer and cut in by Frisby Tilghman and Daniel Boerstler..." *WCLR YY-555.*

Old English Chapel

The first Church erected in the town, was an Episcopal Chapel, which was known as the old English Church, and was struck by lightning and destroyed.[62]

The stone from its walls was used to build the fence that now stands between the old Sager and Stover property, and is the lot upon which the Church stood.

Some years afterwards old "Daddy Moyer," plowed over the graves and raised corn and potatoes.[63] It is not generally known that the lot was ever a grave-yard, and beneath the growing crops, rest the remains of some of the town's early settlers.

Some years afterwards, on the same block, but facing the old grave-yard stood the Union Church, which was jointly used by the Reformed and Lutheran congregations.

By its side, was a long two story log building—the Village school house. The lower story was the school master's dwelling, the upper story the school rooms, and at one end was attached the "Funks-town Library," which was collected mainly through the efforts of a Mr. Curtis, a Yankee school master, who taught school there in 1832.[64]

About the year 1859 the school house caught fire, when both it and the Church were entirely destroyed.

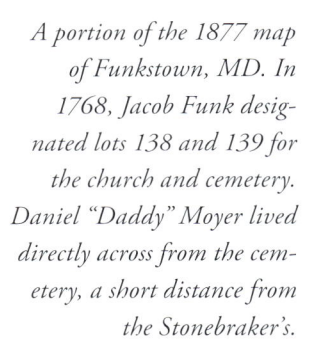

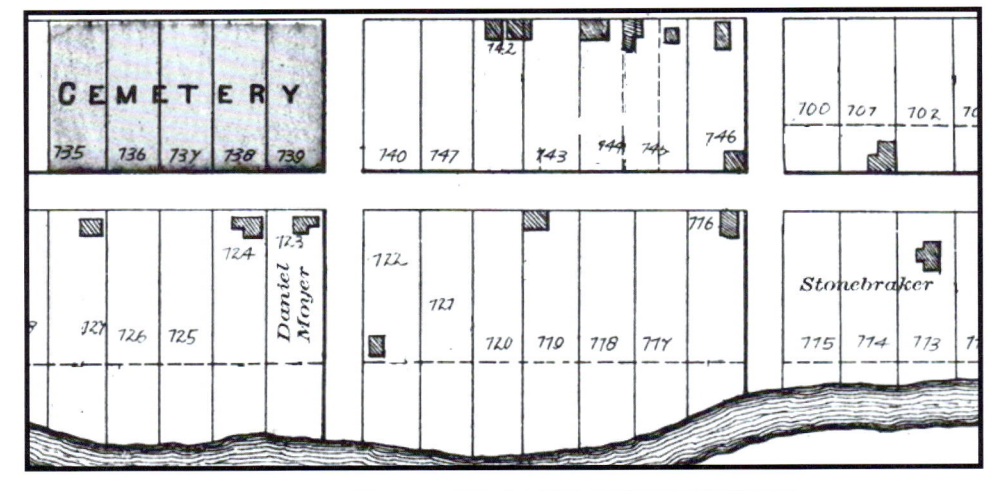

A portion of the 1877 map of Funkstown, MD. In 1768, Jacob Funk designated lots 138 and 139 for the church and cemetery. Daniel "Daddy" Moyer lived directly across from the cemetery, a short distance from the Stonebraker's.

---

62   One of Jacob Funk's first acts in 1768 was to designate a church and burying ground. Reportedly a Union Reformed and Lutheran Church were located there by 1771. A Lutheran Church was built on Baltimore Street in 1850. The German Reformed Church was forced to relocate when their building was destroyed by fire on 3 Aug 1859. The Civil War interrupted completion of the church until 1864.

63   Daniel Moyer (1772-1853) immigrated to Washington County, MD from Germany in 1808. In 1810, he married Margaret Kailor (1768-1854). They had no children. The couple lived in Funkstown from the 1830s through the 1850s, owning lot #123 on present day E. Green Street. *WCLR, NN-198* 20 Apr 1832 and *IN 4-663* 31 Dec 1849.

64   The 1850 US Federal Census lists school teacher Thomas Curtis (1784-?) and his wife Ann L. Curtis (1793-?) residing in downtown Hagerstown above Charles Enoch's ale house. The census notes that Curtis was born in New Jersey, accounting for Stonebraker's comment of "yankee."

A Rebel of '61

Stranger than Fiction

Near this old English Church, at the foot of the hill, towards the creek stood a very old log cabin, which once was occupied by Mrs. Smith and her faithful dog. She, when a mother of eight daughters and two sons, was carried away by the Indians.

One day while she was in the woods just across the Antietam, gathering fagots, a strolling band of Indians came along, and took her with them.[65]

Her captors kept her for some time, in fact so long that her husband had given her up for dead, and was looking around for another help-mate.

She watched long and anxiously for an opportunity to escape, when one night while the Indians were asleep, she stole away and hiding by day and traveling by night, she finally reached her husband's home on the evening of the day, when he was to lead the young and beautiful Polly Hess to the altar.[66]

Polly's disappointment must have been very great, for she never married—yet she did not die with a broken heart. For years afterwards she was a well known character, and spent her declining years in Hagerstown, and was on the best of terms with the Eisenminger's, who were descendants of Mrs. Smith.

---

[65] There are numerous variations on the tale of a man forced to chose at the altar between his abducted wife or his beautiful fiance. One of the more repeated versions is from October of 1755 when George Washington was unable to have his guns repaired at Fort Cumberland by John Fraser because Fraser's abducted bride had escaped her Indian captors and returned in time to force Fraser to choose between her or his fiance. Whisker, James B. *Arms makers of Colonial America* (Associated University Presses, Cranbury, NJ, 1992), 83.

Polly Hess's tale of a broken heart in conjunction with the abduction of Mrs. Smith by Indians is unsubstantiated. The last documented reports in Maryland of an abduction by Indians was in the western part of the county in 1755 and 1756 during the French and Indian War. The capture of a woman by Indians near Hagers-Town and her subsequent return would have been sensational news reported in the *Maryland Gazette*. Mrs. Smith may have disappeared for several years, but it is doubtful Indians were involved.

[66] There is no record of a marriage license for a Smith–Hess wedding in the Washington County Courthouse or in published marriage records.

SHANTY IN CORK

Cork

Cork was a rural village of Irish immigrants located along present day Cool Hollow Road south of Funkstown. Photo from original text.

A portion of the town, just east of where the National Pike makes a turn, and the houses along the road which leads to Beaver Creek, was known as "Cork," so named because a lot of shanties were erected and occupied by the Irish, who were employed in great numbers, when the National Road was under construction.[67]

On the night before Saint Patrick's Day in 1822, some wag hung a stuffed "Paddy," on a sign post of a hotel near where the Irish lived. This so enraged the inhabitants of "Cork," that they refused to go to work, but formed in a body, at the head of which was a fife and drum, and marched through town, caught several of its citizens, which they nearly beat to death, and threatened to destroy the village.[68]

Here it was that Uncle Tom South and Davey Clagett, distinguished themselves, by putting a portion of the mob to flight.[69] Uncle Tom was a

---

[67] The National Road project began in 1811, and the road soon became the main overland route to the west. Made of crushed rock, the road cost up to $13,000 per mile. Toll houses were built about every fifteen miles. Called the Cumberland Road, it was also dubbed the National Pike, or National Road because 'national funds' were used in its construction.

[68] The Saint Patrick's Day Irish riot in Funkstown took place 17 Mar 1823, and was reported by newspapers nationwide. A Paddy was an anti-Irish caricature dummy often decorated with a necklace of stale mackerel, a club, a whisky jug, and dragging a string of potatoes. Williams, William H.A., *Twas only an Irishman's dream* (University of Illinois, 1996), 2.

[69] The 1850 US Federal Census lists Thomas South, age 68 (1782-?), wife Barbara (1784-?) and son David South (1812-?) residing in Funkstown. Davey Clagett is likely David Clagett (1780-

42   *A Rebel of '61*

powerful man, with no end of grit, and for that reason he was waited upon by the leaders of the mob, and asked when he would be ready to take his share of the thrashing. He replied "just give me fifteen minutes," to which they agreed. He in the meantime provided himself with a mowing scythe, and when they called again, he lost no time in joining issue with them, and was soon in their midst, his broad sword gleaming in the sun, as he smote his enemies to the right and the left. His onslaught, backed up by Davey was so vigorous, that the mob soon discovered that the shillalah was no match against such a Goliath, armed with a razor edged weapon and took to their heels, leaving behind the drum and several of their comrades badly wounded.[70]

The persons who made the effigy used a dye stick for the arms, which convinced the mob that some of the factory hands had something to do with its construction.

Later in the day the number of the mob increased, and their rage being greatly inflamed by the use of too much liquor, marched to the factory with the avowed purpose of tearing the building from its foundation.

Upon reaching the place they found that their visit had been anticipated, as the doors of the building were barricaded and men stationed at each window, armed with stones and clubs, awaiting an attack.

Just as the storming party had formed and was ready to move forward to the assault, Captain Geo. W. Barr, from Hagerstown, appeared with his company of dragoons, and reinforced the Yager riflemen—a town organization—when the rioters were put to flight.

It was a notable day in the town's history, and for years afterwards was a subject frequently discussed by the participants to the crowds that nightly congregated around the stores and hotels.[71]

Mr. Thomas Kennedy, a member of the Legislature from Hagerstown, wrote a short but humorous poem, commemorating the event, and I regret very much that I was unable to find a copy to insert here.[72]

Thomas Kennedy (1776-1832) Legislator and writer. Kennedy is buried in Hagerstown, MD. In 1918, some Jewish citizens erected a monument at his grave with the inscription - One who loved his fellow man.

Herald of Freedom and Torch Light, (Hagerstown, MD) 9 Jun 1824.

1850), son of John Clagett, a wealthy landowner with large holdings south of Funkstown.

70   Shillalah is a wooden club or weapon.

71   This battle gained national attention. The *Niles' Register, Baltimore, MD*, 5 Apr 1823 reported: "The exhibit of a Paddy, as it is called, roused the feelings of a number of the natives of Ireland. . . who collected to the amount of 150 persons, provided with shillalahs, etc. with an apparent design to commit violence on the people of the town; the rifle company of which was called out, and soon reinforced by a part of a troop of cavalry and a strong company of militia, from Hagerstown. . . It is wrong to trifle thus with the feelings of any people. . . but it is as wrong. . . for Irishmen to take such hostile notice of what is meant merely as a "piece of fun."

72   Thomas Kennedy (1776-1832) was a Maryland legislator most famous for championing political equality for the Jewish citizens of Maryland. A copy of this very rare poem, *"The Battle of Funks-town,: A Burlesque Poem; Founded on Recent Facts and Circumstances,"* is reprinted on pages 233 to 245.

Ancient Custom

The bell on the old Union Church was cast in England, and had a very fine tone. It was destroyed when the Church burned down, and quite a number of finger rings, were made from its metal as relics.

It was the custom, when any one in the community died, for the Sexton to ring the bell three times. The older the person, the longer the bell was rung.

The belfry was of peculiar construction, and if the bell rope was pulled a little too hard, the bell would upset and get caught in the top of the belfry, when some one would have to climb the steeple and set it right.

When the writer was a mere youth, the sexton was a very nervous man, and never could ring the bell without an accident. The result was that he was often called upon to perform that part of the sexton's duty, much to his delight.

When old Doctor Dorsey died, who was the most celebrated physician of Western Maryland—although his calomel treatment was severely condemned by many—I was called upon to ring the bell as a mark of respect to his memory, and rang it so long that many of the citizens called to learn what extremely old person had died.[73]

Early Funkstown Churches. Top: The Methodist Church at the corner of N. Antietam and Chestnut Streets stands today as a private residence. Bottom: The old Funkstown Lutheran Church.

Mrs. A. R. Johnson, a granddaughter of John Henry Schäfer, and to whom the writer is greatly indebted for much information about the family, tells the following story:[74]

"When a death occurred, the Church bell was tolled, and the age of the deceased announced by the strokes of the bell. A stroke for each year. The town hearse was a large coffin painted black, on four wheels with a raised

---

[73] Frederick Dorsey (1776-1858) was the 'celebrated' physician in Washington County with whom many young doctors studied. He was born in Anne Arundel County, MD and married Sarah Clagett in 1803. His son John Clagett Dorsey (1804-1870) was also a local physician, as was his grandson Frederick Dorsey (1834-1888). Scharf, John Thomas, *History of Western Maryland*, (Philadelphia, PA, 1882), 1238.

[74] Mrs. Anne Rosina Locher Johnson (1819-1909), the author's second cousin, once-removed, was the daughter of George Locher (1789-1831) and Elizabeth Schafer (1793-1851), and a granddaughter of John Henry Schafer. Born in Funkstown, she married Doctor James Johnson (1800-1872) of Hagerstown in 1846. The Johnsons lived in Falling Waters, Berkeley County, VA [WV] where Annie was a teacher. *US Federal Census 1880.*

MRS. ANNIE ROSINA JOHNSON

Stonebraker's second-cousin, once-removed, Mrs. Annie Rosina Locher Johnson. Annie and her husband, Dr. James Johnson, lived in Morgan County and later Berkeley County, VA [WV]. She was a schoolteacher and the source of Stonebraker's genealogical information. The Johnsons had seven children; their sixth child, born in 1860, was amusingly named Hard Times Johnson. Photo from original text.

seat for the driver, and drawn by a diminutive, emaciated horse, which at last succumbed to long service. On the evening of his demise, as the peaceful inhabitants of the quite village were retiring for the night, they were startled by the prolonged tolling of the Church bell. The sexton hastened to the undertaker, to learn who had usurped his exclusive office. The undertaker could not inform him, and both he and the sexton were superstitious, and in the meantime the bell ceased its sounds, when superstition brooded over the village.

"At length it leaked out that some boys, who thought old Shoemaker (the defunct horse) deserved some recognition for his long and weary service, had crept into the Church and announced his departure. The gloom of superstition was lifted by many smiles, and some hearty laughs, and Shoemaker's memory was embalmed."

Scratch

The Pews of the old Union Church, resembled box stalls, being enclosed on all sides with high partitions that reached almost to the back part of the head, and a panel door which closed by a spring latch, with a bang. The main aisle divided the congregation; the men sat on one side and the ladies on the other.

A black velvet bag on the end of a long pole, was used to collect the pennies, and was passed up the pew before the occupants, then raised over their heads to the seat behind.

It took a good eye and steady hand to avoid accidents to the head-gear of the ladies, although sun-bonnets, or pokes, were the prevailing fashion. If the pole was in the hands of a malicious deacon, the heads of mischievous boys were not free from knocks.

The front box, directly opposite the altar, was occupied by the elders, and was known as the elder's Pew, who generally were venerable members of the congregation.

One of the elders, for years had an exceptionally bald head, over which the flies skirmished to the delight of the boys. Shortly after his marriage to a young girl, as wife number two, he appeared among his fellow elders in a dark brown "Scratch," to the surprise of the congregation.[75]

It will never be known whether it was an accident or no, but when the pole passed over the elder's Pew, the bag and "Scratch" became entangled, when a bald head disappeared behind the back, and reappeared again with a full suit of hair. The situation was very embarrassing to him, but it affected the risibles of the beholders.

"Ask nothing but what is right—submit to nothing wrong," was Andrew Jackson's great political maxim. In 1828 he was elected President, and early in the following year he made his way via the Ohio River to Wheeling, and thence over what is now the old National Road to Washington City. He passed through Funkstown, standing in an open carriage, bowing graciously to the citizens, who considered it an event well worth remembering.[76]

The town at one time boasted of a Beneficial Association, but it did not thrive very long. One of its early members became sick and remained on the relief list so long that he bankrupted the treasury, when the association went out of existence.

The box pews in Prince George's Chapel, Dagsboro, DE. with high partition sides comparable to those used in the Union Church of Funkstown in the mid-1850s. Library of Congress, Prints and Photographs, Washington, DC. (hereafter referred to as LOC/P&P HABS DEL,3-DAG,1--9.

---

75   A scratch is an early term for a hairpiece or toupee.
76   Eight years later, at the end of his presidency, Jackson again visited Funkstown. From the *Hagerstown Mail*, 17 Mar 1837: "General Jackson arrived in this county on Thursday, the 9th instant, on his way to Tennessee. . . The General was met at Miller's tavern, on the top of South Mountain. . . He was escorted by his fellow citizens of the Boonsborough district to Beaver Creek, where he was met by a portion of his friends from Hagerstown and Funkstown."

Military

The Yager Riflemen, Capt. Geo. W. Boerstler commanding, was the first military organization of which we have any record. Its Captain was the town's physician, who took great pride in his Company, as well as the town, whose name did not always appear very euphonious to strangers.[77]

One Sunday morning, the old Stage Coach drew up before the Town Hotel, when about a dozen passengers alighted and took a drink. Their conversation showed that many were newly elected members to Congress, on their way to the Capital.

A few drinks put them in good humor, when they commenced to ply some of the by-standers about the name of the town and its enterprises. The Doctor who was standing near by, with face flushed by indignation, stepped up to the crowd and said, "Gentlemen, you have been asking a great many nonsensical questions; let me inform you that this little town was reared by industry, and supported by the economy of its citizens, and I am surprised that they allow a lot of Sunday troopers to pass through unmolested." They lost but little time in shaking the dust of the town from their feet.

Shortly after the Irish riot, Henry I. Schäfer, organized the Kentucky Riflemen, so named because their uniform was modeled after the style of Daniel Boone's dress. This company succeeded the Yagers, with Schäfer as Captain.

Last but not least the Washington Riflemen, Peter L. Huyette, Captain, was the crack company of the section. Huyette was one of the town's merchants, and on muster days, his house was wide open to the members of his company. He was a large pompous man with a voice like a fog horn, and his gay uniform was the admiration of the boys.[78]

The Boerstler house, circa 1792, at 13-17 W. Baltimore Street, Funkstown, MD. Erin Black Photography, Williamsport, MD.

---

77   Doctor George W. Boerstler (1792-1871) was the son of Doctor Christian Boerstler (1750-1833) of Funkstown. Christian Boerstler was the proprietor of a powder-mill in Funkstown as early as 1804. George Boerstler established a woolen factory there in May of 1815 and began practicing medicine in 1820. George Boerstler received a degree from the University of Maryland in 1820. In 1833 he moved to Lancaster in Fairfield County, OH. In 1846, Boerstler became the first president of the Ohio State Medical Society, later the Ohio State Medical Association. Scharf, J. Thomas, *History of Western Maryland*, (Philadelphia, PA, 1882), 1280, Kelly, Howard, Atwood, *A Cyclopedia of American Medical Biography* (Baltimore, MD, 1920), 117-118.

78   Peter Lewis Huyette (1810-1883), son of Daniel Huyette (1786-1869), was a resident of Funkstown in 1850. He married first: Catherine Elizabeth Stonebraker (1813-1838) in 1833, the author's first-cousin, twice-removed. He married second: Elizabeth Ann Clagett (1822-?) in 1840. By 1856, Huyette had moved to Jefferson County, IA, then later St. Joseph, MO. *US Federal Census 1850 to 1880. WCLR 11-244.*

Haunted Hill

This is the picture of an old gristmill that was once operated by Samuel Shafer,[79] one of the third generation. It was situated on Marsh Run, half way between Bakersville and Mount Moriah. John Rentch, who married Catharine Shafer, in connection with his farm owned a large tract of timber, which he utilized by manufacturing barrels and sold them to the surrounding mills and distilleries.[80]

After his death the widow continued the business, with Jesse Banks, as head cooper and general manager. Jesse was a hard-working young man, with an impediment in his speech, and occasionally took too much of old "John Barleycorn."[81]

It was several miles between the mill and the shop; with a very steep hill about midway, upon which the Negroes believed a black headless dog could be seen at mid-night, and whoever the dog barked at, would die before the end of the year.[82]

On Saturday afternoons Jesse generally repaired to the mill to make a report of his week's delivery and get settlement. Here at the distillery, he often met some convivial friends, that were sure to prolong his stay until late at night.

Then it was that Jesse always declared when he reached the foot of the haunted hill the headless dog would jump the fence and follow closely at his heels until they reached a certain tree on the side of the road would suddenly disappear.

OLD GRIST AND SAW MILL, AT MARSH RUN,
OPERATED BY SAMUEL SHAFER

Today there is no evidence of this mill on Marsh Run. Photo from original text.

---

79 **Original Footnote: The third generation Anglicized the name by dropping the "e" and discarding the German umlaut.** Samuel Shafer (1798-?), occupation miller, was the author's granduncle, the brother of his grandmother Catharine Shafer Rentch. *US Federal Census 1850.*

80 John Rentch died in 1822.

81 Master cooper Jesse Dallas Banks (1800-1866), wife Harriett (1816-1901) and five children lived in the Grimes/Bakersville area. They are buried in the Bakersville Cemetery.
"John Barleycorn" is an English folksong. The character of John Barleycorn in the song is a personification of the important cereal crop barley, and of the beer and whiskey made from barley. *US Federal Census 1850 and 1860.*

82 Primarily found in the folklores of the British Isles, virtually every ancient culture has a legend of a fearsome, nocturnal black dog. Often said to be associated with the Devil, its appearance was regarded as a portent of death. It is generally supposed to be larger than a normal dog, and often has large, glowing eyes and is said to be the inspiration for the ghost dog in *The Hound of the Baskervilles* by Arthur Conan Doyle. In this instance it is interesting how a headless dog is able to bark.

Our Eastern Home

Here almost beneath the shadow of "Black Rock," we made our eastern home.[83] Funkstown is located on the old National Pike, two miles south of Hagerstown, and laid out in the bend of the Antietam Creek, which forms a perfect horse-shoe. All the rear or outside lots, northwest and south run to the edge of the creek.

It has a population of about eight hundred people. Its early push and energy had departed before our advent, but there still lingered some evidences of its former sporting elements. Here resided several wealthy families who indulged themselves in almost all manner of sports. They fought chickens, raced horses, and followed the hounds. Although the heads of these families were too old to longer indulge themselves, yet their example was still followed by others, with an occasional bear bait and shooting match.

I saw many of these sports against my mother's wish, and was severely punished when it was discovered that I had disobeyed her commands.

Game cocks of equal weight were matched. Their spurs were cut off, steel gaffs were tied to their legs, and then pitted against each other. The cock that killed his antagonist was declared the winner. As a rule they fought until they died, and if by chance one turned tail and ran, he was considered a "dunghill." It was a barbarous but fascinating sport.[84]

Today there is no evidence of this distillery on Marsh Run. Photo from original text.

OLD DISTILLERY, AT MARSH RUN

---

83   Black Rock is a rocky outcrop on top of the western edge of South Mountain located about seven miles east of Funkstown.
84   Cockfighting was banned in Maryland in 1890, but not made a felony until 2002. *Maryland Criminal Law Code Ann. § 10-608.*

Bear Bait

The bear fight was arranged by driving a stake into the ground and to this the bear was chained, when the spectators formed in a circle around him. Dogs were then put inside of the ring and made to fight, but bruin was always victorious.

We occupied the Bell property. A large white house, with two huge pillars, supporting a porch from the attic, giving it a Colonial appearance.[85]

The house stood on the banks of the Antietam near the old Grist Mill at the head of the island. It was here I spent my boyhood days. What grand days they were too, now that I look back upon them. Fishing and swimming were my chief delight.

The mill had been gutted of its machinery, and father used the second floor as a work shop. What terrors some of its dark places had for my youthful imagination, stimulated by the tales of my colored playmates.

How lasting such impressions seem to be, for when in dreamland now I often see the old mill and flee from some imaginary phantom of my youth.

On the other side of the creek were the ruins of a powder mill that furnished ammunition for the provincial army during the Revolutionary War.[86] Often while standing on its ruins catching black chubs for eel bait, I pictured in my mind the flying timbers and mangled forms that the accident must have caused when the works blew up.

Henry Stonebraker and his family lived in the large 18th century stone home known as Valentia *on Poffenberger Road south of Funkstown, MD. Valentia was a plantation of over 700 acres owned by the Clagett brothers. The house still stands today as a private residence. Erin Black Photography, Williamsport, MD.*

---

85 Directly south of Funkstown, MD at Poffenberger Road is an island in the Antietam Creek and the estate known as *Valentia*. The property has three stone dwelling houses including a large, stone 18th century home fronted by columns. A combination of several earlier patents, in 1819, Samuel Beall [pronounced Bell], David, and Hezekiah Clagett resurveyed over 730 acres into one large plantation they named *Valentia*. The Clagett brothers were successful merchants and politicians of Hagerstown. David Clagett died in 1851, and Hezekiah Clagett and his family did not live at *Valentia* until after 1860. Reasonably, the house would have been available for lease to tenant farmers in the 1850s. *MSA Patents IB G/307:IB E2/74.*

86 The Claggett mill site on the Antietam Creek appears on both the 1794 Dennis Griffin and the 1808 Charles Varle map of Washington County and has a long history as the location of numerous and varied types of mills.

Spring Time

ANTIETAM CREEK AND ISLAND

Photo from original text.

I went to school during the week, but on Saturdays I did small chores about the place. These duties I did with as much grace as boys usually do, until the blue birds began to sing, when I would steal off with my fishing pole and stay away all day, giving my mother many uneasy moments, as she feared that I would be drowned.

When punished, I would promise not to do so any more, but such promises were worthless, for as early in the spring and late in the fall as the fish would bite, I could not resist the temptation. At the first opportunity I would be off with my pole and repeat the same old story.

Bob, our old roan horse, was a sly fox. He would untie any knot that I could make in his halter, get in the corn barrel, and I was often punished for his theft.

He knew I was afraid of him, and when in pasture would not let me catch him, but when hooked to the wagon, he was as gentle as a lamb.

When but ten years old, with "Bob" hitched to a little yellow wheel and green bed wagon, I made many trips to Frick's foundry, near Waynesboro, Pa. During all our companionship he only ran away once, and he was the greatest sufferer, having his legs badly skinned.[87]

---

[87] The industrial revolution of the mid-19th century changed flour and grist mills, tanneries, distilleries, woolen and paper mills, furnaces, forges, marble yards, and sawmills from water power to steam engines power. In about 1853, George Frick opened the Frick Foundry in Waynesboro, PA where he built steam engines and later, threshing machines. *A History of Frick Company, Waynesboro, Pennsylvania* (Kyle Printing Company, 1952).

Pierce and King

In the fall of 1852 I took part in a political demonstration for the first time. It was the campaign in which Pierce, Democrat, defeated Gen. Scott, Whig, for the Presidency.[88]

I carried a flag made by my sisters. It was rather crude and made of cambric. They could not get bright red for the stripes but used dark red. The Whig boys twitted me by saying that the stripes were colored by polkberry juice.[89] However we elected our president, and I was as proud of my flag as if it had been made of the finest silk.

The Democratic farmers of our election district hitched up their teams of four and six horses, some with bells, while others had theirs decorated with fall flowers, now called the chrysanthemum.

The wagons were loaded with men, boys and girls of the town and driven to Hagerstown, the county seat, where a similar delegation from each election district of the county had assembled. They were then marshaled into line, paraded through the principal streets, after which we were taken to a vacant lot, and a lunch of cold meats and bread were served from long tables.

President Franklin Pierce, LOC/P&P. LC-USZ62-13014.

---

88   Franklin Pierce (1804-1869) was a Democrat politician, lawyer, and a "doughface" - a northerner with southern sympathies. Elected the 14th President of the United States, he served from 1853 to 1857. The only President from New Hampshire, he was the first to have been born in the 19th century. His vice-president was William Rufus DeVane King (1786-1853). King died of tuberculosis after 45 days in office. The Pierce-King ticket defeated the Whig candidate "old Fuss and Feather" Winfield Scott (1786-1866), a national hero after the Mexican-American War.

89   Polkberry is also known as poke, pokebush, pokeberry, or pokeroot. The berries yield a red ink or dye, which was once used by American Indians to decorate their horses. Many letters written home during the American Civil War were written in pokeberry ink. The writing in these surviving letters appears brown.

Cow Boy

Nearly every family in town had a cow, and in the summer they were pastured, with the farmers, who lived near the village, charging the owners one dollar per month for the privilege. It was the duty of each boy of the family to drive the cows to the pasture fields in the morning, and take them home in the evening.

The families that did not have boys employed some one to drive their cow, paying one cent a day for such service. I always had a neighbor's cow to take care of, and on Saturday night when paid in copper cents for my week's work, I was very happy, and felt rich, with the big cart-wheel pennies in my pocket.

Mother required us to go to Sunday School and Church regularly. I was so young that I do not remember just when I first commenced to go to either, but I am happy now to state that it was always a pleasant duty. I learned the XXIII Psalm before I could read.

My Sunday School teacher was one of those nice, amiable young women, that can be found in almost every town. She encouraged her class of boys to commit to memory verses from the Bible, and the one that did the best was rewarded with a book. She tried to make a preacher out of me, but when father was approached for his consent, he threw cold water on the project. He evidently knew his boy much better than the teacher.

One of my uncles, a farmer who lived near Sharpsburg, had a boy about my age. I often spent some time with them, on a visit. On Sunday he took us to town to Church, where the Rev. Robt. Douglas officiated, and the one who could remember the most of the sermon received a penny.[90]

At times in every community there are some persons so unfortunate as to imagine that life is not worth living, and end their existence by violence.

In the beautiful month of May, a young farmer living a short distance from town, walked to the Antietam Creek, carefully laid his hat on the bank and threw himself into Clagett's mill dam.

He had the reputation of being a good swimmer, and there were some present who expressed doubts of him suiciding, but I noticed as they fished him out, that his suspender was twisted around his arm.

Child tending grazing cow, Photo by Russell Lee, circa 1940, LOC/P&P. LC-USF33-012804-M2.

---

90 Reverend Robert Douglas (1807-1867) and his family resided at *Ferry Hill* Plantation south of Sharpsburg, MD overlooking the Potomac River.

Harvest Time

Two men cutting grain using scythes with cradles, circa 1900. LOC/P&P. LC-USZ62-51245.

Before machinery had revolutionized the manner of the farmers housing their crops, and the short time in which wheat had to be cut when ready for the sickle, caused such a demand for labor that it depopulated the towns of all able-bodied men and boys. The fields were vast, wages good, and the people happy.

The grain in our section ripened some weeks before the Pennsylvania fields, and many persons journeyed from that state to our valley to help to harvest the crop. In squads, many came from the mountainous portions of Huntingdon and Bedford counties, and were called "backwoodsmen."

A cradle was used, and each one represented three hands. The farmer that employed fewer than five had a small crop.[91]

It was a pleasant sight to see twenty or more cradlers in line mowing down the golden grain, all keeping time to the leader's stroke, and the gleaners in their wake, binding the swath into sheaves.

The boy who followed with the water wagon and "fire-water" was always in demand. How eager we looked for the "ten o'clock bite" and the sound of the dinner horn. For the work was hard and appetites good. When the harvest was over, such a feast. Tubs of lemonade and tables loaded with ginger bread and other good things, the thought of which always makes me wish to be a boy again.

---

91   Harvesting grain with the use of a cradle first came into use about the time of the Revolutionary War. The cradle is a scythe with wooden fingers running parallel with the blade. These wooden fingers hold the stalks of grain, after they have been cut off, in an upright position, and enable the cradler to lay the grain down in a neat row, with the stalks parallel, ready to be gathered into bunches and bound into sheaves. A strong man with a cradle could cut from two to two-and-a-half acres of wheat in a day. A second man following along would gather the grain and bind it into sheaves.

Corn Husking

Often in the fall of the year many farmers made corn husking a social feature. The cornstalk was topped and bladed, instead of cut close to the ground, which is now done.[92] The ears were plucked from the stalk, hauled to the barn and put in a long row. Some afternoon was selected and the neighbors were invited to the shucking. When the company had assembled, two men were appointed as captains, they in turn chose sides, divided the corn in half, when the battle began. The Negroes were always among the shuckers, and did much to enliven the occasion with their quaint songs.

> "Shuck de corn and skin de nubbin, O! Ho, Ho"

and

> "Raccoon tail am ringed all round, and de Possum tail am bare,
> "Old Brer Fox, may fool Bull-Frog, but he didn't kotch de Hare."

When the battle was over, the victorious side elevated their Captain on their shoulders and paraded to the house, where we partook of a sumptuous feast, such only as a farmer's wife can prepare, after which the young people made a night of it with their rural pastimes:

> "Come all young men, in your wicked ways,
> Come sow your wild oats, in your youthful days,
> That you may be happy, That you may be happy,
> When you grow old."[93]

PICKANINNIES

The term Pickaninnies is a potentially derogatory term that refers to children of black descent. It is a pidgin word form, which may be derived from the Portuguese pequenino an affectionate term for small or little one or "small child." Also derived from the Spanish word pequeno, or "little."
Photo from original text.

---

92   In early fall farmers stripped most of the blades or leaves from the corn stalk and tied them into bundles. This 'fodder' was dried, then stored in the 'fodder-loft' and used as food for the livestock throughout the winter. The ears of corn remained on the bare stalks in the field until they were hard and dry. In late fall the ears were gathered and the outer husk removed in a process called 'shucking.' The practice of removing the leaves was thought to focus the plant's energy into the production of enlarged corn ears. In 1835, Luther Tucker in *The Farmer's Register* wisely argued that "the corn plant derives nutriment from the atmospheric air as well as the soil. By depriving it of its top and a portion of its blades, we cut off one source at least of its natural aliment. Such an unnatural practice arrests the natural circulation of the sap, which flows through the stalk. Some farmers may, perhaps believe, that by so doing they can turn or force the juices into the ear by a mode more wisely than that already provided by the Author of nature!" *The Genesee Farmer and Gardener's Journal, Volume 5*, (Rochester, NY, 1835). *The Farmer's Register, Volume 2* (Shellbanks, VA, 1835), 91.

93   A portion of a longer verse from the children's game of joggle or joggling. Gomme, G. Laurence and Alice Bertha, *A Dictionary of British Folk-Lore. Part 1, Traditional games of England, Scotland and Ireland* (London, 1894). 285.

Temptation

Thoreau, says: "It appears that apples made a part of the food of that unknown primitive people whose traces have lately been found at the bottom of the Swiss lakes, supposed to be older than the foundation of Rome, so old that they had no metallic implements."[94]

Whether our first parents were tempted by the apple or no, I never could pass an apple tree, full of ripe, luscious fruit, in an ordinary frame of mind.

On my way to school I had to pass a row of trees red with fruit

"Every twig, apples big,"[95]

jealously guarded by the owner against the predatory habits of the small boy, but it was my special delight to outwit the old man and fill my pockets with the forbidden fruit.

Near where we lived was a group of the "Southern Rambo."[96] Upon one of the trees hung a hornet's nest big as a half-bushel measure. I used to visit this group of trees ostensibly to stone the hornets but really to gorge myself with the fruit. Alas, that variety of apples has become extinct.[97]

At grandfather's, during the long winter nights, what pitchers of cider and baskets of apples were consumed. In the cellar were huge bins, each variety separated by partitions. With that native thrift, peculiar to the German race, we boys, when sent to the cellar for apples and cider, were instructed to get only the "specks."[98]

To me this was worse than foolishness and on the sly would slip a few of the finest in my pockets, and only ate the specked through compulsion.

The bins were so full of fruit, that the apples commenced to decay faster than they could be used, and the result was that the family ate rotten apples the whole winter through.

---

94   From Henry David Thoreau's *Wild Apples, The History of the Apple-Tree.* The article begins with a short history of the apple tree, tracing its path from ancient Greece to America. Thoreau saw the apple as a perfect mirror of man and eloquently lamented where they both were heading. *The Atlantic Monthly, Volume 10, No. 5* (Boston, MA, Nov 1862), 513-526.

95   From a 19th century traditional English Apple Wassailing chant. Wassailing on Twelfth night is said to bless the trees to produce a good crop.

Stand fast root, bear well top,
Pray the God send us a howling good crop
Every twig, apples big.
Every bough, apples now.

Garry Hogg, *Customs and Traditions of England* (Arco Publishing Company, NY, 1971), 11.

96   An 1878 Virginia nursery catalog describes the Rambo apple as "one of the best early winter apples for the piedmont and [Shenandoah] Valley districts." When grown in the cooler climates, Rambo is smaller, more solid, and keeps better than when grown in warmer areas. Calhoun, Creighton Lee, *Old Southern Apples: A Comprehensive History and Description of Varieties for Collectors, Growers, and Fruit Enthusiasts,* (Chelsea Green Publishing Company, White River Junction, VT, 2010), 129.

97   It is estimated that in the 1800s there were over 7,000 apple varieties. Today there are less than 1,000.

98   Specks are cosmetic or disease blemishes on fruit.

Cholera's first Appearance in America

In 1832 Cholera prevailed in France, and within the year caused one hundred and twenty thousand deaths, seven thousand of which occurred in Paris, in the space of eighteen days. In the spring and summer of that year it made its appearance in England, and extended into Ireland—from Liverpool, Cork, Limerick, and Dublin. Five vessels filled with immigrants sailed for Quebec, Canada, and they together lost one hundred and seventy-nine passengers by cholera during the voyage.[99]

On the 7th of June the St. Lawrence steamer, Voyageur, took a load of these immigrants and their baggage from the vessel, which were quarantined two miles below the city, and landed some in Quebec, but took the majority to Montreal. The first case of cholera occurred in an immigrant boarding house in Quebec, on the 8th. The same boat landed persons, dead and dying of cholera, at Montreal, a distance of 200 miles, in thirty hours.

Over this long distance, thickly inhabited on both sides of the St. Lawrence River, cholera made a single leap without infecting a single village or house between the two cities, with the following exceptions: A man picked up a mattress thrown from the Voyageur; he and his wife died from cholera. Another man fishing on the river was requested to bury a dead man from the Voyageur, he and his wife and nephew died from cholera. The scourge continued west along the Great Lakes, and in September it reached our military post, where Chicago now stands, almost depopulating the section through which it passed.[100]

Broadside for Preventives of Cholera. Published by order of the Sanatory Committee, under the sanction of the Medical Counsel (NY, 1849).

---

99   Cholera is an infection of the small intestines caused by the bacterium *Vibrio cholerae*. The main symptoms are profuse watery diarrhea, vomiting and abdominal pain. Transmission is primarily through contaminated drinking water or food. Cholera is a major cause of death in the world. www.ncbi.nlm.nih.gov/.

100   For several years prior to 1832, Americans followed the horrific reports of death by cholera raging across the European and Asian continents. By early spring of 1832 reports of death were diminishing and the plague thought to be contained. The arrival in Jun 1832 of five ships from the United Kingdom at Quebec is credited as the unofficial introduction of the disease to Canada and the United States. By August the disease was reported in almost all major American cities including Washington, Baltimore and Philadelphia. The first cases in Frederick MD were in mid-September of 1832, and by October there were seventeen deaths in Hagerstown as reported in *The Mail*, including: Thomas Kennedy, a member of the Maryland State Legislature. John McIlhenny, father of Edmund,

In 1853 the Asiatic cholera reached our Atlantic coast from Europe for the third time. As heretofore it moved into the interior of the States by the navigable water courses.

The Chesapeake and Ohio Canal, that runs along the Potomac River from Washington, D.C., to Cumberland, conveyed the disease to the western part of the State. In August of this year, two citizens of Funkstown, James Fleming and Jonathan Shilling, Jr., who had been employed on the canal near Williamsport, Md., came home and were stricken down with cholera; and after a few hours illness died; Fleming died one day and Shilling the next.[101] This greatly alarmed the citizens of the town. Quite a number took the disease and many died before the scourge was stamped out. Father closed up the house and took the family to grandfather's farm, where we remained until late in the fall.

Cholera, like war, while full of horrors, has its amusing incidents. Dr. Clagett was the town physician, and a number of the citizens in a body called on the doctor for advice, when he made them a speech from the second-story window of his house, telling them to use brandy freely as a preventive. From his appearance he, no doubt, had been taking his own prescription quite freely.

Uncle Tom South[102] (Geo. Alfred Townsend's Nick Hammer),[103] thought to make himself proof against the disease; and having no very great prejudice against the remedy, took too many large doses and slipped off the bed on the floor, where "Granny," his wife, found him; and thinking him to be dying with the cholera, alarmed the town with her cries. A more careful diagnosis of the case being made, the true state of his condition was discovered, much to her relief.

Father finally purchased the house in which we were living, and it was much out of repair. He being quite a mechanic, spent much of his time in building fences, and making other necessary repairs. He had a fondness for lattice fence, and my little back ached many a night from holding the hammer, while he drove the nails through the pine laths. When the fences were done, they had to be whitewashed, and I did my share of this work. He planted several hundred young fruit trees, and the following summer proving to be a very dry season, when I had to carry water from the creek and give each tree two buckets of water a day—one in the morning and another in the eve-

---

inventor of Tabasco Sauce™, Mr. William Moffett, merchant, John Miller, merchant, William Tritch, John McLaughlin, 3 year old John Schleigh, and Mrs. Daniel Snider.

101   The 184.5 mile long Chesapeake & Ohio Canal stretches from the mouth of Rock Creek in Georgetown, DC to Cumberland, MD.
    Both James Fleming (1821-1853) and John H. Shilling (1829-1853) and their families appear on the 1850 US Federal Census as residents of Funkstown.

102   Thomas South (1781-1873) was listed in the 1860 census, age 78, living in Funkstown MD with his wife Barbara, 77; son David, a butcher; Sarah Crawford, 18; and John South, 13. *US Federal Census 1860.*

103   George Alfred Townsend (1841–1914) wrote the amusing poem *Legend of Funkstown* about a fictitious character named Nick Hammer who mistakes John Brown for the missing founder of Funkstown. Townsend's inspiration for Nick Hammer was Funkstown resident Thomas South and his son. Townsend wrote for newspapers for forty years and was one of the first syndicated correspondents. A war correspondent during the Civil War, Townsend's unique and certainly his most lasting endeavor is a stone monument he had built atop South Mountain in 1896 as a memorial to his fellow war correspondents. See pages 219-220 for full text of the *Legend of Funkstown*.

HENRY STONEBRAKER'S FUNKSTOWN HOME, 1847

ning. This was a herculean task for a boy of my age, and I had many a good cry before the day was over.[104]

In a few years we had our home in fine shape, young orchard, grape arbors, and a yard full of flowers; the most attractive place in the village, when father sold it and formed a co-partnership with Mr. J. C. Hoffman, and opened a general merchandise store on the main street of the town. I was put in the store to do the small errands about the place, such as are usually preformed by a boy.[105]

Some time after the panic of '57, Hoffman went out of the firm, father continuing.[106] The change made it necessary to supply his late partner's place with a clerk, and Geo. S. Miller, of Hagerstown, was selected. Miller was a small, dudish young fellow, who cared more for fine clothes than work,

The Henry Stonebraker home in Funkstown stood on Lot #113 on present day E. Green Street. The house does not stand today. Photo from original text.

---

104   Henry Stonebraker purchased the ½ lot #113, and full lots #114 and #115 on 23 Jan 1855 from Abraham and Caroline White for $75. A short time later he purchased an additional 12 acres for $200 from Elie Beaty, the Washington County Treasurer. *WCLR, IN 9-356* and *IN 11-616*. The Stonebraker home shows on the 1877 map of Funkstown as Lot #113 Mrs. Sager's home, present day E. Green Street. *Illustrated Atlas of Washington County, Maryland 1877* (Philadelphia, PA, 1877).

105   Henry Stonebraker sold his house in Jun 1857 for $600. The 1860 US Federal Census for Funkstown lists: Henry Stonebraker, age 35, merchant; Joseph Stonebraker, age 16, (the author) clerk; John Calvin Hoffman (1832-1895) born in Jefferson County, VA [WV]; and wife Clara Jane Knode Hoffman. *WCLR IN12-426*.

106   John Calvin, or J. C. Hoffman, moved to Hagerstown and continued in the dry-goods business. Eventually Hoffman owned his own business and with his 4 sons he would prosper as J. C. Hoffman's & Sons, selling dry goods, notions, tailoring, and men's clothing. The store continued under several variations of the Hoffman name, the last being Hoffman's Men's Wear. The store closed in 2009. *The Herald Mail* (Hagerstown, MD) 16 Oct 2009.

> WILD WESTERN SCENES:
>
> A NARRATIVE
> OF
> Adventures in the Western Wilderness,
>
> WHEREIN
> THE EXPLOITS OF DANIEL BOONE, THE GREAT AMERICAN PIONEER
> ARE PARTICULARLY DESCRIBED
>
> ALSO,
> ACCOUNTS OF BEAR, DEER, AND BUFFALO HUNTS—DESPERATE CONFLICTS
> WITH THE SAVAGES—WOLF HUNTS—FISHING AND FOWLING
> ADVENTURES—ENCOUNTERS WITH SERPENTS, ETC.
>
> NEW STEREOTYPE EDITION, ALTERED, REVISED, AND CORRECTED
>
> By J. B. JONES.
> AUTHOR OF "THE WAR PATH," "ADVENTURES OF A COUNTRY MERCHANT," ETC.
>
> Illustrated with Sixteen Engravings from Original Designs
>
> PHILADELPHIA:
> J. B. LIPPINCOTT & CO.
> 1875.

John Beauchamp Jones, *Wild Western Scenes: A Narrative of Adventures in the Western Wilderness, wherein The Exploits of Daniel Boone, The Great American Pioneer are Particularly Described*. (J. B. Lippincott & Company, Philadelphia, PA, 1857).

so my duties increased in the rough line. For some reason Miller did not suit the town, or the place was too small to hold him, as he only remained with us a few months.

David Over had been coming through our section with a two-horse wagon, buying old rags for some Pennsylvania paper mill. He was a small, energetic, talkative individual, father taking a great fancy to him, and when Miller left, Over was engaged to take his place. Davy's appearance showed his poverty, and for a time we got on well together. He did his share of rough work and allowed me to wait on some of the big customers once in a while. But it was not long before Davy improved his personal appearance; fine clothes and rough work don't go well together, and as he was the head clerk, all the drudgery fell to me, causing no little friction, and at times open rebellion on my part. Davy finally developed a fondness for the social cup, losing father's confidence, and was discharged. Some years afterwards he met with an accident that injured one of his arms so much that it had to be amputated. He refused to be put under the influence of chloroform, and stood the operation without flinching, but the accident cost him his life.[107]

In certain seasons there are hours between customers in a little country store, and I employed much of my idle time in reading. Jones' *Wild Western Scenes* made its appearance about this time, and was the first book I ever read.[108] How much I admired the cunning of "Sneak" and laughed at "Joe's" stupidity, in putting asafoetida[109] on the soles of his boots while hunting for wolves. This was the beginning of my fondness for books.

Business had been growing from bad to worse ever since the panic, when father closed out his store at auction, leaving him in straightened circumstances.

---

[107] David J. Over (1826-1867) a farm laborer formerly of Bedford, PA, appears on the 1860 US Federal Census as a resident of Funkstown along with his wife Sally, and children Elizabeth, Miller, and Newcomer. The *Herald & Torch Light* of 13 Mar 1867 reported he died from injuries sustained at the paper mill.

[108] John Beauchamp Jones (1810-1866) was a writer whose books featuring the American West and the American South enjoyed considerable popularity during the mid 19th century. Born in Baltimore, MD. Jones also served in the Confederacy. His diary *"A Rebel War Clerk's Diary at the Confederate States Capital"* (J. B. Lippincott & Company, Philadelphia, PA, 1866) was published in two volumes in 1866.

[109] Asifoetida is a resinous gum obtained from the roots of a herbaceous plant used in herbal medicine and Indian cooking. American author John C. Duval (1816-1897) wrote in 1936 that Texans used the odor of asafoetida to bait wolves.

John Brown

One day in June, 1859, while sitting under the trees in front of South's Hotel, a tall, muscular stranger, with a long, full beard, drove up to the tavern and had his horse fed. The wagon was filled with what we supposed to be fork handles, and we wondered what use the old man made of them, and where he was going.[110]

The following October, after Brown had failed to incite the Negroes to insurrection, we learned that the mysterious stranger was John Brown, already notorious as a partisan leader against slavery in Kansas. He had rented a small farm on the Maryland side of the Potomac River, near Harper's Ferry, Va. Here it was that he had stored and fashioned those handles into pikes, with the intention of putting them in the hands of the slaves, to be used against their masters.

One night Brown and his party crossed over the river into Harper's Ferry, took possession of the United States arsenal, made prisoners of many of the citizens, stopped the railway trains, cut the telegraph wires, and held the town until the afternoon of the second day, when the regular troops, under Capt. Rob. E. Lee, stormed and captured the engine house, in which he had taken refuge.[111]

The above incident suggested to Geo. Alfred Townsend to write his poem, "Legend of Funkstown," from which these few verses are selected:[112]

John Brown holding the New York Tribune Newspaper. LOC/P&P. LC-USZ62-89569.

" Nick Hammer sat in Funkstown
    Before his tavern door—
The same old blue-stone tavern
    The wagoners knew of yore,
When the Conestoga Schooners
    Came staggering under their load,

---

110   The 1860 US Federal census indicates the Stonebraker store and home was a few doors east of South's Hotel on the main street of Funkstown. South's Hotel was operated by Benjamin South (1824-?) during the mid-19th century in the stone two-story house built by Funkstown founder Jacob Funk in 1769, at present day 35 W. Baltimore Street. Benjamin South was likely the son of Tom South (1781-1873), the inspiration for Townsend's character in his poem *Legend of Funkstown*. Therefore it would be logical that "'ol Tom South" would be sitting on the front porch of South's Hotel when John Brown passed by.

    John Brown registered at the Washington Hotel on Thursday, 30 Jun 1859 using the alias of "John Smith." *Washington House Ledger*, Western Maryland Room, Washington County Free Library, Hagerstown, MD.

111   This event occurred on the night of 16 Oct 1859.

112   George Alfred Townsend (1841–1914), previously noted footnote 103.

>   And the lines of slow pack-horses
>   Stamped over the National Road.[113]
>
> One day in June two wagons
>   Came over Antietam bridge
> And a tall old man behind them
>   Strode up the turnpike ridge,
> His beard was long and grizzled,
>   His face was gnarled and long,
> His voice was keen and nasal,
>   And his mouth and eye were strong.
>
> One wagon was full of boxes
>   And the other full of poles,
> As the weaver's wife discovered,
>   While the weaver took the tolls.
> Two young men drove the horses,
>   And neither the people knew;
> But young Nick asked a question
>   And the old man looked him through.

Brown and his co-conspirators were turned over to the State of Virginia, taken to Charlestown, tried, convicted and hanged for their crime against the State.[114]

John Smith, a poor wretch, paid the penalty with his life for murdering a young girl. The execution took place in Hagerstown, on a vacant lot near the county jail, and a great crowd of men, women and boys witnessed the tragedy. I had a position within fifty feet of the gibbet. The prisoner had completely lost his nerve, and two men assisted him to ascend the scaffold. As he stood on the trap, his body was convulsed with fear, and he cried like a baby as the black cap was drawn over his head and the noose adjusted about his neck. As I now recall that painful scene, I am forcibly reminded of that similarity of morbid curiosity, as described in the Crucifixion, by the writer of Barabbas: "Fearful and unnatural as it seems, it is nevertheless true, that in all ages the living have found a peculiar and awful satisfaction in watching the agonies of the dying."[115]

In May, 1860, the convention of the Republican party met at Chicago and nominated Mr. Lincoln as its candidate for the presidency. Lincoln was on record as saying, "The Union could not permanently endure, half slave and half free." This was enough to show how he felt toward the South.[116]

---

113   The author identifies Thomas South (1781-1873) of Funkstown as the confused Nick Hammer. Townsend, George Alfred, *Tales of the Chesapeake,* (American News Company, NY, 1880), 60-64. See pages 220 to 224 for the full text of the poem.

114   Brown was tried in Charles Town, VA [WV]. He was executed on 2 Dec 1859.

115   Stonebraker is quoting from Marie Corelli's *Barabbas, A Dream of the Word's Tragedy* (J. P. Lippincott, Philadelphia, PA, 1893), 57.

116   Lincoln's quote is taken from his "House Divided" speech on 16 Jun 1858, in Springfield, IL at the Republican State Convention. There he was selected as the Republican candidate for US

The Washington Hotel on the main street in Hagerstown, MD where John Brown registered as John Smith on Thursday 30 Jun 1859. Image from Harper's Weekly, 5 Sep 1861.

In April, 1860, the Democratic convention met at Charleston, South Carolina, and disagreeing on lines of party policy for the coming campaign, adjourned and met again in Baltimore in June, and again failing to agree, separated and made their respective nominations apart.

Stephen A. Douglas, of Illinois, was nominated by the northern wing of the party. He was the author of the doctrine of "Squatter Sovereignty"—giving the people of the territories the right to determine whether slavery should exist or not, completely ignoring Congress in the matter.[117]

John C. Breckenridge, of Kentucky, was nominated by the southern wing, or States-Rights party. They contended that the territories were open to all the citizens of all the States, and that it was the duty of the General Government to protect both persons and property (slaves), while such territory was under its control, but admitting the right of the people in forming a State, out of such territory, to determine if slavery should exist or not.

In May, 1860, the "Union" party met in Baltimore and nominated John Bell, of Tennessee, as their candidate for the presidency. They ignored the territorial question entirely—declared that they would stand by the "Constitution, the Union, and the enforcement of the laws."

The question whether Congress had the power to legislate slavery into, or exclude it from, the territories belonging to the United States, had been a subject of angry discussion and sectional strife for more than a quarter of a

---

Senate to run against Democrat Stephen A. Douglas. "A house divided against itself cannot stand," is a paraphrase of a statement by Jesus in the New Testament Matthew 12:25.

117   The doctrine of "Squatter Sovereignty" was based on the theory that the people of any state or territory should have the right to regulate their domestic institutions as they might see fit, particularly the institution of slavery. The idea was first suggested by General Lewis Cass on 24 Dec 1847, in a letter to a Mr. Nicholson, of Nashville, TN. Four years later, Stephen A. Douglas embodied the idea into the Kansas-Nebraska bill and was erroneously given the credit of being the originator of the concept. "Squatter Sovereignty" became the slogan of the pro-slavery element. Blackmar, Frank W., *Kansas: A Cyclopedia of State History, Embracing Events, Institutions, Industries, Counties, Cities, Towns, Prominent Persons, Etc.* Volume II, (Standard Publishing Company, Chicago, IL, 1912), 732-734.

One of several patriotic prints issued by Currier & Ives in May 1861, closely following the Confederate bombardment of Fort Sumter and President Lincoln's appeal to the states for troops to suppress the rebellion.
LOC/P&P. LC-USZ62-91516.

century. The split in the Democratic party on the territorial question secured the election of Mr. Lincoln, the Southern States seceded from the Union, and our Civil War began.[118]

On April the 13th ('61) Fort Sumter was bombarded and surrendered to the Confederates. Two days later President Lincoln issued his call for 75,000 troops to put down the rebellion. Two days after this event Virginia passed the ordinance of secession.[119]

Early on the morning of the 19th of April, just as I was opening the office, the United States soldiers, that had been guarding the arsenal at Harper's Ferry, passed hurriedly through the town, going northward, having set fire to the Government property before they left.[120]

After the bombardment of Sumter, it was either Union or Rebel, and much bad blood was displayed by both parties, and this bitter feeling continued to exist long after the war closed.

The village of Funkstown had been overwhelmingly Democratic for years, and in the election just closed, the majority of the party being "States Rights," voted for Breckenridge. The Whigs and what was left of the old "Know-Nothing" party cast their vote for Bell—not a single vote being cast for Lincoln. As a rule the Democrats sided with the South.

John Betts kept one of the hotels and was a rank secessionist.[121] He had a pole erected in front of his house from which floated the Palmetto flag, causing much angry discussion.[122]

---

118   South Carolina adopted the *"Declaration of the Immediate Causes Which Induce and Justify the Secession of South Carolina from the Federal Union"* on 24 Dec 1860. By Feb 1861, Mississippi, Florida, Alabama, Georgia, Louisiana, and Texas had followed suit. These seven states formed the Confederate States of America on 4 Feb 1861.

119   Following the attack on Fort Sumter, President Lincoln called for a volunteer army from each state. Within two months, four more Southern slave states declared their secession and joined the Confederacy: Virginia, Arkansas, North Carolina and Tennessee.

120   On 18 Apr 1861, less than 24 hours after Virginia seceded from the Union, Federal soldiers set fire to the Armory and Arsenal at Harper's Ferry to keep them out of Confederate hands. The Arsenal and 15,000 weapons were destroyed, but the Armory flames were extinguished, and the weapons-making equipment was shipped south. When the Confederates abandoned the town two months later, they burned most of the factory buildings and blew up the railroad bridge.

121   1860 US Federal Census for Funkstown lists hotel keeper John H. Betz (1824-?) age 36, wife Mary E., 34, and children George 12, Thomas 10, Rose 8, Robert 6, and Alfred 2.

122   The Palmetto Flag is the official state flag of South Carolina. By flying the South Carolina flag, Betts was displaying his support for succession.

Candidates for President 1860

Lithograph after the painting of Candidate Abraham Lincoln (1809-1865) by Thomas Hicks (1823-1890). LOC/P&P. LC-USZ62-62946.

Stephen Arnold Douglas (1813 -1861), the Northern Democratic Party nominee for President in 1860. Born in Vermont, he later moved to Jacksonville, IL. Heavyset and only five feet four inches tall, he was dubbed the "Little Giant" by his contemporaries. LOC/P&P. LC-DIG-pga-00785.

John Cabell Breckenridge (1821-1875) 14th Vice-President of the United States (1857–61) under President James Buchanan, unsuccessful presidential candidate of Southern Democrats, and Confederate officer during the Civil War. LOC/P&P. LC-BH82- 3058 B.

John Bell (1796-1869) Senator from Tennessee, the candidate of the "Union" party for President of the United States. During his thirteen terms in Congress, he switched his political party designation five times. LOC/P&P. LC-DIG-pga-00783.

Brave but Toothless

Hanson Beachley, who clerked in Davis' store just below Bett's Hotel, was a Unionist.[123] He paraded around the streets with an old flint-lock musket, boasting that he was ready to go and help to defend the Capital from the Rebels, but later, when Maryland refused to furnish her quota of volunteers,[124] and the conscript officer made his appearance, Beachley was one of the first to get exempt from military service—excuse, false teeth.

This was so good that young Kerfoot,[125] the town rhymer, immortalized Beachley's patriotism:

> "Where's your Hanson Beachley,
>   the man that was so brave,
> He swore he'd fight the Rebels,
>   this Union he would save,
> But where is he now,
>   in the time he's needed most,
> He pulls out his false teeth,
>   and looks like a ghost."

Early in the summer of '61 a brigade of Federal soldiers from Rhode Island passed through the town and went into camp in Hunter's field.[126] Col. Burnside was in command of one of the regiments.[127] This was the first large

---

123   Jacob Hanson Beachley, (1838-1905) is inaccurately listed as J. H. Benkley, age 22, a clerk in Joseph F. and Angela Kirkham Davis's store in the 1860 US Federal Census for Funkstown. In her memoirs, Mrs. Davis wrote of the young clerk 'Mr. Beachley' who defended the National flag in front of her store with his pistol. Beachley was later a clerk in the Funkstown store of Simon Knode (1811-1868), and married Knode's daughter Anne. In 1870, he was still a merchant in Funkstown. He later moved to Hagerstown, opening the wholesale produce business of J. H. Beachley & Company. Hanson's father was Daniel Beachley (1803-1874), whose home farm was on present day Alternate US #40, a large two-story stone dwelling on the east side of South Mountain. The home was in the direct line of the Union Army's advance toward Turner's Gap during the Battle of South Mountain on 14 Sep 1862. After the war, his sons successfully petitioned Congress for almost $9,000 as reimbursement for rails, corn, hay, wheat, wood, and oats, supplied by their father or taken by the Union soldiers during and after the Battle at Antietam. *1860 through 1900 US Federal Census and Miscellaneous Documents of the House of Representatives for the second session of the fifty-first Congress, 1890-91* (Washington DC, 1891), 65.

124   The *Herald of Freedom & Torch Light* of 5 Nov 1862, reported the county's enrolled militia was 5,251, with 324 coming from Funkstown.

125   Richard Kerfoot (1832-?) was a shoemaker residing in Funkstown in 1860. *US Federal Census 1860*.

126   The second division of Colonel Burnside's Rhode Island Regiment encamped at Funkstown, MD on the 7th of June. Hunter's field was the farm of Ranney Hunter (1813-?) and his wife Elizabeth Rowland Hunter just south of Funkstown on the east side of the National Pike. The Hunter farm bordered the creek, providing an ample water supply for both the soldiers and their stock. Scharf, John Thomas, *History of Western Maryland,* (Philadelphia, PA, 1882).

127   Union General Ambrose Evertt Burnside (1824–1881) ranked a colonel in 1861. After the Antietam campaign under McClellan, Burnside was promoted to commander of the Army of the Potomac. After the war he was elected governor of Rhode Island in 1866, 1867, and 1868. From 1875, until his death he was a US Senator. He is credited with originating the fashion of wearing long side whiskers, thus the term burnsides or sideburns.

A Rebel of '61

This is the type of four-horse coach Henry Stonebraker would have used during his short term as postmaster. LOC/P&P. LC-DIG-det-4a25792.

body of troops I had ever seen, and they impressed me greatly. I thought all the men in the United States north of Mason and Dixon's line were in that body of troops until I ascertained their number. They were in camp but a short time, when they came to town in small squads and amused themselves by making the prominent Southern sympathizers hang the American flag from their houses.

Father was Post-master at this time, and I assisted in the office and made up the mail, which was carried daily by a four-horse stage coach between Hagerstown and Frederick.[128] The camp nearby greatly increased the office work, notwithstanding that some of our Union friends reported us to be Rebels, and intimated that we would destroy the letters instead of mailing them.[129] The camp broke up just before the first battle of "Bull Run."[130]

---

128   In Mar 1860 the Post Office Department advertised in the *Herald of Freedom & Torch Light* for proposals for conveying the mail for four years from Frederick, by Middletown, Boliver, Boonsboro, Benevola, Funkstown, Hagerstown, Conococheague, Clear Spring, Indian Springs, and Millstone Point, to Hancock, a trip of fifty-five miles and back.

129   The announcement of Henry Stonebraker's appointment as postmaster appeared in the *Herald of Freedom & Torch Light* (Hagerstown, MD) newspaper 2 Jan 1861. An announcement of his resignation followed on 10 Jul 1861.

130   The first Battle of Bull Run was fought on 21 Jul 1861.

Tow Boy

A canal boat from the era of the Canal Towage Company in Washington County, MD circa 1905. The boat is only partially loaded, and, since there is no one at the tiller, it is parked. There are sacks piled on the hatch covers. Photo from the Newman-Bucci Collection, Washington County Free Library, Hagerstown, MD.

Some time before the War, an uncle, Daniel S. Rentch, of Shepardstown, Virginia, had been operating several boats on the Chesapeake and Ohio Canal.[131]

After Virginia seceded, to prevent the boats from being confiscated he transferred them to his brother-in-law, John Eckert Knode, who had always been a Whig, and was now considered a Union man.[132]

Knode was married to father's sister, and in the following fall he and father put the boat "Ellen Rentch" in order, purchased wheat from the farmers, taking the first load from near the old Buchanan place, south of Downsville, and freighted it to Georgetown, District of Columbia.[133]

It might as well be recorded here that Knode was a farmer, and resided on the old Michael Stonebraker's homestead, adjoining Bakersville, near the Potomac River.

Being a Whig, he may have been a "Union man," but he had married a Stonebraker, and all the world knew where they stood as long as their tongues could wag.

However, in the following winter, some of his enemies—and they were not Southerners, either—set fire to his barn, destroyed all his crops, many of his horses and cattle, and all his farming implements. It cost something in those days to be joined to a Southern woman in wedlock.[134]

---

131   Daniel Shafer Rentch (1821-1918), the son of John and Catherine Shaeffer Rentch, was Stonebraker's maternal uncle who married the author's paternal aunt Savilla Stonebraker. The 1860 US Federal Census indicates Daniel was a merchant in Shepherdstown, VA [WV].

132   John Eckert Knode (1814-1875) married Hester Anne Stonebraker (1821-1906), Stonebraker's paternal aunt.

133   The canal boat the "Ellen Rentch" was named for Daniel and Savilla Stonebraker Rentch's eldest child, Eleanor "Ellen" Barbary Rentch (1846-1918). Ellen Rentch was named for her aunt Eleanor Margaret Rentch (1819-1840), Daniel's sister. Ellen Barbary Rentch married George Newton Byers (1834-1904) of Shepherdstown, WV in 1871. Sergeant Major G. Newton Byers enlisted as a private in the Confederate Army in 1861, Company 1st, Virginia Rockbridge 1st Light Artillery Battery.

    The "old Buchanan place" is *Woburn Manor,* a circa 1800 mansion located on present day Dam #4 at Shaffer Road just south of Downsville, MD.

134   The Christmas day Hagerstown newspaper reported two arson fires set Saturday night 21 Dec 1861. In a barn fire near Bakersville, John Eckert Knode lost 1,200 bushels of wheat, and other winter forage, 10 or more horses, cattle, and all his farming implements. In Hagerstown, the stone barn on the grist mill property of William H. Hager was torched. At the time of the fire the Hager's 17 year old son Jonathan was living there. William H. Hager was a descendent of Jonathan Hager, founder of Hagerstown. He was a prosperous merchant who divided his time between his home near Hagerstown and his offices at the corner of Howard & Pratt Streets in Baltimore, MD. Jonathan Hager was Stonebraker's age and enlisted in the 1st Maryland Cavalry in Jun 1863. See footnote 418 and photo page 171. *American and Commercial Daily Advertiser*, Baltimore, MD, 3 Sep 1853. *Herald of Freedom & Torch Light*, (Hagerstown, MD), 25 Dec 1861.

They employed Captain Wade to steer the boat. He was an industrious but a very stubborn man; this latter trait proved to be very unfortunate for them, as we shall hereafter see.

The farmers hauled the wheat to the landing in wagons, and I helped to carry, weigh and empty it into the boat. When the boat was loaded, we started on our journey, I driving the team which consisted of three horses, and they pulled the loaded boat at the rate of two miles an hour. Fourteen to sixteen hours was a day's work; to ac-

MICHAEL STONEBRAKER'S HOMESTEAD, BUILT IN 1804.

Above: The Michael Stonebraker house still stands today on Tommytown Road near Bakersville, MD. In 1861, Michael Stonebraker was living in Baltimore and the farm in the tenancy of John Eckert Knode and his wife Hester Anne Stonebraker Knode. Photo from original text.
Left: The Michael Stonebraker home as it stands today along Tommytown Road.
Below: The south end gable of the main section has a date stone inscribed MSB 1804. The two-bay stone addition is dated 1833 with the initial W attached to the north end wall. Erin Black Photography, Williamsport, MD.

complish this, we had to be up early in the morning and go late into the night.

I soon discovered it to be a very disagreeable occupation. The men that followed the canal for a living did not hesitate to steal anything they could get their hands on, and the one who could use the foulest language was considered the most accomplished boatman.

When near our destination the boat sprung a leak, but we kept her afloat by pumping until we reached the two-mile level, had the water drawn off and corked up the leak, the cargo being but little damaged.

It was Sunday when we reached Georgetown. As the dome of the Capitol looked as though it was but a short distance away, I hurried up the avenue only to find that it was miles instead of blocks before reaching that majestic pile of marble. While here I went to the theatre for the first time. They were playing the "Colleen Bawn." What a grand and imposing sight for a country boy.[135]

We made several trips from various points along the canal before cold weather closed navigation. The next spring we took the boat on the Virginia side, two miles above Dam Number 4, which was in big slack water.[136] We received the farmer's wheat at Harrison's Landing, and took them on our return trips groceries, etc.

Father had been informed that some of the Unionists had threatened to give him trouble if he continued to trade with the people. We finished loading the boat about five o'clock, but father had left some time before to attend to some business, expecting to meet us the next morning further down the river. Before leaving he instructed Wade to take the boat over on the Maryland side of the river, as soon as she was loaded. This Wade failed to do for no other reason than to have his own way. Some time during the night a squad of Yankee soldiers, led by a citizen, came and ordered us to get up and put on our clothes, go back into Maryland, and not come to Virginia until the War was over.

After we left they untied the boat, pushed her out into the current, when she floated down the river and over Dam Number 4 and broke in half. Part of the wreck drifted down the stream and lodged against an island, just opposite where father had agreed to meet us. I shall never forget his distress and the sight of the big tears that rolled down his cheeks when we explained to him how it occurred. The money loss to him was about $4,500.00.[137]

---

135   The *Colleen Bawn*, also sometimes referred to as *The Brides of Garryowen,* is a melodramatic play written by Irish playwright Dion Boucicault. It was first performed at Miss Laura Keene's Theatre in New York City, NY on 27 Mar 1860.

136   Big Slackwater is a section of the Chesapeake & Ohio Canal in Washington County, MD between Dam No. 4 (mile 84.6) and McMahon's Mill (mile 88.1). The towpath here follows the bank of the Potomac River, allowing boats to be towed along a quiet, or "slack," part of the river.

137   The *Herald of Freedom & Torch Light of* April 30, 1862 reported: "An Outrage—Heavy Loss. We learn that Henry Stonebraker of Funkstown, and John E. Knode, living near Bakersville, met with a heavy loss one night last week. They had been purchasing wheat at Harris' Mills, above Dam No. 4, in Va., and transporting it to Georgetown via the Canal. They had just freighted a Canal Boat with 3300 bushels of the article, intending to start for Georgetown the following day. That night some malicious scoundrels cut the boat loose from its moorings, and it drifted down over the dam, a total loss of boat and cargo to the owners. The boat cost $1100, which added to the wheat, entails a loss of near $5000 to the owners. The editor follows this with these words: We copy the above from the Mail who says the sufferers are sympathizers with the South, and attributes the outrage upon them to sectional bitterness. We don't know whether this is true or not, but we do know that it is but one of the many natural consequences of insurrection in every country. When a Government is about to be subverted by violence, no man is safe either in life, liberty, or property."

John E. Knode lost his suit against Jacob Williamson to recover $10,000 in damages for the destruction of the Ellen Rentch canal boat and her cargo in the District Court of West Virginia. That decision was reversed by the US Supreme Court in Nov 1873. Williams, Stephen K., *Cases Argued and Decided in the Supreme Court of the United States,* Volume 21, (Lawyers Co-Operative Publishing Company, Rochester, NY, 1883), 586-589.

Political Prisoner

Hagerstown is the county seat of Washington County.[138] For some days Prof. Light had been advertised to make an ascension in a balloon from the public square (August 9, 1862).[139] Boy-like, I was anxious to see the air ship make the trip, and on the afternoon of that day I went to town for that purpose.

The town had been occupied by Federal soldiers for some time, and was under martial law, and governed by a provost–martial.[140] I had been in town but a short time when I was arrested by a soldier and taken before the "provo." He said that I had been reported to him as being a rebel sympathizer, and must take the oath of allegiance. The oath at that time was known as "iron clad," and no one who had friends South, or sympathized with them, could possibly subscribe to it without mental reservation or perjury.[141]

Many of our citizens, with Southern proclivities, had been arrested and required to take the oath or go to jail.[142] I told the

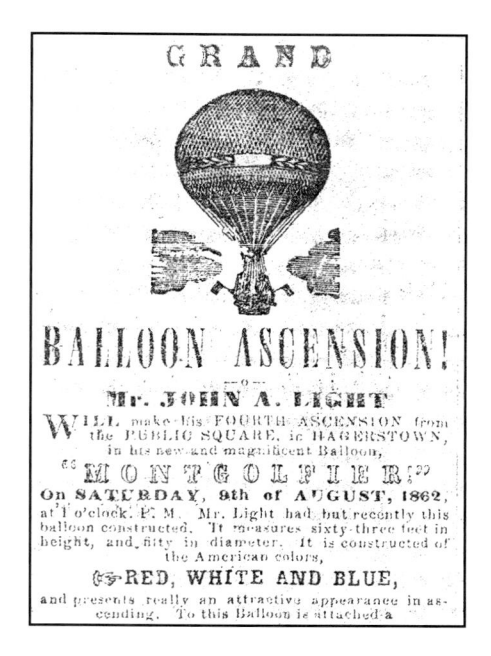

Advertisement in the Herald of Freedom & Torch Light (Hagerstown, MD) newspaper 30 Jul 1862 for Professor Light's Hot Air Balloon ascension in downtown Hagerstown. While attending this event, 18 year old Stonebraker was arrested as a rebel sympathizer.

---

138   Washington County was formed from Frederick County on September 6, 1776, and Hagerstown named the county seat on that day. According to most sources, Hagerstown was established in 1762 by Jonathan Hager, a German immigrant. Originally named Elizabethtown, after Hager's wife, the City Council voted to change the name to Hagerstown on 5 Dec 1813.

139   On an extremely hot Saturday afternoon a huge crowd gathered in the public square of Hagerstown to watch aeronaut John A. Light ascend in his hot-air balloon. After several attempts that extended well into the evening, the balloon refused to rise. Hot air balloons rise when the heated air inside the balloon is lighter than the surrounding air. The air temperature of Saturday, 9 Aug 1862 was extremely hot as reported by soldiers of both armies fighting in the Battle of Cedar Mountain south of Culpeper, VA. The heat was so intense that soldiers "fell out of ranks because of the high temperature, some suffering fatal heat stroke." Kennedy, Frances H., *The Civil War Battlefield Guide, 2nd Edition* (Houghton-Mifflin Company, NY, 1998), 105. *Herald of Freedom & Torch Light*, 30 Jul 1862 and 13 Aug 1862.

140   Officers of the 29th Pennsylvania Regiment were acting Provost Marshals.

141   Nineteenth-century Americans took oaths very seriously. Early in the war, Congress enacted a series of oath laws in reaction to widespread defections of federal soldiers and other government workers. As the war continued, in Jul 1862 Congress enacted the "ironclad oath," that required a pledge of both past and future loyalty. Those suspected sympathizers of Maryland who refused the oath were sent to Fort McHenry. Ranney, Joseph A. *In the Wake of Slavery: Civil War, Civil Rights, and the Reconstruction of Southern Law* (Paeger Publishers, Westport, CT, 2006), 36.

142   *Habeas corpus* represents the legal right of persons in a free society not to be detained or punished by the authorities without cause and a fair hearing in court and the opportunity for self-defense. Article I, Section 9 of the Constitution says the writ of habeas corpus shall not be suspended "unless when in cases of rebellion or invasion the public safety may require it." President Lincoln was worried that if Maryland joined Virginia and seceded from the Union, the nation's capital would be stranded amid hostile states. On 27 Apr 1861, about a week after the Fort Sumter surrender, President Lincoln ordered General Winfield Scott, then head of the nation's military, to arrest anyone between Washington and Philadelphia suspected of subversive acts or speech, and his order specifically authorized suspension of the writ of habeas corpus. The following summer on 8 Aug 1862, at Lincoln's behest, Secretary of War Edwin Stanton issued sweeping orders suspending habeas corpus nationwide—the first time the writ was suspended beyond a narrowly defined emergency area. Stanton decreed that anyone "engaged, by act, speech, or writing, in discouraging volunteer enlistments, or in any way giving aid and comfort to the enemy, or in any other disloyal practice against the United States" was subject to arrest and trial "before a military commission." The exceedingly broad mandate precipitated a civil liberties disaster. It allowed local sheriffs and constables to decide arbitrarily

marshal that I was but a boy, not yet out of my teens,[143] that I could not help being born and raised in the South, that it was only natural that my feelings were in that direction, but at the same time I had never committed any overt act against the Government, and thought it both unfair and unreasonable to be required to take the oath. He said, "take the oath or go to jail," so to the jail under an escort of a body of soldiers I went. While on the way, one of my fellow townsmen followed on behind crying, "hang him." It was he that had put the soldiers on my track. Some months prior to this event, in a street fight, I gave this same fellow a sound thrashing. Now he had a coward's revenge. When I reached the jail, I found Jos. E. Williams and S. J. Keller, citizens from my town, who had been incarcerated a few days before, besides many more from all over the county.[144] In fact the jail was so full that many of us were huddled together in the yard, where I slept the first night, with the cellar door for my

Circa 1860 photo of the Baltimore Central Police Station on the southeast corner of Holiday and Saratoga Streets in Baltimore, MD where Stonebraker and other political prisoners were housed on their way to Fort McHenry. Courtesy of the Maryland Historical Society.

who was loyal or disloyal. *New York Times* (NY) 9 Aug 1862.

143 Born 1 Feb 1844, Stonebraker was eighteen-years-old.

144 In Aug 1862, the *Herald of Freedom & Torch Light* reported the following six men of Washington County, MD were sent to Fort McHenry for having refused to take the oath of allegiance:
<u>Judge John Thomson Mason</u>, age 47; Confined 19 Aug 1862 for disloyalty. Released 4 Aug 1862 by "taking Special Oath by Gen. Wool." Interestingly, the records of Fort McHenry reflect that Judge Mason was released prior to his incarceration. Judge Mason (1815-1873) was born at the estate of *Montpelier* near Clear Spring in Washington County, MD. Two years after graduating from Princeton in 1836, he opened a law practice in Hagerstown, MD. He was elected to the Maryland House of Representatives in 1838 and 1839, and in Congress from 1841 to 1843. He was appointed Judge of the Court of Appeals from 1851 until 1857, and the collector of customs at Baltimore from 1857 until 1861. In later years he lived in Annapolis, MD where he died 28 Mar 1873. He is buried in Hagerstown, MD.
<u>Solomon J. Keller</u>, age 22; Confined 19 Aug 1862 for disloyalty, released 8 Nov 1862. Keller was the son of John Henry and Elizabeth Newcomer Keller of present day 6 S. High Street, Funkstown, MD. Stonebraker and Keller were second-cousins, once-removed, and became brothers-in-law when Keller married Clara Stonebraker in 1864. The 1880 US Federal census indicates Keller's son, C. Harry Keller, was born in Canada in 1865, suggesting the family may have temporarily moved there during the later part of the war.
<u>Josiah Williams,</u> age 31; Confined 19 Aug 1862 for disloyalty, released 12 Nov 1862. The 1860 US Federal census lists Josiah E. Williams (1831-1925) living near Funkstown, MD with his mother Mary Williams, and sisters, Ellen and Catherine Williams. See footnote 165, photograph page 80.
<u>David R. Protzman,</u> age 37; Confined 19 Aug 1862 for disloyalty, released 12 Sep 1862. Protzman (1825-1907) and his wife Sarah Sanger Protzman lived in Ringgold, MD. Listed as a laborer on the 1870 and 1880 US Federal Census, at the time of his arrest he was married and the father to several small children. The 1863 Union Draft Registration Records list David Protzman as "blind in one eye" and unfit for service in the Union army.
<u>Samuel J. Price,</u> age 21 (1841-?); Confined 19 Aug 1862 for disloyalty, released 8 Sep 1862. Price was the son of a cabinetmaker from Smithsburg, MD. Private Samuel R. Price of Smithsburg, MD, unit unknown CSA, is noted in Roger J. Keller's *Roster of Civil War Soldiers from Washington County, Maryland* (Clearfield Company, Baltimore, MD, 1993), 199.
<u>Joseph Stonebraker,</u> age 18 (1844-1903); Confined 19 Aug 1862 for disloyalty, released 10 Nov 1862.
 The Torch Light expressed their opinion that these men "too cowardly to go into the rebel lines. . .and too disloyal to defend the Government under which they live," should be kept alive on a diet of only bread and water. The editor feared that without punishment of some kind, the fort would soon overflow with those who wished to "repose in luxurious ease, far out of harm's way." *Herald of Freedom & Torch Light* (Hagerstown, MD) 20 Aug 1862. *US Civil War Draft Registrations Records, 1863-1865, 4th Congressional District of Maryland*. Vol. 6. Civil War Prisoner Database, http://fortmchenrylibrary.org/index.cfm?action=1861.

bed and the Heavens for my covering. It rained during the night, much to my discomfort.

The next day my parents called to see me, and brought some bedding, which made me more comfortable. Our jail companions in the yard were Negroes, horse thieves, and deserters from the Federal Army.

August the 18th, 1862, in company with five others, I was marched to the Cumberland Valley Depot, under a guard of soldiers, and sent to Harrisburg, Pa.[145] Here, by permission of the officer who had us in charge, we dined at the United States Hotel.[146] This was the first time I had ever been on the cars, or dined at a large hotel. Judge Mason had much fun at my expense, and said I ought to thank Uncle Sam for giving me a free ride.

After dinner we were put on the cars, reached Baltimore about dark, and marched to the Central Police Station on Saratoga Street near North. Here we were confined in a dirty little cell hardly big enough for two. Judge John T. Mason, ex-Judge of the Court of Appeals of Maryland, who was one of our party, protested so vigorously and sent out so many notes to his friends surreptitiously that we were finally removed to another room up stairs, with a cot for each person.[147]

The next day, about noon, two hacks drove to the station, with a policeman on each hack as a guard.[148] Three of our party got in each carriage and drove to a restaurant on German Street near Sharp and got something to eat. After which we were driven to Fort McHenry, which is situated on a point of land between the harbor and the Patapsco. It was successfully defended against the British fleet in 1814, and Francis Scott Key wrote the "Star Spangled Banner" while a prisoner on a British vessel but a short distance down the bay.

SOLOMON J. KELLER, POLITICAL PRISONER, 1862

Solomon J. Keller (1840-1899), Stonebraker' second-cousin, once-removed, and future brother-in-law. Photo from original text.

---

145   Located on the western edge of town, the Cumberland Valley Railroad was the earliest railroad into Hagerstown. The train trip from Hagerstown to the Pennsylvania Railroad Station at Harrisburg, PA was just under three hours. From there the detainees were likely put on the North Central Railroad line for a three-and-a-half hour ride south into Baltimore. The Western Maryland Railroad direct line from Hagerstown to Baltimore was under construction and would not be completed until 1872.

146   The 100 room United States Hotel in Harrisburg, PA was opposite the Pennsylvania Railroad Station and the Philadelphia & Reading Depots. *The Rand-McNalley Official Railway Guide and Travelers Hand Book,* (The National Railway Publication Company, Chicago, IL, 1886), 481.

147   Judge John Thomson Mason (1815-1873) previously noted footnote 144. In his biography published in John Thomas Scharf's 1882 *History of Western Maryland*, it was noted the Judge was jailed twice for his southern sympathies, once at Fort McHenry, and one time on his farm in Western Maryland. Despite his sympathies, the judge was an influential man with influential friends. It is doubtful that he spent much time in Fort McHenry. After the war, the Judge was appointed Secretary of State of Maryland under Governor William Pinkney Whyte. Scharf, J. Thomas, *History of Western Maryland* (Philadelphia, PA, 1882), 1115.

148   A hack is a carriage for hire, short for hackney or hackney carriage.

More than 260 American citizens were held at Fort McHenry during the war, most of whom would never be formally charged or tried for a crime. Portion of a lithograph of Fort McHenry, by E. Sachse, 1862. Fort McHenry, Baltimore, MD. LOC/P&P. HABS MD,4-BALT,5--19.

Upon our arrival at the fort, we were taken before General Morris, the commandant.[149] He being busy, we were allowed to stroll through the grounds, admiring their beauty. I was especially delighted and watched the soldiers fishing and crabbing from the wharf, congratulating myself upon the change from the dirty jailyard to this delightful place; but alas for human hopes so soon to be blasted. The Captain of the prison took and put us in a building which had been used for a horse stable, but now the guard house. It was filthy with dirt and alive with vermin. The stalls where the horses once stood were shelved off in bunks for the men who slept there without bedding, unless they provided blankets for themselves. We found in this den of misery about twenty prisoners, a few Confederate soldiers, the balance citizens from Baltimore. We were fed by the Government; our breakfast consisted of a tin cup of black coffee and a few crackers, called "hard tack,"[150] boiled beef, and soup well seasoned with flies for dinner, supper being the same as breakfast. We were much depressed the first few days, but it is wonderful how soon one can become reconciled to almost anything. In a few days kind friends from the city sent us mattresses and blankets, improving our condition and reviving our spirits.

---

149   Brigadier General William Walton Morris (1801-1865) was born in Ballston Springs, NY and graduated from the US Military Academy in 1820. A capable military lawyer, he was commander of Fort Kearny in the Nebraska territory and Fort Ridgely, MN before being transferred to Fort McHenry in 1861. Fort McHenry was the key to holding Baltimore and Maryland during the Civil War. As commander of Fort McHenry, Morris played a pivotal role in the suspension of habeas corpus, the imposition of martial law, and the arrest and detention of more than 260 American citizens, many, if not all, of whom would never be formally charged or tried for a crime. *The American Annual Cyclopaedia and Register of Important Events of the Year 1865, Volume V,* (NY, 1869), 594. Marshall, John A., *American Bastille: A History of the Illegal Arrests and Imprisonment of American Citizens in the Northern and Border States on Account of Their Political Opinions During the Late Civil War,* (Thomas W. Hartley & Company, Philadelphia, PA, 1883).

150   Hard tack is made from flour and water baked together for an extended period of time. This baking time extends its shelf life considerably, making it useful as a trail food.

The Confederate soldiers enlivened our prison with their War songs and stories. In a few days I was taken before General Morris, a rough, uncouth Irish soldier, who said you take the oath, and I will let you out. I declined and went back to the stable.

August 27th, 1862, a sergeant and six soldiers halted in front of our prison, when Williams, Keller, and three others, including myself, were put under guard of this squad and marched out Fort Avenue to Light Street and thence into the city. Soon as we got well into its limits a crowd of men and boys, both black and white, followed after us, the crowd increasing as we proceeded towards the center, and the sergeant becoming alarmed, and fearing that there might be an attempt made to take us from him, called lustily for the police.

When we reached the corner of Holliday and North Streets we were taken into General Wool's headquarters. He was a little, old, gray-headed, withered-looking man, 73 years old and weighing about 90 pounds.[151] He was of the old school, gentlemanly and mild-mannered in deportment. Williams acted as our spokesman and gave him a history of our arrest. He said that our imprisonment was certainly illegal, and had he been in the city when we first arrived, he would have released us, "but you now must take the oath, so I can have some excuse when the administration at Washington wants to know why I set you free." We declined and were marched back to the fort.

During the months of our incarceration, many persons were put in our prison—political prisoners, Confederate soldiers, blockade runners, and horse thieves. Political prisoners predominated; these embraced all persons who had Southern proclivities.

Very few remained with us long; there was a constant coming and going. The Confederates were either exchanged or transferred to some other prison; the political prisoners, after a few days' confinement, generally took the oath. Some declared they would subscribe to anything rather than remain in this "hell-hole;" they contended that no moral law could bind a person to respect an oath that you were forced to take—the very fact that force being used justified one in taking it with mental reservation.

It took me a long time before I could make up my mind to take this view of the matter. A Mr. Sullivan from the city had been one of the inmates of our room, and after his release, sent to our party a lot of pipes and tobacco;

Major General John Ellis Wool (1784 -1869), commander of Fort McHenry during Stonebraker's incarceration. LOC/ P&P. LC-DIG-ppmsca-08354

---

151   Major General John Ellis Wool (1784 -1869) was an officer in the US Army during three consecutive wars: the War of 1812, the Mexican-American War, and the Civil War. He was 78 years old and the highest ranking Union officer in Baltimore when Stonebraker and his fellow detainees were brought before him. From the conversation, the General did not agree with incarceration of southern sympathizers.

I took a smoke which made me so sick that I remained in bed two days, and now at the age of more than fifty years, I consider that it was the most fortunate spell of sickness I ever had, as it no doubt saved me from acquiring that senseless habit of smoking.[152]

The prisoners passed their time in reading and various other ways— many gambled from morning until night, and often fought over the game. Shortly after the battle of Antietam was fought, many sick and wounded Confederates were sent to the fort, and a number put into our room.[153] This increased our misery; one soldier, with a wound in the head, being delirious with fever, roamed all around our room, crying in a mournful voice, "Joe, Loy is here." This poor fellow died from sheer neglect. The Confederates were destitute of shoes and clothing and many were so sick that they could scarcely walk. The ladies from Baltimore— among which was a Mrs. Egerton, whom I shall always remember with much pleasure, and I am sure many others from all over the South-land remember her acts with gratitude—distributed clothing among the soldiers and brought many nice things to eat.[154] The Federals had a convalescent camp in the fort-yard. They became jealous of the attentions the ladies paid to the Confederates, and stoned their carriages from the grounds.

The Rev. Rob. Douglas, whose home was on the banks of the Potomac River, opposite Shepherdstown, Va.—the same person that Uncle Henry Reel took me to hear preach when but a small boy[155]—shortly after the battle of Antietam, was arrested and confined in several prisons, finally reaching Fort McHenry.[156]

---

152   Franklin Sullivan was incarcerated on 15 Sep 1862 for 4 days for the crime of "Denouncing the government of the United States and expressing a wish that the Rebels would burn Philadelphia or New York expressing a hope that the God damned Yankees would be driven out of Baltimore." *Selected Records of the War Department Relating to Confederate Prisoners of War, 1861-1865. Fort McHenry Military Prison, Register No. 1* (National Archives, Washington, DC, M598, Roll 96, Vol. 305), 68.

153   The Battle of Antietam was fought at Sharpsburg, MD 17 Sep 1862, about fourteen miles south of Stonebraker's hometown of Funkstown, MD. Incarcerated in Baltimore, Stonebraker missed one of the most notable events in the history of his home county.

154   Mrs. Adeline L. P. McRea Egerton was born in New York in 1832 and later married to Baltimore merchant Abraham Dubois Egerton (1820-1874). Mrs. Egerton was intricately involved in efforts during and following the Civil War to supply needy southerners with clothes, money and other goods. She likely did this through the Soldiers' Relief Association, Southern Aid Society, Southern Relief Association, and other organizations in the Baltimore area. The Library of Virginia, East Broad Street, Richmond, VA has a collection of letters written to Mrs. Egerton, predominately from appreciative Confederate soldiers.

155   In Jan 1849, Henry Reel (1815-1873) married Barbara Ann Stonebraker (1823-1880), the author's aunt. The Reels were farmers in the Sharpsburg, MD district.

156   In Oct 1862, Irish-born Reverend Robert Douglas (1807-1867), father of Confederate officer Henry Kyd Douglas, was arrested on suspicion of signaling the enemy across the Potomac River from a window in his home at *Ferry Hill*. He spent several days at a prison in Harper's Ferry before being transferred to Fort McHenry. A wealthy and important member of his community, the Reverend acquired *Ferry Hill* Plantation through marriage to his second wife, Helena Blackford (1821-1882), the daughter of Colonel John Blackford. Prior to his incarceration, the "old rebel preacher" and his family were made prisoners in their home by Federal officers. The house was frequently entered and ransacked, his barn, fences, and outbuildings were burned, horses and cattle were stolen as a consequence of his affiliation with the Southern cause. After the Battle of Antietam in September of 1862, the Federal forces encamped on the plantation destroyed the remainder of his personal and agricultural property. Marshall, John A., *American Bastille: A History of the Illegal Arrests and Imprisonment of American Citizens in the Northern and Border States on Account of Their Political Opinions During the Late Civil War*, (Thomas W. Hartley & Company, Philadelphia, PA, 1883), 156-164. Pow-

He had been with us about a week, when, on Sunday evening (November 2, 1862), he, by request, preached to us, his subject being "The duty of children to their parents, and man's duty to God as a parent." The Doctor was a remarkable looking man and an eloquent speaker. He stood six feet two in height, form erect as an Indian, black eyes, clean cut, ruddy features, his long white hair brushed behind his ears, almost reaching his shoulders.

He stood in the middle of our pen, one foot resting on a bench before him, with no light save the reflection of the lamp from the outside, and as his Irish blood warmed to the surroundings, his clear, musical voice penetrated beyond our prison walls, attracting the attention of the guards, who suddenly became silent and listened attentively. He gave me a Testament, which I read through, still have and greatly prize.

Where Sparrows Point Steel Works are now located was a woods. As the early frost turned the leaves their autumn color, it made my heart sad, as I thought of home and its glorious forests, and longed to be free.[157]

Judge Mason had been released for some days; he took a great interest in us and endeavored to secure our release without taking the "iron-clad oath." He and Mr. B. F. Newcomer drew up a paper which Keller and I agreed to sign; they took us before Gen. Morris and submitted it to him for approval; he said: "I consider it an insult to bring such a paper for my inspection; if I had my way with these people, I would choke the oath down

Ferry Hill Plantation, *circa 1810, overlooking the Potomac River south of Sharpsburg, MD. The home of Reverend Robert Douglas and his wife, Helena Blackford Douglas. Photographs from 1950 and as the home is today. Courtesy the National Park Service.*

---

ell, Michael A., and Bruce A. Thompson, *Mid-Maryland: a crossroads of history*, (The History Press, Charleston, SC, 2003), 104.

157   Sparrows Point, a promontory that juts into the Chesapeake Bay east of Baltimore, MD was named for Thomas Sparrow, who obtained the land in 1652. In 1887, Frederick Wood, working with an industrial combination of the Pennsylvania Steel Company and the Bethlehem Iron Company, began the construction of the enormous works that would become Maryland Steel and later Bethlehem Steel.

Benjamin Franklin Newcomer (1827-1901), Stonebraker's second-cousin, once-removed. An influential businessman of Baltimore, Newcomer attempted to negotiate Stonebraker and Solomon Keller's release from Fort McHenry. Photo from Men of Mark in Maryland *(Washington, DC, 1907).*

their throats or send them to Botany Bay and keep them there until the War is over."[158]

Keller and I had long debated whether we should take the oath and leave our "den of misery." We finally concluded to swallow the pill. Williams could not make up his mind to do what we were about to do; an intimacy had formed between Williams and myself; I bade him good-bye with a full heart.

When we reached Gen. Wool's headquarters, we complied with his terms, just what they were I do not now remember, but it was the objectionable oath. Keller said, "General, our taking the oath, does not change our sentiments." "Oh," replied the General, "I don't expect it will; if it does, we have changed a great many in the past few months." To me, it seemed the height of foolishness to force a person to do an act against his will and expect him to respect it. I certainly had no such intention.[159]

We remained in Baltimore a few days taking in the sights and went to the fort to see Williams, before leaving for home. We proceeded to Frederick by the B. & O. R. R., and from there took the

---

[158] The *Herald of Freedom & Torch Light* and the *Baltimore Sun* reported that Judge Mason was released from Fort McHenry on Monday, 25 Aug 1862. The Judge was granted a parole by General John E. Wool (see footnote 151), the highest ranking Union officer in Baltimore, not General Morris commandant of Fort McHenry. The "special oath" administered by General Wool required the Judge swear he would not take up arms against the US Government or "in any manner either directly or indirectly aid or abet the Enemies." This was not the "ironclad oath" administered to other detainees. Judge Mason and Benjamin Newcomer tried unsuccessfully to use the "special oath" a second time in securing the release of Stonebraker and Keller. General Wool may have been obliged for political reasons to release the older, influential judge by altering the words of the oath, but the "rough, uncouth Irish soldier" General Morris (see footnote 149) could not be convinced to do the same for young, healthy 18 and 20 year old Stonebraker and Keller, regardless of their influential relatives. *Herald of Freedom & Torch Light* (Hagerstown, MD) 27 Aug 1862. *Civil War Prisoners Database Fort McHenry*, http://fortmchenrylibrary.org/index.cfm?action=1861&id=473.

Benjamin Franklin Newcomer (1827-1901) was born at Beaver Creek, Washington County, MD the son of John Newcomer (1797-1861) and Catherine Newcomer (1802-1883). He was Stonebraker's second-cousin, once-removed, and cousin to Solomon Keller. At the time he negotiated for Stonebraker's release, Newcomer and his family lived in Baltimore where he was a partner in the grain commodities firm of Newcomer & Stonebraker with yet another of the authors relatives. Newcomer was a director in the Corn & Flour Exchange of Baltimore (1853), a director at the Union Bank (1854), and a director of the Northern Central Railroad Company (1861). He later served as President of the Safe Deposit & Trust Company of Baltimore for thirty-three years and was heavily invested in the numerous Baltimore railroad companies – Mr. Newcomer decidedly had influence in Baltimore. Spencer, Richard Henry, *Genealogical and Memorial Encyclopedia of the State of Maryland*, (The American Historical Society, Inc, NY, 1919), 378-385. Steiner, Bernard C., *Men of Mark in Maryland: Biographies of Leading Men in the States, Volume 1*, (Johnson-Wynne Company, Washington, DC, 1907), 266-273.

Since 1788, Botany Bay was an infamous British penal colony in Australia.

[159] The Civil War prisoners records at Fort McHenry indicate Solomon J. Keller was released on 8 Nov 1862, Joseph Stonebraker released 10 Nov 1862, and Josiah E. Williams released 12 Nov 1862 by order of General Wool on taking the oath of allegiance. *Civil War Prisoners Database Fort McHenry*, http://fortmchenrylibrary.org/index.cfm?action=1861&id=473.

old four-horse stage coach, reaching home the evening of November the 11th, 1862, to the surprise and joy of our friends.[160]

As the War progressed, the Federal authorities at Washington issued permits to persons whose loyalty was unquestioned, to establish stores south of the Potomac, and trade with the Southern people who lived with in the Federal lines. Such a store had been located in Shepherdstown, Va., in the winter of 1862, and managed by H. N. Bankard, of Baltimore.[161] He employed Daniel S. Rentch to assist him. Early in the year of '63 uncle wrote for me to come and help them about the store.[162] The store was located on the main street, one door from where uncle lived, and with whom I boarded. Bankard slept in the store, but took his meals at the same place where I did. One night about two o'clock I was aroused out of my sleep by a most unearthly noise—by some one beating on a tin pan and crying, "Rentch! Rentch! The Rebels have robbed the store."

Upon investigation, we found that a squad of Blackford's mounted scouts had induced Bankard to open the store door, when they walked in and helped themselves while one of their number stood guard over him.[163]

Shortly before they had secured what plunder they wanted, Bankard slipped into a side room at the rear of the warehouse, where a window opened into the back yard. Fortunately for him, one of the 14 x 16 panes was broken, over which paper had been pasted, and through this he jumped head first into the yard and thence to the kitchen of our house, where he secured the tin pan with which he roused the household.

They took about two thousand dollars worth of the stock, when the parties who owned the store sent William E. Woody, from Baltimore, to look after their interest, and I lost my position.[164]

In less than two months they made another raid on the store, when, after helping themselves, they made Bankard go though the same performance at the point of the pistol, and it was thereafter known as "Bankard's hole." This last raid ended the project.

---

160   Stonebraker and Keller were in prison in Sept 1862 during the Battle of Antietam.

161   Henry Nicholas Bankard (1832-1903) was a real estate broker with offices at 5 St. Paul Street, Baltimore, MD. He was very outspoken in his loyalties to the Union. Scharf, John Thomas, *History of Baltimore City and County, from the earliest period to the Present Day* (Philadelphia, PA, 1881), 775.

162   Daniel Shafer Rentch (1821-1918), the author's maternal uncle, married Savilla Stonebraker (1825-1867), the author's paternal aunt. Rentch was a merchant on Shepherdstown's main street before and after the war. His skills as a merchant and knowledge of the locals would have made him a valuable employee to Bankard. *1860* and *1880 U. S. Federal Census.*

163   Confederate scout Captain John Corbin Blackford (1839-1864) was born in Berkeley County, VA [WV] but lived most of his life in Jefferson County, VA [WV] near Shepherdstown. He enlisted in Company Glenn's, Virginia 7th Cavalry Regiment on 26 Jun 1861, transferring to Company A, Virginia 12th Cavalry (Laurel Brigade) on 15 Jun 1862. Blackford had a great many relatives in the Jefferson County area and, across the river in Maryland, *Ferry Hill* plantation was the home of his aunt Helena Blackford Douglas and her husband Reverend Robert Douglas (previously noted footnote 156). The ford across the Potomac River at Shepherdstown was once known as Blackford's Ford. Blackford was killed at Newtown [Stephens City] VA in Jan 1864. French, Steve, *Rebel Chronicles: Raiders, Scouts, and Train Robbers of the Upper Potomac,* (New Horizons Publishing Company, 2012).

164   William E. Woody (b. 1830) appears on the 1850 US Federal Census as a printer in Baltimore, MD. Like Bankard, Woody was an outspoken Unionist.

Wandering

JOS. E. WILLIAMS, POLITICAL PRISONER, 1862

Josiah E. Williams (1831-1925) of Funkstown, MD was incarcerated at Fort McHenry with Stonebraker and Solomon Keller. Photo from original text.

During the dreary and monotonous days that I spent in Fort McHenry as a political prisoner, I formed an attachment for one of my fellow sufferers which ripened into friendship as the years increased.[165]

Although some years my senior, we were much together enjoying the beautiful scenery of the garden spot of the State, as we wandered along the banks of the Antietam and over the hills and through its fields and forests.

One of our favorite walks took us by a fine spring, which flowed from beneath a green slope and emptied into the creek at one of its bends.

At this picturesque spot, under the shade of a noble elm, we often rested and were delighted with the melodious notes of the birds as they sang to their mates during nesting time.

The wild grape had a peculiar fascination for me. How I loved to draw near a dense clump of trees made more so by this clinging vine, when the air was freighted with the aroma of its bloom. No perfume could equal its fragrance, not even the delicate odor of the palmetto, in which the bees hum the whole day long. When fall had stripped the vine of its leaves and the frost had mellowed the wild flavor of its fruit, I was a frequent visitor, to the dismay of the birds.

A visit to the spring a short time since showed that the woodman's axe had destroyed much of the timber and changed the whole face of nature. The elm had lost its vigor, and, like an old man, commenced to decay at the top. Time had thinned it of so many of its branches that it no longer shaded the green slope from the July rays of the noonday sun.

"The spring that bubbled 'neath the hill, down by the spreading beech,
Is very low but once so high that we could scarcely reach,
On stooping down to get a drink, dear Tom. I started so,
To see how greatly I had changed since twenty years ago."

"Near by the spring, upon an elm, you know, I cut your name;
Your sweetheart's just beneath it, Tom, as you did mine the same:
Some heartless wretch had peeled the bark, 'twas dying, sure but slow,
Just as the one whose name was cut, died twenty years ago."[166]

---

165   Although Stonebraker does not specify the identity of his "fellow sufferer" in *Wandering*, it is assumed to be Josiah E. Williams (1831-1925) of Funkstown as he inserted William's image near the text. Josiah E. Williams was thirteen-years older than Stonebraker, but he would survive him by twenty-two years. He lived until age ninety-four, dying 1 Apr 1925, at Fahrney Home at San Mar near Boonsboro MD. His *Daily Mail* front page obituary noted that he was "Probably Oldest Resident in County." Born on Death Curve Farm, formerly the Adam's farm along the Boonsboro Pike, he never married. His mother was an Emmert before her marriage. Ella and Catherine Williams were his sisters.

166   Excerpt from the poem *"Twenty Years Ago"* by Dill Armor Smith (b.1812).

Retreat from Gettysburg

The battle of Gettysburg was fought on the first, second and third days of July, 1863. General Lee retired from the field on the night of the fourth, moving towards Williamsport, where he intended to cross the Potomac. General Hill's corps preceded everything through the mountain pass at Monterey;[167] the main portion of the wagon trains and ambulances followed under the special charge of General Imboden.[168] To General Stuart was assigned the duty of protecting the flank of this train. He moved his column by Emmitsburg and thence through Harbaugh's Valley via Zion Church. Here he divided his command in order to make the passage of the mountain more certain. Chambliss'[169] brigade, under his immediate command, moved to the right, towards Leitersburg, while Col. Ferguson,[170] with Jenkin's[171] brigade, passed to the left towards Smithburg. Before reaching the west entrance of this pass, General Stuart found that it was held by Kilpatrick's Cavalry[172], so he dismounted a portion of his command and fought from crag to crag before they were dislodged. He forced the passage of the mountain late in the afternoon and moved to Hagerstown.

General Kilpatrick retired to Boonsboro, where he and General Buford[173] arranged a plan to renew the fight the next day.[174] Kilpatrick was to move against Stuart at Hagerstown, while Buford was to attack and capture the trains, which had assembled at Williamsport, the late rains having made the ford impassable at that point.

---

167   Monterey Pass is a mountain pass through South Mountain at the Mason-Dixon Line. In 1863, a toll house connected five major roads that intersected there.

168   Confederate Brigadier General John Daniel Imboden (1823–1895) of Staunton, VA was a lawyer, teacher, and Virginia state legislator. After the war he returned to practicing law in Richmond, VA.

169   Confederate General John R. Chambliss, Jr., (1833–1864) of Greenville County, VA was a career military officer, serving in the United States Army. He was killed in action during the Second Battle of Deep Bottom in Aug 1864.

170   Confederate Colonel Milton Jameson Ferguson (1833-1881) practised law in Wayne County, VA [WV] and was a member of the Wayne County militia before the war. An imposing 5'11," the cavalryman sported a spectacular, nearly waist-length beard. Ferguson succeeded to the command of General Albert Jenkins brigade after Jenkins was wounded on 2 Jul 1863 at Gettysburg, PA.

171   Confederate Brigadier General Albert Gallatin Jenkins (1830-1864) of Cabell County, VA [WV] was an 1850 Harvard graduate, later an attorney, planter, and representative to the US Congress and First Confederate Congress. Jenkins was mortally wounded in May 1864 at the Battle of Cloyd's Mountain near Dublin, VA.

172   Union General Hugh Judson Kilpatrick, (1836–1881) of Deckertown, NJ was also known as "Kilcavalry (or Kill Cavalry)" for his reckless disregard for both the soldiers in his command and the enemy.

173   Union Major General John Buford, (1826–1863) was born in Kentucky but raised in Rock Island, IL the son of a prominent Democratic politician. A captain in the 2nd Dragoons at the start of the war, he was soon promoted to commander of a cavalry brigade. He is most noted for his contributions at Gettysburg. He died 16 Dec 1863 from typhoid fever.

174   **Original footnote: July 6, 1863.**

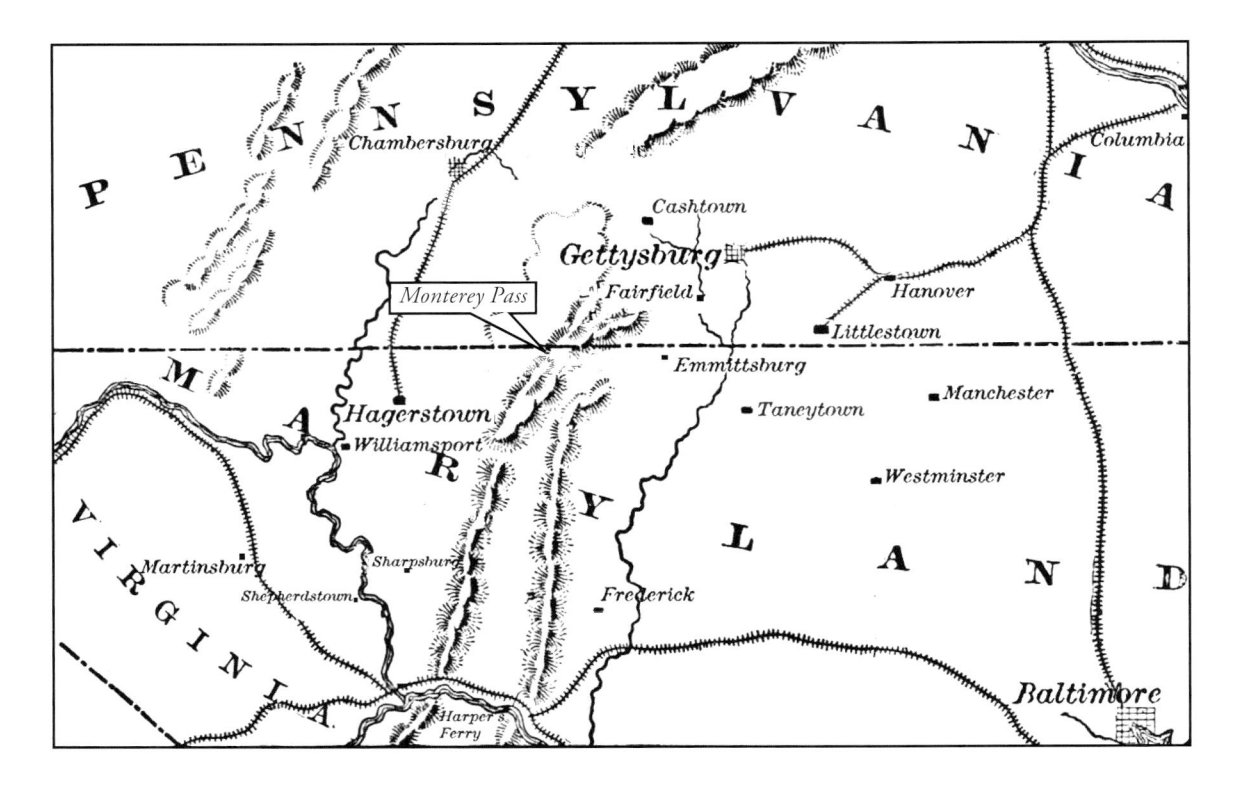

In 1863, Monterey Pass was one of the few improved road gaps along South Mountain.

Gen. Jeb. Stuart,[175] in his report, says:

> "Having heard from the commanding general about daylight the next morning, and being satisfied that all of Kilpatrick's force had gone to Boonsboro, I immediately, notwithstanding the march of a greater portion of both the preceding nights, set out for Boonsboro. Having reached Cavetown, I directed Gen. Jones[176] to proceed on the Boonsboro road a few miles, and thence proceed to Funkstown, which point I desired him to hold, covering the eastern front of Hagerstown. Chambliss' brigade proceeded direct from Leitersburg to Hagerstown, and Robertson's[177] took the same route, both together a very small command. Diverging from Jones' line of march at Cavetown, I proceeded with Jenkin's brigade

---

175   Confederate Cavalry General James Ewell Brown "Jeb" Stuart, (1833–1864) commanded brilliantly at the battles of Bull Run in 1861 and 1862, Antietam, and Fredericksburg in 1862. His tactical error at Gettysburg contributed to the Confederate defeat there. Stuart was mortally wounded at Yellow Tavern, VA during the Wilderness Campaign of 1864.

176   Confederate General William Edmondson "Grumble" Jones (1824-1864) was a planter from Washington County, VA. A graduate of the US Military Academy in 1848, he was a career US Army officer before the war. Court-martialed by General Stuart in late 1863 for his insults and attitude, General Imboden acknowledged that Jones ". . .was an old army officer, brave as a lion and had seen much service, and was known as a hard fighter. He was a man, however, of high temper, morose and fretful. He held the fighting qualities of the enemy in great contempt, and never would admit the possibility of defeat where the odds against him were not much over two to one." Jones was killed in the Battle of Piedmont in Jun 1864. Eicher, John H., and David J. Eicher. *Civil War High Command*, (Stanford University Press, Stanford, CA, 2001).

177   Confederate General Beverly Holcombe Robertson (1827-1910) of Amelia County, VA was an 1849 graduate of the US Military Academy and a Captain in the regular US Army before the war. He commanded two North Carolina cavalry brigades at Gettysburg.

by way of Chewsville toward Hagerstown. Upon arriving at the former place, it was ascertained that the enemy was nearing Hagerstown with a large force of cavalry from the direction of Boonsboro, and Col. Chambliss needed reinforcements. Jenkin's brigade was pushed forward, and arriving before Hagerstown, found the enemy in possession; made an attack in flank by this road, Jones coming up further to the left and opening with a few shots of artillery. A small body of infantry, under Brigadier Gen. Iverson,[178] also held the north edge of the town, aided by the cavalry of Robertson and Chambliss. Our operations here were much embarrassed by our great difficulty in preventing this later force from mistaking us for the enemy, several shots striking very near our column. I felt sure that the enemy's designs were directed against Williamsport, where I was informed by Gen. Jones our wagons were congregated in a narrow space at the foot of a hill near the river, which was too much swollen to admit their passage to the south bank. I therefore urged on all sides the most vigorous attack, to save our trains at Williamsport. Our force was perceptibly much smaller than the enemy's, but by a bold front and determined attack, with a reliance on that help which has never failed me, I hoped to raise the siege of Williamsport, if, as I believed, that was the real object of the enemy's designs.

"Hagerstown is six miles from Williamsport, the country between being almost entirely cleared, but intersected by innumerable fences and ditches. The two places are connected by a lane, a perfectly straight macadamized road.

"The enemy's skirmishers fought dismounted from street to street, and some time elapsed before the town was entirely clear, the enemy taking the road first towards Sharpsburg, but afterwards turning to the Williamsport road. Just as the town was cleared I heard the sound of artillery at Williamsport.

"The cavalry, except two brigades with Gen. Fitz. Lee,[179] was now pretty well concentrated at Hagerstown, and one column, under Col. Chambliss, was pushed directly down the road after the enemy, while Robertson's two regiments and Jenkin's brigade kept to the left of the road, moving in a parallel direction to Chambliss. A portion of Stuart's Horse

Confederate Cavalry General James Ewell Brown "Jeb" Stuart, (1833–1864). LOC/ P&P. LOT 14043-2, no. 33.

---

178   Confederate Brigadier General Alfred Iverson, Jr., (1829–1911) was born in Clinton, Jones County, GA the son of US Georgia Senator Alfred Iverson, Sr. Iverson attended the Tuskegee Military Institute and served in the Mexican-American War. After his less than distinguished performance at Gettysburg, General Lee removed Iverson from combat command.

179   Confederate Brigadier General Fitzhugh Lee (1835–1905) of Fairfax County, VA was a cavalry officer and the nephew of General Robert E. Lee. A graduate of the US Military Academy in 1856, he was a career officer until the secession of Virginia in 1861. After the war he served as the 40th governor of Virginia.

The retreating Confederate army could cross the rugged South Mountain range through only two gaps, the Fairfield Gap or the Monterey Pass. The wagon train consisting of soldiers, artillery, equipment, thousands of wounded, ambulances, supply wagons, mules, and horses was over 17 miles long when it arrived at Williamsport, MD. Drawing by Edwin Forbes entitled "Pursuit of Lee's Army. Scene on the read near Emmittsburg." LOC/P&P. LC-DIG-ppmsca-22572.

Artillery also accompanied the movement. The Ninth and Thirteenth Virginia Cavalry participating with marked gallantry. The column on the flank was now hurried up to attack the enemy, but the obstacles, such as post-and-rail fences, delayed its progress so long that the enemy had time to rally along a crest of rocks and fences, from which he opened with artillery, raking the road. Jenkin's brigade was ordered to dismount and deploy over the difficult ground. This was done with marked effect and boldness, Lt. Col. Witcher[180] as usual, distinguishing himself by his courage and conduct. The enemy thus dislodged, was closely pressed by the mounted cavalry, but made one effort at counter charge, which was gallantly met and repulsed by Col. James B. Gordon,[181] commanding a fragment of the Fifth North Carolina Cavalry, that officer exhibiting under my eye individual prowess, deserving special commendation. The repulse was soon after converted into a rout by Col. Lomax's[182] regiment, the Eleventh Virginia Cavalry, of Jones' brigade, which now took the road under the gallant leadership of its colonel, and with drawn sabers charged down the turnpike under a fearful fire of artillery.

"The enemy was now very near Williamsport, and the determined and vigorous attack in his rear soon compelled him to raise the siege of the place and leave by the Downsville Road."

---

180   Confederate Lieutenant Colonel Vincent Addison Witcher (1837-1912) of Pittsylvania County, VA commanded the 34th Virginia Cavalry that suffered over 70% losses at Gettysburg. "I shall never, no never, forget that eventful night . . . I full of grief and bitterness, rode to the barns in our rear and saw with tears in my eyes, my brave fellows from away over the mountains in West Virginia, laid out in windrows, torn and bleeding. I shall never forget that night or the next morning's parade when I could muster but 96 enlisted men. Brave fellows, not a slave holder among them."

181   Confederate Brigadier General James Bryon Gordon (1822–1864) of Wilkes County, NC was a college graduate, successful businessman, and North Carolina legislator. For his actions at Hagerstown, MD Gordon was promoted from Colonel of Cavalry to Brigadier General in command of the North Carolina Cavalry Brigade. On 11 May 1864, General J.E.B. Stuart was killed at Yellow Tavern, VA and Gordon assumed the role of defending Richmond. On 12 May 1864 Gordon's cavalry held Union General Sheridan's troops, but Gordon was mortally wounded and died within the week.

182   Confederate Major General Lunsford Lindsay Lomax (1835–1913) was born in Newport, RI the son of a Virginia-born ordnance officer. He graduated from the US Military Academy in 1856 with Fitzhugh Lee and also resigned his commission to join the Confederacy in 1861 as a Colonel in the 11th Virginia Cavalry. In the aftermath of Gettysburg he was promoted to Brigadier General. After the war Lomax returned to farming, then was appointed president of the Virginia Polytechnic Institute for five years, later working for the War Department assembling and editing the Official Records of the war.

In this engagement Gen. Stuart lost 254 officers and men, exclusive of Jenkins' brigade, from which no report was received.

Kilpatrick and Buford lost 401, and Gen. Buford says in his report:

> "While our hottest contest was in progress, Gen. Kilpatrick's guns were heard in the direction of Hagerstown.
>
> * * * Just before dark, Kilpatrick's troops gave way, passing to my rear by the right, and were closely followed by the enemy.
>
> * * * The expedition had for its object the destruction of the enemy's trains, supposed to be at Williamsport. This, I regret to say, was not accomplished. The enemy was too strong for me, but he was severely punished for his obstinacy."[183]

The next day, the 6th, the United States Cavalry, under the command of Lt. Col. Noland,[184] advanced against Funkstown and drove the Confederates into town. Lt. Col. Thos. Marshall,[185] with Companies F and G of the Seventh Virginia Cavalry, attacked and drove them several miles down the pike, killing and capturing 59 of their number.

General Stuart, now being sorely pressed by greatly superior numbers, asked for infantry to support his artillery. General Longstreet sent him two brigades—Semmes', under Col. Bryan[186], and Anderson's, under Col. W. W. White.[187]

I have detailed the movements of General Stuart from Gettysburg thus far in order to give a description of the engagement which took place on July the 10th, 1863, as the

Union Cavalry General John Buford, Jr (1826–1863). LOC/ P&P. LC-B813- 2171 A.

---

183 The "he" General Buford refers to here is the rebel enemy.
184 Union Second Lieutenant Nicholas Merritt Nolan (1835-1883) was born in Ireland and began his military career as a private in 1852. He rose through the ranks and was commissioned an officer in 1862. Nolan and other members of the Union Cavalry spent the first half of the war proving Union "horse soldiers" were the equals of the more dashing Confederate Cavalry. After the war Nolan continued his service in the regular army, eventually promoted to Major.
185 Confederate Lieutenant Colonel Thomas Marshall (1836–1864) of Fauquier County, VA was the grandson of Chief Justice John Marshall. He attended the University of Virginia before volunteering in the 7th Virginia Cavalry in 1861. A daring officer, Marshall had six horses shot out from under him during the war. He was killed at Nineveh, VA in Nov 1864.
186 Confederate Brigadier General Paul Jones Semmes (1815-1863) of Wilkes County, GA was a banker and businessman in Columbus, GA. He was the cousin of *CSS Alabama* Captain Raphael Semmes, and half-brother to Albert Gallatin Semmes, Associate Justice of the Florida Supreme Court. Semmes was mortally wounded at Gettysburg on July 2nd and died 8 days later in Martinsburg, VA [WV]. Command of Semmes brigade fell to Lieutenant Colonel Goode Bryan (1811-1885) of Hancock County, GA a graduate of the US Military Academy in 1834. Bryan was promoted to Brigadier General in Aug 1863 to officially replace the deceased Semmes.
187 Confederate Colonel George "Tige" Thomas Anderson (1824-1901) of Georgia served as a lieutenant of Georgia cavalry during the Mexican-American War. In 1861 he was made Colonel of the 11th Georgia Regiment. After he was wounded at Gettysburg command of his brigade fell to fellow Georgian, Colonel William Wilkinson White (1835-abt 1869). Wilkinson survived the war, married, and died a few years later.

Battle of Funkstown

On Friday morning, four guns of Company A, First North Carolina Artillery, under Capt. Manly,[183] were placed on the crest of the hill in Gilbert's field,[184] directly east of the town. Two brigades of infantry from Longstreet's Corps supported this battery,[185] Semmes' brigade being placed on the north side and Anderson's on the south side of the turnpike that leads from Funkstown to Beaver Creek.[186] On the flank of each of these brigades dismounted cavalry was placed—the right resting on the National Pike near the Antietam, just north of Hauck's large stone barn,[187] and Chew's battery of Stuart's Horse Artillery supported these troops.[188] The left rested on the road that leads to Smithburg, and near the old Kemp house.[189] Sharpshooters being posted in the large stone barn belonging to John W. Stonebraker and the line of battle being in the shape of a crescent.[190]

---

183   Confederate Captain Basil "Baz" Charles Manly (1839-1882), the son of former North Carolina Governor Charles Manly, was commissioned 1st Lieutenant of Company A of the 10th North Carolina State Troops Apr 1861. After the war Manly was elected Mayor of Raleigh in 1875 for seven consecutive one-year terms.

184   Fifty-six year-old John Gilbert (1807-1885) and his wife Susan (1798-1885) owned numerous small land parcels in the Funkstown and Cavetown area, including a triangular parcel of 13 ½ acres situated at the intersection of the roads from Funkstown to Beaver Creek and Cavetown. The Gilbert's lived on a small farm off present day Robinwood Drive very near Chewsville. Their two grown sons had recently moved to Ogle County, IL, and the senior Gilbert's would follow in Dec 1864. In Feb 1865, Gilbert sold the 13 acres to Samuel Stouffer whose property was contiguous. *1860 US Federal Census, Thomas Taggert, A Map of Washington County, 1859, LOC MSA SC 1213-1-471, WCLR IN11-74* and *18-365*.

185   Confederate Major General James Longstreet (1821–1904) graduated from West Point in 1842 and served on Indian campaigns and in the Mexican War. One of the foremost Confederate generals of the war, General Lee called him his "Old War Horse."

186   Confederate General Paul Jones Semmes and Colonel George "Tige" Thomas Anderson were both out of action due to battle injuries from Gettysburg. General Semmes would die from his wounds a few days later in Martinsburg, VA [WV]. At Funkstown, Lieutenant Colonel Goode Bryan commanded Semmes brigade, and Colonel William Wilkinson White commanded Anderson's brigade.

187   Jacob Hauck (1813-1904) and his wife Sabina Brewer Hauck (1820-1907), originally of Franklin County, PA, lived just south of Funkstown on Alternate Route 40. The barn still stands on the east side of the road.

188   Confederate Captain Roger Preston Chew (1842-1921), a native of Charles Town, VA [WV], attended the Virginia Military Institute where he studied artillery tactics under Professor Thomas J. Jackson before the opening of the war.

189   The 1860 US Federal Census notes three generation households of Kemps in or near Funkstown: Andrew Kemp (1792-1866); his son George Kemp (b.1810) and family on lot #21; and George's son David (1835-1910) and his family. As Stonebraker refers to the house as the "old Kemp House," he most likely is referring to the home of Andrew Kemp. Kemp rented the property where he lived and is listed as a "blind pauper" on the 1860 census. Most of the adult family members of the Kemp families worked at the nearby woolen mill as managers, weavers, and spinners. *US Federal Census 1860 Funkstown, WCLR OHW2-598*.

190   John W. Stonebraker, the author's first-cousin, twice-removed, was the owner of the *Fox Deceived* 1793 stone farm house and 1825 stone barn on the southwest corner of present-day Dual Highway and Edgewood Drive, Hagerstown, MD. The house was built by Colonel Conrad Hogmire (1725-1797), the barn built by Gerrard Stonebraker, who installed a plaque "GS 1825" on the west gable. Gerrard Stonebraker purchased the farm in 1808, title later transferred to his son, John W. Stonebraker. The farm remained in the Stonebraker family until 1937. In Feb 1991, the farmstead presented an insurmountable obstacle to a proposed shopping center on the site and was mysteriously demolished in the dead of the night. Today the property is the Hagerstown Commons Shopping Center.

Early in the morning, the first division of Major Gen. Pleasonton's Cavalry,[191] three brigades commanded by Brig. Gen. Buford were dismounted and formed in line as follows: The reserve brigade, under Gen. Merritt,[192] being on the right, the first, under Col. Gamble[193] in the center, and on both sides of the National Pike, the second under Col. Devin,[194] on the left. This line was supported by two sections of Tidball's Light Horse Artillery.[195] They advanced up the Boonsboro pike, driving the Confederate skirmishers before them and made a vigorous attack on Stuart's right, but were repulsed in fine style. Lt. Col. Witcher's dismounted cavalry,[196] who were posted behind a stone fence, south of the town, on the Hauck farm, sustained the brunt of this assault. These troops behaved gallantly and held their ground with unflinching tenacity.

Directly in front of Manly's battery, some eight hundred yards distant, was a piece of heavy timber, known as Stover's woods, the reserve brigade of Buford's right, in its advance, swung around and occupied a portion of this timber.[197]

Gustav William Lurman, Jr. (1844-1927), a fellow member of Company C, 1st Maryland Cavalry, CSA. This rare CDV photo was taken at E. J. Rees Studio in Richmond, VA shortly after Lurman enlisted there in Sep 1862. Lurman was the son of a wealthy Catonsville, MD businessman. He was paroled at Appomattox Apr 1865. Photo from authors collection.

---

191   Union Major General Alfred Pleasanton (1824–1897) of Washington, DC graduated from the US Military Academy in 1844. He commanded the Cavalry Corps of the Army of the Potomac during the Gettysburg Campaign, and later the largest predominantly cavalry battle of the war, Brandy Station.
192   Union General Wesley Merritt (1836-1910) was born in New York City, NY. He graduated from the US Military Academy in 1860 and was commissioned a second lieutenant in the 2nd US Dragoons under General John Buford. Merritt took over command of the 1st Division of the Cavalry Corps following the death by typhoid fever of General John Buford in Dec 1863.
193   Union Colonel William Gamble (1818-1866) was born in County Fermanagh, Ireland. A civil engineer, he immigrated to the US in 1838. After some service in the US Dragoons, he retired in 1843 to Evanston, IL. In 1861 Gamble was appointed Lieutenant Colonel of the 8th Illinois Cavalry. Due to ill health, Gamble had just returned to field duty in Jun 1863. He ended the war a Brigadier General.
194   Union Colonel Thomas Casimer Devin (1822-1878) was born in New York City, NY to Irish parents. Devin descended in a family with ancestors who fought in the American Revolutionary War and French and Indian War. He became a favorite of General Buford's, and his rugged leadership style earned him the nickname "Buford's Hard Hitter," while his own men referred to him as "Uncle Tommy." Ending the war with the rank of Brigadier General and Brevet Major General, Devin became a Lieutenant Colonel assigned to the 8th US Cavalry. He died of stomach cancer and exposure in 1897 and was initially buried on Long Island, NY, but later interred in West Point Cemetery at the US Military Academy very near his old friend and commander John Buford.
195   Union Captain John Caldwell Tidball (1825-1906) was born near Wheeling, VA [WV] and grew up on a farm in eastern Ohio. He graduated 10th in the US Military Academy class of 1848. A career officer, he entered the war as 1st Lieutenant of an artillery regiment, rapidly being promoted to Captain of the "flying" battery of the US Horse Artillery Brigade. He was briefly commandant of West Point 1864, but returned to the field leading artillery in the Appomattox Campaign. He became a brigadier general of volunteers and a brevet major general in 1865. When he retired, he was regarded as the army's premier artillerist.
196   Confederate Lieutenant Colonel Vincent Addison Witcher (1837-1912) previously noted footnote 180.
197   The woods was on the eastern end of the Samuel Stouffer (1796-1871) and Sarah Schneider Stouffer's (1802-1888) farm. The Town of Funkstown acquired the western part of the farm in 1953 for a community park.

Major General Sedgwick,[198] commanding the Sixth Corps, says: "The enemy was posted near Funkstown, and the corps moved up and took position after crossing Beaver Creek. The Vermont brigade, Grant's,[199] of the Second Division, were deployed as skirmishers, covering a front of over two miles, and during the afternoon repulsed three successive attacks made in line of battle."

The left of the Vermont brigade occupied a portion of Stover's woods, its line running in a northwesterly direction through Stockslager's[200] and Baker's[201] land, its right resting on the road east of Stonebraker's barn. The Third New York battery, under Capt. Harn,[202] and Company C, First Rhode Island battery, under Capt. Waterman,[203] supported this line of infantry.

From this woods sharpshooters had been advanced in force to Stover's barn, which was about four hundred yards from the Confederate line. Colonel White, with Anderson's brigade,[204] pushed forward and drove the Federals out and from behind the barn and through two open fields to the edge of the woods. Just as they reached the fence of the second field, Manly's battery exploded several shells among them, killing and wounding six of their number. It is bad enough to have to face the determined fire of the enemy, without having death lurking in your rear. This accident was caused by a defective fuse in the Confederate shells, and somewhat disconcerted and checked their advance, but they soon rallied, climbed a post and rail fence, and pushed half way across a newly plowed corn field to within two hundred yards of the woods in which Grant's and Buford's men were sheltered behind trees and large rocks. Here they met with a more determined resistance and sustained their heaviest loss. General Fitz. Lee, seeing no advantage to be gained by a further advance, ordered them to desist and return to their original position.

---

198 Union Major General John Sedgwick (1813–1864) of Litchfield Hill, CT was a career military officer, the grandson of an American Revolutionary War general who served General Washington. Killed by a sniper in 1864 at the Battle of Spotsylvania Court House, Sedgwick has the unfortunate distinction of being the highest ranking Union casualty of the Civil War.
199 Union Colonel Lewis Addison Grant (1828-1918) of Winhall, VT was a school teacher and part-time lawyer prior to the war. He assumed command of the famed Vermont Brigade and led it during the 1863 Gettysburg Campaign.
200 Peter Stockslager (b.1808) and Sarah Carnes Stockslager (b.1816) lived next door to Conrad Stockslager (1817-1881) and Rebecca Laudenslager Stockslager. The relationship between the families is not known.
201 Samuel Baker (1815-1892) and Lavinia Thomas Baker (b.1821) farmed just east of Funkstown. In Mar 1865 they sold their livestock and equipment, yet by 1880 they were still listed as farmers near Funkstown. *US Federal Census 1860* and *1880*, *Herald and Torchlight*, (Hagerstown, MD), *1 Mar 1865*.
202 Little is known of Union Captain William A. Harn (1834-1889) until he assumed command of the 3rd New York Battery late in 1862. He survived the war and became a lighthouse keeper in St. Augustine, FL.
203 Union 1st Lieutenant Richard Waterman (1841-1900) of Providence, RI was a lineal descendant of his namesake who helped Roger Williams found the state of Rhode Island. Waterman survived the war and graduated from Harvard School Law in 1867. He practiced law in Cook County, IL where he died.
204 Confederate Colonel William Wilkinson White commanded Colonel George "Tige" Thomas Anderson's brigade.

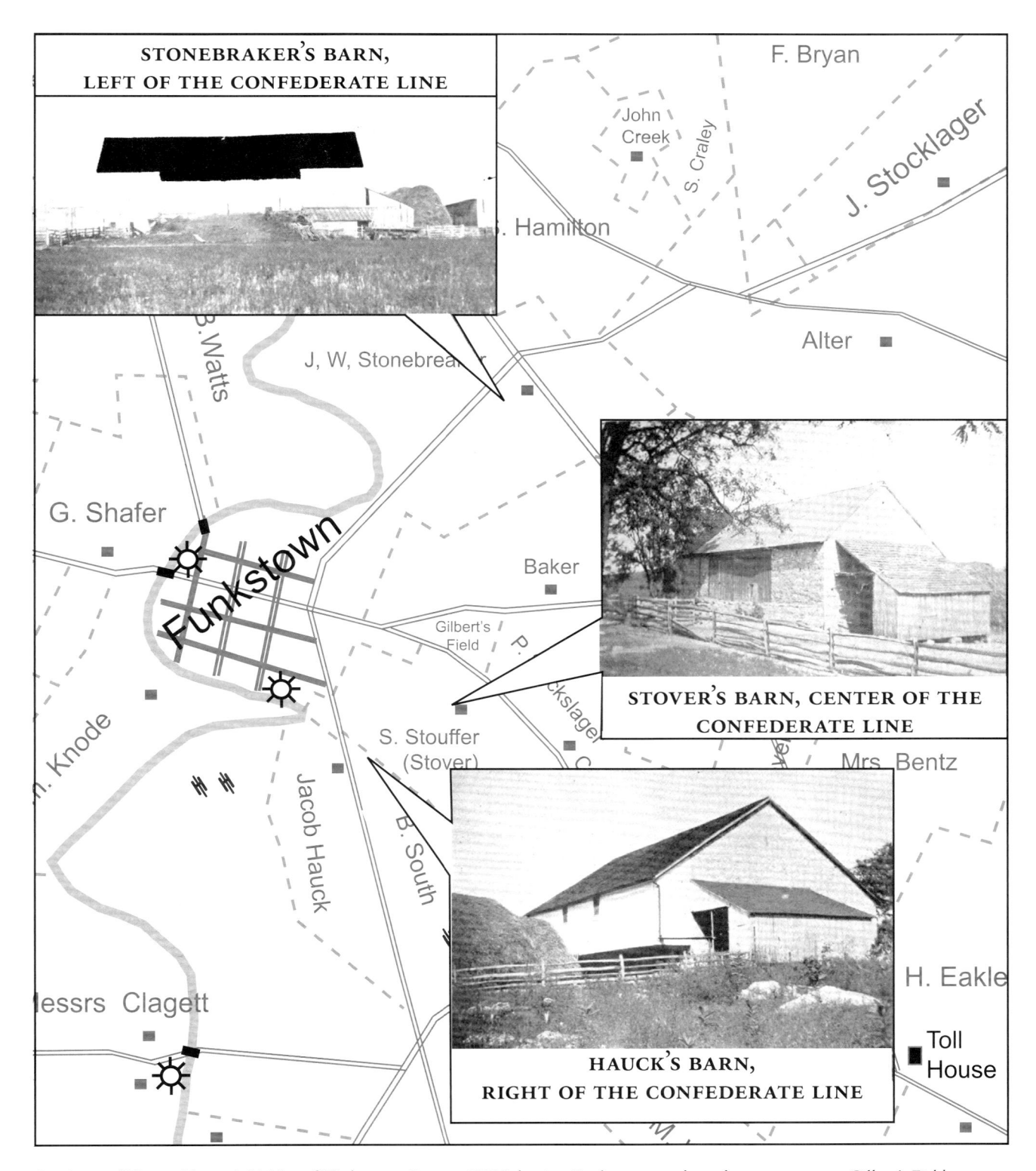

STONEBRAKER'S BARN, LEFT OF THE CONFEDERATE LINE

STOVER'S BARN, CENTER OF THE CONFEDERATE LINE

HAUCK'S BARN, RIGHT OF THE CONFEDERATE LINE

Rendition of Thomas Taggert's "A Map of Washington County, 1859" showing Funkstown, roads, and property owners. Gilbert's Field was added to this map after being identified. The barn photos are from the original text.

Top barn: John W. Stonebraker's 1825 stone barn on the National Highway on Fox Deceived Farm. Today the property is Hagerstown Commons Shopping Center.

Middle barn: The property was owned by Samuel Stouffer (1796-1871) and wife Sarah Schneider Stouffer (1802-1888). The author is anglicizing the German name of Stöuffer to Stover. Today there remain only traces of a barn foundation.

Bottom barn: Jacob Hauck's barn along US Alternate 40 is the only barn standing today.

89

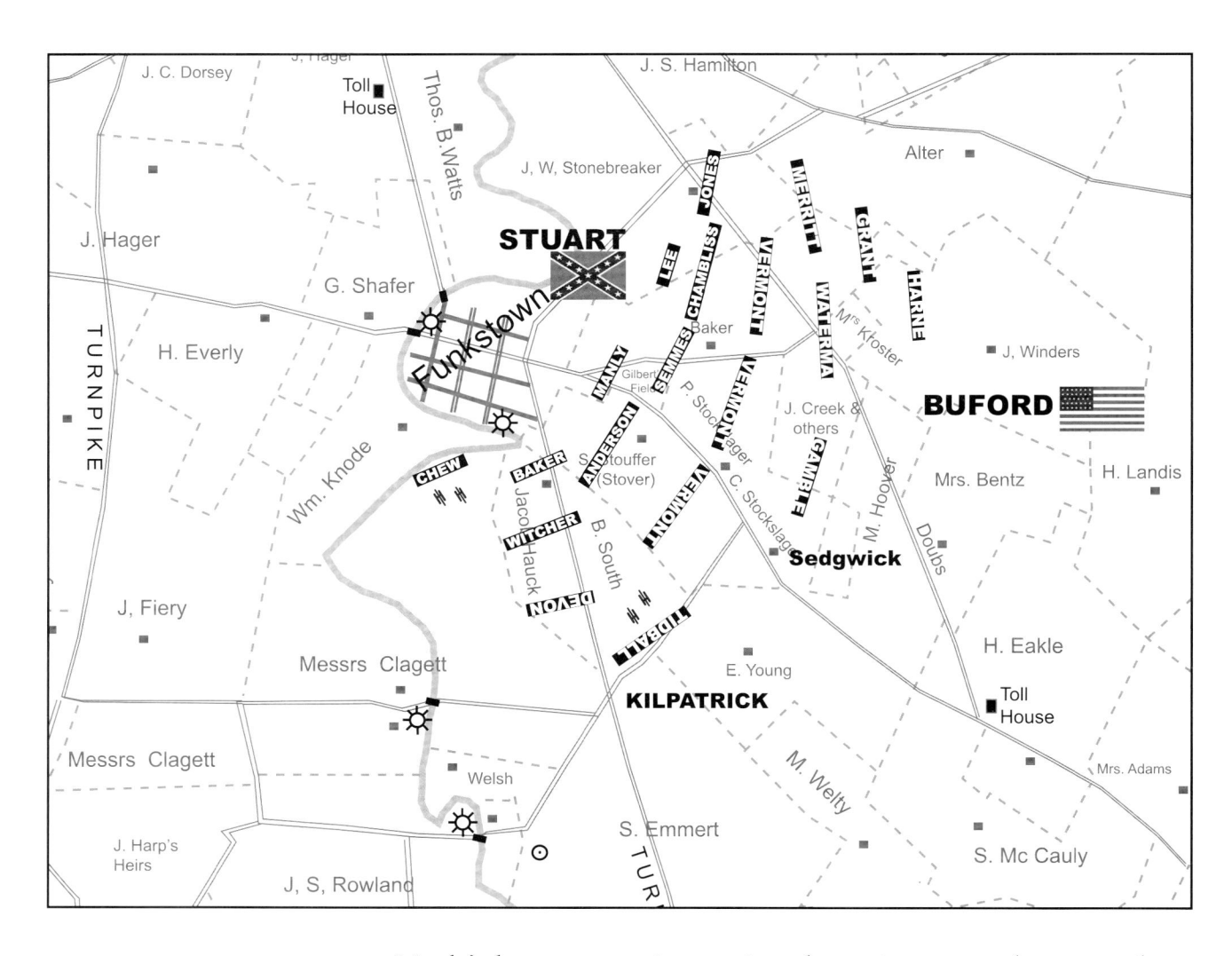

Property owners and parcels are taken from the 1859 Taggart Map of Washington County, MD. Troop positions are based on Stonebraker's writings.

Manly's battery went into action about six a.m., and continued engaged until late in the afternoon. He shelled Stover's woods at a furious rate and fought Tidball's battery with effect,[205] compelling them to change their position several times during the engagement. While the fight was raging on the right and center, a portion of Gen. Fitz. Lee's brigade under Capt. Wooldridge,[206] was hotly engaged on the left with Grant's right, finally compelling them to seek shelter in Stonebraker's woods, better known as "The Cedars."

The killed and wounded on both sides in this engagement was 479, as follows: Vermont brigade, Federal, 97; Buford's, Federal, 99. On the Confederate side, Anderson's, 127, and Stuart's, 156.

The advance of the Federals met with such a stubborn resistance at the hands of the Confederates that they withdrew from the woods and fell back to the "Hoop-pole" woods during the night.[207]

---

205   Confederate Captain Basil "Baz" Charles Manly (1839-1882) previously noted footnote 183. Union Captain John Caldwell Tidball (1825-1906) footnote 195.

206   Confederate Lieutenant Colonel William B. Wooldridge (1825-1873) of Tennessee was a member of the 4th Virginia Cavalry. He is noted in the Wooldridge family histories as a "one-legged confederate cavalry colonel."

207   A hoop-pole refers to a straight slender length of green sapling wood usually of hickory or white oak used as stock for barrel hoops.

From the garret of Mrs. Keller's house I saw a portion of this fight.[208] The wounded were brought into town, and Mrs. Chaney's large dwelling was taken for a hospital.[209] The surgeons had a table in the yard under some trees, and amputated arms and legs like sawing limbs from a tree. It was a horrible sight.

Major McDaniel,[210] of Georgia, was among the wounded. He was brought to Mrs. Keller's on a mattress and laid on the pavement. He had a fearful looking wound in his abdomen, the entrails protruding to an alarming extent. As I stood looking, with pitying eye, a surgeon came and examined the wound. McDaniel had an impediment in his speech and asked the Doctor to tell him the truth, did he think the wound was mortal?

The Doctor said he didn't know, but he thought it was. McDaniel then said, "*Dulce et decorum est, pro patria mori.*"[211] A brave and patriotic sentiment, but I could not help but think it was sweeter to live.

He was taken into the house and placed on a table, when an army surgeon tried to push the entrails back into the wound with his fingers; this he could not do. Doctor Boteler,[212] our town physician, who was about half drunk, being in the room and seeing the difficulty, said, "Damn it, Doctor, dilate the wound." This was done and the wound was dressed.[213] Major Mc-

Confederate Major Henry Dickerson McDaniel (1836-1926) of Walton County, GA circa 1862. His command of the 11th Georgia lasted only eight days when he was shot in the abdomen at Funkstown. He survived and spent the remainder of the war in an Ohio prison camp. After the war he returned to Georgia where he served in both the House and Senate, ultimately becoming the 52nd Governor of Georgia from 1883 to 1886. Photo courtesy of Vanishing Georgia, Georgia Archives, Morrow, Georgia.

---

208   The Keller House, circa 1750, at 6 S. High Street is diagonally across High street from the Chaney House. At the time of the battle the house was owned by Elizabeth Newcomer Keller (1808-1879), the widow of John Keller (1800-1854). The Kellers purchased the property in Apr 1851 from the heirs of John Knode (1780-1848). In Nov 1863 Mrs. Keller deeded the house and lot to her son William N. Keller (1829-1880). *WCLR YY-55, IN5-708, IN17-414. US Federal Census 1850, 1860, 1870* and *1880.*

209   The elegant brick Chaney house was built about 1847 by Elias Chaney (1794-1859). In 1863 it was home to his widow Sarah Eastburn Chaney (1808-1881), her 26 year old son Elias (b.1834), son Doctor Joseph Penn Chaney (1830-1910) and his wife Mary (b.1827), and Doctor Jenrous K. Fleming and his wife Clorinda Chaney Fleming (1835-1910).

210   Confederate Major Henry Dickerson McDaniel (1836-1926) of Monroe, GA assumed command of the 11th Georgia after the wounding of Colonel Francis H. Little and Lieutenant Colonel William Luffman at Gettysburg. Eight days later in Funkstown, McDaniel was shot in the abdomen and spent the remainder of the war in an Ohio prisoner of war camp.

211   Latin phrase "It is sweet and right to die for your country."

212   It is not clear if Stonebraker is referring to sixty-nine year old Doctor Edward L. Boteler, his thirty-year old son, Doctor Robert H. E. Boteler (1833-1892), or twenty-four year old Doctor George W. Boteler (1839-1881). The Boteler family was from southern Washington County near Sandy Hook where they owned several large tracts. Both Robert Boteler and his son owned town homes in Funkstown where they practised medicine. In some census they appear as residents of the southern Washington County district, while in other census they are listed as residents of Funkstown. Interestingly, in 1868, Robert Boteler and his wife Rebecca Chaney Boteler (1837-1905) purchased the Knode-Keller home and used this as their town residence until a few months before his death in 1892. *US Federal Census 1850, 1860, 1870* and *1880. WCLR WMcKK 1-108.*

213   Doctor Elisha James Roach (1833-1890) was a surgeon in the 18th Georgia. Roach was born in Somerset County, MD later moving to Atlanta, GA where he married McDaniel's cousin, Nancy Mitchell (1835-1910). At McDaniel's request, 18 Jul 1863, Dr. Roach wrote McDaniel's girlfriend, Miss Hester Felker, describing the intestinal injuries and McDaniel's subsequent removal to Doctor John Absolom Wroe's (1817/19-1874) home at 27 S. Prospect Street in Hagerstown for continued medical care. When the Union Army occupied Hagerstown, McDaniel became a prisoner of war. His injuries required that he stay in Hagerstown until 15 Sep 1863. He was then moved to a

Daniel not only got well, but survived the War, and afterwards was elected Governor of the State of Georgia.[214]

As fast as the wounded were dressed, they were carried into the house and laid on the floor in rows. The citizens administered to their wants; many died and their cries and suffering were distressing to behold. Simon Knode,[215] an old Methodist deacon, added very much to the confusion as he prayed and sang to the dying.

That night, standing near Mrs. Keller's house, I could hear the cries of the wounded that had been left on the battlefield to die.

On Sunday, after the battle, some of our citizens buried the Confederate dead that had been left in the corn field just where they had died. They were in such a decomposed state that we could not move them, but dug holes just where they laid and rolled them in and covered them over with earth. It was a very disagreeable undertaking.

While the Confederates were in town, father had General Stuart to breakfast. After the meal was over, the General stood on the porch in the rain with uncovered head, viewing his troops as they passed down the National Pike.[216] Father got an umbrella and attempted to protect the General from the rain. He pushed it aside, saying that he would not be seen with that over him when his men were marching through the rain.

While General Stuart engaged the federals east of Funkstown, General Lee's Infantry and Artillery took up a strong position one and a half miles west of Funkstown and two miles south of Hagerstown. The left wing of his line of battle commenced in a piece of woods on the Stockslager farm, near the Downsville pike, just south of where the Williamsport road crosses, and due east through Stover's land to and across the Sharpsburg Pike into a piece of timber on the Eyerly farm.[217] Here it turned and ran south past the

---

hospital at Chester, PA just south of Philadelphia. On 2 Oct 1863 McDaniel was moved by steamer to Hammond hospital at Point Lookout, St. Mary's County, MD. By Dec 1863 McDaniel had recovered sufficiently to be moved to the Union prison camp at Johnson's Island, Sandusky Bay, OH at Lake Erie, a prison almost exclusively housing Confederate officers, where he remained imprisoned until the end of the war. McDaniel, Henry D., Hester Felker McDaniel, and Anita B. Sams., *With Unabated Trust: Major Henry McDaniel's Love Letters from Confederate Battlefields As Treasured in Hester McDaniel's Bonnet Box*, (Historical Society of Walton County, GA), 1977.

214   Henry Dickerson McDaniel (1836-1926) returned to Georgia and served in both the House and Senate, ultimately becoming the 52nd Governor of Georgia from 1883 to 1886. During his administration he established the Georgia School of Technology (Georgia Tech) and began construction of the new state capitol in Atlanta. He died six weeks shy of his 90th birthday. Today, the McDaniel-Tichenor house in Monroe, GA is run by the Georgia Trust for Historic Preservation.

215   "Old" Simon Knode (1811-1868) was fifty-two at the time of the battle. Listed in both 1850 and 1860 US Federal Census as a merchant in Funkstown, he was also an enthusiastic Methodist.

216   Henry Stonebraker and his family lived in a rented home in downtown Funkstown along the National Pike two doors down from Betz's Hotel. *1860 US Federal Census.*

217   The John W. Stouffer [Stover](1802-1877) and Henry Eyerly (1801-1859) farms lay on the south side of the present day West Oak Ridge Drive west of Funkstown. The George Stockslager (1828-1879) farm lay due west of Stouffer and Eyerly along a no longer existing road that extended from Funkstown west to present day Virginia Avenue. That farm today is the Oak Ridge housing development south of Oak Ridge Drive. *US Federal Census 1860.*

THE KELLER HOUSE
FUNKSTOWN, MD

The Keller House at 6 High Street, Funkstown, MD, the home of the widow Mrs. Elizabeth Newcomer Keller and her children during the war.

For many years the Keller House was erroneously believed to be 32 E. Baltimore Street; however, at the time of the battle, that home was owned and occupied by Lewis and Julia Repp. Solomon Keller purchased the property in April of 1876, many years after the war.

The impressionable nineteen-year-old Joseph Stonebraker had an excellent vista of the battle from Mrs. Keller's two large east-facing attic (garret) windows.

In the aftermath of the Battle of Funkstown, Joseph Stonebraker watched as wounded and dying soldiers from both armies were tended at the Funkstown home of Doctor Joseph Penn Chaney and his brother-in-law Doctor Jenrous K. Fleming. Today, the circa 1847 Chaney House is the home of Hudson House Antiques.

93

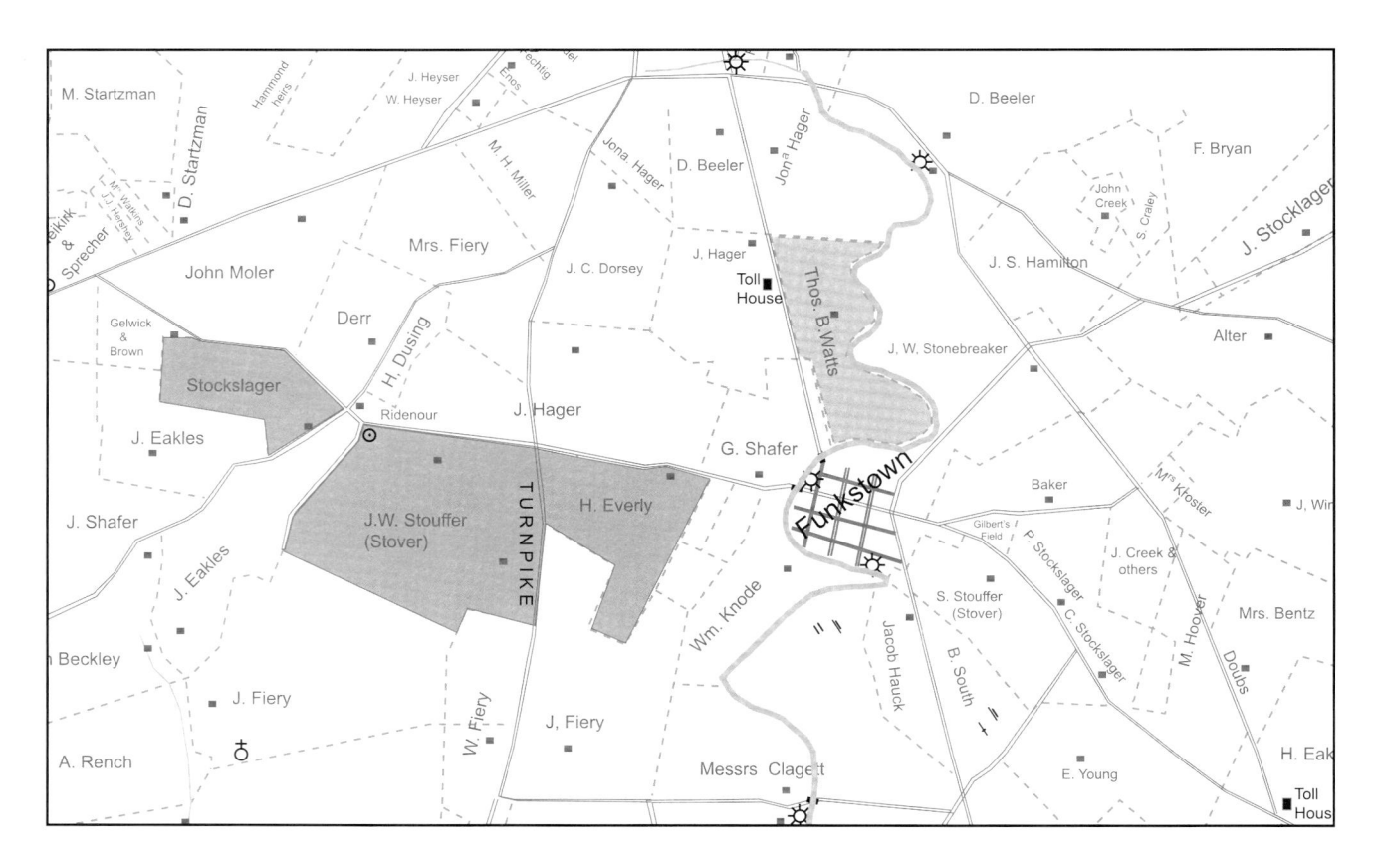

Rendition of the 1859 Thomas Taggart map of Washington County, MD showing roads and land owners. The identified farms shaded in gray are those of Stockslager, Stouffer (Stover) and Eyerly noted by Stonebraker as the position of the Confederate army. Part of the Union army occupied the farm of Thomas B. Watt.

St. James College,[218] the right resting on the Potomac, below Downsville,[219] near Falling Waters, where a pontoon bridge had been constructed.[220]

This line was about nine miles long, and the troops had securely entrenched themselves and now awaited the Federal attack. Longstreet's corps was on the left, Ewell's in the center, and A. P. Hill held the right.[221]

General Stuart having succeeded in masking Gen. Lee's main line until the entrenchments were completed, withdrew his cavalry from east of Funkstown, on the morning of the 12th and massed them on the left of the main body, facing north, the line extending west, the left resting on or near Conococheague.[222]

---

218   Founded in 1842 by Bishop William Whittingham, Saint James School is the oldest Episcopal boarding school founded on the English model in the United States. Saint James College continues today as Saint James School, a coeducational college preparatory school. The campus lies five miles southwest of Hagerstown in the village of Saint James, formerly known as the village of Lydia.
219   Named for the first postmaster Charles Downs in about 1857, Downsville lies eight miles south of Hagerstown, MD at the crossroads of the road from Hagerstown to Dam #4, and the road from Sharpsburg to Williamsport.
220   A pontoon bridge is a portable, relatively easy to build structure consisting of multiple flat-bottomed boats, or other floating devices, linked together.
221   Confederate General Richard Stoddert Ewell (1817-1872) was born in Georgetown, DC and raised on an estate in Prince William County, VA. He graduated from the US Military Academy in 1840 and was known to his friends as "old bald-head" or "baldy." A career military officer, he served in the Mexican War, but when Virginia seceded, he resigned his commission to join the Virginia Provisional Army. After the war Ewell retired as a gentleman farmer in Tennessee.
    Confederate General Ambrose Powell Hill (1825–1865) was born and raised in Culpeper, VA. A graduate of the US Military Academy in 1847, he was a career officer. In March of 1861, he resigned his commission and was appointed colonel of the 13th Virginia Infantry. He was killed just seven days before General Lee's surrender at Appomattox.
222   Conococheague Creek flows south out of Pennsylvania into Maryland and eventually emp-

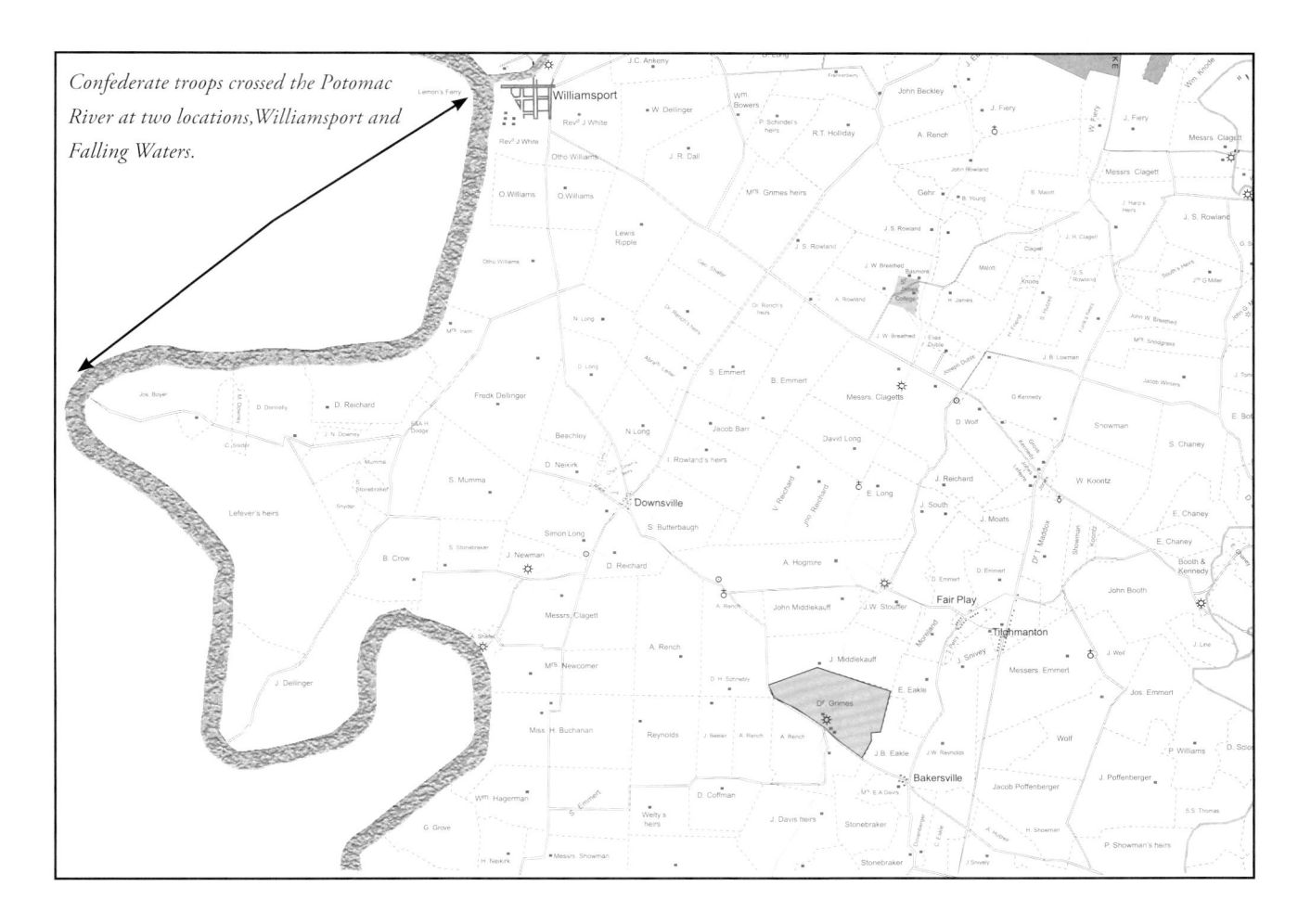

Confederate troops crossed the Potomac River at two locations, Williamsport and Falling Waters.

General Meade now advanced his line of battle to a position parallel with that of the Confederates.'[223] His right resting on the Antietam Creek, facing Hagerstown, and running west through the Watts farm,[224] to and across the National Pike at the top of the big hill just south of the Toll gate,[225] through Grosh's land and thence in a southwesterly direction to the west of Jones's Cross Roads,[226] the left resting between Fair-Play and Bakers-

Rendition of 1859 Thomas Taggart map of Washington County, MD. Dr. William Henry Grimes farm near Bakersville and St. James College is shaded in gray.

---

ties into the Potomac River at Williamsport, MD.

223   Union Brigadier General George Gordon Meade (1815-1872) was born in Cádiz, Spain, the son of a wealthy Philadelphia naval agent for the US Government. He graduated from the US Military Academy in 1835 and was promoted from captain to brigadier general of volunteers a few months after the start of the Civil War. Following the costly victory at Gettysburg, Meade was criticized by President Lincoln for not aggressively pursuing the Confederates during their retreat. The Army of Northern Virginia was extremely vulnerable with their backs to the rain-swollen, almost impassable Potomac River. Lincoln believed that General Meade's inaction wasted an opportunity to end the war.

224   Thomas B. Watt (1817-1896), his wife Lydia (1823-?), and son William Watts (1847-?) are listed as residents of Funkstown in the 1860 US Federal Census. From 1855 through 1858, Watts purchased several land parcels along the Hagerstown-Boonsboro Turnpike bordering the Antietam Creek, including 134 ¾ acres just north of Funkstown on the west side of present day Frederick Street. *WCLR IN10-368, IN12-772,* and *IN13-403*.

225   The toll gate house was at the intersection of the National Pike (US Route 40) and the road from Funkstown to Beaver Creek.

226   Funkstown resident Frederick Grosh (1774-1862) regularly bought and sold property in and around his hometown throughout his lifetime. Grosh died 17 Jun 1862 just a few months before the Battle of Antietam. In Jul 1863, the "Grosh's land" was part of his estate.

William Jones (1802-1892) and his wife Sarah Ann South Jones operated a tavern and a ville. The First corps occupied the right, then came the Sixth, Eleventh, Second, Third, and Twelfth, the latter being the left wing.

Buford's Cavalry covered the flank of the Twelfth corps and was posted near Grime's Mill.[227] Kilpatrick, with his command, was posted on the right, in and about Hagerstown.

Soon as the Federals got into line they commenced to entrench their position. On July the 11th, General Lee issued to his army General Order No. 76, which shows that he expected and was ready for Meade's attack. That he had every confidence in his ability to meet such an attack, his letter the next day to President Davis plainly indicates. But now seeing that Meade did not mean to attack until reinforced, and the waters in the river having receded, he recrossed the Potomac on the night of the 13th.[228]

"GENERAL ORDERS" No. 76.
HEADQUARTERS ARMY OF
NORTHERN VIRGINIA,
July the 11th, 1863.

After long and trying marches, endured with fortitude that has ever characterized the soldiers of the Army of Northern Virginia, you have penetrated the country of our enemies and recalled to the defense of their own soil those who were engaged in the invasion of ours.

You have fought a fierce and sanguinary battle, which if not attended with the success that has hitherto crowned your efforts, was marked by the same heroic spirit that has commanded the respect of your enemies, the gratitude of your country, and the admiration of mankind.

Commander of the Army of Northern Virginia, General Robert Edward Lee (1807-1870). LOC/P&P. LC-DIG-ppmsca-35446.

---

blacksmith shop at the intersection of the "road from Hagerstown to Sharpsburg" and the "road from Williamsport to Boonsboro" that they had purchased in Feb 1848. Jones' heirs sold their interest in the property at public auction in Jan 1893 after 45 years of ownership. At that same crossroads, Alexander H. Lappan purchased a parcel in Oct 1843. He died in Mar 1844. His widow sold the property to William Jones in 1846. The Jones family lived there for 45 years, Lappan for less than 3 years, yet today the crossroad is called "Lappan's Crossroads." WCLR OHW1-626, IN3-188, IN1-923, 107-597, *Herald and Torch Light*, 8 Dec 1892.

227   The grist and saw mill on Marsh Run just northwest of Bakersville, MD was owned by Dr. William Henry Grimes (1822-1892). Grimes graduated from the University of Maryland School of Medicine in 1842 and began his practise at his farm he called *Marshton*. In 1855 he married Sarah Rentch, the daughter of neighboring landowner Andrew Rentch. In 1874 Grimes was elected to the Maryland State Legislature. Scharf, John Thomas, *History of Western Maryland*, (Philadelphia, PA, 1882), 1286.

228   Warner Emmerson, a resident of Hainesville, Berkeley County, VA [WV] recounted the crossing event in a letter to his brother Frank Emmerson of Lousiana, MO: "The evening it rained powerful so that by morning the river was high and the army on the other side with no pontoon bridge to cross on and too deep to ford anyway, so that they had to wait until they put up another pontoon bridge at Falling Waters, or till the river fell again, which it did not do, as it rained every day or so. They kept crossing their wounded day and night in the ferryboat at Williamsport and also in other boats, until they got another bridge put up at Falling Waters, which they made up at Williamsport and floated down the river. As soon as the last plank was laid down, they commenced crossing on it. Lee, Longstreet, and Hill crossed on it, while Ewell forded it up at Williamsport. Keller, S. Roger, *Crossroads of War, Washington County, Maryland in the Civil War*, (The Burd Street Press, Shippensburg, PA, 1997), 199.

Invasion of Maryland - Lee Retreating Across the Potomac to Virginia, above Williamsport, July 13. - From a sketch by our Special Artist, C. E. H. Bonwill. Frank Leslie's Illustrated Newspaper, 1 Aug 1863, 305.

To facilitate their retreat from Maryland Confederate soldiers constructed a pontoon bridges over the Potomac River. The temporary bridge at Falling Waters would have been similar to this bridge built over the James River at Jones Landing, VA. LOC/P&P. LC-DIG-cwpb-01896.

97

President of the Confederate States, Jefferson Finis Davis (1808-1889). LOC/P&P. LC-DIG-ppmsca-23852.

Once more you are called upon to meet the army from which you have won on so many fields a name that will never die.

Once more the eyes of your countrymen are turned upon you and again do our wives and sisters, fathers, mothers and helpless children, lean for defense on your strong and brave hearts.

Let every solider remember that on his courage and fidelity depends all that makes life worth having—the freedom of his country, the honor of his people, and the security of his home. Let each heart grow strong in remembrance of our glorious past, and in the thought of the inestimable blessings for which we contend, and, invoking the assistance of that Divine Power which has so signally blessed our former efforts, let us go forth in confidence to secure the peace and safety of the country. Soldiers, your old enemy is before you! Win from him honors worthy of your righteous cause—worthy of your comrades dead on so many illustrious fields.

R. E. LEE, General.

On the next day, the 12th, he wrote to President Davis the following letter:[229]

"The army is in good condition, and occupies a strong position covering the Potomac, from Williamsport to Falling Waters. The enemy seems to be collecting his forces in the Valley of the Antietam, his main body stretching from Boonsboro to Sharpsburg. But for the power he possesses of accumulating troops, I should await his attack, expecting that in our restricted limits, the means of obtaining subsistence are becoming precarious.

"Should the river continue to subside, our communication with the south bank will be open to-morrow. Had the late unexpected rise not occurred, there would have been no cause for anxiety, as it would have been in my power to recross the Potomac on my first reaching it without molestation."

---

[229] Jefferson Finis Davis (1808-1889) of Christian County, KY moved to Mississippi at an early age. A graduate of the US Military Academy in 1824, he entered politics after a short career as an army officer. Davis was appointed Secretary of War under President Franklin Pierce. Following the secession of Mississippi, Davis was unanimously elected Provisional President of the Confederate States.

Border State

It is a trite saying, when speaking of a positive character, that he has the courage of his convictions. How little does the present generation know what that meant, to the Southern sympathizer, who lived in the Border States during the dark days of '61 to '65.

In those trying times, the writer's family almost suffered martyrdom, because of their convictions, and strange as it may seem, the greater the persecution, the firmer the faith. So it has been in all ages, and so it will continue until the end of time. The mighty oak of the forest is stronger after each storm, and all true men and women hold more tenaciously to their faith and friends when persecuted.

If the Unionist was not the most vindictive, he at least appeared to be, for he more frequently took advantage of the opportunity to annoy his neighbor by having the Federal troops oftener and longer among us.

Father's house was ransacked time and again, looking for that which he never had, a "Rebel Flag," his horses and wagon taken and never returned; his property taken and never paid for; mother and sisters often insulted, and once after dark driven from their home, are some of the many trials we had to endure. The chief offenders were men, who had enlisted in the Federal army from our town and section.

Searching for Arms in a Rebel's House in Southern Maryland, Harper's Weekly 16 Nov 1861.

99

Brutal Treatment

On Sunday, July the 26th, 1863, while taking dinner at Mr. Samuel Emmert's,[230] two miles south of our village, two soldiers, members of Cole's Cavalry,[231] forcibly and with much abuse, marched me to Hagerstown. I was taken before the Provost Marshal, who ordered me to be confined in a room above his office. Here I found father and several of our neighbors, Wm. Harper being one of the number.[232]

Father was much depressed and would not accompany us in the evening, when we were marched under guard to another part of the town for supper—coffee and dry bread. At night we slept on the bare floor. I was young and could stand almost anything, but father had a tough night of it, much to my sorrow.

The next morning we breakfasted at the same place, receiving the same kind of grub, father going with us.

Harper was a rough diamond, but true as steel to his convictions and friends. He was noted for his dry wit and flow of spirits. During the day their wives called with heavy hearts and tearful eyes. Harper greeted them with smiles and said to mother, "your husband is a very poor bed fellow. I awoke last night to find that he had robbed me of all the feathers and covering, leaving me the bare floor only." Soon his pleasantry dried their eyes.

Later in the day we were taken before the Provost Marshal and asked what we had done. Not having been informed of the cause of our arrest, we could only say we were entirely ignorant of having committed any offense. He said, "Well, you can go home."

The arrest of a suspected Confederate sympathizer by Union troops. From John A. Marshalls, American Bastille: A History of the Illegal Arrest and Imprisonment of American Citizens During the Late Civil War *(Philadelphia, PA, 1876).*

---

230 Samuel Emmert (1808-1885), his wife Mary Newcomer Emmert (1810-1884), and their numerous children lived on 237 acres about two miles south of Funkstown just south of Poffenberger Road. Henry Stonebraker and Mary Newcomer Emmert were first-cousins, once-removed. Samuel Emmert purchased the 237 acres lying on both sides of the Boonsboro Turnpike from John Stonebraker 11 Apr 1843. Emmert had six sons ranging in age from 17 to 32 years old, yet none served in either army. *WCLR OHW1-64.*

231 The Union 1st Maryland Cavalry Companies A, C & D were organized in Frederick MD and Company B at Cumberland, MD from 10 Aug to 27 Nov 1861. Company A was called "Cole's Cavalry" after its founder Captain Henry Alexander Cole. The four companies consolidated into a battalion, and Captain Cole was promoted to Major and given command of "Cole's Cavalry."

Most of the men in the original four companies of Cole's Cavalry were from Western Maryland, with some from Virginia and Pennsylvania as well. These men were farmers and planters, young, unmarried, and accustomed to both firearms and riding. Cole's Cavalry spent much of their time patrolling along the Potomac River and Shenandoah Valley, their extensive knowledge of Western Maryland and nearby regions a great asset to the Union cause. Newcomer, C. Armour, *Cole's Cavalry, or, Three years in the saddle in the Shenandoah Valley,* (Baltimore, MD, 1895). Wert, Jeffery D., *Mosby's Rangers,* (Simon & Schuster, NY, 1990), 131.

232 William Harper (1811-1883) and his wife Ann Rebecca Shawen Harper lived in Funkstown on lot 146 that Ann purchased 16 Oct 1849. William Harper's vocation in 1860 is listed as a "turnpiker." In 1880, Harper "works on Pike." William Harper purchased lots 117 & 118 in Funkstown 23 Dec 1863. *US Federal Census 1860 and 1880, WCLR IN4-572* and *IN18-70.*

When confined in Fort McHenry, as a political prisoner, one of the inmates of our room was a very old man, beyond 70, named Ramsburg, from Shenandoah Valley, Virginia.[233] He was released from prison some weeks before I was.[234]

One day, while in a field near his home, he noticed a squad of Federal Cavalrymen approaching. The remembrance of his former treatment caused him to flee to the house and secrete himself in the cellar, unobserved as he thought, but he was discovered and shot to death in the presence of his aged wife.[235]

The soldier charged with brutally murdering the old man was one of the two cavalrymen who marched me past my home with drawn pistols in their hands and foul oaths in their mouths.[236]

The early part of July, 1864, while in the field helping my brother-in-law to harvest his wheat, the farmers were seized with a panic, by a report that the Rebels had crossed the Potomac, and were taking all the horses that they could lay their hands upon. A number of panic-stricken men passed the field in which we were at work, going towards the Mountain with their horses in great haste.[237]

Hamilton being much alarmed, quickly unhitched the team from the reaper, and got the balance of his stock together. I, by his request, took them to the Blue Ridge, some eight miles distant, without changing my clothes. When I reached Wolfsville, a little town in the heart of the mountain,[238] I

---

233   Ezra Ramsburg (1805-1863) of Martinsburg, VA [WV] was 57 years old in 1862. He married first: Barbara in 1834 and had three children; married second Margaret Jane Waggoner in 1849. Waggoner was 23 years his junior. They also had three children. In 1860, Ramsburg lived near Martinsburg VA next door to George H. Fellows (1837-1893). Ramsburg was incarcerated as a political prisoner at Fort McHenry from 20 Aug 1862 until 15 Dec 1862 when he took the oath of allegiance. Fort McHenry records indicate Ramsburg "Twice violated his parole. Witness Geo. F. Fellows, Mrs & Miss Ramsburg. Ramsburg is an infamous character. Will take the oath of allegiance." It is not clear if George H. Fellows and the Ramsburg ladies were witnesses for his arrest or defense. A widower, George Fellow later married Ramsburg's daughter, Miss Harriett Anne Ramsburg (1842-1899) 20 Dec 1863. *West Virginia, Marriages Index, 1785-1971 [database on-line]. Provo, UT, USA: Ancestry. com Operations, Inc., 2011, US Federal Census 1850* and *1860. Civil War Soldiers and Sailors System (CWSS) Civil War Prison records of Fort McHenry. Selected Records of the War Department Relating to Confederate Prisoners of War, 1861-1865.*

234   Stonebraker indicated earlier he arrived home in Funkstown, MD on 11 Nov 1862 (see page 79), yet according to the records of Fort McHenry, Ramsburg did not swear the oath of allegiance until 15 Dec 1862. http://www.nps.gov/civilwar/search-prisoners-ftmchenry-detail.htm?prisoner_id=1396&PRRecordSet=F.

235   Mrs. Margaret Jane Waggoner Ramsburg (b.1828) was 34 years old when her 58 year old husband was shot by Federal troops. Likely Stonebraker assumed Mrs. Ramsburg was elderly.

236   Stonebraker uses the term "charged with brutally murdering" yet there are virtually no accounts of Civil War soldiers charged with war crimes against civilians. In the middle of the Civil War, an American law professor, German-born Francis Lieber (1800–1872) suggested a code of the law to restrain excesses by the military against civilians and prisoners, treatment of prisoners, and captured enemy property. In Apr 1863, Lieber's code was issued by the Union government under the title "Instructions for the Government of Armies of the United States in the Field." US War Department, *The 1863 Laws of War* (Stackpole Books, Mechanicsburg, PA, 2005), xiii.

237   Charles T. Hamilton (1826-1893) married Stonebraker's eldest sister Ann E. Stonebraker (1838-1934) in 1857 in Washington County, MD. They lived in Funkstown on lot #171 which Charles T. Hamilton purchased for $1200 in Nov 1853. In 1860, Hamilton is listed as a grocer; in 1880 he owned a feed store. *WCLR IN8-267. US Federal Census 1860* and *1880.*

238   Wolfsville is located in Frederick County, MD on the east side of South Mountain approximately 12 miles by highway from Funkstown.

joined quite a number of refugees that had assembled there from all parts of the County. We grazed and bought hay for our horses, and slept in the barns during the night; but some of the party were always detailed to do picket duty both day and night. I finally put my horses in the care of another person and walked home, when I learned that General Early had crossed the Potomac July the 6th with his Army at Shepherdstown, passed through the South Mountain to the north of Harpers Ferry, and on the 9th met and defeated the Federals at Monocacy, three miles south of Frederick, advanced against the defenses of Washington, but finding them too strong to attack with his small force, withdrew and recrossed the Potomac River at Leesburg, Va.[239]

July the 24th General Early, having fought and defeated Generals Crook and Averill at Kernstown,[240] again moved towards the Potomac, which he crossed August 6th, and took up a position between Sharpsburg and Hagerstown.

This move of Gen. Early was to cover the retreat of a retaliatory expedition that had been sent into Pennsylvania, with instructions to levy a contribution upon the City of Chambersburg, and in case of a refusal, McCausland was to burn the town, which they did July the 30th.[241]

General Grant had instructed Hunter, who was operating in the Valley of Virginia, before Early had driven him out, to make "all the Valley south of the Baltimore and Ohio Railroad a desert as high up as possible." It was Hunter's acts of brutality, that exceeded even Grant's barbarous order, that provoked the burning of Chambersburg.

---

239 Confederate General Jubal Anderson Early (1816–1894) of Franklin County, VA graduated from the US Military Academy in 1837. He practised law in Virginia in the 1840s and served in the Virginia House of Delegates. Opposed to the secession of Virginia, he accepted a commission as a brigadier general in the Virginia militia, later commanding the 24th Virginia Infantry as a colonel. Short tempered and critical, he fought in most of the major battles of the war. Early's nearly successful invasion of Washington in Jul 1864 caused considerable panic. When General Lee surrendered at Appomatox, Early refused to surrender and escaped to Texas on horseback. He was pardoned in 1868 by President Andrew Johnson, but he remained an unreconstructed rebel. He returned to Lynchburg, VA where he practised law and promoted the "lost cause."

240 The Second Battle of Kernstown was fought on 24 Jul 1864, at Kernstown, VA outside Winchester, VA. Confederate Lieutenant General Jubal A. Early soundly defeated the Union Army of the Kanawha under Brigadier General George Crook (1828-1890) and Lieutenant General William Woods Averell (1832-1900) and drove them from the Shenandoah Valley back over the Potomac River into Maryland. As a result, Early was able to launch the Confederacy's last major Confederate raid into northern territory.

241 Confederate General John McCausland (1836-1927) of St. Louis, MO graduated from the US Military Academy with first honors in 1857. He was commissioned colonel of the 3rd Kanawha Regiment on 16 Jul 1861, fighting predominately in southern Virginia and Kentucky. In May 1864 he was promoted to brigadier general in the Valley Campaigns of 1864. In the summer of 1864, Union General David Hunter permitted his troops to loot and burn private property in the Shenandoah Valley. In retaliation, General Early concluded "it was time to open the eyes of the people of the North to this enormity, by example in the way of retaliation," and ordered General McCausland to Chambersburg, PA. Residents were offered the chance to hand over $100,000 in gold, or $500,000 in currency to compensate people in the Shenandoah Valley for the loss of their homes and property. The townspeople didn't believe the threat, chose not to raise the money, and about two-thirds of the town was torched. "They burned the core of town, and over 500 structures were burned — over 2,000 people were left homeless." The result was about $1.5 million in damages to real estate and personal property. *http://www.naco.org/newsroom/countynews/Current%20Issue/5-9-11/Pages/Counties-NorthandSouthmarkCivilWarsesquicentennial.aspx/*.

Off for Dixie

The time had now arrived for me to consummate a determination, long since formed, to cast my lot with the Southern people. Knowing that my parents were opposed to such a move, because of my youth, and to prevent a scene, I went to my room at the usual hour and waited until the family had retired.[242]

I threw myself on the bed, and before I knew it, was fast asleep but awoke just as the clock was striking three. With my boots in my hand I silently left the house.

Oh, how dark and silent was the night; so dark, that for fear, the Katydids had ceased to chirp; so still, that it recalled to my mind Byron's lines on death:[243]

> "The first dark day of nothingness,
> The last of danger and distress."

I started down the main street, but my foot-falls resounded so that I retraced my steps and took one of the back streets, for fear of running into a Federal picket post.

I hurried across the old stone bridge, and up and over the same hill that Braddock's troops had climbed more than a century before.[244]

I met the Confederate's out-post about a mile north of Williamsport, which point I reached at sunrise, and waded the Potomac River.

At noon I overtook the rear guard of Gen. Early's Infantry, moving southward, when I joined and entered into conversation with a ragged and weary-looking veteran, who, upon learning my purpose, said "You take the advice of an old soldier, and go back to your home."

No doubt my youthful appearance had excited his pity, but his advice did not dampen my ardor, for I pushed on through Martinsburg and halted for the night just south of Darkesville, being both tired and homesick, having walked 26 miles since leaving home.[245]

The three-arch stone bridge along the Old National Pike in Funkstown is still in use today. The western facade looks much as it did in when constructed in 1823, and in 1864 when Joseph Stonebraker crossed it leaving home to join the Confederate Army. The eastern facade has been heavily modified with concrete as a reinforcement to accommodate modern traffic.

---

242 Joseph Stonebraker turned twenty-years-old on 1 Feb 1864.
243 George Gordon (Noel) Byron, 6th Baron Byron (1788-1824), better known as Lord Byron, was an Anglo-Scottish poet and a leading figure in Romanticism. In 1813 he wrote *The Giaour, a Fragment of a Turkish tale*. "He who hath bent him o'er the dead, Ere the first day of death is fled, The first dark day of nothingness, The last of danger and distress."
244 The early two stone arch bridges that cross the Antietam Creek at Funkstown are still in use today. Stonebraker's reference to General Braddock would indicate he exited Funkstown using the three-arch stone bridge on the Old National Pike leading north to Hagerstown. The bridge was built in 1823 by James Lloyd when the Old National Pike was built through Funck's Town. Stonebraker is erroneously assuming General Braddock's forces used this road in 1755 enroute to the disastrous Battle of Monongahela. Braddock's forces did use a portion of what would later be the Old National Pike, but further south.
245 Stonebraker crossed the Potomac River just west of Williamsport, MD along today's Bot-

CAPT. A. S. STONEBRAKER

Confederate Captain Doctor Abraham S. Stonebraker (1831-1885), Stonebraker's uncle. Mrs. Cora Schnebly Keady, Stonebraker's cousin, noted in her copy of Rebel of '61, *"Captain A. S. Stonebraker was mother's cousin and we all called him Uncle Abe. Cora S. Keady." Cora's inscribed copy is located in the Allen County Public Library in Fort Wayne, IN. Photo from original text.*

Here one of Gen. John C. Breckenridge's couriers shared his blanket with me.[246] The General occupied a tent nearby; his imposing presence and soldierly bearing excited my admiration. The fact that he had been the presidential candidate of the "States-Rights" party in 1860 greatly increased my interest.

I met a young man, who had lately left his home in Baltimore; we journeyed together by leaving the pike and taking the road that ran parallel but farther to the west. We thought our chances would be better to get something to eat by getting away from the main thoroughfare, as we had to depend upon the kindness of the citizens to supply our wants. We reached Winchester late in the day and parted company. My object now was to find Dr. Stonebraker, an Uncle,[247] whom I knew was in the Army. I learned he was encamped near Bunker Hill, but Winchester being under martial law,[248] it was much easier to get in than out—a pass was required, and by the time I overcame the difficulty, it was nearly dark; but so anxious was I to reach Uncle's camp, nothing but force could prevent me from immediately retracing my steps. I had proceeded about three miles when it became so dark, and being very tired, that I laid down on the porch of a deserted house and went to sleep. I awoke during the night, being quite chilly; for the first time I realized the great mistake I had made by not bringing a blanket from home, and no longer wondered at the old Veteran's advice.

When I reached the camp, Uncle gave me a warm reception, which was very agreeable in my worn-out condition. He was Quartermaster of the "Stonewall" Brigade with the rank of Captain; had charge of ten four-horse teams, two orderlies, and a Negro boy as a cook.

---

tom Road. Once in West Virginia, he traveled south along US Route #11 through Martinsburg to Darkesville, an unincorporated village north of Inwood. Founded about 1791, the community was listed on the National Register of Historic Places in 1980 for its historic architecture that includes about twenty-five 1810, or earlier, log cabins.

246   John Cabell Breckenridge (1821-1875) previously noted footnote 33, photograph page 65. After his unsuccessful bid for the presidency in 1860, Breckenridge entered the Confederate Army as a brigadier general and soon became a major general, originally commanding the 1st Kentucky Brigade. In early 1864, Breckenridge was put in charge of Confederate forces in the Shenandoah Valley. Breckenridge participated in Lieutenant General Jubal Early's Raid on Washington and fought at the Battle of Monocacy.

247   Confederate Captain Doctor Abraham S. Stonebraker (1831-1885) was the younger brother of Stonebraker's father Henry. A First Lieutenant in Company S, 2nd Virginia Infantry Regiment on 19 Jun 1861, he also served as regiment quartermaster. In Apr 1864 he was promoted to Full Captain, quartermaster to the Stonewall brigade. After the war, Dr. Stonebraker and family moved for a short time to Chicago, IL, then Baltimore, MD. In 1876, he moved his family to Waco, TX.

248   It is estimated Winchester, VA changed hands more than 70 times in the course of the Civil War. As Stonebraker could enter, but not exit, it may be assumed the Confederates occupied the city at that time.

It was arranged that I should remain with him until I could equip myself to enter the Cavalry service, as only those who furnished their own horses were admitted to that branch.

In a few days I secured a horse, but he was nearly broken down, yet I hoped by care and plenty of feed to get him in condition for service. For over a month the opposing Generals maneuvered for position from Strasburg to Charlestown, each expecting to secure some advantage by a false move of his adversary. These movements kept the train in almost constant motion. I made several attempts to reach Shepherdstown, and when near Leetown I came upon General Bradley T. Johnson's picket post. After being with them a short time, one of the soldiers asked me to go with him, as Gen. Johnson wanted to see me.[249] After a few moments of conversation, I learned that one of his men had suspected me of being a Yankee spy.

My horse had been sick with the distemper for some time,[250] and the hard riding I was compelled to do completely broke him down. I left him on the road, put the saddle on my back and walked until I found the train.

Captain Stonebraker offered to make me a loan of Confederate money, to be paid when the war was over, which I accepted and paid six hundred dollars for a horse, fifteen dollars for a second-hand gum blanket, and five dollars for a pair of spurs.[251]

Col. A. R. Boteler, the Captain and I made another effort, but failed to reach Shepherdstown, as the Yankees were there in force.[252] On our return

---

[249] Confederate Brigadier General Bradley Tyler Johnson (1829-1903), previously noted footnote 10, photograph page 16. Johnson assumed command of the Maryland Line and was promoted to brigadier general in Jun 1864. After General John McCausland and General Bradley T. Johnson led the burning raid on Chambersburg, PA on 30 Jul 1864, they traveled to Hancock, MD, then south to Moorefield WV where on the night of Aug 7 they were routed in a surprise attack by Union General William W. Averell. Official reports indicate 38 Confederate officers and 388 enlisted men were captured. After the rout General Johnson's brigade must have retreated back to Leetown, WV where Stonebraker encountered the picket post. Johnson's brigade participated in the 1864 Shenandoah Valley campaign, and, in November, he was relegated to command a prison at Salisbury, NC where he served until the close of the war. Beach, William H., *The First New York (Lincoln) Cavalry* (New York, 1902), 409-410.

[250] Horse distemper, which also is known as *strangles*, is a highly contagious disease of horses. The disease is caused by the bacteria Streptococcus equi, which infects the upper respiratory tract of equine species. The disease gets the name strangles from the swelling of the lymph nodes under the jowl and around the throatlatch area, which interferes with a horse's ability to breathe.

[251] A gum blanket is a rubber coated canvas.

[252] Colonel Alexander Robinson Boteler (1815-1892) was born south of Shepherdstown, VA [WV] on his father's estate of *Fountain Rock*. He was raised in Baltimore by his maternal grandmother, a daughter of the famous Maryland artist, Charles Willson Peale (1741-1827). After receiving his master's degree from Princeton he returned to Shepherdstown and, after several unsuccessful campaigns, was elected to the US House of Representatives in 1858. When Virginia seceded from the Union, Boteler's service in the US Congress ended. He was elected to the First Confederate Congress in 1862 and served from Feb 1862 until Feb 1864. When the Confederate Congress was not in session, Boteler, with the rank of colonel, served in the army as an aide on the staff of Thomas J. "Stonewall" Jackson. Boteler often took Jackson's appeals to Congress and, when Jackson threatened to resign because of War Department interference in his command, Boteler persuaded Jackson to withdraw the resignation. After Jackson died Boteler became an aide on the staff of General J. E. B. Stuart. Boteler served with Stuart until 12 May 1864. He surrendered at Appomattox with the Army of Northern Virginia. After the war Boteler served as an assistant attorney in the Department of Justice as a pardon clerk. Later in life he took up painting and, although not quite as preeminent as his great-grandfather, he did complete oil paintings of the principal Confederate military heroes. He also wrote historical articles, including a detailed account of Jackson's Valley campaign. He died in Shepherdstown, WV in 1892.

to camp, the Colonel became very nervous for fear of being captured by the enemy, as we were on the flank of our army.

The Captain's Headquarters was a rendezvous for Shepherdstown people. Colonel Boteler was a frequent visitor and a man of brilliant parts; we enjoyed his talks very much. His was one of the three prominent citizens' houses near Shepherdstown that Hunter had selected and burned. Hunter's officer turned out the lady occupants, refusing them permission to save anything from the flames.[253]

Col. Boteler and Chas. J. Faulkner lived in the same Congressional district and often were opposing candidates for Congressional honors.[254] His description of their joint debates in those campaigns and Stephen A. Douglas' great speeches in the U.S. Senate, when the Southern members withdrew from the National halls of legislation, in the early days of '61, were very entertaining.

When the train was not in motion I did writing for the Captain, hunted, read and foraged. Squirrels were very plentiful near one of our camps. The Captain had a double-barreled shot gun, but no ammunition. Powder could be had from musket cartridges, but how to procure shot was the question. Our blacksmith came to my assistance by punching a small hole through a bar of iron, then heated the bar red hot, laid bullets on the holes and let the melted lead drop in cold water. The lead formed in all shapes and sizes and the squirrel that was hit by this Confederate shot met a mangled death.

---

[253] Against orders prohibiting such depredations, Union General David Hunter (1802-1886) ordered the burning of three homes in Jefferson County VA [WV] in reprisal for the burning by rebels of a home in Maryland of a member of Lincoln's cabinet. Hunter first burned the Charles Town home of his cousin, Andrew Hunter, the lawyer who prosecuted and tried John Brown. Second, he burned the Boteler mansion of *Fountain Rock* in Shepherdstown, followed by the burning of the mansion *Bedford*, on Flowing Springs Road south of Shepherdstown, the home of Edmund Jennings Lee II, Confederate General Robert E. Lee's first cousin. *The Burning of Bedford, justjefferson.com/20Bedford.htm*, National Park Service, National Register of Historic Places Registration Form for the Old Charles Town Historic District, Section 7, 63.

[254] Charles James Faulkner (1806-1884) was born in Martinsburg, VA [WV] and graduated from Georgetown University in Washington, DC in 1822. A career politician from 1829 through 1860, he served in the Virginia House of Delegates, the Virginia Senate, and the US House of Representatives. Appointed by President Buchanan to France, he was arrested in August of 1861 on charges of negotiating the sale of arms for the Confederacy. He was exchanged in December and returned home where he enlisted in the Confederacy. After the war he was elected back to the House of Representatives from West Virginia, later returning to Martinsburg where he practised law until his death in 1884.

In the spring of 1864, one of the elements in Lieutenant General Ulysses S. Grant's plan for "total war" against the rebel army was to disrupt and destroy the continued flow of supplies provided to the rebel army by the citizens of Virginia's Shenandoah Valley, specifically Jefferson County. On 19 Jul 1864, Union General David Hunter ordered the burning of three homes in Jefferson County, WV: Hunter Hill *near Charles Town, the home of his cousin Andrew Hunter who had prosecuted John Brown;* Fountain Rock *near Shepherdstown, the home of Confederate Congressman Alexander Boteler; and* Bedford *also near Shepherdstown, the home of Edmund Jennings Lee, General Robert E. Lee's first cousin.*

Right: Built in 1820, Hunter Hill *in Charles Town, WV was the home of attorney Andrew Hunter (1804-1888). The home was rebuilt in 1865 and stands today on E. Washington Street at Samuel Street in the Charles Town Historic District.*

Left: Post Civil War photo of the shell of Fountain Rock *mansion in Shepherdstown, WV, former home of Colonel Alexander Robinson Boteler. Today the remnants of the foundation can be seen at the Morgan Grove Park.*

Right: Bedford, *home of Edmund Jennings Lee and his wife Henrietta Bedinger Lee. The home was not rebuilt. This pastel drawing of* Bedford *hangs in the Entler Hotel, the home of the Historic Shepherdstown Museum in downtown Shepherdstown, WV. Image courtesy of Historic Shepherdstown Commission.*

Battle of Winchester

Early's army now held a position fronting Winchester, he having failed to bring on an engagement because of Sheridan's extreme caution,[255] and General Lee being hard pressed by Grant, Kershaw's division was detached and sent to Richmond on Sept. 14th.[256] A few days later Early sent a portion of his command to Martinsburg to destroy the railroad. Sheridan becoming aware of these movements, hoping to defeat that part of the army remaining, attacked it on the morning of the 19th, but he was repulsed and driven back some distance in the direction of Berryville. In the meantime the detached portion came up, the fight raging all along the line and, at times, it seemed as if Sheridan's great army was about to yield to the fierce onsets of Early's troops. Late in the afternoon the Cavalry under Gen. Fitz Lee, which held the left, were badly defeated and stampeded. Sheridan taking advantage of the situation, massed his infantry on our center and moved forward with flags flying, while our artillery plowed lanes through their ranks. On they came and simply overwhelmed our thin line by numbers. I watched the battle with much interest, riding from point to point, making a very narrow escape, as a shell struck and exploded near enough to cover me with dirt.[257]

---

255   Union General Philip Henry Sheridan (1831-1888) reportedly harbored presidential aspirations from an early age and claimed he was born in Albany, NY. However evidence suggests he may have been born in County Caven, Ireland. Standing only 5'5" President Lincoln described his appearance as "A brown, chunky little chap, with a long body, short legs, not enough neck to hang him, and such long arms that if his ankles itch he can scratch them without stooping." A graduate of the US Military Academy in 1853 he was a career US Army officer. His career is noted for his rapid rise to major general and his association with Lieutenant General Ulysses S. Grant who unleashed Sheridan's forces in the Shenandoah Valley in 1864, destroying the economic infrastructure. After the war Sheridan applied the same destructive tactics against the plains Indians, destroying their supplies and livestock and killing those who resisted. In 1883, he was promoted to Commanding General, US Army. Morris, Roy, Jr., *Sheridan: The Life and Wars of General Phil Sheridan.* [Crown Publishing, NY, 1992]

256   Confederate Brigadier General Joseph Brevard Kershaw (1822-1894), an attorney from Camden, SC, was a member of the South Carolina Senate from 1852 to 1856. At the start of the war he commanded the 2nd South Carolina Volunteer Infantry Regiment. He participated in most of the major eastern battles of the war from the First Battle of Bull Run, Antietam, Fredericksburg, Gettysburg, Shenandoah Valley, until his capture at Saylor's Creek, VA on 6 Apr 1865. After the war he returned to South Carolina and politics and in 1865 was chosen as president of the State Senate. He died in Camden, SC and is buried there in the Quaker Cemetery.

257   The third battle at Winchester VA on 19 Sep 1874, also referred to as the Battle of Opequon, was considered a turning point in the Shenandoah Valley in favor of the Union. The battle was particularly damaging due to the number of casualties among key commanders. In the Union Army, Brigadier General David A. Russell was killed and Brigadier Generals Emory Upton, George H. Chapman, and John B. McIntosh were seriously wounded. Confederate Major General Robert E. Rodes was killed and Major General Fitzhugh Lee, Brigadier Generals William Terry, Archibald Godwin, and Colonel William Wharton were wounded. Also among the Confederate dead was Colonel George S. Patton, Sr. His grandson and namesake would become the famous US General of World War II, George S. Patton, Jr.

Our wagon trains, which had been parked south of Winchester, on both sides of the Valley Pike, now moved off with some haste, and as the Federals exploded a shell now and then among them, almost caused a stampede. The army fell back during the night and occupied the entrenchments at Fisher's Hill, which had been constructed by them a few weeks previous. I became separated from the train, when Docter Magill and I bunked together in a fence corner about midnight.[258]

Sheridan's final charge at Winchester, by Thure de Thulstrup, published L. Prang & Company, 1886. LOC/P&P. LC-DIG-pga-04046.

---

258   Confederate Doctor Charles Griffith Worthington Macgill (1836-1907) was born in Hagerstown, MD the son of Doctor Charles Macgill. He earned his medical degree from the University of Maryland in 1856 and practiced in Hagerstown until 1863 when he joined the Confederate Army. Macgill served as regimental surgeon to the 2nd Virginia Stonewall Brigade. After the war, Macgill moved to Catonsville, MD where he became one of only two instructors at the Maryland Military Institute. Keller, Roger, *Roster of Civil War Soldiers from Washington County, Maryland*, (Clearfield Company, Baltimore MD, 1993), 7.

Fisher's Hill

I found the train encamped south of Fisher's Hill, near Tom's Brook, where we remained for several days.[259] On the afternoon of the 22nd day of September, I rode to Three Top Mountain,[260] upon which our signal corps was stationed, and had a fine view of the Federal army as they skirmished with our troops. The officer at the station said to me that he thought that Sheridan was massing troops on our left, under cover of the timber. Shortly after returning to the train, straggling squads of horsemen came by hurriedly and reported that our Cavalry, which held the left of the line, had been defeated and were in full retreat up the back road. The Captain ordered the teams hooked up and sent me to ascertain the truth of the report.

I had not gone far before I met our troops in full retreat and many of them in a semi-panic condition. When I returned the trains were moving up the Valley Pike in the utmost confusion.

Some of the stragglers from the army mixed among the teamsters, and the reports that they circulated only increased the excitement and alarm. Finally some of the drivers became panic-stricken and dashed off at full speed; others caught the contagion, when a disgraceful stampede began without any reason.

Their terror would have been very amusing had not their mad run up the Valley been attended with such disastrous results to some of the wagons and accidents to themselves.

I saw one poor fellow, who had both legs broken, and another dead, both caused by being run over. Broken down wagons were abandoned all along the road, from which the soldiers helped themselves. I came across some army clothing, secured 17 gray jackets and a lot of shirts, which I turned over to the Captain.

We retreated all night, reaching Mount Jackson about daylight with our entire brigade train, which we parked a few miles south of the town, where we remained all day while our army was in line of battle at Rude's Hill, a few miles north of us.[261]

---

259 Fisher's Hill is just west of Strasburg, VA. On 21-22 Sep 1864, Lieutenant General Jubal Early was outgeneraled by Major General Philip Sheridan. Although the casualty figures were not high, this battle was a masterpiece of maneuver and surprise. Sheridan's flanking attack brought Crook's corps to the left rear of Early's position on Fisher's Hill and threw the Confederate Army into a panic. The Confederate defeat at Fisher's Hill, following the defeat at Opequon, opened the Shenandoah Valley to a Union advance. *National Park Service, Battle of Fisher's Hill.* http://www.nps.gov/history/hps/abpp/shenandoah/svs3-13.html.

260 Now known as Signal Knob, Three Top Mountain is located in the George Washington National Forest in Shenandoah County and Warren County, VA. It is the northernmost peak of Massanutten Mountain, with an elevation of 2,106 feet.

261 Rude's Hill was named after the Danish Lutheran minister Anders Rudolph Rude (1812-1883), who immigrated to the United States in 1836. Ordained as a minister, he located in Woodstock, VA marrying the widow Elizabeth Steenbergen of *Locust Grove* plantation. The house and plantation saw a great deal of activity during the war. In Sep 1862 General Stonewall Jackson used *Locust Grove* for his headquarters. In Oct 1864, the mortally wounded partisan Confederate Captain John Hanson McNeill lay in *Locust Grove* for several days before being discovered by Sheridan's

Sheridan's decisive victory at Fisher's Hill lead to Union control of the Shenandoah Valley. Confederate prisoners captured at the battle under the charge of the rear guard. LOC/P&P. LC-DIG-ppmsca-15835.

At sunrise on the 24th the train was put in motion, but Dr. Magill and I rode to the front, and saw the Federal infantry advance through Mount Jackson and form into line of battle. They posted their artillery on a hill to the west of the town. A puff of smoke would flash from and hang over the gun for a moment, then the screech of the shell and the report from the gun would reach us almost simultaneously. Shells fell uncomfortably near, but we shifted our position to get out of their range, and watched them shell our troops as they slowly fell back. We now passed through the garden spot of the Valley, nature was smiling with abundance, orchards laden with fruit, fields full of corn and sugar cane. From the latter a syrup was made called sorghum.

The retrograde was continued all day;[262] halted the train about dark but did not unhook the teams; put the train in motion at midnight, reaching Port Republic at sunrise the 25th; crossed the south fork of the Shenandoah River, and passed over the Mountain through Brown's Gap into eastern Virginia.[263] This Mountain is divided at Harper's Ferry where the Potomac

---

troops. Rude's son William Steenbergen Rude (1845-1938) served in the Confederate Army. Having lost everything in the war including his wife in 1862, Rude and his son relocated to Texas about 1869. Wayland, John Walter, *A History of Shenandoah Valley,* (Shenandoah Publishing House, Inc, Strasburg, VA, 1927), 329-330, 504. Pedersen, Lisbeth and Mads Findal Andreasen, *West-Zealanders in the American Civil War,* http://www.kalmus.dk/civilwar/westzealanders1.htm#_edn32.

262   *Retrograde motion* is motion in the direction opposite to the movement of something else. In this instance, Stonebraker refers to the withdrawal of the Confederate in the face of the Union Army's advance into the Shenandoah Valley.

263   Brown's Gap has an elevation of about 2,600 ft. In 1750 Benjamin Brown began to buy land

passes through. That portion of the range which extends north into Maryland and Pennsylvania is called South Mountain, while the branch that runs south is known as the Blue Ridge, and divides the Valley from eastern Virginia. When I reached the top of the ridge a view from both sides met my gaze, and great was the contrast—to the east all was serene, the peaceful look of all nature made a beautiful region more beautiful, while to the west all was confusion, death and destruction, war in all its horrors, immense trains of wagons moving rapidly up the mountain, droves of cattle and sheep with panting sides were hurried along by their anxious drivers, as a shell now and then struck too close for comfort; just beyond Port Republic, our troops in line of battle, slowly falling back, but nobly disputing every inch of ground given up.

As soon as all the trains had crossed the river our army followed and took up a strong position at the foot of the mountain, which ended the retreat.

We parked the train on the eastern side, where our teamsters found Apple Jack in abundance, which they used freely. I made some purchases for the mess—butter $7, and soap $2 per pound, washing $1.50 per piece. I was my own washerwoman.

After Early's defeat at Winchester, Kershaw's division, which was en route for Richmond, was ordered to return to the Valley and rejoin Early and check Sheridan's advance. Part of this division reached us late in the afternoon of the 26th, the balance early the following morning, when Early began a forward movement. Sheridan declined battle and slowly retreated down the Valley, burning everything in the way of grain in his route, and did not stop until he reached the north branch of Cedar Creek.

About midnight the train was put in motion, recrossed the mountain, forded the river at sunrise and parked the train northwest of Waynesboro, where we remained two days. On this march we passed a great many dead horses and some unburied Federals--the result of a fight the day before. The next move took us through Fisherville, Staunton and down the Valley Pike, where we parked the train in a piece of woods nine miles south of Staunton, near an old stone church; here we remained six days.[264]

Rev. Mr. Bowman was the pastor of Augusta Church, who informed me that it was one of the oldest churches now standing in Virginia, having been erected in 1740. The early worshippers took their rifles to defend themselves against the Indians just where the breastworks, that surrounded the Church in those days, could now be plainly traced.[265]

---

in the western part of Albemarle County, VA, including more than 6,000 acres on both sides of what is now Doyle's River. An influential family in the county, Benjamin Brown had eight sons, seven of whom are known: Benjamin, Barzillai, Benajah, Bernard, Bernis, Bezaleel, and Brightberry. In 1805-06 Brightberry Brown and William Jarman built a turnpike across the Blue Ridge here. It was a principal route for taking farm produce from the Shenandoah Valley to Richmond until it was closed to traffic by the formation of the Shenandoah National Forest about 1918.

264   The Augusta Stone Church is located near Fort Defiance, VA about 9 miles *north* of Staunton, VA. This may be a case of a misprint by the publisher.

265   The Augusta Stone Presbyterian Church was established in 1740 by Reverend John Craig, who served as pastor from 1740 until 1774. Still in use today, it has the distinction of being the oldest Presbyterian house of worship in continuous use in the State of Virginia. Reverend Francis Henry Bowman (1833-1873) from Charlottesville, VA served as pastor from 1861 until 1868. He moved to Mem-

The devastation of the Valley has been complete. Rev. Bowman says that on the night of the 29th of September he counted twenty fires south of him, all burning at the same time; a neighbor, who was on a higher point, counted 48. We broke camp on the 7th of October, moved slowly down the pike, passed through Harrisonburg, and parked the train north of Lacy's Springs. The next day we continued down the Valley, encamped southeast of New Market, where we remained three days. Our next move was through New Market, forded the north branch of the Shenandoah, passed through and parked the train north of Mount Jackson on the 12th.

The outrages and cruelties which marked the path of Sheridan's army down the Valley were truly appalling. Aug. 26th Gen. Grant wrote Sheridan: "Do all the damage to railroads and crops you can. Carry off all stock of all description, and negroes, so as to prevent further planting. If this war is to continue another year, we want the Shenandoah Valley to remain a barren waste."

When Sheridan received this letter, it is said he boasted that when he was through with the Valley a crow could not pass over it unless he carried his rations. How terribly he executed his threat his letters to Grant will show. Sept. 29th he writes:

> "This morning I sent Merritt's and Custer's divisions via Piedmont to burn grain, etc., pursuant to your instructions. The destruction of the grain and forage, from here to Staunton, will be a terrible blow to them. In moving back to this point (Woodstock), the whole country from the Blue Ridge to the North Mountain has been made untenable for a Rebel army. I have destroyed over 2,000 barns filled with wheat, hay and farming implements, over seventy mills filled with flour and wheat, have driven in front of the army over

The 1740 Augusta Stone Church along US Route 11 near Fort Defiance, VA where Stonebraker camped for six days with his uncle, the quartermaster Captain Abraham Stonebraker, and part of a wagon train. LOC/P&P. HABS VA,8-FORDEF,1--1.

---

phis, TN in 1868 and died in 1873 of yellow fever.

Lieutenant General Philip H. Sheridan (1831-1888). LOC/P&P. LC-USZ62-131934.

4,000 head of stock, and have killed and issued to the troops not less than 3,000 sheep. This destruction embraces the Luray Valley and Little Fort Valley, as well as the main Valley. A large number of horses have been obtained, a proper estimate of which I cannot now make. Lieut. John R. Meigs, my engineer officer, was murdered beyond Harrisonburg, near Dayton. For this atrocious act all houses within an area of five miles were burned."[266]

In devastating the country, Sheridan's cavalry was scattered over a vast section of territory. That our cavalry followed these incendiaries and shot some of them, when caught in the act of firing houses which were only occupied by innocent women and children, will not be denied, but that Lieut. Meigs was murdered is not true.[267]

While Sheridan's army was in the neighborhood of Harrisonburg three of our cavalry scouts got in his rear; they encountered Lieut. Meigs with two soldiers. These parties came upon each other unexpectedly, and a fight ensued. Meigs was ordered to surrender, but like a brave man he replied by shooting and wounding his opponent, who in return fired and killed Meigs. One of the men with Meigs was captured, the other escaped. This, then, is the "atrocious act" that gave Sheridan the excuse to exceed even Hunter's barbarities.[268]

---

266   The letter is a combination of two separate messages sent from Major General Philip Sheridan in Harrisonburg, VA to Lieutenant General Grant. The first was on 29 Sep 1864, the second on 7 Oct 1864. *The War of the Rebellion: v. 1-53 [serial no. 1-111] 1880-98. 111v,* (US Government Printing Office, 1893), 29-30.

267   Born in Washington, DC, Union Lieutenant John Rodgers Meigs (1841-1864) was the eldest son of Major General Montgomery Cunningham Meigs (1816-1892), quartermaster general of the US Army, and grandson of Commodore John Rodgers, a naval officer in the War of 1812. In 1859, Lieutenant Meigs received an appointment to the US Military Academy. He took a leave of absence to serve as an aide-de-camp to General Sheridan during the First Battle of Bull Run. After returning to West Point, he graduated first in his class in 1863. He participated in the pursuit of the Confederate Army following the Battle of Gettysburg, the Battle of New Market, and operations in the Shenandoah Valley. In Aug 1864, Sheridan appointed him his Chief Engineer. *Personal Memoirs of P. H. Sheridan, General United States Army,* Volume II (Charles L. Webster & Co., NY, 1888), 51-52. Giunta, Mary A., *A Civil War Soldier of Christ and Country, The Selected Correspondence of John Rodgers Meigs 1859-64* (University of IL Press, 2006).

268   The Union soldier who escaped and reported the incident to General Sheridan claimed Meigs was shot without provocation by three Confederates dressed in Union uniforms behind enemy lines. Convinced the Confederates were receiving aid from friendly locals, Sheridan ordered "all the houses within an area of five miles to be burned" by General George Armstrong Custer. The three Confederates involved in the affair gave a different version of the incident, claiming the fight had been fair. Many such occurrences took place during the war, but Meigs' prominence made his case famous. Unwilling to accept that his son had been a casualty of war, General Meigs offered a reward of $1,000 for his son's killer.

In 1864, with Union dead piling up throughout the Washington area, Quartermaster General Meigs recommended that General Lee's former estate in Arlington, VA be seized for use as a military burial ground. The site became the Arlington National Cemetery. A Georgia native, Meigs reportedly selected the Custis-Lee estate as the site for the cemetery to demonstrate his animosity toward General Lee for his service to the Confederate cause. Ironically, among the first to be buried at

We remained in the Mount Jackson camp for more than a week. Captain Estell, the brigade ordnance officer, always accompanied our train and pitched his tent near the Captain's.[269] His orderly was a young man about my age; we became warm friends and were much together. We made it a point to attend Church at every opportunity; the chaplains of the army generally officiated when near a town.

The Captain had many hunts for birds but met with poor success, not having a dog. Near the camp was a young one for which the owner wanted fifteen dollars. I induced him to go with me to the camp, when the Captain purchased him.

On the morning of the 19th of October we heard cannonading in the direction of Fisher's Hill, which continued nearly all day.[270] Finally a message came from Col. Allen, saying that our army had gained a great victory, ordering the trains moved to Strasburg, where the battle had been fought. We put the train in motion about sunset and proceeded to Woodstock, when we met a great many stragglers from the army, who reported that the morning's victory was more than offset by the evening's defeat. The train was halted and turned southward, moved all night, reaching Rude's Hill at sunrise the next morning, where we halted for a short time, but continued up the Valley until we reached New Market and parked the train southwest of the town (Oct. 21).[271]

Civil War era photo of Lieutenant John Rodgers Meigs (1841-1864), eldest son of Major General Montgomery Cunningham Meigs. LOC/P&P. LC-USZ62-120547.

Arlington Cemetery in Section 1 was Meigs' own son. *http://www.arlingtoncemetery.mil/*.

269   Both Captain Abraham Stonebraker, quartermaster, and Captain C. P. Estill, ordnance officer, were under the command of General John Brown Gordon. Brock, R. A., *Paroles of the Army of Northern Virginia, Southern Historical Society Papers. Volume XV.* (Southern Historical Society, Richmond, VA, 1887), 212 (hereafter cited as *SHSP*).

270   The Battle of Fisher's Hill near Strasburg, VA was fought 21-22 Sep 1864 as part of the Valley Campaign. Union Major General Philip Sheridan had almost 30,000 men opposing Confederate Lieutenant General Jubal Early with just under 10,000 men. The battle was a victory for the Union Army. Of the 1,763 casualties, 1,235 were Confederate soldiers.

271   Rude's Hill previously noted footnote 261.

Battle of Cedar Creek

Confederate Major General John Brown Gordon (1832-1904). LOC/P&P. LC-DIG-cwpb-06185.

Our army reached Fisher's Hill on the 13th of October, 1864, and took up their old position.[272] Sheridan's troops occupied a position on the north bank of Cedar Creek, which they had fortified, and it was too strong for Early to attack with his small force.

There was some skirmishing at Hupp's Hill for several days, and Early watched Sheridan, hoping that he would either come out and attack or move back from his strong position,[273] but Sheridan did not seem disposed to do either.

Early now planned to surprise him by moving against and attacking his rear and left wing. On the afternoon of the 18th he called together his division commanders and communicated to them his plan of attack, which was to be carried into effect the next morning at 5 a.m. Gen. Gordon,[274] with three divisions of the Second Corps, was to move around in Sheridan's rear, taking a position near the Cooly house, and attack the enemy promptly at the time named.[275] Kershaw with his division was to assault the enemy's breastworks on the left as soon as he heard Gordon's guns.[276] Wharton with his division and the artillery was to occupy Hupp's Hill and be ready to second the

---

[272] For the second time in less than a month, Fisher's Hill provided an ideal Confederate defensive position for General Early. The wayside marker at Fisher's Hill today refers to the heights as the "Confederate Gibralter."

[273] Defensible and affording an excellent lookout, Hupp's Hill was occupied at various times by both Confederate and Union troops. George F. Hupp, the owner of Hupp's Hill, was a man of wealth and influence in the valley and owner of several charcoal furnaces. The Hupp plantation was over 1,000 acres and included Hupp's Hill, and also Hupp's Cavern, known today as Crystal Caverns. Stonebraker did not know that about 100 years earlier Hupp's plantation had been owned by Jacob Funk, founder of Stonebraker's home town of Funkstown, MD. Wayland, John W., *A History of Shenandoah County, Virginia* (Shenandoah Publishing House, 1927). Bly, Daniel W., *Identification of the Earliest Owners and Residents Of the Site Now Called "The Frontier Fort,"* (Strasburg, VA, 2011) http://www.vagenweb.org/shenandoah/hom/w_hupp.html/.

[274] Confederate Major General John Brown Gordon (1832-1904) of Upson County, GA was a graduate of the University of Georgia. Before the war, he was a practising attorney in Atlanta with lucrative investments in coal-mines in Georgia, Tennessee, and Alabama. In 1904, Gordon published his memoirs of service in the Confederate Army in *Reminiscences of the Civil War* (Charles Scribner's Sons, NY, 1904).

[275] The Cooly House is *Belle Grove*, a late 18th century plantation about a mile southwest of Middletown, VA. Built between 1794 and 1797 for Major Isaac Hite, the property remained in the Hite family until 1860 when it was sold to John W. Cooley and Benjamin C. Cooley. The large Federal-style manor house is a National Historic Landmark and was opened to the public as a historic house museum in 1967. *A Visitor's Guide to Belle Grove Plantation* (Fort Valley, VA, 2000). Umstattd, Elizabeth Madison Coles, *Hite Family Homesteads, Neckar to Shenandoah,* (Published privately by Meema Publications Ink for Hite Family Association Publications; Revised edition, 1999).

[276] Confederate General Joseph Brevard Kershaw (1822-1894) see footnote 256.

attack,[277] while Rosser,[278] with his cavalry, was to move down the back road, near North Mountain, and detain the enemy's cavalry.

Shortly after dark Gordon crossed the Shenandoah River and marched around Three Top Mountain by a blind path. This path was too rough and narrow for artillery and ambulances. Swords and canteens were left in camp, so as to make as little noise as possible. He again had to cross the river at Bowman's Ford before reaching the position assigned him.

Wharton and Kershaw, with the artillery, under the immediate command of Early, moved at 1 a.m. down the turnpike and passed by Strasburg. Wharton's division, with the artillery, took their position on Hupp's Hill, while Kershaw moved by Bowman's mill, directly in front of Sheridan's left, where he awaited Gordon's attack.

Rosser's advance having been discovered by the enemy, he was therefore compelled to attack at once. Kershaw hearing Rosser's guns did not wait for Gordon, but moved forward, swept over the works in his front, capturing a battery of artillery, which he at once turned against the flying enemy. Gordon, owing to the difficulties which he met on the march, had but one division in position, and upon hearing Kershaw's attack, put his men in motion, striking the enemy in the rear, driving everything before him.

Belle Grove Plantation near Middletown, VA. From 1860 until 1867, the home was owned by John Cooley and Benjamin Cooley. LOC/P&P. HABS VA,35-MIDTO.V,2--4.

---

277   Confederate General Gabriel Colvin Wharton (1824-1906) of Culpeper County, VA was a graduate of the Virginia Military Institute in Lexington, VA. After graduating he became a civil engineer and moved to the Arizona Territory. In 1861 he returned to Virginia and was appointed a major in the 45th Virginia Infantry. By 1864 he had been promoted to brigadier general. After the war he became a legislator in the Virginia General Assembly and returned to his pre-war career as an engineer.

278   Confederate General Thomas Lafayette "Tex" Rosser (1836-1910) born in Campbell County, VA, moved with his family to Panola County, TX in 1849. Attending the US Military Academy, he resigned two weeks before graduation when Texas seceded from the Union on 22 Apr 1861. Rosser traveled to Montgomery, AL where he enlisted in the Confederate Army. Several times wounded, Rosser was an aggressive and daring participant in most of the major eastern battles from First Manassas to Appomattox. After the war he worked for several railroad companies. In 1886 he retired to a farm in Charlottesville, VA. In 1898, President William McKinley appointed Rosser a brigadier general of US Volunteers during the Spanish-American War, training young cavalry recruits.

Numerous paintings and lithographs were created to immortalize General Philip Sheridan's 20 mile ride from Winchester to Middletown, VA 19 Oct 1864. This chromolithograph was created by artist Thure de Thulstrup (1848-1930), published by L. Prang & Company, circa 1886. LOC/P&P. LC-DIG-pga-04047.

So far the movement was a great success. Crook's and the Nineteenth Corps were completely routed and driven two miles north of Middletown,[279] losing twenty-five pieces of artillery, sixteen hundred prisoners, and leaving behind many killed and wounded, and a camp full of small arms and supplies.

Early halted the troops about noon to reform their lines, as many of the men had dropped out of the ranks while passing through the enemy's camp to plunder, which thinned our lines to an alarming extent—a detachment being sent to clear the camp and drive the stragglers back to their commands.

Sheridan came up with the Sixth Corps and a portion of his cavalry, neither of which had been in the morning's engagement, and seeing the disorganized condition of Early's troops, attacked them, when the whole line gave away just before dark and retreated.[280] The bridge near Spangler's mill

---

[279] Union Brigadier General George Crook (1828-1890) was born near Taylorsville, OH and graduated from the US Military Academy in 1852. A career army soldier, he was promoted to colonel of the 36th Ohio Volunteer Infantry in 1861. Defeated by General Early at the Battle of Kernstown in Jul 1864, at the Battle of Cedar Creek he was saved from defeat a second time by the arrival of General Sheridan from Winchester, VA. In Feb 1865, General Crook was captured by Confederate raiders at Cumberland, MD and briefly imprisoned until he was exchanged a month later. At the end of the war, George Crook received a brevet as major general in the regular army, but reverted to the permanent rank of lieutenant colonel, serving with the 23rd Infantry on frontier duty in the Pacific Northwest. He spent his last years speaking out against the unjust treatment of his former Indian adversaries.

[280] When the Battle of Cedar Creek began, General Sheridan was about 20 miles north at Winchester, VA. As reports of the battle arrived he ordered his horse Rienzi to be saddled. Accompanied by a 300-man cavalry escort, he left Winchester about 9 am, arriving in time to rally the Union

118 *A Rebel of '61*

broke down, which stopped our trains, making their capture an easy matter for the enemy's cavalry.

By this movement Sheridan not only recaptured all the guns he had lost in the morning, but took 23 guns, over one thousand prisoners and many wagons from Early.

It was a great victory given up, by our troops becoming demoralized, by plundering the enemy's camp. Human nature is frail under the most favorable conditions. Soldiers are prone to plunder when not in need. Our men in their half fed, half clad, and scantily equipped condition, would have been more than human had they resisted the temptation to help themselves from the great abundance everywhere to be found.

It is very difficult to ascertain the number of troops engaged in the Battle of Winchester, but after much care and research I found in the official records of the War of the Rebellion, Vol. 63, Sheridan's report for the month of August, present for duty, as follows: Crook's Corps, 21,006; Sixth Corps, 11,956; Nineteenth Corps, 12,504; Gen. Torbert's Cavalry, 8,502;[281] total, 53,968. Deduct 6,000 for guard duty and 3,000 added for sickness and absent, between the date of the report and the battle, Sheridan had not less than 45,000 men engaged. Sheridan lost in the campaign, from Winchester to Cedar Creek, killed, 1,938; wounded, 11,893; missing, 3,121; total, 16,952.

The Southern Historical Society Papers, Vol. IX, extracts from Colonel Taylor's book,[282] gives Early's troops present for duty Aug. 31st, as follows: Breckenridge's Division, 2,104; Rhode's Division, 3,013; Gordon's Division, 2,544; Ramseur's Division, 1,909; Cavalry and Artillery, 3,000; total,

---

forces into a defensive line north of Middletown, VA.

Both writers Thomas Buchanan Read (1822-1872) in *"Sheridan's Ride"* in 1864, and Herman Melville in *"Sheridan at Cedar Creek"* in 1866, immortalized Sheridan's 20 mile ride from Winchester. The general took notice of the widespread public acclaim and renamed his horse "Winchester." In 1908, Gutzon Borglum created an equestrian statue of Sheridan and Winchester riding to Cedar Creek, which stands in Sheridan Circle, Washington, DC. Stevenson, Burton Egbert, *Poems of American History*, (Houghton Mifflin Company, MA, 1908), 521-522. Wert, Jeffry D., *From Winchester to Cedar Creek: The Shenandoah Campaign of 1864*. (Simon & Schuster, NY, 1987), 248.

281   Brigadier General George Crook (1828-1890) previously noted footnote 279.

    Union General Alfred Thomas Archimedes Torbert (1833-1880) was born in Georgetown, DE. He graduated from the US Military Academy in 1855, and was a career army officer. Appointed a colonel of the 1st New Jersey Infantry, by Aug 1862 he was a brigade commander in the VI Corp of the Army of the Potomac. In Apr 1864 following the death of General John Buford, Torbert was given command of the 1st Division of the Cavalry Corp. Sheridan was unhappy with the performance of the cavalry at the time of the Battle of Fisher's Hill. He is said to have told Torbert to go out and "whip or be whipped." After the war Torbert served in a number of diplomatic posts: as US Consul to El Salvador in 1869; US Consul General in Havana in 1871; and US Consul General in Paris in 1873. Torbert drowned off Cape Canaveral, FL in the sinking of the *SS Vera Cruz* on 29 Aug 1880. Eicher John H., and David J. Eicher. *Civil War High Commands*. (Stanford University Press, 2001). Longacre, Edward G., *The Cavalry at Appomattox: A Tactical Study of Mounted Operations During the Civil War's Climactic Campaign, March 27 – April 9, 1865*. (Stackpole Books, Mechanicsburg, PA, 2003), 29.

282   Confederate Lieutenant Colonel Walter Herron Taylor (1838-1916) of Norfolk VA graduated from Virginia Military Institute in 1857. He became a merchant and banker in Norfolk. Taylor enlisted in the Confederate Army when Virginia seceded in 1861 and joined the staff of General Robert E. Lee. Taylor became General Lee's Aide-de-camp, a position he executed competently for the entire war. In 1877, Taylor wrote his war memoirs entitled *Four Years with General Lee* where he listed the numbers of General Early's troops. The information was noted by General Jubal Early in his work, *"The Advance on Washington in 1864, a Letter from General J. A. Early"* that appeared in *SHSP*, Vol. IX,1881, 297-312. Taylor, Walter H., *Four Years with General Lee* (NY, 1878), 178.

12,570.[283] The cavalry is Early's estimate, and I am disposed to think it is too low, but I am satisfied that Early's force did not exceed 15,000 at the Battle of Winchester.

General Early was terribly criticized for his several defeats. Soldiers, like men in all other walks of life, are measured by the success they attain; the difficulties that make success impossible are not considered, as men seldom take the time to investigate the cause of failure in others. At Winchester, with less than 15,000 troops, he fought Sheridan's 45,000 to a standstill for nearly a whole day, inflicting upon them fearful loss. After his rout at Fisher's Hill, when reinforced by Kershaw's 2,700 infantry and Rosser's 600 cavalry, which about made up his loss in those two engagements, he followed Sheridan down the Valley, planned and attacked him at Cedar Creek, which, for brilliant conception and daring execution, when numbers are considered, should rank him among the great captains of the War. In the campaign just closed Sheridan lost over sixteen thousand men, being more than Early had in his entire army.

Our camp was near the Massanutten Mountain; the early frost had given its forests their autumn tints, presenting that combination of gorgeous color only to be seen in a Southern clime.

One of the teamsters being boisterous by too much Apple Jack was tied up to a limb of a tree. This was the first and only case of punishment inflicted by the Captain while I was with the train. I was on the best of terms with the teamsters. Some of them were expert foragers, especially Richards, the blacksmith. One day an old farmer came to the camp and complained that some one had killed his sheep; that he had tracked the offender by the blood to our camp. The Captain called up the men, when they denied the accusation, but to satisfy the farmer and himself, he searched the camp and wagons without success. Richards was busy at the forge making horseshoes, the very picture of innocent indignation, while the search was in progress. Soon as the old man had left and the Captain gone in his tent, Richards called to me, threw the anvil to the ground, raised the hollow block upon which it rested, when a bucket of fresh mutton met my astonished gaze.

---

283   Confederate Brigadier General John Cabell Breckenridge (1821-1875) previously noted footnote 33, photograph page 65.

    Confederate General Robert Emmet Rodes (1829-1864) was born in Lynchburg, VA and a graduate of Virginia Military Institute. Rodes was killed in Sep 1864 at the Battle of Opequon.

    Confederate Major General John Brown Gordon (1832-1904) previously noted footnote 274 and photo page 116.

    Confederate General Stephen Dodson Ramseur (1837-1864) of Lincolnton, NC attended Davison College before graduating from the US Military Academy in 1860. He was commissioned a second lieutenant and assigned to the 3rd and 4th USS Artillery Regiment before the war. At the outbreak of war he joined the Confederate Army in Alabama, later transferring to the 10th North Carolina Militia when North Carolina seceded. Ramseur was one of the youngest Confederate generals in the war. He was mortally wounded at the Battle of Cedar Creek.

A Rebel of '61

Soldier

On October the 26th, having ascertained that the command I had selected to join was in the Luray Valley, I bade good bye to the Captain's camp, where I had formed some strong attachments, mounted my horse and proceeded in a northeasterly direction, with two mountains in my path.[284] The early part of the ride took me over Fort Mountain and through a Valley of the same name.[285] In this Valley the ruins of Sheridan's devastators were everywhere to be seen. War must make men demons. Only devils could inflict so much misery on innocent women and children, as the destruction of their property must, of necessity, lead to much suffering before winter is over.

It was late in the day when I crossed the Massanutten Mountain. The air was full of autumn-colored leaves, and the sun in golden streams drifted through the half-bare branches under which I rode. The clear, crisp atmosphere and the grandeur of the scenery calmed and soothed the indignation that had raged within my breast while passing through Sheridan's path of wanton destruction and cruelty.

I halted on the east bank of the Shenandoah River, where I remained over night, sleeping in a barn by the owner's permission. He had been boiling sorghum, and the young people of the neighborhood had a party during the evening.[286] The girls in their homespuns were there in numbers; the male portion was composed of youths, about 14 years and under. They had a good time and sung their homely Mountain songs with much vigor until late in the night.

I rode through rain and mud nearly all the next day, reaching the First Maryland Cavalry shortly before dark, when I became a member of Co. C, Lieut. Watters commanding.[287] This company had a number of boys in its

JOS. R. STONEBRAKER, IN CONFEDERATE UNIFORM

Stonebraker commissioned this painting of himself after the war. His will bequeathed the painting to his youngest son, Joseph R. Stonebraker, Jr. who died in 1972 in Brookfield CN. The location of the painting today remains unknown. Photo from original text.

---

284   Joseph R. Stonebraker enlisted in the Confederate Army as a private in Company C of the 1st Maryland Cavalry.
285   Fort Valley is a 23-mile long mountain valley in Shenandoah County, VA. This valley-within-a-valley lies between the two arms of the northern Massanutten Mountain range. At the north end is a very narrow gap through which Passage Creek flows and Fort Valley Road SR 678 runs. The valley opens in the center, about three miles wide at its widest point.
286   Sweet sorghum syrup is the boiled-down juice from sweet cultivars of *Sorghum bicolor,* a tall grassy plant. Traditionally called sorghum molasses, the syrup is sweet and light brown in color like maple syrup, but has a mild touch of the distinctive flavor of cane molasses. Like molasses, sorghum carries a lot of calories and offers some nutrition in the form of iron, calcium and other minerals. Each October, Amherst County, VA hosts an annual Sorghum Festival.
287   Confederate Lieutenant James D. Watters (1834-1908) of Harford County, MD was a

ranks from Hagerstown.[288] In the spring of '63, at Brandy Station, the battalion numbered 650 men, but now it did not have over 90 in its ranks, and they were poorly mounted and badly equipped. They were doing picket duty on the south branch of the Shenandoah River, at Burner's Ford, just north of Milford.[289]

It had been raining all day and continued all night, and being without shelter I tried to sleep, but the water getting between me and the blanket about midnight compelled me to get up, when I stood around a half-smothered fire until daylight in a most uncomfortable frame of mind.

Both men and horses fared badly for food, as the section was a mountainous and non-productive country, and Sheridan's incendiaries had destroyed what little crops they found in their path, making foraging very difficult, especially when we had orders only to take from those who were willing to part with their corn for Confederate money.

I had been with the command about a week, when I received a letter from Captain Stonebraker, requesting me not to enlist, but come to him at once.[290] I submitted the letter to Lieut. Watters, who not only gave me permission to leave, but full liberty to act as circumstances might suggest. I left camp on Nov. 4th, passed through the town of Luray, forded the Shenandoah River, and crossed the Massanutten Mountain, reaching the Captain's tent just at dark.

The Captain offered to make me his Orderly, saying that it would be a much easier position and freer from danger than a private in the regular army. I thanked him very much, but declined his offer because I felt that I ought to be in the ranks. I remained with him a few days, reading and resting my horse. While here he gave a dinner to some of his officer friends. Roast turkey, beef and mutton in profusion; no sweets, but plenty of Apple Jack. After the dinner they played poker, and continued the game all night.

The Captain received a letter from his wife, who lived in Montgomery County, Maryland[291]—it came through the lines via Flag of Truce. I

---

graduate of Dickinson College, PA. Watters moved to St. Louis, MO, where he passed the bar and practiced law. In 1861 he returned east and enlisted in the 1st Virginia, later transferring to 1st Maryland Cavalry, where he served until the end of the war. After the war, Watters practiced law in Harford County, but is best remember for having served for 32 years as Judge of the 3rd Circuit Court of Harford County.

288   Other Company C, Hagerstown residents were privates William D. Macgill (1835-1889), David Macgill (1838-1897), and James Macgill (1844-1923), the sons of Hagerstown physician Dr. Charles Macgill (1806-1881). Stonebraker was well acquainted with the Macgill family, having traveled briefly with the fourth Macgill brother, Dr. Charles G. W. Macgill (1836-1907), a surgeon in the Stonewall Brigade previously noted in footnote 258. Keller, C. Roger, *Roster of Civil War Soldiers from Washington County, Maryland*, (Clearfield Company, Baltimore MD. 1993). 5-7, 173.

289   Today Milford is known as Overall, VA. In 1864, Milford was a small commercial center on the Luray-Front Royal Turnpike and the site of several engagements, including a cavalry battle on 25-26 Oct 1864. Outnumbered two-to-one, Confederate Colonel Thomas T. Munford's cavalry met and stalled the Union cavalry forces of General James H. Wilson long enough for the confederates under General Early to retreat after their defeat at Fisher's Hill. The Milford Battlefield Historic District was listed on the National Register of Historic Places in 2004. Stonebraker arrived at Milford to join Company C just as the Battle of Milford was ending.

290   Confederate Captain Abraham Stonebraker, the author's uncle, previously noted see footnote 247. Photo page 104.

291   Captain Abraham Stonebraker married Catherine E. Pearre (1827-1882), daughter of William and Catherine Marian Springer Pearre, in Sep 1856 at the Pearre plantation near Comus, Mont-

wrote home by the same channel. One of the conditions was that all letters should be unsealed. I afterwards ascertained that my letter went through all right, much to the gratification of my parents, who, while suspecting, did not know of my whereabouts.

Since my absence all the able bodied teamsters had been sent to their respective commands, and disabled men put in their places, much to the disgust of the Captain, as it disorganized his trains, but the Confederacy was in such straits for soldiers that they had to recruit their ranks from all and every source.

I rejoined the battalion 9th of November, and on the afternoon of the next day our brigade made a forward movement, marching through and encamping for the night two miles north of Milford. At daylight we were in the saddle again, our battalion taking the advance, reaching Front Royal about noon, where we halted and grazed our horses for a short time. We crossed the Shenandoah and formed in line of battle, on the right of the pike until the balance of the brigade came up, when we moved again and encamped for the night three miles north of Middletown. The next morning, with heavy firing in our front we continued our advance, reaching and taking a position on the right of Newtown. Here fifteen of our company and five of B Company were detailed as videttes.[292] We were dismounted and placed in line about three hundred feet apart, when we were advanced some distance in front of the battalion where we remained until sunset when we rejoined our command, which retreated nearly all night, halting some miles south of Front Royal. The next day we reoccupied our old camp which we had left three days ago. If anything was accomplished by the move it is more that I was able to learn, but supposed it was a reconnaissance to ascertain if Sheridan had sent part of his force to Grant at Richmond, as reported. The next morning one-third of the battalion was sent on a foraging expedition; we rode all day without success and returned to find that the command had moved, but we stayed all night in the old camp and rejoined them the next day.

Both men and horses have had little or nothing to eat for some days; in fact the horses are in a starving condition. A small party from our company stole corn during the night. I am free to confess that I felt like a thief ought to feel when so engaged, but necessity knows no law; the Government can't feed our animals and it is steal or walk. Horses are selling from five to eight thousand dollars apiece, and only those captured by a soldier can be had at any price. The next morning we went to the river and did picket duty for two days; it rained and snowed the best part of the time, with the mud knee deep.

---

gomery County, MD. The large estate had been in the Pearre family since the 1720s. Catherine's father, William Pearre, died in Mar 1864, followed by his wife in May 1864, and the farm was purchased by Catherine's sister Sarah Ellen Pearre (1830-1900). While her husband served in the Confederate Army, Catherine E. Pearre Stonebraker left their home in Shepherdstown, WV and stayed with her sister on the family farm.

The Pearre house was still standing in 1974, but badly deteriorated. Today, only the Pearre cemetery remains of the once fine plantation. Maryland Historical Trust Inventory, *William Pearre Farm and Cemetery, www.msa.md.gov/megafile/msa/stagsere/se1/../msa_se5_16392.pdf*. Obituary of Catherine Pearre Stonebraker, *Waco Daily*, Waco, TX, 8 Aug 1882.

292   A mounted sentry on picket or guard duty was called a vidette. Also spelled "vedette," the word derives from the Latin meaning to "watch" or "see."

The Federals having advanced against our position, we were hurried to the front and formed into line of battle, mounted, just in the rear of our breastworks, while the balance of the brigade were dismounted and manned the works. The enemy came up, and after exchanging a few shots with our outposts, fell back, but we remained in position until long after dark, in case of an emergency.

We went back to camp both cold and hungry. To make matters worse, neither men or horses got anything to eat, having fasted all day. At sunrise the next morning we broke camp and moved off. We crossed the Blue Ridge at Thornton's Gap,[293] where we found snow two inches deep, the weather bitter cold, the men suffering because of their destitute condition. During the march we passed many orchards full of frozen apples, which the men devoured ravenously being the only thing they got to eat on the march. We encamped for the night near Sperryville, but resumed the march early the next morning, the men still eating frozen fruit. We went into camp seven miles south of Sperryville and received a half ration of flour for each man, which we made into dough by mixing with water, spread the dough on flat stones and set them before the fire to bake. Most excellent "Johnnie Cake" out of corn meal was made in the same manner. Instead of stone, we baked it on a board or broad flat chip cut from a tree when a board could not be had. When brown on one side, we gently struck the corner of the board, which loosened the cake; it was then reversed and browned on the other side. The end of the next day, Nov. 25th,[294] we reached Little Washington, encamping in a piece of woods east of the town and received two and half rations of flour.

We were now encamped near the county seat of Rappahannock. The county was full of corn and forage, but the citizens were loth to part with anything they had for Confederate money. Some of us continued to forage after night to keep our horses from starving. I was shot at by one of the guards on one of my marauding expeditions. The country was full of little stills, all turning apples into brandy; many of the men spreed for a week.[295]

Mosby and his men occupied Loudon County and vicinity from the beginning until the close of the War.[296] He not only gave General Lee valu-

---

[293] Thornton's Gap is a wind gap located in the Blue Ridge Mountains separating the Shenandoah Valley from the Piedmont region of the state and is at the border of Page County and Rappahannock County, VA. The gap was named for Colonel Francis Thornton III (1711–1749), owner of the land to the east. In 1740, Thornton built the mansion known as *Montpelier* outside Sperryville in Rappahannock County. The privately-owned Thornton's Gap Turnpike Company was formed to build a road over the mountains at Thornton's Gap. The toll road opened in 1806.

[294] Washington is the county seat of Rappahannock County, VA. The site of this town was surveyed by George Washington in Jul 1749. It is noted for being the oldest of the 28 towns and villages by the name of *Washington* in America. It is nicknamed *Little Washington* to avoid confusion with Washington, DC, which lies 70 miles to the east.

[295] Stonebraker has applied an unusual past tense to the noun "spree." Spree (sprē) *noun*. - a session of considerable overindulgence, especially in drinking, squandering money, etc.

[296] Confederate Colonel John Singleton Mosby (1833–1916), of Powhatan County, VA was a graduate of Hampden-Sydney College. Nicknamed the "Gray Ghost," Mosby commanded the partisan brigade known as *Mosby's Rangers* or *Mosby's Raiders* noted for its lightning quick raids and its ability to elude Union Army pursuers and disappear, blending in with local farmers and townsmen. The area of northern central Virginia in which Mosby operated with impunity was known during the war and ever since as *Mosby's Confederacy*. After the war, Mosby worked as an attorney and supported his former enemy's commander, President Ulysses S. Grant, serving as the US consul to Hong Kong

A Rebel of '61

Wonderfully arrogant period photo of Colonel Mosby posed beside a captured Yankee officers uniform. LOC/P&P. LC-DIG-cwpbh-03240.

Above left: Harper's Weekly, 5 Sep 1863 depict Mosby and his men as unprincipled guerrillas who steal from honest sutler merchants. LOC/P&P. LC-USZ62-93015. Map depicting Mosby's area of operations as published by Major John Scott in Partisan Life with Col. John S. Mosby, *1867. The region was also known as "Mosby's Confederacy."*

125

able information as to the movements of the enemy, but annoyed the Federals by capturing small parties of soldiers and the destruction of many of their transportation trains. All efforts to capture or dislodge them from their mountain homes failed.

Sheridan having made his path through the Shenandoah and adjoining valleys a barren waste by the torch, now turned his attention to the section occupied by Mosby. Speaking of the Shenandoah campaign, he says:

> "During this campaign, I was at times annoyed by guerilla bands, the most formidable of which was Mosby, who made his headquarters east of the Blue Ridge in the section of the country of Upperville. I had constantly refused to operate against these bands, believing them to be, substantially, a benefit to me, as they prevented straggling and kept my trains well closed up, and discharged such other duties as would have required a provost guard of at least two regiments of cavalry. In retaliation for assistance and sympathy given them, however, by the inhabitants of Loudon Valley, General Merritt,[297] with two brigades of cavalry, was directed to proceed on the 28th of November, 1864, to the valley under the following instructions: 'They were to cross the mountain at Ashby's Gap,[298] concentrate at Snickersville[299] on the 29th and operate both east and west, moving towards the Potomac. He says: 'To clear the country of these parties that are bringing destruction upon the innocent, as well as their guilty supporters, by their cowardly acts, you will consume and destroy all forage and subsistence, burn all barns and mills and their contents, drive off all stock in the region, the boundaries of which are above described.'"[300]

---

and in the Department of Justice.

297   Union General Wesley Merritt previously noted footnote 192.

298   Ashby's Gap is a wind gap in the Blue Ridge Mountains on the border of Clarke County, Loudoun County, and Fauquier County, VA. The gap is traversed by US Route 50. The earliest known use of the gap was as part of a trail of the Native Americans. It was later named "Ashby's Bent" when Thomas Ashby received lands along Goose Creek, and settled Paris, VA at the eastern entrance to the gap. Later it came to be called Ashby's Gap.

299   Snickersville is today known as Bluemont, an unincorporated village in Loudoun County, VA located at the base of Snickers Gap in the Blue Ridge Mountains. The town and gap were named after Edward Snickers (1735-1790), who operated a ferry across the nearby Shenandoah River.

300   This letter is combination of two documents – General Sheridan's official report, and the order from Sheridan's Chief of Staff, Lieutenant Colonel James W. Forsyth to Brevet Major General Wesley Merritt in command of the 1st Cavalry Division. General Grant had ordered General Sheridan to "destroy and carry off all the crops, animals, negroes and all men under fifty years of age capable of bearing arms" in Loudoun County, VA as early as 16 Aug 1864. Although Sheridan endorsed Grant's harsh methods, convinced that "Death is popularly considered the maximum of punishments in war, but it is not: reduction to poverty brings prayers for peace more surely and more quickly than does the destruction of human life," he feared such action might agitate anti-war advocates and negatively impact the reelection of Abraham Lincoln. In late November, with Lincoln's reelection assured, Sheridan decided he could safely conduct operations against Mosby. On the 26th he wrote Union Chief of Staff Henry Halleck, "Now there is going to be an intense hatred of [Mosby] in that portion of the Valley which is nearly desert. I will soon commence on Loudoun County, and let them know there is a God in Israel." Chamberlin, Taylor M. and John M. Souders, *Between Reb and Yank: A Civil War History of Northern Loudoun County, Virginia* (McFarland & Company, Inc, NC, 2011), 283, 297. Moore, Frank, editor, *The Rebellion Record: a diary of American Events, with documents, Volume*

Information of Merritt's devastating expedition reached our camp late on the 30th. Early the next morning our brigade, under Gen. Davidson,[301] moved rapidly towards Loudon, with the hope of striking the raiders. Ten of our battalion, under Lt. Ditty,[302] were detailed as an advance guard. We kept some distance in front of the command, and when we left the main road we cut branches of cedars and strewed them in our tracks, so the command would follow our path. When we reached Piedmont, on the O. & A. R. R.,[303] we were ordered to report to the command. When we returned to the command the General was drunk and denied ordering our return, said we should go back and not return until we struck the "Yankees." We rode all day and the best part of the night, in all about sixty miles. When near Bloomfield we hid our horses in the bushes,[304] and being inside of the Federal lines, could not make fire. We remained here until daylight. Lt. Ditty, with one man, left us during the night to ascertain something about the enemy's movements.

Having ascertained the position of the Federals, we returned to report to the command, but found that they had retraced their steps, as it was impossible to reach the raiders, as they had too much start. During the first day's march we saw many of Mosby's men, who kept in the distance until they found out who we were. As we neared a little village, and being some distance in advance of the detail, I noticed several ladies on a veranda in an unusual state of excitement, and as I passed a stable one of Mosby's men rushed out with a pistol in each hand demanding that I surrender. The blue overcoat that I wore made him take me for a Federal. The situation was so comical that I laughed in his face. Explanations followed, and instead of showing his sweetheart a "Yankee" prisoner, he called to them that the old regulars were coming, when there was general rejoicing among the ladies.

II, (NY, 1868), 728.

301   Confederate General Henry Brevard Davidson (1831-1899) of Shelbyville, TN graduated from the US Military Academy in 1853 and received a brevet commission of 2nd Lieutenant in the dragoons. Davidson enlisted in the Confederacy in 1861 after the secession of Tennessee. By Aug 1863 he was commissioned a brigadier general and appointed command of a cavalry brigade at Rome, GA. Transferred to Virginia during the Valley Campaign, he was given command of five cavalry units including the 1st Maryland Cavalry. After the war, Davidson worked as a deputy sheriff in New Orleans, LA, later moving to California where he worked as a civil engineer. Evans, Clement, ed. *Confederate Military History, Vol. XII,* (Confederate Publishing Company, Atlanta, GA, 1899).

302   1st Lieutenant Cyrus Irving Ditty (1838-1887) of the 1st Maryland Cavalry was born at West River, south of Annapolis, MD in 1838, the son of George T. Ditty of Virginia and Harriet Winterson Ditty. He graduated from Dickinson College in 1857 and for many years practiced law in Baltimore. He entered the Confederate Army with Colonel Ridgely Brown as a corporal in Company K, 1st Virginia Cavalry, later transferring to Company A, 1st Maryland Cavalry. Ditty did not surrender at Appomattox, escaping with many other soldiers of the 1st Maryland Cavalry. He finally surrendered a month later at Beaver Dam, VA on 3 May 1865. Irvington, a suburb of Baltimore, takes its name from Ditty. Warfield, J. D., *The Founders of Anne Arundel and Howard Counties,* (Baltimore, MD, 1905), 324. Driver, Robert J., *First and Second Maryland Cavalry, C.S.A.* (Charlottesville, VA, 1999), 219-220 (hereafter cited as Driver, *1st & 2nd MD Cavalry*).

303   Piedmont Station is known today as Delaplane in Loudoun County, VA. Stonebraker is using the later name of the railroad. During the war, Piedmont was along the Manassas Gap Railroad line, not the Orange & Alexandria Railroad (O&ARR). In 1867, the O&A merged with the Manassas Gap Railroad to become the Orange, Alexandria and Manassas Railroad.

304   Bloomfield, VA is an unincorporated hamlet in Loudoun County, VA.

Rations from the Stalk, by Allen C. Redwood depicting Confederate soldiers gnawing on the only available rations of raw field corn. As published in Battles and Leaders of the Civil War, (Century, NY, 1884-1887).

We returned by way of Rectortown,[305] the party dividing in pairs so as to get something to eat by begging from the citizens, as our rations were exhausted. We rejoined our command, December 3rd, at the camp at Little Washington.

The Confederate soldier always selected a piece of timber, when available, for his camping place. Why this was so I have never seen explained. The first men in the ranks of the Southern army came from the Gulf States, and being poorly provided in camp equipage, naturally, to shield themselves from the heat of the noon-day sun, sought the shade of the forest. The individuality of the Confederate soldier was such that it was impossible to make a machine of him, as he would not submit to discipline. He fought as a matter of duty and acknowledged no one as his superior. As a rule, both officers and men were on an equal footing, and this often impaired his efficiency when in battle.

The Federals preferred an open space for their camp. Being magnificently equipped, they laid out their camps in regular order, their tents fronting on broad avenues. Their officers were strict disciplinarians, and no one could pass in or out without permission. They also prized the "Pomp, pride, and circumstance of glorious War."[306] At the battle of Antietam, McClellan's troops marched into line, under fire, with bands playing, banners flying and lines dressed. It is said that Caldwell's brigade relieved Meagher's brigade from one of the hottest contested portions of the field, the one breaking by companies to the front and the other by companies to the rear.[307]

Had it been a Confederate movement, they would not have wasted the time nor exposed their men in any such regular movement, but the front brigade would have laid flat on the ground while the rear brigade marched over them.

The woods certainly had many advantages over an open space for a camp. It not only protected the men from the heat in the summer, but in

---

305   Rectortown, VA is an unincorporated community in Fauquier County, VA.

306   Excerpt from Act III, Scene III of Shakespeare's Othello:
Farewell the neighing steed and the shrill trump,
The spirit-stirring drum, th'ear-piercing fife,
The royal banner, and all quality,
Pride, pomp, and circumstance of glorious war!"
The "Pomp and Circumstance Marches" for orchestra, composed by Sir Edward Elgar in the early 1900s, takes its title from the same passage.

307   Bloody Lane is considered the "hottest contested portion[s]" at the Battle of Antietam 17 Sep 1862. Convinced he faced a significantly larger Confederate force, the piecemeal attacks orchestrated by Union General George McClellan almost nullified his 2-to-1 troop advantage. Union General Thomas Francis Meagher's Irish Brigade, and Union General John C. Caldwell's brigades were especially hard hit against Confederate General T. Anderson's brigade entrenched in Bloody Lane. Attacking over the same ground time and again, they made no headway against the Confederates until Colonel John Brooks's five-regiment united force drove the Confederates from the lane.

winter fuel was always near at hand. The men divided themselves into groups of four to eight men each; the rations of these men were issued together, and the labor, such as cutting wood, and carrying water, was divided among the members of the mess. When the weather was very cold, a large tree was felled to the ground, and after all the small wood was cut into the length desired, the trunk was used as a back log to build a fire against, which was kept going both day and night, the men spreading their blankets on the ground. Lying with their feet towards the fire, and whoever first awakened replenished it during the night.

In the next three days but one day's rations of corn meal was issued to the men, and its quality was such that the officers pronounced it only fit for horse feed. Forage was so scarce that we turned our horses out to graze on dead grass and bushes. Something shortly had to be done or they would starve. Just as I was spreading my blanket for the night I noticed some of the company mounting their horses, preparatory for a raid on some corn field. I hurried to join the party, but by the time I got my horse saddled they were well under way and I put my horse in a run to overtake them. As I crossed the road south of our picket post, I met one of Company B's men who had taken a near cut, on foot, running to catch up with the party. The man on the picket post seeing the raiders and thinking them to be Federals, reported that a squad of the enemy had passed by the camp and taken a man from the lower post, going in a westerly direction. This led General Davidson to conclude that we were a reconnoitering party of the enemy who intended to attempt to surprise his camp.[308] He ordered the Twenty-sixth battalion under arms and posted two companies behind the stone fence on the crest of the hill just where we had crossed the road. While these preparations were in progress, we had secured what corn we wanted and were returning to camp. As we ascended the hill we were met by a command to "halt, halt," and the next instant saw a flash of fire, followed by the report of carbines from the men behind the fence. Our party was much scattered, and that some were not killed was owing to the darkness and the aim of the men being a little too high, as the bullets passed over our heads.

I _____, with an exclamation, fell from his horse and rolled into a ditch, and I supposed he was shot.[309] B _____and I were captured.

The firing had aroused the whole camp, the General riding up to where we were in a full run, and when he ascertained that we were part of his command the air was full of brimstone for a while.

He demanded the names of those who escaped and ordered us to be taken to the provost guard and tied up until we did tell. B ____ showed signs of

---

308   Confederate General Henry Brevard Davidson (1831-1899) previously noted footnote 301.
309   Stonebraker indicates he is foraging with members of Company C. The only member of Company C with the initial of *I* is Charles E. Inloes (1839-1873). The son of wealthy Baltimore merchant Joshua S. Inloes, Charles served 1861-1862 in 1st Maryland Infantry Company H, transferring to 1st Maryland Cavalry Company C in Aug 1864. Inloes was captured three months later on 13 Mar 1865 and spent the remainder of the war imprisoned at Point Lookout, MD. He was paroled 12 Jun 1865 and returned to Baltimore. Inloe married Mary Carroll in 1869 and died in 1873 at age 33. There were at least 11 members of Company C with the initial of *B*.
Driver, *1st & 2nd MD Cavalry*, 244. *Statewide County MD Archives Military Records, 1st Maryland Cavalry, CSA*, http://files.usgwarchives.net/md/statewide/military/civilwar/rosters/1stcav.txt/.

Confederate Lieutenant Colonel Gustavus Warfield Dorsey (1839-1911) of Montgomery County, MD, field commander of Stonebraker's brigade. Colonel Dorsey took the credit of catching General Stuart as he fell from his horse when he was shot. "The General rode up, giving words of praise to the men in my company. We were dismounted, and as the General shouted from his steed, waving his saber above his head, he was shot in the stomach. I caught him as he fell and took him from his horse. His last words were, 'Dorsey, leave me here and save your men.'" (Baltimore Sun, 12 Sep 1911).

flinching, but I shamed and threatened and he held his tongue. It was a bitter cold night, but the lieutenant of the guard was a gentleman and executed the order as leniently as possible. He tied our hands loosely together and drew them over our head and fastened them to a limb of a tree and had a fire built near us. The rope was so loose that we slipped one hand out and warmed it by the fire; when it was warm we exchanged it for the other. He pretended not to see us, but the situation was one of great hardship, and we had the sympathy of the entire guard. The next morning two of the general's staff called to see if we were ready to tell and got no for their answer. One of the guards took a message to one of my friends, and when our company learned of our predicament they were much incensed and immediately formed into line and were marching to take us from the guard by force.

Lt. Dorsey,[310] who commanded the battalion, prevailed upon the men to desist until he could see the General. We were finally released on condition that we should pay for the corn, estimated by some of the officers to be four bushels. Having found the owner, I paid him twenty dollars and accepted his invitation to dinner, but he never knew that I was one of the raiders.

When I _____ rolled from his horse and secreted himself in a ditch, his horse was taken to the camp with us. Some of his messmates teased him unmercifully, because he returned to the camp without horse or corn and intimated that our account of his escape reflected upon his courage. He approached B _____, whose mess was but a short distance from where I was standing, and in a loud and abusive manner offered to fight. B _____, acted as though he was afraid and did not arise from a sitting posture. I _____ then said, "Perhaps Stonebraker will fight," and came up to me and said, "Stonebreaker, if you said so and so (repeating something that was never said) you are a d _____, "Whack," I took him in the eye, down he went and I on top of him. We were parted; he carried a black eye for some time.

A few days afterwards we talked the matter over, when he said, "When I offered to fight you, I meant at the muzzle of the musket." I replied "that you came to me as a blackguard and I met you as such, but I now hold myself ready to give you any satisfaction you desire." The fact of the matter is

---

310   Confederate Lieutenant-Colonel Gustavus Warfield Dorsey (1839-1911) of Montgomery County, MD enlisted as a private in Company K, 1st Virginia Cavalry on 14 May 1861. He was quickly promoted to lieutenant, and by 1 Oct 1863 he was a captain. In Aug 1864 the company transferred to the 1st Maryland Cavalry. On 17 Feb 1865, Dorsey was promoted to lieutenant colonel for "Valor & Skill." He was wounded at Fredericksburg and Fisher's Hill. When General J. E. B. Stuart fell at the Battle of Yellow Tavern, Dorsey reportedly caught him as he fell from the saddle. Dorsey returned to Brookfield after the war and married Margaret D. Owens. Krick, Robert K. *Lee's Colonels: A Biographical Register of the Field Officers of the Army of Northern Virginia* (Morningside, Dayton, OH, 1991), 121. *Richmond Times Dispatch* (Richmond, VA) 23 Feb 1908. *US Federal Census, 1850, 1860, 1870, and 1880.*

he had more mouth than courage and he never forgave me for meeting his bluff as I did.

The weather continued very cold, greatly to the discomfort of the men, as they were without shelter of any kind, and being scantily fed, receiving one-half ration of corn meal to each man about every other day. The horses were worse off than the men and I determined not to let my horse starve as long as forage could be had; and from that time until the end of the war I raided hay and fodder stacks whenever the Government failed to furnish feed for my horse.

On Dec. the 12th we broke camp, moving in a southeasterly direction, passed through and encamped south of Sperryville. Not having our axes we made fires with fence rails and cleaned the snow from the ground before we could spread our blankets. Both men and horses went to sleep on empty stomachs. The march was continued the next day; we moved along Robinson's River. We passed through Criglersville and encamped at the foot of the Blue Ridge, near Milam's Gap.[311] The weather was so cold that I dismounted and took hold of my horse's tail and walked the greater portion of the day to keep my feet from freezing.

We remained in this camp for several days, the men getting about a half a pound of corn meal each day. We had to rely upon our wits to get an occasional meal from the citizens. This was not always an easy matter, as they had suffered so much from the War and many were very poor. If you met the man of the house, nine times out of ten he would turn you away with an empty stomach.

One day while on the march Dall and I left the command and approached a fine looking plantation.[312] All the surroundings indicated that the owner was a man of wealth. He met us at the door and when we made our wants known, he became very indignant and said, "Do you think I can feed the whole world?" But when he learned how great was our distress he sent us to his wife. The family and guests had just finished their meal, and the sight of the table, with its white linen cloth, cut glass and bright silver, almost paralyzed us. Mrs. Chaplain, with the grace of a true Southern woman, gave us a magnificent meal.[313] I can not recall a single instance of ever being turned away from a house empty handed by a woman, either rich or poor. When returning from the Loudon County expedition, our rations gave out, and the men scattered to forage on the country through which they passed. I

---

311   It is approximately 15 miles south from Sperryville along VA-231 Fort Valley Road to Robinson's River at VA-670/Old Blue Ridge Turnpike crossing over the Rappahannock County into Madison County, VA. From Criglersville to Milams's or Fisher's Gap is another 10 miles.

312   Confederate Private Horatio McPherson Dall (1839-1903) of Virginia enlisted Company B of the 21st Virginia Infantry Regiment in 1861 before transferring to the 1st Maryland Cavalry.

313   The best candidate for Mrs. Chaplain is Ann O. *Chapman*. The Chapman family owned a large estate in Madison County, VA along the Robinson River near Criglersville, VA. The US Federal census for 1860 indicates Edmund G. Chapman (1802-abt 1873) and his wife Ann Chapman (1816-?) owned real estate valued at $15,000, their personal property at $18,800, including several slaves. The Chapman family settled in Madison County as early as 1820. Edmund Chapman was related to Lieutenant Colonel William Henry Chapman, an officer under Colonel John Mosby. Bonan, Gordon Blackwell, *The Edge of Mosby's Sword: The Life of Confederate Colonel William Henry Chapman*, (Southern IL University, 2009), 10. LOC, Geography and Map Division Washington, DC. *Hotchkiss Map collection,: no 46.*

took the road that ran along the foot of the Blue Ridge. Some distance from the road, on the side of a hill, I noticed a column of blue smoke curling above the bare branches of the trees. I turned my horse's head in that direction and soon came upon a one-story log cabin. As I neared the place not a sign of life was to be seen except the smoke from the chimney, not even a dog. Everything denoted extreme poverty and the place looked so forlorn that I debated with my self before knocking. A tall, slender woman with a pale, sad face opened the door, and when I asked her for something to eat she looked me full in the face for a moment, then turned and gave me a piece of cold ash cake, shut the door, and never a word escaped her lips. I have often wished that I had learned her name and knew her story.

We scoured the country in every direction for forage for the horses, but no one was willing to sell, and we were forced to take fodder without the owner's consent on very many occasions.

Having exhausted the country of supplies, the march was resumed through rain, sleet and slush. We passed through Madison Court House and encamped on the Stannardsville Road a few miles southeast of the town.[314] The next day I was ordered to report at headquarters, mounted, where I joined a small squad of men detailed for special duty. I was assigned to guard the premises of a Mr. Urtz, a farmer who resided a few miles from our camp. That night I slept in a feather bed, and had ham and eggs, warm cakes, and sorghum for breakfast. The madam and several daughters were weaving plaid dress goods with a hand loom, and I was much impressed with the beauty of some of the patterns. Several small children were barefooted, and it made the cold chills run up my back to see them run through the snow with their little feet. I was congratulating myself upon securing such a delightful place when Sergeant Jones came on the following day and informed me that the command had marching orders, and that I was to join them at Stannardsville. [315]

We passed over the mountain via Wolftown, and when near the place of meeting, learned that the command had gone to Madison Court House, where the Federal cavalry were reported to be advancing.[316] It was late in the day when we reached our troops and found the division dismounted and in line of battle just east of the town, skirmishing with the enemy.

Just before dark our battalion was formed into column of fours and ordered to drive the enemy from the town. It was a very cold day and the ground was covered with snow and ice. I think making preparations to go into action is the most trying time of a fight—no two men are affected alike,

---

[314] About 6.5 miles southeast of Criglersville on VA 231, Madison Court House or Madison is the county seat of Madison County. The US Federal Census of 1860 indicates there were several families of Utz/Urtz/Urz living in the region including: Gustavas Urz; Michael Utz; George Utz; Julius Utz; and Fielding Fisher Utz (1814-1881) and his wife Harriet Margaret Smith Jones (1819-1887), who had 11 children of whom 7 were daughters.

[315] The 1st Maryland Cavalry had two officers named Jones: Corporal Pembroke Jones of Company B, and Sergeant Albert Jones of Company D. *Statewide County MD. Archives Military Records, 1st Maryland Cavalry (CSA) Civilwar - Rosters.* http://files.usgwarchives.net/md/statewide/military/civilwar/rosters/1stcav.txt.

[316] Wolftown, VA in Madison County is 6.3 miles southwest of Madison, VA along VA 230.

MARYLAND BATTALION ON THE WAR PATH, DECEMBER 1864

if you can judge by their demeanor. This being my baptism of fire, my feelings partook more of curiosity than fear. I watched the faces of the men with much interest, and some of them would have made a study for an artist.

As we moved toward the enemy, our horses being in a trot, the veterans realized more fully than I did the serious business in front, but the woebegone expression on the face of one of my set of fours was so comical that I could not help but laugh. He turned to me and said, "Why, you seem to like it?" "No, no," I replied.

We approached the town from the east, going directly west, then turned to the right and passed through a field so as to attack them from the north.

It was now quite dark and the enemy's bugle sounded the alarm, and the voices of their officers could be plainly heard as they gave orders to their troops. Our horses were in a full run, the men cheering as we moved forward, when suddenly the whole hill was illuminated by the flash from the enemy's guns, and the next moment my horse was down, mixed up with the several others. The fall was so sudden that I scarcely had time to think, but was much gratified to find that neither were hurt. We had tumbled into a ditch which the darkness prevented us from seeing. The column was reformed, but it was too dark to proceed further and the charge had only been made so our dismounted men could withdraw from their position and mount their horses while we attracted the attention of the enemy.

An illustration by Allen Christian Redwood, 1898. The production date and subject matter indicate that Stonebraker commissioned this image for this book. Photo from original text.

133

We fell back some ten miles and encamped for the night at Jack's Shop.[317] The night was intensely cold, and we cleaned the snow from the ground and made a fire out of fence rails which we carried about a half mile. By daylight the next morning we were in the saddle, slowly falling back. We crossed the Rapidan River, burned the bridge, and formed in line of battle at Liberty Mills.[318]

In the absence of infantry, a portion of the cavalry were dismounted and fought on foot, especially in rough and mountainous sections. When this was the case, one man took charge of four horses, including his own. These horses were taken to the rear and kept in some sheltered place of easy access to the owners.

The enemy came up about ten o'clock and engaged our men, who had been posted behind some hastily constructed defenses at such places where the river was fordable. Our battalion remained in the saddle and was transferred from point to point, as our services seemed most needed, being constantly on the move the whole day.

Just before dark we moved into a piece of timber and were making preparations to camp for the night, when we were ordered to remount and attack the enemy who had crossed the river some distance above and were moving against the town on the Stannardsville road. As we moved south in a trot, we could see the Federals forming in line on both sides of the town about a half mile distant. We were hurried towards those on the east while our supports were moving to our right. As we neared the party which we were to attack, a post-and-rail fence separated us, and we had to pass through a gate to reach them. A short distance further we discovered that they had formed on the edge of a ravine, which checked our advance, and we righted into line and commenced to fire upon each other, being about one hundred yards apart. In a short time our troops to our right broke and ran, and the Federals seeing our only way of retreat was by the gate, attempted to block our way by moving rapidly to our rear. Our command broke and ran, every man for himself, all trying to get through the gate at the same time. This only made matters worse, and rather than add to the difficulty, I held my horse back, and was the last one to get through. Three of the enemy were now within hailing distance, demanding that I surrender. I gave my horse his head and for a quarter of a mile it was a tight race, one of the enemy's horse's nose almost touched my horse's tail while he was trying to reach me with his saber.

I rejoined my command, which was forming behind a regiment that had not been engaged, but by the time we got our line in shape it was too dark for further operations. The enemy held the town and had possession of the road that led direct to Gordonsville but seven miles distant,[319] which was a

---

317 Jack's Shop is today Rochelle, VA in Madison County at VA 231 and VA 621 or Jack's Shop Road, about 8.7 miles southeast of Wolftown, VA. Named for an earlier blacksmith's shop, Jack's Shop was the scene of an earlier cavalry skirmish between Major General J. E. B. Stuart and Union Brigadier General John Buford 22 Sep 1862.

318 Liberty Mills at Somerset, VA on the Rapidan River is about 5.7 miles southeast of Rochelle, VA on the Madison and Orange County line following the South Blue Ridge Turnpike VA 231.

319 Gordonsville, VA is a town on the Louisa and Orange county border. About 1787, Nathaniel Gordon purchased 1,350 acres and applied for a license to operate a tavern. 18th century travelers leaving Charlottesville followed the "Fredericksburgh Great Road" northward to Gordonsville.

railroad center and their objective point. The only road open to us was via Orange Court House, fourteen miles. The men were at once put in motion; the night was dark and cold, the road full of ice and snow; to keep from freezing I walked a good portion of the road, guiding myself by taking hold of my horse's tail.

We reached the vicinity of Gordonsville in the after part of the night with orders not to unsaddle our horses, and made a roaring fire with fence rails. I cleaned the snow from the front of the fire, laid down on my gum blanket, was soon asleep and in the land of dreams. I was wandering over a strange, cold country which turned warmer by degrees, as the surface became less firm, when suddenly I sank into a pit of fire; sprang to my feet to find the soles of my shoes on fire.

South West Mountain rises at Orange Court House and runs in a southwesterly direction towards Lynchburg. Gordonsville is situated at the foot of the east side of this range. Our troops had been dismounted and placed on the west side of the mountain and fortified their position with logs, rails, etc., the best they could in the limited time at their command.

Ten members of our battalion were detailed to act on General Lomax's staff and reported at his headquarters at daylight.[320] About nine o'clock the Federals reached our front and skirmished with our outposts. As the firing became general, headed by General Lomax, we rode rapidly to the apex of the range, where we had a fine view of the field. The ground was covered with snow, the branches of every bush and tree encased in ice from the sleet and rain of the past few days. The sun was shining brightly and the valley below looked like a sea of ice fringed by a crystal forest, over which the men in blue were deploying. As the Federals pressed forward their superior numbers began to tell on our line. General Lomax turned to me, and after explaining the whereabouts of Gen. McCausland,[321] said, "Tell him to hold out ten minutes longer and I will have infantry up." A few jumps of my horse brought me in full view of the enemy's line; they at once tried their marksmanship on my blue coat. As the bullets passed over my head, they cut the icicles from the branches, raining ice all over me. I found Gen. McCausland but a short distance in the rear of his troops, sitting on a stump holding the rein of his horse's bridle, both protected by a depression in the ground, with the bullets passing through the trees in a lively manner. When I delivered my message, he replied, "Tell the General if he will come here he can see how they are deploying."

I received another volley as my horse flew back to Gen. Lomax and told him what McCausland said, when he replied, "I can see them well enough from here."

On the track near the town was an engine under full head of steam, with a train made up ready to pull out at a moment's warning, should we be defeated. As the enemy steadily pressed forward, the General directed one of

---

320   Confederate Major General Lunsford Lindsay Lomax (1835–1913) previously cited footnote 182.
321   Confederate General John McCausland (1836-1927) previously cited footnote 241.

Following the death of General John Buford in Apr 1864, Union General Alfred Thomas Archimedes Torbert (1833-1880) was given command of the 1st Division of the Cavalry Corp. LOC/P&P. LC-DIG-cwpb-04935.

his staff to go into town and instruct the engineer to run his train up and down the track and blow the whistle. Next came a report that the ammunition was giving out. Several of us collected cartridges from the men who had charge of the horses, which the General directed me to distribute among the men. I tied my horse to a small tree and proceeded along the line, and while so engaged many soldiers were shot, the wounded passing to the rear. One soldier came running through the bushes, greatly excited, being shot in the head; the blood was running down his face; his actions almost bordered on the ludicrous. Another came out leaning on the shoulders of two men, who was shot in the leg, six inches above the knee; his pants were well worn and skin tight. The bullet had cut a hole through them as round and clean as a punch. There was something peculiar about these two men that impressed me very much that I could never explain.

The fighting along this portion of the line became quite fierce, and there was great commotion where I had left my horse. Upon looking in that direction I saw many of our troops coming out of the timber in great haste. The General and his staff were not slow to follow, while my horse, in an excited state, was winding his bridle around the tree, going first to the right and then to the left. I dropped the sack and ran towards him, taking my knife from my pocket as I ran, and cut the bridle. The Federals were too close for me to mount, and he scampered after the others, almost dragging me off my feet. Things now looked so critical that the General dispatched another courier to town to instruct the telegraph operator to have his instrument ready to move at a moment's warning. Had the Federals followed up this charge it would have ended the day. The engine was now making a great fuss; the pressure of the Federals grew less and soon they withdrew and commenced to retreat when victory was within their grasp—the engineer's whistle saved the day. Some hours afterwards, infantry arrived from Richmond, but their aid was not needed. So ended General Torbert's expedition against Gordonsville. His report says:

> "With two divisions of cavalry, five thousand men, he left Winchester Dec. the 19th, '64, crossed the Blue Ridge on the 20th, and moved on Madison Court House, via Little Washington, reaching Gordonsville the 23rd, but failed to take the town because of superior numbers."[322]

---

[322] General Torbert's official report of 28 Dec 1864 agrees with Stonebraker's account of the engagement at Gordonsville, although Torbert never states "superior numbers," rather that the enemy was "strongly posted behind rails and earth breast-works where a few men could hold three times their number in check. I attacked the position with nearly half my force, but could not carry it. . ."
The War of the Rebellion: a compilation of the official records of the Union and Confederate Armies, Series I, Volume XLIII, Chapter LV (Washington Government Printing Office, 1893), 677-679.

Our division that opposed him consisted of Jackson's and McCausland's brigades, and they did not number fifteen hundred men.[323]

Late in the afternoon the General instructed me to find Colonel Jackson and direct him to take the twenty-sixth battalion and push on after the retreating foe.[324] It took me several hours to find Jackson, and from his manner, the duty was anything but pleasant. Oh, what a trying day. I was so tired and thankful when it was over. We took up quarters in a house near the depot and got supper about ten p.m., the first food that I had tasted since leaving Madison Court House, some sixty hours. My stomach had been empty so long that it ceased to feel hungry, but weak and nauseated.

I spent Christmas day in carrying dispatches to Colonel Jackson and fasting, as we did not get any rations, but one of the men who had been fortunate enough to be invited out to dinner brought me two small cakes. We moved our quarters about a mile from the town and were thoroughly drenched that night by a rain, being without shelter.

The next day I reported to my company, and after a march of two days through the rain, with the mud knee deep to the horses, we encamped near Liberty Mills, where we remained about four weeks, having intolerable weather. It rained and snowed for eight days, and between the freezes and thaws our camp was in a wretched state, our little fly tents being our only shelter. We knew it was not to be a permanent camp, and expected orders to move at any moment, or we might have improved our condition.

Rations for the men and forage for the horses came at irregular intervals, compelling the men to exercise their wits to supply the deficiency. Wharton, of our company, was a man of great drollery and a good storyteller.[325] He

WILLIAM F. WHARTON, CO C., MARYLAND BATTALION

Photo from original text.

---

323 Confederate Colonel William Lowther Jackson (1825-1890) of Clarksburg, VA [WV] was the third Lieutenant Governor of Virginia from 1857 until 1860. After the outbreak of the Civil War, he joined the Confederate Army as a colonel and served on the staff of General Stonewall Jackson, his second cousin. He was promoted to brigadier general in 19 Dec 1864. At the war's end Jackson fled to Mexico, later returning to Kentucky where he became a judge. Jackson is referred to as "Mudwall Jackson." In his research published in *Blue & Gray,* Vol. VIII, No.1, Gregory R. Walden convincingly argues the title "Mudwall" belongs to a different General Jackson – Tennessee born Confederate General Alfred Eugene Jackson (1807-1889).

Confederate General John McCausland (1836-1927) previously cited footnote 241.

324 Stonebraker is again referring to Colonel William L. Jackson commanding a cavalry brigade under General Lomax although Jackson had been promoted to brigadier general just days before the engagement.

325 The same age as Stonebraker, and also born in Washington County, MD, Private William Fitzhugh Wharton (1844-1889) was the son of Doctor John Overton Wharton (1805-1875) and Elizabeth Ann Armistead Thomson Mason (1803-1857) of *Montpelier* in Clear Spring, Washington County, MD. For a brief time after their marriage the couple lived in Tennessee, returning to Washington County by 1835. In 1860, the Whartons were living near Beltsville, Prince George's County, MD, likely due to Doctor Wharton's active political career. In 1863, 19 year old William F. Wharton enlisted in Company C, 1st Maryland Cavalry. Wharton had a short and uneventful military career

Above: Authentic reproduction of camp shoe available from a company specializing in historic footwear. www.robertlandhistoricshoes.com.

Right: The two-tone Victorian spectator boots fashionable in the late 1890s when Stonebraker was writing his memoirs.

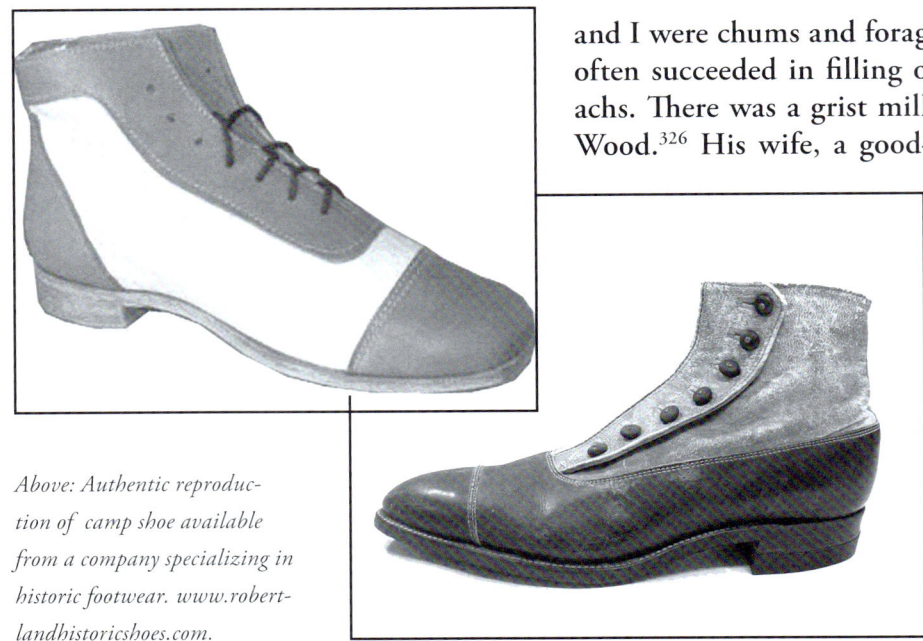

and I were chums and foraged much together. His stories often succeeded in filling out the wrinkles in our stomachs. There was a grist mill near the camp run by a Mr. Wood.[326] His wife, a good-natured, big hearted, fat old woman, took a great fancy to Wharton, and the latch string was always out to us.[327] In a three-legged "Dutch oven," she baked a short cake which she named "Leather hoe cake", and which she shared bounteously with us on many occasions.[328]

The only pay day came while in this camp, but my name not being on the pay roll, the Confederate Government still owes my salary. I was more fortunate as to clothing, receiving, while in the service, a pair of pants, two pairs of drawers, three pairs of socks, two pairs of shoes—one of them tan colored, being just thirty years ahead of the present fashion.[329] A review of the troops by General Fitz Lee was the most important event of the camp.[330]

At the close of each campaign it was customary to issue a certain number of "horse details" to each company. Men who had lost their horses came

---

overshadowed dramatically by the heroics of his older brother, Colonel John "Jack" Thomson Mason Wharton (1833-1902) of the 6th Texas Cavalry, known as Wharton's Cavalry. After the war William F. Wharton practised law in Towson, MD. He died at age 45 in Baltimore, but is buried in the Saint Johns Episcopal Church Cemetery in Hagerstown, MD along with all the other members of his family including his famous older brother. Neither William nor John married. *Hagerstown Mail,* 14 May 1875 and 12 Sep 1902. *US Federal Census of 1850, 1860, and 1880. The Gettysburg Compiler,* 14 Jan 1887. Johnson, Sidney Smith, *Texans who wore Grey,* (Tyler, TX), 138. WCLR PP-671.

326   Zach Wood (1815-?) and his wife Nancy (1810-?) are listed as "millers" in the 1860 US Federal census for Orange County, VA.

327   The latch was a wooden bar that secured the door. It was lifted by means of a leather thong run through a small hole above the bar called a "latch-string." To lock the door, one pulled the latch-string inside. There was no way to lock the door when everyone left the house. If the latch-string is always out, one is always welcome.

328   A Dutch oven is a thick-walled, usually cast iron, cooking pot with a tight-fitting lid. A hoe cake, also known as a Johnnycake, is a cornmeal flatbread. According to the *Oxford English Dictionary,* the term *hoecake* first occurs in 1745. The name is derived from the method of preparation where field hands often cooked on a shovel or hoe held to an open flame.

329   Stonebraker is comparing the two-tone Victorian spectator boot with the two-tone, late-war "camp shoe." In the 1890s the spectator boots combined the effect of the protective "spatterdashes" or "spats" into a two-toned, ankle-high fashion boot. Late in the war some soldiers in both armies were issued "camp shoes." They combined white canvas with leather on the toe and lacing reinforcement. There is some controversy whether these boots were an invention of Union ingenuity or the Confederacy's lack of leather supplies.

330   Confederate General Fitzhugh Lee previously cited footnote 179. The whole of Robert E. Lee's cavalry was dependent upon Fitzhugh Lee. Three horses were shot under him, and he was severely wounded at the Battle of Third Winchester 19 Sep 1864. This review was likely the first time his cavalry corp had seen their general after his difficult 3 month convalescence at Charlottesville, VA. Longacre, Edward G., *Fitz Lee: a military biography of Major General Fitzhugh Lee, C.S.A.* (Da Capo Press, Cambridge, MA, 2005), 176.

first on the list, next, those whose horses were worn out or in bad condition. It was a thirty days' furlough, in which the men were expected to secure better mounts for themselves. To those whose homes were within the lines or had friends to whom they could go, such a detail was very desirable. Few of our command were so situated, and the more who could get away, the better those fared who remained. So when orders came to our command for the names of those who wanted details, Wharton had his horse examined in my name.

An 1864 Timothy H. O'Sullivan photograph of a captured Confederate encampment at Petersburg, VA. Stonebraker's company erected similar cabins at Ellisville, VA in Jan 1865. LOC/P&P. LC-DIG-cwpb-00382.

The unexpected joys of this life are by far the sweetest. The underground railroad brought me an unsigned letter from Shepherdstown, Va., which I recognized to be the writing of Uncle Rentch, containing news from my dear ones at home.[331]

Jan. 26th, '65, we broke camp, moved down the "plank road,"[332] passed through Orange Court House and encamped at Orange Springs, twenty miles to the east of Gordonsville.[333]

Dall and I were sent to guard some old gentleman's property near the camp.[334] It proved to be what the boys termed a "soft snap." We had a large room to ourselves, a Negro boy to keep the logs blazing in a big, old-time fireplace and to attend to our wants, with plenty to eat for ourselves and horses. Much to our sorrow the command had continued on its march and we had to follow.

They had selected a camp near Ellisville in a fine piece of timber near a small stream.[335] The men at once commenced to prepare shelter of a substantial nature by felling trees and building small cabins with chimneys. I was much interested in the one that was to be my home. Just as it was finished,

---

331   Today the term "underground railroad" is used almost exclusively to identify the network of secret routes and safe houses used by slaves to escape to free states. In this instance, Stonebraker is applying the railroad term as a method by which soldiers secretly passed mail through Union occupied territory by "conductors" along "lines" with stops at "stations."
    Daniel Shafer Rentch (1821-1918) of Shepherdstown, WV previously cited footnote 131.
332   A plank road is a dirt road covered with a series of boards, logs, or planks. The Orange Turnpike, a gravel toll road built circa 1812, connected Fredericksburg with Orange Court House. The Orange Plank Road was planked only on one side.
333   Orange Springs, about 13.5 miles east of Orange, VA, was also known as "Healing Springs." The natural mineral springs was a licensed tavern as early as 1794. During the Civil War, the former hotel was the private residence of the Coleman family and a frequent camp location for troops from both armies. National Register of Historic Places, Orange Springs, *http://www.dhr.virginia.gov/registers/Counties/Orange/068-0066_Orange_Springs_1992_Final_Nomination.pdf*
334   Confederate Private Horatio M. Dall (1839-1903) previously cited footnote 312.
335   Ellisville was on the North Anna River at Hickory Creek north of Louisa Court House. It appears on both the 1871 Hotchkiss *"Map of Louisa County, Virginia,"* and *"Preliminary map of Orange County, Virginia."* Today there is an Ellisville Road and an Ellisville Drive in the vicinity, but no town of Ellisville. *LOC, Geography and Map Division, Washington, DC 20540-4650 dcu.*

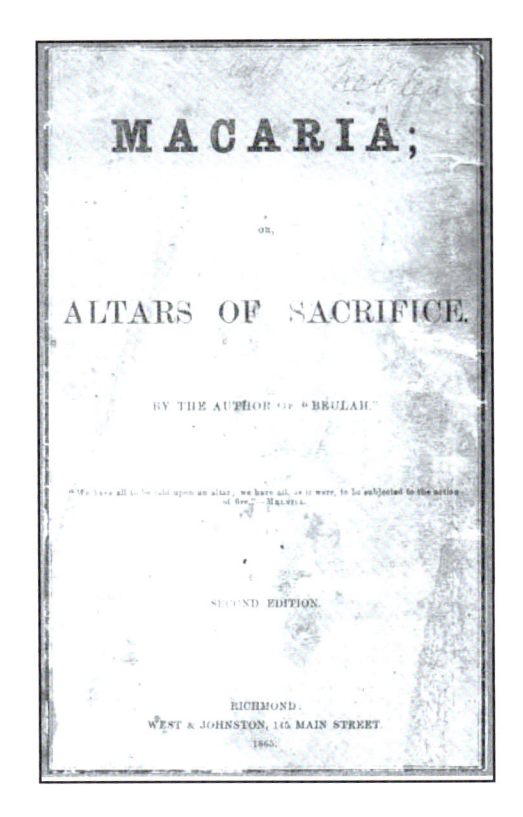

Augusta Jane Evan's 1864, Macaria, Alters of Sacrifice became a best seller in the Confederate states, selling over 20,000 copies by war's end.

Dall and I were detailed to establish a courier post between our camp and Wickam's brigade near Barboursville,[336] some thirty miles south.

We were instructed to locate at a private house, if we could get the consent of the owners, half way between the two camps. After many attempts we took up quarters in an old log cabin near a Mr. Willis, who had two handsome daughters of a literary turn of mind, they sending us books to read and an occasional meal.[337] We remained here five days, first one then the other carrying dispatches. Neither rations for ourselves or forage for our horses came from the command, so we supplied our wants by begging something to eat for ourselves and stealing forage for our horses. This was more than we could stand when we wrote to the Colonel to either send us supplies or relieve us from duty, which was finally done.

We rejoined our battalion the 6th of February. The weather had been intensely cold for several days, followed by a rise in temperature and eight inches of snow, making our cabins, with their fire places and chimneys, a luxury. Subsistence was our greatest trouble. We lived mainly on "black-eyed peas" which we boiled in an iron kettle over a slow fire that took from early in the morning until three in the afternoon before they reached the proper consistency. Having but one spoon in the mess, the men sitting around the kettle used small chips to convey the beans to their mouths by scraping them up the side of the kettle as a miniature elevator. We scoured the country for books and spent most of my time in reading. "Macaria" was considered the great Southern novel.[338] There being but one copy in the camp, it was in great demand.

I read while others slept, using pine knots for a light.[339] About this time a letter with a fifty dollar Confederate bill came from Capt. Stonebraker,

---

[336] Richmond, VA born Confederate General Williams Carter Wickham (1820-1888) descended from the prominent Virginia families of Carter, Nelson, Lee, and Wickham. A graduate of the University of Virginia, he was admitted to the bar in 1842. Following the secession of Virginia, Wickham and his company of the Hanover Dragoons enlisted in the Confederacy. Wickham fought in virtually every major battle in the eastern theater of the war. In Sep 1863 he was commissioned a brigadier general in command of "Wickham's Brigade" of General Fitzhugh Lee's division. Wickham was not with his brigade near Barboursville, VA as he had resigned his commission 5 Oct 1864, attending the Second Confederate Congress in Richmond, VA. On 3 Feb 1865, Wickham was participating in the Hampton Roads Conference at Newport News, VA in an attempt to bring an end to the war. Barboursville is an unincorporated community in Orange County west of Gordonsville and is renowned as the birthplace of President Zachary Taylor (1784-1850).

[337] Willis is a common family name throughout Orange County, VA with approximately 10 large families in the region appearing on the 1860 US Federal Census.

[338] First published in 1864, *Macaria; or, Altars of Sacrifice* was the third novel by Augusta Jane Evans, a leading female writer of nineteenth-century domestic fiction. Printed in Richmond, VA, *Macaria* was a wartime best seller, with more than 20,000 copies in circulation before the war's end. The novel was also well received along the Union front, so much so that some northern officials thought it should be banned. The tale focuses on a pair of strong-minded heroines who grapple with questions of individual morality and contribute to the war against the "Cain-cursed race of New England."

[339] Pine knots, or "fat wood," are made from the heartwood of pine trees. The resin-impregnated heartwood is hard, rot-resistant, and prized for use as kindling in starting fires. Pine knots light quickly even when damp and are wind resistant.

who was near Petersburg, with an invitation to spend my expected furlough with him.[340]

The "horse details" which had been granted to our battalion reached us on the 24th. The next morning, in company with Willie Redwood, we bade good-bye to our comrades and left the camp.[341] It had been raining for some days; the roads were in a horrible condition and the streams high. We crossed the North Anna River at Ellisville, passed through Louisa Court House, remaining over night at a Mrs. Barrot's, who had two very agreeable daughters, with whom we spent a pleasant evening at cards and enjoyed some fine music on the piano.[342]

It seemed almost a shame to put two dirty "Confeds." in a clean feather bed, the snow white sheets being scented with lavender leaves; but such was our luck. With many thanks for their kindness, we continued our journey, crossed several streams much swollen by the continued rains. Redwood, swimming his horse as we crossed the South Anna River at Ambler's Bridge,[343] passing into Goochland County and remaining over night at a Mr. Straughn's, formerly of Baltimore.

WILLIE REDWOOD, CO C, MARYLAND BATTALION

James William "Willie" Redwood (1846-1871), younger brother of artist Allen Christian Redwood. Photo from original text.

---

340   Confederate Captain Abraham Stonebraker, the author's uncle, previously cited see footnote 247. Photo page 104.

341   James William "Willie" Redwood (1846-1871) and his older brother, artist Allen Christian Redwood (1844-1922), were members of Company C, 1st Maryland Cavalry along with Stonebraker. Allen Redwood first enlisted in the 55th Virginia Infantry 24 Jul 1861, then transferred to 1st Maryland Cavalry, Company C on 12 Jan 1864. Willie Redwood enlisted in Company C on 25 Apr 1864. Another brother, Henry Redwood (1848-1923) was a member of Company B, 3rd Local Defense Troop of Richmond. Henry Redwood's Confederate uniform is on display at the Museum of the Confederacy in Richmond, VA.

    Their father, William H. Redwood (1812-1891), was a salesman, and the family moved often. Allen was born in Lancaster, VA in the northern neck, while Willie was born in Baltimore, MD. By 1860 the Redwood's were living in Brooklyn, NY as Allen attended Polytechnic Institute in Brooklyn that had opened in 1853. After the war, Willie died at age 25 in Fredericksburg, VA. Allen returned to Baltimore where he and his father opened studios in Baltimore and New York City. Allen illustrated and wrote articles about the Civil War for *Century*, *Scribner's*, and *Harper's* magazines. He also wrote *Stonewall, Memories from the Ranks and Other Places, Jackson's Foot Cavalry at the Battle of Second Bull Run, Following Stuart's Feather, A Boy in Grey,* and co-authored *Our March Against Pope* with General James Longstreet. Redwood traveled to the West in 1882. In 1898, Harper's magazine sent him to Cuba to cover the Spanish American War. Redwood's works are featured in the collections of the De Young Museum in San Francisco, the Phoenix Art Museum, and the Virginia Historical Society. *US Federal Census 1850, 1860, 1880*. Wagner, Margaret E. *The Library of Congress Civil War Desk Reference* (Simon & Schuster, NY 2002), 823. *Museum of the Confederacy-Collection no. 0982.14.2.*

342   The 1860 US Federal Census lists several families of Barrot/Barrett's living in Louisa County VA.

343   Ambler's Bridge does not appear on the maps of the Civil War era. However, William Marshall Ambler (1813-1896), a wealthy farmer and lawyer, owned a large plantation 10 miles south of Louisa Court House just east of Yanceyville, VA. The 1851 *Livingston's Law Register* indicates William M. Ambler lived in Louisa County at "Ambler's Mill." Today Ambler Road runs south from Shannon Hill Road. The fact that Willie Redwood swam his horse across the South Anna River in the presence of a bridge would indicate the young men did not wish to be noticed. Livingston, John, *Livingston's Law Register containing the Name, Post Office, County and State of Every Lawyer in the United States,* (NY, 1851), 196.

Our horses had to fast, as he could not furnish us with any feed for them. We paid our bill and took up the march, being joined here by another soldier who was going to Petersburg.

At Cartersville we paid three Negroes forty-five dollars to ferry us across the James River, passing into Cumberland County and thence into Powhatan County, remaining over night with a Mrs. Webb, just south of the Court House. She and several daughters were busily engaged making plaids for dress goods, hats from corn husks and window shades from dried grass.

The South was a purely agricultural section, and before the War they received nearly all their supplies either from Europe or the Northern States, other than what their land produced.

Reared in luxury, but when shut off from the outside world, the sacrifice and ingenuity of the Southern women was one of the marvels of the war.

They made buttons from Persimmon seeds.[344] When on the children's clothes they were more durable than pearl or porcelain. Shoe blacking from China berries.[345] Home made dyes from bark of trees—sassafras produced a yellow, laurel a drab; willow produced slate color in cotton and blue black in wool and linen; red oak a chocolate brown, white oak a lead color.[346]

Clothed in their home-made "Butternut," a brigade of Confederate soldiers possessed all the above colors, multiplied by the different shades, presenting a queer sight to one not accustomed to their presence.[347]

Tea was made from sassafras bark and blackberry leaves. Coffee from parched rye, carrots and sweet potatoes.[348] These are only a few substitutes from hundreds that can be named.

Rare surviving examples of Civil War era persimmon seeds and a complete persimmon seed button. From the authors collection.

---

344   The fruit-bearing American Persimmon (*Diospyros virginiana*) is native to the eastern United States. Early settlers and explorers probably learned of the many beneficial uses of the persimmon from Native Americans. Welch, William C., and Greg Grant, *Heirloom Gardening in the South: Yesterday's Plants for Today's Gardens*, (Texas AgriLife Research and Extension Services Series, 2011), 235.

345   The Chinaberry (*Melia azedarach*) is a member of the mahogany family introduced to the United States about 1830. This fast-growing tree forms dense thickets and is today considered an invasive species. The fruit is poisonous to both humans and small mammals. Chinaberry is similar to, and often confused with, the native shrub of common elderberry (*Sambucus canadensis*). The mature fruit of both the elderberry and chinaberry is dark-purple. The *Confederate Veteran Magazine* of 1916 noted that chinaberries mixed with soot made an excellent shoe dressing. *Confederate Veteran Magazine*, Volume 24, (Cunningham, S.A. Nashville, TN, 1916), 218. National Park Service, *Plant Conservation Alliance, Weeds Gone Wild, Alien Plant Invaders of Natural Areas*, http://www.nps.gov/plants/alien/fact/meaz1.htm.

346   For further reading on wartime hardships of everyday life in the south see: *The New York Times*, 19 Jul 1886, *War Days in the South, Curious details of enforced economy. Great dearth of necessary things, especially salt, leather, and iron – newspapers and wooden shoes.*

347   The butternut tree (*juglans cinerea*), or white walnut, is native to eastern North America. Like its close relative the American black walnut (*juglans nigra*), the kernel nut is edible, and the hull, when boiled down, creates an exceptionally strong fabric dye. Later in the war, the term "butternut" is homogeneously applied to homemade, hand-dyed Confederate uniforms, regardless of color variations.

348   A post-war editorial by "Chemicus" appeared in Georgia's *The Southern Banner* listing coffee substitutes recipes used during the war. Soldiers roasted various substances including: almond, acorn, asparagus, malted barley, beechnut, beetroot, carrot, chicory root, corn, cottonseed, dandelion root, fig, boiled-down molasses, okra seed, pea, persimmon seed, potato peel, rye, sassafras pits, sweet potato, wheat bran. Chemicus concluded: "For the stimulating property to which both tea and coffee owe their chief value, there is unfortunately no substitute; the best we can do is to dilute the little stocks which still remain, and cheat the palate, if we cannot deceive the nerves." *The Southern Banner*, (Athens, GA), 15 Mar 1865, 1.

Through the rain and mud, with the roads almost impassable, we traversed Chesterfield County, remaining over night with Dr. Walker, a wealthy gentleman who lived twenty miles northwest of Petersburg.[349] The next morning Redwood and I parted, he going to North Carolina.

I reached Petersburg about noon, crossed the Appomattox River on a pontoon bridge, passing through the northwestern portion of the city, arriving at Capt. Stonebraker's headquarters a little before sunset on March the 1st, 1865, and was made happy by the warm welcome I received.[350]

The Captain was stationed at Jarrett's Station on the South Side Rail Road, some seven miles from Petersburg, where he received and distributed supplies and furnished transportation over the road.[351]

I remained here for nearly three weeks, reading and noting the troops and trains passing up and down the road and getting my horse in good condition.

The reports of victory and defeat, the plans of this and that General that were daily circulated and discussed in and about camp would fill a volume.

March the 10th was set apart by President Davis for thanksgiving and prayer.[352] Instead of going to Church I read John Marchmont's Legacy.[353] St.

Stonebraker and Willie Redwood stayed at Physic Hill, *the home of Dr. John Wistar Walke. The circa 1815 home still stands today near Winterpock in Chesterfield County, VA.*

349   Confederate Surgeon Dr. John Wistar *Walke* (1824-1885) was born at *Physic Hill* in Chesterfield County, VA, the son of Dr. John Robertson Walke (1790-1863). Walke was assigned to the 59th Virginia Infantry, also called the 2nd Regiment Wise Legion. Physic Hill is listed in Dennis William Hauck's *Haunted Places: The National Directory (Penguin Group, NY, 1996), 423.* Moore, Josiah Staunton, *Reminiscences, letters, poetry and miscellanies* (Flanhart Printing Company, Richmond, VA, 1903), 367-368, 553. *US Federal Census 1850-1870.*

350   Confederate Captain Abraham Stonebraker, the author's uncle, previously cited see footnote 247. Photo page 104.

351   In Mar 1865, the siege at Petersburg, VA had been ongoing for over nine months as the Confederacy continued to defend the critical railroad supply trains between Petersburg and Richmond. Weakened by desertion, disease, and shortage of supplies, the rebel soldiers were outnumbered almost four-to-one. Jarrett's Station or Depot had been burned by Union forces 9 Dec 1864. *Harper's Weekly, A Journal of Civilization* Volume 8, No. 418, 31 Dec 1864.

352   In the second year of the Civil War, both Union President Abraham Lincoln and Confederate President Jefferson Davis began issuing "national" thanksgiving proclamations in response to victories in battle. These were the first presidential proclamations since James Madison's presidential proclamation of 1815. After the Confederate victory at Manassas, Jefferson Davis proclaimed a thanksgiving day for 15 Nov 1861. Lincoln followed suit by appointing a thanksgiving day in Apr 1862. After the Confederate victory at Second Manassas, Davis proclaimed 18 Sep 1862 as a "day of prayer and thanksgiving." Following Gettysburg, Lincoln appointed 6 Aug 1863 as a "day of national thanksgiving," and another for the last Thursday in November. This last proclamation is considered the first in an unbroken series of Presidential autumn proclamations that officially created the holiday of Thanksgiving in America. Pilgrim Hall Museum, America's museum of Pilgrim possession, *http://www.pilgrimhall.org/ThanxProc1862.htm.*

353   The Victorian novel *John Marchmont's Legacy* by British novelist Mary Elizabeth Braddon (1835-1915) was published in 1863. The story is a dramatic love triangle set in an English manor.

A rustic form of matches, pitch pine sticks light remarkably well even when damp.

Patrick's Day was celebrated by moving the train into Petersburg, encamping near the Fair Ground. We left the Captain at the depot, but he rejoined us in a few days, when we took possession of a vacant house near by for headquarters.

The beautiful pink of the peach trees and fresh, bright green of the lawns showed that spring was near at hand. A few more days of sunshine will dry up the mud, when the campaign of '65 will begin.[354]

As I wandered through the city from day to day, noting the various phases of life, I saw a crowd of old men and women, youths and little children, both white and black, around a grist mill. Upon investigation, I found that at stated periods they sold to the poor corn meal. Each one took their turn to be admitted, but they were only allowed to have one peck at a time. Their pinched faces and ragged clothes plainly indicated much want and suffering.

Lamps and candles were a luxury that the poor could ill-afford, but instead they used "pitch pine" sticks, which the negroes put up in bundles of one dozen each, about eighteen inches long and an inch square, which they sold at one dollar each.[355]

In the section where the better class lived were some fine residences with lawns in front and flowers in bloom. Handsome dressed ladies promenaded the streets. They seemed so unconcerned. Had it not been for the almost constant booming of the artillery, both day and night, one would never suspect that the city was and had been under siege for months.

On Sycamore Street some of the stores had a fair display of wares. In one window the following placard had a conspicuous place: "Genuine Coffee $30.00 per pound. Apples 50 cents a piece."[356]

The eastern portion of the city was much damaged by the shells from the Federal batteries. Not a single house escaped, and some were a total wreck.

On the morning of March the 25th, a few hours before daylight, we were aroused by a most terrific artillery duel. The sky was full of flying and bursting shells—a magnificent sight, and the rattle of small arms told of an early morning attack.

---

354   The nine-month siege at Petersburg, fought from 9 Jun 1864 to 25 Mar 1865, was coming to a close. The battle at Fort Stedman (25 Mar 1865) and Five Forks (1 Apr 1865) dramatically weakened the Confederate resources. Only a heroic defense by 600 Confederates against 5,000 federal troops at Fort Gregg (2 Apr 1865) allowed General Lee time to withdraw the Confederate forces from Petersburg and Richmond the night of 2 Apr 1865. Lee's plan was to resupply his army at Lynchburg, then turn south and join General Joseph E. Johnston's army in North Carolina. The Confederate withdraw from Petersburg and Richmond, VA resulted in the Appomattox Campaign. The National Park Service, American Battlefield Protection Program CWSAC Battle Summary, *http://www.cr.nps.gov/hps/abpp/battles/va084.htm.*

355   Pitch Pine (pinus rigida) is a small to medium sized, slow-growing native pine mainly found in the northeastern United States. It grows well in poor conditions and has a high resin content that is very flammable. Most sources indicate the pitch pine sticks were crude matches lit with a flint and steel. Aldrich, Charles, *Things Remembered, Iowa Historical Record,* Vol XI, No. 3, (Iowa City, IA, 1895).

356   Sycamore Street is a major north-south street running through the center of Petersburg, VA and was a busy commercial district before and during the war. The Petersburg Courthouse off Sycamore Street was the Confederate headquarters during the siege.

A Rebel of '61

The elegant Spotswood Hotel on the corner of Main Street and 8th Street, Richmond, VA. The hotel survived the war only to burn on Christmas Day in 1870. Photograph Apr 1865 by Alexander Gardner (1821-1882). LOC/ P&P. LC-DIG-cwpb-00458.

As soon as it was light the Captain and I rode to the front and learned that General Gordon had assaulted and carried Fort Steadman, situated on Hare's Hill, opposite the city, but was unable to hold it longer than a few hours.[357] This precipitated fighting all along the line. About noon, hearing very heavy firing to the southwest, I rode in that direction and saw some severe fighting near Battery 45—charges and counter charges, without any decisive results to either side.[358]

I bade good-bye to my friends and started to rejoin my command. When near Richmond, I met Paine's Brigade of Cavalry going to Petersburg,[359] when General Fitz Lee informed me that he expected my regiment to join him at Petersburg in a few days.[360] Being anxious to see the Confederate capital, I rode into the city and stopped at the Spottswood.[361] After taking

---

357   Fort Stedman was a Union stronghold and the focus of an attack by Confederate Major General John Brown Gordon on 25 Mar 1865 in General Lee's attempt to relieve pressure west of the city. General Brown previously cited footnote 274, photograph page 116.

358   Battery 45, or Fort Lee, was along the Plank Road just east of Fort Gregg on the west side of Petersburg, VA.

359   Confederate General William Henry Fitzhugh Payne (1830-1904) of Fauquier County, VA attended Virginia Military Institute, later studying law at the University of Virginia. He served as the Commonwealth's Attorney for Fauquier County for several years. A capable cavalry officer under General J. E. B. Stuart in the famed Black Horse Cavalry, he was wounded and captured several times. In the final months of the war he commanded a cavalry brigade under Brigadier General Thomas l. Munford in General Fitzhugh Lee's division.

360   In Mar 1865, the 1st Maryland Cavalry was instructed to make quick hit-and-run attacks on General Sheridan's flank as he moved from Charlottesville to White House on the York River. From White House the 1st Maryland made their way to Richmond, arriving on 2 Apr 1865. The following morning, after viewing the destruction of Richmond, they continued south to Petersburg where they found the Army of Northern Virginia battling for its life. Driver, *1st & 2nd MD Cavalry*, 114.

361   The Spotswood, or Spotswood Hotel, on the corner of Main and 8th Street, in Richmond, VA opened 19 Jan 1861. Only a block from the Virginia State Capital building, the grand hotel quickly became the hotel of choice for officers visiting the capital, diplomats, and a platform for speeches for both President Davis and General Lee. Some short term uses for the hotel included the housing of important captured Union officers, a hospital for wounded, and a post office. After the Confederate withdrawal, the *Richmond Whig* 7 Apr 1865 reported the "last rebel and first Union patrons at the Spotswood." The hotel survived the war only to burn on Christmas Day 1870. *Richmond Enquirer*, 19 Jan 1861. *Richmond Dispatch*: 15 Apr 1861, 20 Apr 1861, 23 Apr 1861, 30 May 1861, 1 Jun 1861, 20 Jun 1861, 24 Jul 1861, 10 Feb 1862, 17 Apr 1861, 2 Jul 1862, 4 Sep 1862, 26 Dec 1870. *Richmond Examiner:* 5 Jul 1862, 11 Jul 1862. *Pittsburgh Gazette,* 17 Jul 1862, *Richmond Sentinel:* 14

The commercial business district along Sycamore Street near the Petersburg Courthouse in 1865. The courthouse was the Confederate headquarters during the siege. The circa 1840, classical revival Petersburg Courthouse still stands today and was listed on the National Register of Historic Places in May 1973. LOC/P&P. LC-DIG-cw-pb-02773.

a look at the State House I overtook the First Virginia Cavalry, remaining over night with them. The next day I reached Petersburg to find that the Captain had moved his quarters near the Poor House.[362] It was full of little boys and girls. While reading, a little "tot" came running into our tent, threw his arms around my neck and asked for a piece of bread.

As if by general consent quiet prevailed all along the line until 2 a.m. on the morning of the 30th, when the Federals commenced to shell our position at a furious rate. Soon as our artillery replied the sky was full of shells flying and bursting like hundreds of rockets—a truly grand and thrilling sight if one could shut from his mind the death and destruction that such a display caused. This artillery duel continued well into the following day and did not cease amidst a heavy thunder storm. The sharp clap of lightning and the heavy boom of cannon produced a combination not soon to be forgotten.[363]

Information now reached us that severe fighting and some reverses had overtaken our troops on our right at Hatcher's Run, causing us to move our train to the north side of the Appomattox River.[364] Screeching and bursting shells now rained into the city; extensive warehouses, full of tobacco, poured forth smoke and flame, having been fired by General Lee's order; non-combatants, with their valuables in small tin boxes, hurrying through the streets; women standing in their doors with blanched faces; all told that some dire calamity had overtaken our army. While riding through the streets amidst such scenes, a little girl hailed me, "Say, Mister, look at your horse." As I turned in my saddle, "April fool" she cried. Did Nero do more?[365]

Mar 1863, 28 Jul 1863, 5 Dec 1864. *Richmond Whig:* 2 Jan 1864, 7 Apr 1865.

362 For more information on the poorhouse of Petersburg, VA see Fleming, Patricia W. *A poorhouse tale: a history of the Petersburg poorhouse.* (Manakin-Sabot, VA: Dementi Milestone Publishing, 2011).

363 Union forces had besieged General Lee's army around the city of Petersburg since Jun 1864. Lee was withdrawing from Petersburg and Richmond, moving his army westward in an attempt to resupply, then join forces with Confederate General Joseph E. Johnston. The artillery Stonebraker heard was the opening shots of General Grant's spring offensive and the beginning of the Appomattox Campaign.

364 Hatcher's Run flows through Dinwiddie County about halfway between Petersburg and Five Forks. An earlier, two-day battle had taken place at Hatcher's Run beginning 5 Feb 1865 when Union Brigadier General David McMurtrie Gregg's cavalry set out to the Boydton Plank Road to destroy as many Confederate supply wagons as they could find while the Union II and V Corps provided support and kept the Confederates occupied to the north and east.

365 Foolishness on April 1st can be found as early as the 1500s. The reference to the Roman Emperor Nero is that he remained idle, or fled, while fire destroyed or damaged ten of the fourteen Roman districts in the year 64. Boese, Alex, *The Origin of April Fool's Day*, www.museumofhoaxes.com (2008).

A Rebel of '61

Petersburg to Appomattox

The disaster of Five Forks and Hatcher's Run cut Lee's right wing in half, separating General Pickett with three brigades of infantry from the main army.[366] This doubled Lee's right back on Petersburg, causing him to re-form his lines. This was on the second day of April and the first time I saw the peerless Rob. E. Lee. He and Gen. Longstreet were on their horses together, and from Lee's movements I could see he was directing Longstreet where to place his troops, which were but a short distance in their front, forming on the crest of a hill to the west of the city.

The Federals were slowly advancing and shells were bursting in the vicinity, but the generals were partially sheltered by a fine large suburban mansion.[367] Lee, while pointing towards the troops with his right hand, held in his left a biscuit which he had taken from the rear pocket of his coat and ate while they conferred.

It was very evident that Petersburg was lost. I rode back to the train and found preparations in progress for a retreat. As soon as darkness set in the train was put in motion, and continued to move slowly all night, passing through Chesterfield County, reaching Clover Hill at daybreak, when Capt. Stonebrak-

The Confederate army evacuated the capital city of Richmond on 2 Apr 1865. The warehouses and arsenal buildings were burned by the retreating confederates to prevent the supplies from falling into the hands of the Union army. Photograph Apr 1865 by Alexander Gardner (1821-1882). LOC/P&P. LC-DIG-cwpb-00436.

---

366   General Lee realized Five Forks was his last supply line to Petersburg along the Southside Railroad and ordered General George Pickett to "Hold Five Forks at all hazards. Protect road to Ford Depot and prevent Union forces from striking the South-side Railroad." Union General Sheridan launched an assault at Five Forks on 1 Apr 1865. What began as a promising victory for the Confederates resulted in the Federals pushing the Confederates back and piercing their line. Picket, La Salle Corbell, *Pickett and his Men* (J. B. Lippincott Company, Philadelphia & London, 1913), 266.

367   From 23 Nov 1864 until 2 Apr 1865, General Lee was headquartered at *Edge Hill*, the home of William Turnbull along the Boydton Plank Road on the west side of Petersburg. From *Edge Hill* on 2 Apr 1865, Lee sent a letter to Secretary of War General J. C. Breckenridge, "It is absolutely necessary that we should abandon our position to-night or run the risk of being cut off in the morning." *Edge Hill* was almost entirely destroyed by fire during the retreat.

     William Turnbull (1824-1889) was the magistrate of Dinwiddie County, VA. One year after the war, Turnbull wrote to General Lee: "Feeling that you would like to hear from me & knowing that you deeply sympathized with me in my misfortunes, I send you a few lines to let you know that I am again doing well. I am now quite comfortably situated on my farm - Have a fine prospect for a crop. I only allude to the fact, to inform you, that I will ever remember with pleasure & will love & honor my farm because it was your Headquarters. An attempt was made to entirely destroy it - But "Phoenix like" it blooms out of its ashes. . ." Confederate General Robert E. Lee. *Petersburg Progress [Newspaper]*, (Petersburg, VA.) 16 Apr 1865, Long, A. L. *Memoirs of Robert E. Lee, His Military and Personal History* (J. M. Stoddart & Company, New York, Philadelphia and Washington, 1886), 691. 2 Apr 1866 letter from William Turnbull to Robert E. Lee. *Robert E. Lee Collection* Leyburn Library, Washington and Lee University, Lexington, VA.

On the morning of 3 Apr 1865, Stonebraker and his uncle breakfasted at Clover Hill *Plantation in Chesterfield County, VA, the home of Judge James Henry Cox, his wife Martha, daughter Catherine Virginia Cox, and youngest son John. Two older Cox brothers, Henry and James, were serving in the Confederacy, another son Lieutenant Joseph Edwin Cox was buried in the family cemetery having died in the service in Dec 1861. In 1932, the daughter of Catherine Virginia Cox Logan published her mother's civil war era diary as "My Confederate Girlhood," reminiscing that General Robert E. Lee had dined at* Clover Hill *on 2 Apr 1865. Photo from* My Confederate Girlhood *(Richmond, VA, 1932)*

er, Major Rawl, and myself took breakfast with Doctor Walker.[368] He gave us peach brandy mixed with honey, and when I sat down at the table the plates were spinning around before me.

Everything was now in confusion. Troops and trains moving in the direction of Amelia Court House, where the Federals are reported to be. We halted at the coal mines for a short time,[369] then moved down the Woodpecker Road and parked the train near the Appomattox River.

About midnight we moved the train and tried to cross the river, but the pontoon bridge was broken and we were detained until sunrise before get-

---

[368] *Clover Hill* Plantation, located in the Winterpock area of Chesterfield County, VA was the home of Judge James Henry Cox and his wife Martha Reid Cox. He had been given the land by his father, Henry Cox, after his graduation from Hampdon-Sydney College in 1829. After coal was discovered on the land, a railroad was built to transport coal along the eastern seaboard. During the war, much of the coal was shipped to the ironworks in Richmond to help the Confederate cause. *Clover Hill* remained in the Cox family until the 1920s. Chesterfield Historical Society of Virginia. Doctor Walke, previously cited footnote 349, lived at nearby *Physic Hill* Plantation.

[369] In the year 1837, legend has it that a slave named Moses found coal on the land following a heavy rain, and this important discovery led to the operation of several mines at *Clover Hill*. The Clover Hill Railroad was built in the 1840s to haul Cox's coal to Manchester, where it was loaded onto steamships bound for the gasworks in New York and Philadelphia. The name Winterpock was later applied to the mining community that grew up a mile from the house. The community peaked at around 1,000 residents in the 1870s, but dwindled down to nothing when the mines closed late in the 19th century. Dallmeyer, Diane, *A Short History Lesson on Winterpock and Clover Hill*, Chesterfield Observer [Newspaper], 9 Apr 2008.

148   *A Rebel of '61*

ting over. With skirmishing at Deep Creek we passed slowly through Amelia County, halting from time to time, all the trains from Richmond followed by infantry being in our front.[370]

The troops were silent and seemed depressed, except the Second Corps, who cheered vigorously as General Lee rode along their moving columns.[371] He gravely raised his hat in recognition of the compliment. I never saw that great soldier again, but his handsome face and form is enshrined in my heart and memory. We parked the train four miles east of Amelia Court House, where we remained all night. It was here that General Lee expected to receive supplies for his army, but the Federals having destroyed the railroad in our front frustrated that desired relief. The constant moving of the trains began to tell on our stock. Rather than abandon some of his wagons, the Captain left to scour the country to the north for horses to take the place of those that showed signs of breaking down.[372]

The next morning, April the 5th, my regiment, First Maryland Cavalry, came passing along, when I rejoined my company. We pushed ahead and upon reaching Amelia Court House we found that the Federal Cavalry had struck our wagon train near Flat Creek. As we approached they began to retreat, when a running fight commenced. We pursued them for several miles, killed and wounded quite a number and took seventy prisoners. The road was strewn with guns, sabers, and knapsacks, which they threw away in their flight.[373]

Fortunately we reached the train before the enemy had time to do any serious damage, but we found evidences of great panic among the teamsters—wagons upset, others with poles broken, and many without teams, the drivers having cut their horses loose and fled. The dead that laid among the ruins only made the scene more ghastly, with their bloody heads and gaping wounds.

We encamped for the night at Amelia Springs, being tired and hungry, the rain during the night adding very much to our discomfort. Daylight the next morning found us in the saddle moving westward. Soon report reached us that the enemy was in our front trying to block General Lee's progress by burning bridges, when we pushed forward in a trot and found a body of infantry, supported by cavalry, within one mile of . . .

---

370   Most sources agree that much of the Confederate army crossed the Appomattox River into Amelia County at the Goode's Bridge crossing on present day US-360.

371   Officially created and named in 1862 following the Battle of Antietam, the Second Corp of the Army of Northern Virginia gained the reputation as hard fighters under the leadership of General Thomas J. "Stonewall" Jackson. In Dec 1864, the remaining troops were placed under the command of Confederate Major General John B. Gordon. By Apr 1865 very little remained of the Second Corp.

372   The Union army had destroyed the railroad at Jetersville, VA. A battle would be fought there the following day.

    The Captain was Captain Abraham Stonebraker, the author's uncle.

373   Also known as the Battle of Amelia Springs, the Confederate cavalry divisions of Major General Thomas L. Rosser and Brigadier General Thomas T. Munford counterattacked Union Brigadier General Henry E. Davies, Jr's. brigade that was attempting to destroy the Confederate supply wagons in the vicinity of Painesville, VA. Considered an inconclusive, minor battle with estimated casualties of 250, the running fight started about three miles north of Amelia Springs and continued through Amelia Springs almost to Jetersville, VA.

High Bridge near Farmville, VA. Photograph Apr 1865 by Timothy O'Sullivan. LOC/P&P. LC-LC-DIG-ppmsca-33390.

Painting of the 4th Massachusetts Cavalry at the Battle of High Bridge, VA. by Frederick Mortimer Lamb. This huge painting hangs in the Brockton Massachusetts City Hall, Brockton, MA. Photo by Wayne Burkholder, Middleton, MA.

A Rebel of '61

High Bridge

on the South Side Railroad near Farmville.[374] A part of General Fitz. Lee's division had been dismounted and placed in line of battle behind a fence skirting a piece of timber, while we, in a brisk trot, were hurried to the enemy's rear by the left flank. The battle commenced as we came upon the field, and in less than an hour we bagged the whole outfit, killed and wounded quite a number, capturing 780 prisoners, two stands of colors and a full brass band.[375]

This was Major-General Ord's bridge-burning expedition under the command of his chief of staff, Brig.-Gen. Theo. Read, and consisted of two regiments of infantry—Fifty-fourth Pennsylvania and One Hundred and Twenty-third Ohio, with 13 officers and 67 men of the Fourth Massachusetts cavalry.[376] The fight was sharp and determined on both sides, the Federal Gen. Read being among the killed. Gen. Geo. A Hundley, in Vol. XXIII, Southern Historical Society Papers, describes Gen. Read's death:[377]

---

[374] The 1854 South Side Railroad trestle bridge was an engineering marvel of the mid-19th century. Twenty-one brick piers supported the rail tracks with a span of 2,400 feet and height of 125 feet. A smaller wagon bridge ran parallel to the towering railroad trestle, and both bridges offered an escape route for the retreating Confederates across the 75 foot wide Appomattox River.

[375] On 6 Apr 1865, Confederate General Longstreet dispatched cavalrymen under Major General Thomas L. Rosser to protect the bridges from Union forces. Union Major General Edward O. C. Ord, commanding the Army of the James, ordered Brigadier General Theodore Read, leading the 54th Pennsylvania, the 123rd Ohio, and three companies of the 4th Massachusetts Cavalry, to take the bridge. The Union accounts declared the battle at High Bridge tactically inconclusive, despite the fact that two entire Union infantry regiments surrendered to retreating Confederate cavalry. The Confederates captured almost 800 Union soldiers, six regimental flags, an ambulance, and even a brass band, versus only about 100 Confederates captured or killed. Salmon, John S. *The Official Virginia Civil War Battlefield Guide.* (Stackpole Books, Mechanicsburg, PA, 2001), Welsh, Richard F., *Burning High Bridge: The South's Last Hope, Civil War Times,* March/April 2007.

[376] Union Major General Edward Otho Cresap Ord (1818-1883) of Cumberland, MD was a career army officer. A graduate of the US Military Academy in 1839, he saw action in the Seminole War and the Indian Wars. At the outbreak of the Civil War, Ord was assigned to Fort Vancouver in the Washington Territory. By May 1863, Ord was promoted to major general and assigned command of the 2nd Division of the Army of Tennessee. After the fall of Vicksburg, he was transferred to the eastern theater of the war. General Ord was inside the McLean house at Appomattox when General Lee surrendered and is often pictured in paintings of this event. After the surrender ceremony, General Ord paid $40 to Wilmer McLean for the mahogany, marble-top table at which General Lee had sat. The table is now on display in the Chicago History Museum (formerly Chicago Historical Society).

[377] Confederate General George Jefferson Hundley's account of Battle at High Bridge was published in "*The Beginning and the Ending: Reminiscences of the First and Last Days of the War.*" This account was published in the *Richmond Times* (Richmond, VA) newspaper in two parts on 26 Jan and 2 Feb 1896. The complete story later appeared in the *SHSP, Vol. XXIII,* 294-313, (hereafter cited as Hundley, *Reminiscences, SHSP*).

Personal accounts of the Battle at High Bridge indicate General Read and his officers pressed well ahead of the main corps and were flanked by Confederate cavalry and infantry. Eight of the eleven Union officers were killed or wounded in the action. In addition to General Theodore Read, Captains Hodges and Goddard, and Lieutenant Davis were killed. Lieutenant Colonel Jenkins, Captain Caldwell and Lieutenants Belcher and Thompson were severely wounded. Colonel Francis Washburn later died from his wounds. "Was your colonel drunk or crazy this morning, that he attacked with less than one hundred men the best fighting division of the Confederate cavalry?" reportedly asked a Confederate officer of a wounded captain of the 4th Massachusetts, "We have seen hard fighting, but we never heard of anything like this before!" Bouve, Major Edward T., U.S.V. *The Battle at High Bridge, Civil War Papers read before the Commandery of the State of Massachusetts,* Vol. 2 (Gilson Company, Boston, MA, 1900), 403-412. Sorenson, Michael K. *Biography of Francis P. Washburn* http://www.2mass.reunioncivilwar.com/References/Hist-Washburn,%20Francis.pdf, *Official Records: Series 1, Vol. 46, Part 1 Appomattox Campaign,* 1168.

Three Desperate Men.

Union Brevet Brigadier General Theodore Read (1835-1865) has the unfortunate notability of being the last Union general killed in the war, three days before the Confederate surrender at Appomattox.

"The enemy's cavalry charged that part of the line where I stood three times. They were mounted and we dismounted. A single, well-directed volley scattered them each time, but the second time three Federal officers stood their ground and attempted to cut their way out. We were not much more than a skirmish line, and here these three desperate men came down right amongst us, whilst our men were reloading, cutting, and slashing with their sabers as they came. A sight so unusual puzzled our men at first, but soon finding these fellows to be in earnest, some one cried out, 'kill the d_____d Yankees,' and instantly the three men went down as if they had suddenly melted away. I remember seeing the dust fly from their coats behind as the bullets passed through their bodies. One of these officers proved to be General Theodore Read."[378]

Shortly after this fight I met Major James Breathed riding along the road, bare headed and minus a boot. He told me that he had lost them in hand to hand fight with a "d_____d Yankee" who unhorsed him in the struggle, and while his horse was dragging him over the ground, with one foot in the stirrup; some one shot his antagonist, which saved his life.[379]

Gen. Hundley, who was an eye witness to this duel says:

---

[378] Most first hand accounts of this battle identify the "three desperate men" as Union officers General Theodore Read, Captain John D. B. Goddard of Company L, 4th Massachusetts Cavalry, and Colonel Francis Washburn also of the 4th Massachusetts Cavalry. Colonel Washburn was shot in the mouth and sabred as he fell from his horse. He was found on the field the following day with the other dead and wounded, and taken to a hospital. He was sent home to Massachusetts where he later died.

Union Brigadier General Theodore Read of Athens, OH was an 1854 graduate of Indiana University and a practising attorney prior to the war. He entered the service as a private in the 12th Illinois Infantry and served in various staff positions. He was promoted to lieutenant colonel, assistant adjutant general, and finally chief of staff of the Army of the James. Read was brevetted a brigadier general 29 Sep 1864 "for gallantry before the enemy." General Read has the unfortunate distinction of being identified as the last Union general killed in the war, the fatal shot delivered by Confederate Brigadier General James Dearing (1840-1865) of Campbell County, VA. Reportedly, General Dearing was mortally wounded while firing at General Read and also fell dead to became the last Confederate general killed in the war. Sorenson, Michael K., *Biography of Francis P. Washburn*, http://www.2mass.reunioncivilwar.com/References/Hist-Washburn,%20Francis.pdf.

[379] Confederate Major James Breathed was born near present-day Berkeley Springs, VA [WV] on 15 Dec 1838. About 1848, the Breathed family moved to the farm adjacent to the Saint James School (see footnote 218) where they lived in the large and elegant Greek Revival home known today as *Bai Yuka*, the Indian words for Fountain Rock. James Breathed attended Saint James School, afterwards graduating from the University of Maryland medical school. During the Civil War, he served first as a lieutenant in the 1st Virginia Cavalry under General J. E. B. Stuart. Breathed so distinguished himself in the battles of Chancellorsville, Brandy Station, Gettysburg, Spotsylvania Court House, and Yellow Tavern, that General Lee regarded him as "the hardest artillery fighter the war produced." After the war he practiced medicine in Hancock, MD, where he died in 1870 at age 32. For additional reading on Major Breathed see: Bridges, David P., *Fighting with JEB Stuart* (Breathed Bridges Best, Inc., Arlington, VA, 2006). *US Federal Census 1850 and 1860. Thomas Taggart Map of Washington County, MD, 1859, District 10.*

A Rebel of '61

A Brave Federal Officer.

"Soon the same cavalry came charging down again, and this time one officer stood his ground after a volley had again scattered his men. Major James Breathed, our Chief of Artillery, who will never be forgotten as long as a cavalryman of the Army of Northern Virginia lives to think of his dash and courage, came up in the meantime and rode through our line, accompanied by _____Scruggs, a courier. As Breathed rode towards the brave Federal, who quietly awaited him, he seemed to make a motion with his drawn sabre as if to convey a challenge, which the Federal accepted, and every man stood still to witness the tilt between two such gallant men. They went at it and fought for some minutes pretty evenly matched, whilst _____Scruggs sat on his horse close by. Soon the Federal wounded Major Breathed in the arm and seemed to get some advantage, when _____Scruggs shot the brave fellow dead. I was not near enough to hear whether _____Scruggs demanded his surrender or not, but I am sure he evinced no intention of surrendering. I passed him as he lay gasping his last, and looked with pity into the dying face of a foeman so brave."[380]

---

380 There are several published accounts of Major Breathed's duel with a "brave federal officer." Most of those accounts identify Breathed's combatant as Union Captain William Townsend Hodges of Company I, 4th Massachusetts Cavalry as he lead the third and final charge at High Bridge. In his memoirs of the 35th Virginia Cavalry, Captain Frank M. Myers recorded Breathed's duel, but did not identify his rescuer. Lieutenant Colonel R. Preston Chew in his article for *Confederate Veteran* recounted the same incident; however, he credited Lieutenant W. B. Conrad of the 12th Virginia Cavalry as the shooter of Hodges.

In this account of the duel, Confederate General George J. Hundley identifies Breathed's defender as James Egington Scruggs (1833-1901). Born in Fluvanna County, VA, Scruggs was the fourth child of fifteen children born to Joseph C. and Francis Parks Shepherd Scruggs. Seven Scruggs brothers enlisted in the Confederacy: Joseph A., Calvin S., James E., Samuel M., William P., Abram E. T., and Albea E. Scruggs. Three of the brothers enlisted in Company C, 2nd Virginia Cavalry. Only Calvin Scott Scruggs (1830-1863) died during the war; the other brothers survived. On 1 Oct 1861, James transferred to the 2nd Virginia Cavalry from the 19th Virginia. From about Nov 1863 to Apr 1864, Scruggs was detailed to Brigadier-General Williams Carter Wickham as a courier. Confederate records note Scruggs as a "courier; most efficient; always well mounted." According to Scruggs family legend, James E. Scruggs captured the sword of the deceased Union General Theodore Read at the Battle of High Bridge. However, another account noted that after the battle Confederate cavalry commander Major General Thomas L. Rosser rode back into General Longstreet's camp on a fine black horse carrying a new saber. "It was a gallant fight," he announced to Longstreet. "This is Read's horse and this is his saber. Both beauties aren't they?" Myers, Frank M., *The Comanches: A History of White's Battalion, Virginia Cavalry,* (Kelly, Piet & Co.,Baltimore, MD, 1871). *Confederate Veteran, Vol XVI, Defense of High Bridge, Near Farmville,* (Cunningham, S.A., Nashville, TN, Aug 1908), 394. Hundley, *Reminiscences, SHSP, Vol. XXIII,* 294-313. National Park Service, *Civil War Soldiers and Sailors Database,* http://www.nps.gov/civilwar/soldiers-and-sailors-database.html/. Welsh, Richard F., *Burning High Bridge: The South's Last Hope, Civil War Times,* March/April 2007. Marvel, William, *Lee's Last Retreat, The Flight to Appomattox,* (University of NC Press, 2002), 77.

Captain William Hodges (mounted) led the third and final charge of the 4th Massachusetts Cavalry at High Bridge. During the melee he engaged in a mounted saber duel with Major James Breathed. After Captain Hodges knocked Major Breathed from his horse, a nearby Confederate came to Breathed's aid and fatally shot Captain Hodges in the chest. Adjutant George Foster Hodges (1837-1862) and Captain William Townsend Hodges (1833-1865), oil on canvas 1866, by William Sharp. Harvard University Portrait Collection, Gift of Anne C. Hodges, 1935, H459.

Confederate Major James Breathed (1838-1870) of Washington County, MD. The rural village of Breathesville near St. James College is named for the Breathed family.

Major Breathed was born in Morgan County, Virginia, and raised in Washington County, Maryland, near St. James College. After the surrender he located in Hancock, Maryland, and became a successful physician.

Our division having been ordered to cover the retreat, by 4 a.m. we were in the saddle and in line of battle. At sunrise the enemy pressed steadily forward and we slowly fell back, stubbornly disputing every inch of ground as we moved. Just before we reached Farmville we crossed a small but deep stream, the bottom being full of rocks, making it a most difficult place to ford, while the enemy had a battery on the hill above trying to get our range, dropping shells dangerously near. Once over we drew up in line to the west of High Bridge, where we remained until the enemy's guns succeeded in getting our range, when we moved back into a piece of timber for protection. It was not long before they knocked the woods all to pieces, exposing us to a most terrific fire. It takes nerves of steel to stand without flinching, hundreds of screeching shells plowing through a woods, smashing tops and creating havoc generally. Demoralizing as such a shelling as we underwent, yet I could stand that with much better grace than to have the enemy shooting into our backs as we retreated in a snail-like pace, and was always relieved when ordered to right about face and charge the enemy when they got too persistent.

Slowly we moved through Farmville, turning and showing our teeth when too hard pressed. We forded the Appomattox River, the bridge being in flames, exposed all the while to a galling fire from the enemy's guns.

Our battalion was posted at the ford, which we held for hours, while the balance of the division passed on and took a position to our right.

Although being in a very exposed position we were not molested, the larger body of troops stationed elsewhere making a better target for the enemy's guns. We had a clear view of the field and saw the conflict as it raged all around. Just to the northwest six hundred wagons were on fire, the animals had played out and they were fired to prevent them from falling into the enemy's hands.

Finally, the smoke from the wagons, the bridge and the guns began to settle near the earth, obscuring our view, but the heavy firing on our right told where the conflict was the thickest. Soon we were hurried in that direction, and as we neared the point a mighty cheer went up, which told us the enemy had been repulsed.

Gen. Fitz. Lee says:

"On the 7th a portion of the enemy's cavalry having crossed the river again, made an attack on the wagon train moving upon our right line of march. They were met by Munford in front, whilst Rosser attacked their flank, and

A Rebel of '61

were driven back with considerable loss, including amongst the captured, their commanding general, J. Irving Gregg.[381] Our position was held near this point of attack until 12 p.m., when the march was resumed towards Appomattox Court House."[382]

When we reached the point of attack Gen. Munford took charge of the battalion, the men being formed into a column of fours, were stationed with drawn sabres in a road fringed with stunted pines.[383] The smoke was now so dense you could not see over ten yards in your front, and being so close to the enemy, the men were ordered not to speak above a whisper. We remained in this position for more than an hour, expecting the enemy to renew the attack at any moment.

As darkness set in the retreat was resumed, and continued nearly the whole night. We passed through Prince Edward County, both men and horses showing signs of utter weariness from lack of rest and food. Some time in the after part of the night we tied our horses to some trees and laid down, but at daylight we were again in the saddle and on the move. I secured some corn, as I passed a crib, and later in the day, when our command halted and moved to the side of the road to allow a column of Federal prisoners to pass, I slipped the bit from my horse's mouth and fed him while we waited. One of the prisoners asked me for some corn, when I told him to help himself; he picked up an ear which the horse had already bitten, munching the raw grains as he moved along. They were a woe-begone looking set, and were nearly starved, and so were we. The following incident, as related by Gen. Hundley, graphically describes the condition of our own men:

> "Soon a tired, dusty, foot-sore soldier came up to the fire and asked if he could parch some corn. I said, 'Yes, certainly.' I watched the poor fellow, by the flickering light, as he drew a handful of corn out of his dirty old haversack and put it in his pan. I said, 'My friend, is that all you have?' he said, 'Yes, and I have had nothing better for three days.' 'Are you going

---

381   Union General John Irvin Gregg (1826-1892) of Bellefonte, PA was a career army officer. Gregg saw action during the Mexican-American War and was honorably discharged with the rank of captain. When the Civil War broke out, Gregg was commissioned a captain in the 3rd US Cavalry. Gregg commanded many different brigades in the various reorganizations of the Army of the Potomac. By 1 Aug 1864, he was promoted to brevet brigadier general. On 7 Apr 1865, Gregg was slightly wounded at the Battle of Saylor's Creek, captured the next day north of Farmville, VA and released two days later. Eicher, John H., and Eicher, David J., *Civil War High Commands*, (Stanford University Press, Palo Alto, CA. 2001).

382   Report of Major General Fitzhugh Lee, 22 Apr 1865, *The War of the Rebellion: A Compilation of the Official Records of the Union and Confederate Armies*, Series I, Volume XLVI. Report No. 277.

383   Confederate Brigadier General Thomas Taylor Munford (1831-1918) of Richmond, VA graduated from Virginia Military Institute in 1854. Prior to the war, Munford was a cotton planter in Mississippi and a farmer in Bedford County, VA. In May 1861, Munford mustered into the Confederate Army as a lieutenant colonel with the 30th Virginia. He participated in most major campaigns in the eastern theater. After the war, Munford worked as an iron manufacturer, writer, and cotton planter. He served as President of the Virginia Military Institute Board of Visitors from 1884 until 1888. Evans, Clement A., *Confederate Military History*, Volume III, (Atlanta, GA. 1899), 639–641.

Modern Civil War re-enactors often refer to Allen Christian Redwood's very detailed sketches for accuracy in their period attire. Redwood's Confederate troops under Cobb and Kershaw behind a stone wall on Marye's Heights, Fredericksburg, Virginia. LOC/P&P. LC-USZ62-134479.

to stand by Marse Bob to the last?' The light that flashed up in the old soldier's face from the fire of a noble spirit almost outshone that thrown out by the dying embers beneath, as he proudly straightened up and replied: 'Yes, sir, to the last.'"[384]

This was on the night preceding the battle of High Bridge, two days and a half before the one related by myself; the men had not received any rations in the meantime. We moved slowly over roads, along which were scattered broken down wagons and ambulances, dead and worn-out mules and horses, and the remains of whole wagon trains that had been fired by our people.

Just before sunset we had a slight brush with the enemy, but they seemed loath to press matters, and we were only too glad to be let alone. Soon we went into camp for the night, among some stunted oaks through which the road ran, and built our fires. I parched some corn and fell asleep while watching the thin, jaded, weary-looking lines of our infantry, as they silently trudged along.

About midnight, being chilled to the marrow by the damp air, we mounted our horses and moved into. . .

---

[384] Hundley, *Reminiscences SHSP, Vol XXIII*, 308.

Appomattox Court House

and shortly before daylight on April the 9th, 1865, we formed into line of battle, to the right of the line, near the Village Church. As the sun made its appearance in the east the Federals, who occupied the Lynchburg Road directly in our front, commenced to shell our position. In a short time infantry relieved us, when we moved directly north through a piece of timber, the enemy shelling us as we slowly ascended to the top of the hill. When on the other side the column headed west through an open field beyond; the enemy's guns, being within easy range, swept the plain with grape and canister as the men, in small squads, passed over on a run.

The division was reformed by the time we got over, attacking the Federal Cavalry, capturing two pieces of artillery and clearing the Lynchburg road of the enemy.

Two divisions of the enemy's infantry now made their appearance, causing us to withdraw, taking a position on the edge of a piece of timber, while the Federal Cavalry reformed in another piece just to the east, with an open field between the two lines, about a half a mile wide.[385]

Federal soldiers at Appomattox Court House, VA. Photo by Timothy H. O'Sullivan, Apr 1865. LOC/P&P.LC-DIG-cw-pb-03908.

---

385   In a final attempt to reach the supply depot at Lynchburg, VA, early on 9 Apr 1865, General Robert E. Lee ordered the remnants of Confederate Major General John B. Gordon's corps and Brigadier General Fitzhugh Lee's cavalry to form a line of battle at Appomattox Court House. At dawn the Confederates advanced and initially gained ground against Union General Sheridan's cavalry. Gordon's troops charged through the Union lines and took the ridge, but as they reached the crest they saw the entire Union XXIV Corps in line of battle with the Union V Corps to their right. Lee's army was surrounded on three sides.

When asked for his assessment of the battle by a member of General Lee's staff, Gordon replied, "Tell General Lee I have fought my corps to a frazzle, and I fear I can do nothing unless I am heavily supported by Longstreet's corps." Gordon's reply forced General Lee to the inevitable, "Then there is nothing left for me to do but to go and see General Grant, and I would rather die a thousand deaths." http://www.nps.gov/hps/abpp/battles/va097.htm, Longstreet, James, *From Manassas to Appomattox*, (J.B. Lippincott Company, Philadelphia, PA, 1903), 624.

Last Charge and the Last Man Killed in the Army of Northern Virginia

Hostilities now ceased for several hours. The sun was shining brightly, and being almost dead for want of rest, I threw myself from my horse, laid down on some dry leaves and was soon fast asleep. I do not know how long I slept, but upon awakening, some member of the command had hold of my arm, shaking the sluggishness from my tired body, as the Battalion was forming into a column of fours.[386]

I fell into line as the men moved out on the Lynchburg Road; then came the order by fours right about charge. As we moved towards the enemy in a trot, I looked to our rear and saw the division moving on our left within supporting distance, also in columns of fours.

From a trot to a run soon brought us within easy range of the enemy, the bullets from their Spencer's making that peculiar Zip! Zip! so familiar to an old veteran.[387] The next moment down went my file leader, Private Price, a member of Co. E, our horses almost treading on his prostrate form.[388]

---

[386] Stonebraker slept as General Lee surrendered the Army of Northern Virginia to General Grant at the Wilmer McLean home near Appomattox Court House. General Lee arrived shortly before one o'clock, followed thirty minutes later by General Grant. The meeting and surrender lasted approximately ninety minutes. National Park Service, Appomattox Court House: *http://www.nps.gov/apco/the-surrender.htm*.

[387] The Spencer repeating rifle was a manually operated, lever-action, repeating rifle fed from a tube magazine with cartridges. The Spencer carbine was a shorter and lighter version. The Spencer showed itself to be very reliable under combat conditions, with a sustainable rate-of-fire in excess of 20 rounds per minute. Compared to standard muzzle-loaders, with a rate of fire of 2-3 rounds per minute, this represented a significant tactical advantage. Confederates soldiers occasionally captured some of these weapons and ammunition, but were unable to manufacture the cartridges because of shortages of copper limiting their ability to take advantage of the weapons. In the late 1860s, the Spencer Company was sold to the Fogerty Rifle Company and ultimately to the Winchester Repeating Arms Company. Walter, John, *The Rifle Story: An Illustrated History from 1776 to the Present Day* (MBI Publishing, St. Paul, MN, 2006), 69-71. *https://en.wikipedia.org/wiki/Spencer_repeating_rifle*.

[388] Several states vied for the distinction to claim the honor of "last man killed" in the Army of Northern Virginia. Virginians claim that John William Ashby of the 12th Virginia Cavalry was the last man killed. North Carolinians contend that Sergeant Ivy Ritchie of the 14th North Carolina State Troops was the final Confederate killed. William W. Goldsborough, author of *The Maryland Line in the Confederate Army*, agrees with Stonebraker that William C. Price of Maryland was the last man killed. Confederate records indicate that in Nov 1862, 18 year old Price enlisted as a private in Company E, 1st Maryland Cavalry. By Jul 1863 he was promoted to corporal. Price was captured 27 May 1864 at Pollard's Farm near the engagement at Dabney's Ferry on the Pumunkey River, Hanover County, VA when his horse was killed. After surviving almost nine months in the prison at Point Lookout, MD, he was exchanged 13 Feb 1865 and would live another 53 days. Of the eighteen Confederate soldiers buried in the Confederate Cemetery at Appomattox, only eight are identified. Interestingly, J. W. Ashby of Virginia is identified by a tombstone, but not William C. Price of Maryland. *Compiled Service Records of Confederate Soldiers*, NARA M321, roll 0004, National Archives, (Washington DC) (hereafter cited as *CSRV*). *SHSP, Vol. XXXIV*, 218-220. Hardy, Michael C. *North*

Soon the battalion halted, the men began to waver and some started back, when Herman Heimiller of our Company shouted, "Come, boys, rally around our flag."[389]

The next instant I was by his side, when we with two others, whose names I do not remember, overtook John Ridgely, our color-bearer, who had pushed some distance ahead, stood waving our banner and calling to the men to follow him.[390]

As we reached his side the color-bearer of the Seventh Virginia Cavalry joined the group, when our little party drew the entire fire of several thousand of the enemy, who held an elevated position, enfilading our right flank. The noise from their bullets sounded like a swarm of bees, interspersed by the dull thud, as they hit the rails of the fence at our side. I remember, when a boy, in reading of Braddock's defeat, that the writer intimated that it took the weight of a man in lead for every soldier killed in battle.[391] I am almost compelled to endorse that writer's statement, extravagant as it may seem, as we all escaped unhurt, except a slight wound of Heimiller's horse.

The firing suddenly ceased, as an officer rode from their ranks towards us with a white handkerchief on the point of his sabre, with the information that Gen. Lee had surrendered several hours before, and wanted to know why we persisted in continuing the conflict. In clearing the Lynchburg Road of the enemy's cavalry in the morning we became separated from the main army, and this was the first information to reach us of the dire calamity, which ended the Southern Confederacy.[392] Heimiller burst

HERMAN HEIMILLER,
CO. C, MARYLAND BATTALION

German born Heimiller (1841-1930) immigrated to the US in 1854. After the war he served as a Baltimore City Police officer. Photo from original text.

Carolina in the Civil War, (Charleston, SC, 2011), 113. Goldsborough, William Worthington, *The Maryland Line in the Confederate Army, 1861-1865* (Baltimore, MD, 1900), 225. Marvel, William, *A Place called Appomattox,* (University of NC Press, 2000), Wright, Catherine M., *Lee's Last Casualty* (University of TN Press, 2008).

389   Confederate Private Herman Heimiller (1841-1930) of Company C, 1st Maryland Cavalry was born in Germany in Feb 1841 and immigrated with his family to the United States in 1854. He became a naturalized citizen in 1860. After the war he returned to Baltimore MD where he was employed as a city police officer. *US Federal Census, 1880, 1900, 1910, and 1920.*

390   Confederate records indicate there were two John Ridgelys in the 1st Maryland Cavalry, both were color-bearers. Private, later Sergeant John T. Ridgely (1842-1929) of Company A, was from a prominent family of Howard County, MD. After surrendering at Appomattox, VA he returned to the family plantation of *Bowling Green* near Sykesville, MD. He died in 1929. Private John Ridgely (1841-1911) of Company C to whom Stonebraker refers was from Baltimore, MD. He and Stonebraker did not surrender at Appomattox. After the war Ridgely returned to Baltimore where he lived for many years. By 1910, Ridgely had moved to Berrett, Carroll County, MD, where he died the following year. *Sykesville Herald* (Sykesville, MD) 12 Dec 1929. *CSRV,* microcopy M321, roll 0004 and 005, *US Federal Census, 1850, 1860, 1880, 1910, and 1920.*

391   In his 1883 works, *Society and Solitude,* Ralph Waldo Emerson wrote of "Marshal Saxe's rule, that every soldier killed costs the enemy his weight in lead," paraphrased from Comte Hermann Maurice de Saxe (1696-1750). The quote appeared in the *New York Commercial Advertiser* (New York, NY) 21 May 1861, in *"Poetry, Rumors and Incidents,"* and became a well-used adage during the Civil War. Emerson, Ralph Waldo, *Society and Solitude,* (Cambridge Riverside Press, 1883), 248.

392   It is questionable if this was the first word of a surrender to reach the 1st Maryland Cavalry. In March 1865, command of the General Lee's cavalry corps was assigned to his very capable nephew, Major General Fitzhugh Lee. At a council of war the evening of 8 Apr 1865, General Lee discussed battle strategy for the next day with his high command which included Fitzhugh Lee,

At the Confederate veterans Bazaar in Baltimore in April 1885, Stonebraker produced a journal he had kept during the war. This entry from his journal was published in the Sun Newspaper, *(Baltimore, MD) 15 Apr 1885.*
The location of the original journal is unknown.

Saturday, April 8, 1865 – We have been retreating slowly in the direction of Lynchburg. Broken-down wagons and ambulances, worn-out horses and mules are being left along the road. Both men and animals are fast wearing out. I am almost dead for want of rest and food. Our army is sadly dwindling away, and what is left is in a pitiful condition. We have a great many prisoners, who are nearly starved, but their condition is no worse than ours. When they were passing our command one poor fellow asked me for a ear of corn I was feeding to my horse.
Have been retreating all day. I am completely broken down! Will the sun never set? No Federals come up to us until near sunset.
Went into camp shortly after dark, with order not to unsaddle our horses. Was soon asleep, but the refreshing slumber was of short duration, as we soon had orders to mount and take up our line of march. About midnight we halted at Appomattox Court House.

Sunday, April 9, 1865 – We were aroused at sunrise by the bursting of shells which were thrown into town by the Federals. We formed in line of battle on the western side of the town, and soon discovered that the enemy had possession of the road between us and Lynchburg. We held our position until relieved by infantry, when we cut our way out by the right flank doing some hard fighting. We were compelled to pass over an open field within easy range of the enemy's artillery, exposed all the while to a terrific fire from their guns. We crossed this field in squads of fifty men at a time, in full run, until we reached a road near by, where we again formed in line of battle and drove the Federal troops back and took possession of the Lynchburg road. Hostilities now ceased for several hours, we remaining in one piece of woods and the Northern troops in another, with an open field of half a mile width between us.
We were ordered to charge the enemy who were seen coming out of the woods toward us, and as we did so were met with a volley of musket balls, which whistled through the air, making a noise like a swarm of bees. Our color-bearer – John Ridgley, I think it was – and the color-bearer of the Second Virginia Regiment, and besides myself three others who names I have forgotten, refused to fall back and held our ground for some time, but being closely pressed, the flag was torn from its staff, and we made our escape with it. Shortly afterward the Federals send in a flag of truce announcing Gen. Lee's surrender. During this engagement we became separated from the main army and did not know what had taken place, but soon afterward Gen. Fitz Lee received a communication from Gen. R. E. Lee informing us that he had surrendered. Gen Fitz Lee turned his cavalry over the Gen. Munford, who ordered us to fall back and halt until the officers of the command held a consultation. Soon afterward we were informed by our officers the end had come."

from the journal of Joseph R. Stonebraker

LAST CHARGE — MARYLAND BATTALION AT APPOMATTOX

out crying as we slowly rode back, passing four men having our unfortunate comrade in a blanket, carrying him to the rear. The poor fellow was dead, having been shot in the thigh, the bullet penetrating the femoral artery.

I felt dreadfully sorry that he had been killed after the conflict was over, but mused that it might be some consolation to his family to know that though he was dead, he died in the last charge made by the Army of Northern Virginia.

While the officers held a consultation, the men stood around in groups hardly knowing what to think, being almost paralyzed at the disaster that had overtaken General Lee's Army. Many sun-burned faces were wet with tears. Who can wonder, for the sun was just setting and down with it went the hopes of the Southern people.[393]

The Last Charge (1899) by Allen Christian Redwood was commissioned by Stonebraker for publication in this book. The mustached private leading the charge in the foreground bears a striking resemblance to the painting of Stonebraker in his Confederate uniform (see insert). In 1901 Stonebraker's sons would publish a calender featuring this work, suggesting they were in possession of the original work.

---

and informed them of his correspondence with General Grant for terms of surrender. Fitzhugh Lee would have related this information to his subordinate generals and the information of a potential surrender likely filtered through the cavalry ranks. Marvel, William, *Lee's Last Retreat, The Flight to Appomattox* (University of NC Press, 2002), 152. *Paroles of the Army of Northern Virginia, SHSP, Vol. XV,* Introduction VIII.

393 There are numerous glorified accounts of the Confederate Cavalry's defiant departure from Appomattox to Lynchburg at the time of surrender, and their decision to continue the fight. However, General Fitzhugh Lee's 22 Apr 1865 official report to General Robert E. Lee leaves very little doubt that the positioning of the cavalry along the Lynchburg Road at the extreme west at Appomattox had been contrived by General Lee and his commanders the evening of 8 Apr 1865 at the council of war. Should General Lee be forced to surrender his army the following day, the cavalry commanders had the option of surrender or flight, with the optimistic hope they would be of further service to

161

JOHN RIDGELY, COLOR BEARER OF THE MD BATTALION, C.S.A

John Ridgely (1841-1911), Company C, 1st Maryland Cavalry, CSA. Photo from original text.

We reached Lynchburg in the early part of the evening where we found great confusion, and the Government warehouses, surrounded by crowds of men, women and children, both white and black, clamoring for the supplies which they contained. Upon reaching the Fair ground we went into camp until midnight, when we crossed to the north side of the James over the bridge.[394]

When about half over I unbuckled my sabre from the saddle and threw it into the river. The next morning at daylight we were formed into line, when Colonel Dorsey informed us that it had been determined at yesterday's conference to disband the Cavalry for a short time.[395] Acting upon that agreement we were now free to go where we pleased until April the 25th, when he would expect every man to meet him at the Cattle Scales in Augusta County, Va.[396]

We broke ranks, when Ridgely stripped our beloved Flag from its staff and put it in his haversack,[397] the men

the Confederacy by joining with General Joseph Johnson's army in North Carolina. Additionally, General Fitzhugh Lee was convinced that if the army surrendered, the cavalry would be forced to surrender their horses – horses that each man personally owned. "It will be recalled that my action was in accordance with the views I had expressed in the council the night before – that if a surrender was compelled the next day, I would try to extricate the cavalry, provided it could be done without compromising the action of the commanding general . . ." After receiving word of the surrender "Fitz Lee and his cavalry rode unmolested on the Lynchburg road." Official report of General Fitzhugh Lee to General Robert E. Lee, 22 Apr 1865, Evan, General Clement A., Editor, *Confederate Military History,* Volume III, (Confederate Publishing Company, Atlanta, GA, 1899), 555-556. Jones, Thomas Goode, *The Last Days of the Army of Northern Virginia; an address delivered before the Virginia Division of the Virginia Division of the Association of the Army of Northern Virginia at the annual meeting,* 12 Oct 1893 (Richmond, VA), 27, 29.

394 Located on a triangular-shaped plot of land on the southwest side of town, the Lynchburg fairgrounds served numerous roles during the war. First as an assembly point for organizing Confederate units, a prison, a hospital, and a supply depot. In 1938, side-by-side football and baseball stadiums were constructed on grounds. Today, the site is the Lynchburg City Stadium grounds. General Munford's rebel cavalry arrived at Lynchburg the evening of 9 Apr 1865 where "large supplies had been gathered at this point." Goldsborough, William Worthington, *The Maryland Line in the Confederate Army, 1861-1865* (Baltimore, MD, 1900), 225-226.

395 On the morning of 10 Apr 1865, north of Lynchburg, the General Munford disbanded his renegade cavalrymen for 15 days. Munford and his officers needed time to determine if they could march the cavalry south and join General Joe Johnston still fighting in North Carolina. While disbanded, but not having surrendered, the men would have to fend and forage for themselves as the supplies in Lynchburg would be quickly exhausted. This arrangement was convenient for the cavalrymen of the 2nd Virginia who, almost without exception, lived in the area. However, the men of the 1st Maryland Cavalry were forced to forage from an exhausted, war ravaged countryside. Additionally, it seems incongruous that Colonel Dorsey ordered the weary soldiers of the 1st Maryland Cavalry to forage over 60 miles north from Lynchburg to Waynesboro if the later objective was to travel south into North Carolina. Confederate Lieutenant-Colonel Gustavus Warfield Dorsey (1839-1911) previously noted footnote 310.

396 Often noted as the "breadbasket to the Confederacy," Augusta County and the surrounding counties in the Shenandoah Valley remain today ideal grazing grounds for cattle. Prior to the Union Army's 1864-65 destruction of valley resources, there were numerous cattle scales, most near the important Virginia Central Railroad. Farmer's cattle were weighed, then shipped by rail to the coastal cities. By spring 1865 the cattle scales and the railroad tracks at Waynesboro, VA had been destroyed. The remaining cattle scale was about 5 miles north of town along a county road today known as "Cattle Scales Road."

397 **Author's footnote 4—Ridgely carried the flag to Redlands, Albemarle County, and kept it in his possession until the Battalion assembled at the Cattle Scales. When the command was disbanded at Cloverdale, by vote of the officers and men, the flag was turned over to**

A Rebel of '61

scattering in every direction. A few of us rode to Amherst Court House where we got dinner, after which Ridgely and I proceeded north on the Charlottesville Road through a drizzling rain, encamping along the road just where night overtook us.[398]

The next morning we silently folded our small fly-tent, mounted our horses, when an old gentleman came along and kindly took us to his home and gave us breakfast.

We continued on our way in a thankful mood, arriving at Nelson Court House, where we found the place full of excited soldiers and citizens discussing the surrender and circulating all kinds of reports.[399] Here Ridgely and I parted, he going towards Charlottesville while I headed for Augusta County without any fixed destination.[400]

Being now alone with my thoughts, not knowing where to go or what to do with myself in the next fortnight, I began to realize that I was without friends and among strangers, who were sadly impoverished by four years of war. The more I thought the greater I was perplexed, when an unutterable feeling of loneliness entered my soul, producing the blackness of despair. The Blue Ridge laid in my path; soon I was among its hills and lost in its winding roads, with no habitation in sight, being entirely indifferent as to where they led, as all places would be the same when night overtook me.

Redlands, *Albemarle County, VA, was built by Robert Carter about 1789, completed about 1809. During the war Margaret Smith Carter, formerly of Maryland, having five brothers in the Confederacy, made* Redlands *a sanctuary for Maryland Confederates. Redlands had the honorary title of "Camp Maryland." LOC/P&P. LC-DIG-csas-04256.*

Colonel Dorsey. He gave it to a young lady in Nelson County, who subsequently married Judge Horsely of Nelson, and years ago she returned it to me and now it is at Soldier's Home, Pikesville, Baltimore County, Maryland. — General Bradley T. Johnson.

Redlands in Albemarle County, VA is a Federal mansion built by Robert Carter in 1789, completed in 1809. During the Civil War it was owned by Robert Hill Carter and his wife Margaret Smith Carter, formerly of Baltimore, MD. Margaret Smith Carter was the daughter of John Spears Smith (1804-1867), and granddaughter of General Samuel Smith (1752-1839), major general of militia in the defense of Baltimore during the War of 1812. Five of Margaret's brothers served in the Confederacy, giving her strong sympathies to Maryland Confederate soldiers. During the war a great many Confederate Marylanders found their way to *Redlands,* either voluntarily or because they were wounded, giving *Redlands* the honorary title of "Camp Maryland." Today *Redlands* continues to be the residence of the Carter family and is said to be haunted by the ghost of a Confederate soldier. Carter II, B. Noland, *A Goodly Heritage, A History of the Carter Family in Virginia* (Virginia Genealogical Society, Richmond, VA, 2003). *Historic American Buildings Survey* (HABS) National Park Service, Washington, DC. *http://lcweb2.loc.gov/pnp/habshaer/va/va1400/va1463/data/va1463data.pdf.*

See footnote 390 for information on the two John Ridgely's of the 1st Maryland Cavalry. John T. Ridgely of Company A surrendered at Appomattox 10 Apr 1865. John Ridgely, color-bearer Company C, accompanied Stonebraker to Waynesboro. VA. He surrendered 7 May 1865 at Harrisonburg, VA.

The "young lady in Nelson County," guardian of the 1st Maryland Cavalry flag for many years, was Miss Florence Massie (1848-abt 1910). She married first John L. Tunstall of Nelson County, VA. After his death, she married Judge John Dunscombe Horsley (1848-1909) of Lynchburg, VA. Judge Horsely attended Virginia Military Institute for the greater part of the war, enlisting in the Confederacy in 1865. He attended the University of Virginia, later practicing law in Nelson County. He was elected in 1886 as Judge of the 5th Circuit Court. Mrs. Florence Massie Tunstall Horsley was active in the Society of Colonial Dames, Daughter of the American Revolution, and served as historian for the Lynchburg, VA chapter of the United Daughters of the Confederacy.

398   Amherst, VA is approximately 15 miles north of Lynchburg, VA.
399   Nelson Court House is Lovingston, VA, about 17 miles northeast of Amherst, VA.
400   Stonebraker and Ridgely parted company near present day Woods Mill, Nelson County, VA at the intersection of US 29 and SR 6.

A Narrow Escape

A young Mulatto came down the Mountain side and was very talkative as he jogged along at my horse's side. His conversation showed that he was familiar with the events of the past few days and was anxious to know if I thought the "Yankees" would soon be in the neighborhood. Although he tried to conceal his joy, I saw he was elated—and justly so. He greatly admired my Carbine, as it hung by my side, finally asking that I let him see if it was very heavy, and without thinking, I unslung the gun and handed it to him.

It was a breech-loader.[401] As he tried to adjust a shell in the barrel, I in a moment divined his motive and forcibly took the gun from him, clearly convinced that to his ignorance alone in the use of firearms I am now living and able to relate this incident.

I was now in Timber Ridge, a spur of the Blue Ridge Mountain. By the invitation of a little boy whom I met, I went with him to this home, where I remained all night. His mother was a widow, her husband having died in the army. Three children and a niece comprised the family. She owned fifteen acres of land in Deep Gully, through which ran a small stream called Hickory Creek.[402] The house was a one-story log cabin, with a door and three windows; the whole ground floor was in one room, with a large fire-place at the west end, where the cooking for the family was done, which also furnished heat in the winter. At the other end was an open pair of steps which led to the attic, which was divided into two rooms, where the family slept. The next morning the Madam said: "You want a place to stay, and I need a horse to plow my corn patch." I accepted her proposition and the boys hitched "Bill" to a single shovel plow and commenced to scratch the ground.

---

401 Cavalry in both the Union and the Confederate Armies employed a variety of breech-loading, single-shot, rifle-barreled weapons known as carbines. The carbines, because their barrels were several inches shorter than the rifle-muskets the infantry carried, also had a shorter range. In addition, the cavalry weapons had a brutal recoil when fired, and—despite their advantages in loading—most still required the cavalry soldier to manipulate a tiny cap in order to fire. Confederate cavalry often brought sawed-off shotguns and cut-down hunting rifles from home. Others used the standard infantry rifle-muskets, though the longer barrels were awkward and muzzle-loading was difficult on horseback. The favorite firearm of the Confederate cavalry was the "Maynard" rifle, a lightweight breech loading carbine patented by Dr. Edward Maynard in 1856. The Maynard factory in Chicopee, MA was shipping the weapons south to southern "sportsman" as late as four months after the start of the war. One Confederate cavalryman stated that the weapon was "warrented to shoot twelve times a minute, and carry a ball effectley to 1,600 yards. . . Nothing to do with the Maynard rifle but load her up, turn North and pull the trigger." Small Arms of the Civil War, http://www.civilwar.org/education/history/warfare-and-logistics/warfare/smallarms.html?referrer. Niepert, Robert, *Carbines, Revolving Rifles and Repeating Rifles*, http://www.floridareenactorsonline.com/carbinesetc.htm.

402 Hickory Creek in Nelson County, VA is a long, meandering tributary that flows south along Hickory Creek road, then crosses under US 29, roughly following Irish Road (SR 6) toward the town of Farber, VA where it merges into Cove Creek. This stream flows between Rock Springs, Diggs, Archer, and Boaz Mountains, creating numerous "deep gullies" as described by Stonebraker. The 1866 *Map of Nelson County, Virginia* prepared by Hotchkiss & Robinson show only a few families living in the region in 1866; Roberts, Hare, Moore, Newton, Watson, Harris, and Heiskell. Of those families, only the widow Harris is listed on the 2002 *Nelson County Confederate Pension Rolls, Veterans and Widows* as prepared by Joan Ackerman Renfrow, http://files.usgwarchives.net/va/nelson/military/civilwar/pensions/roles.txt.

"Bill" was a short coupled, bright bay, about 900 pounds, with a fine disposition. His face was very wide between the eyes, denoting much horse sense. He hated the Zip of a bullet and the screech of a shell almost as much as I did. He had learned to be very watchful, and when passing through the woods alone he kept his head moving from side to side, as though he expected a surprise, and would startle whenever a bird flew across his path.

For months he had been part of myself, and it almost broke my heart to see him in the plow. At first he protested by balking and refusing to pull, but "Mr. Man" was too much for him, and his good sense told him the easiest way was the best, and in due time his task was done.

I remained at my new home about twelve days, and although the widow was very poor, she was a refined and big-hearted lady and gave the best she had—corn bread, butter and sorghum.

From a gentleman in the neighborhood I had the loan of Fielding's and Goldsmith's works,[403] which helped me to pass the time. On April the 23d information reached us of the assassination of President Lincoln and the assault on Mr. Seward, which no one believed.[404]

The next morning I bade good bye to my new friends, leaving Miss Fannie in tears. When well on the road I met Lieut. Ditty and Private Johnson, both of my command.[405] Together we crossed the Blue Ridge at Rockfish Gap, and upon reaching Waynesboro I left them and proceeded five miles further to our appointed . . .[406]

---

403   Henry Fielding (1707-1749) was an 18th century novelist and dramatist. He is most noted for his 1749 work of *Tom Jones*. Novelist and playwright Oliver Goldsmith (1730-1774) is best known for his work *The Vicar of Wakefield*, 1766.

404   President Lincoln was assassinated in Ford's Theater in Washington, DC on 14 Apr 1865 by John Wilkes Booth of Harford County, MD. Co-conspirator Lewis Powell attacked Secretary of State William Henry Seward as he lay in bed severely injured after being thrown from his carriage. *New York Times* [NY], *Terrible Tragedy in Washington: Murder of the President, Attempted Murder of Mr. Seward,* 17 Apr 1865, 2.

After the assassination of President Lincoln in Washington, DC by John Wilkes Booth of Harford County, MD, Maryland Confederates became extremely cautious about returning to their home state. Attorney General James Speed initially held a moderate view of how the government should deal with the secessionists, but the assassination of the President by a Marylander caused him to develop a less forgiving stance. After the assassination, Speed maintained that "the rebel officers who surrendered to General Grant have no homes within the loyal states and have no right to come to places which were their homes prior to going into rebellion." Several Maryland counties followed suit. The "loyal men" of Havre de Grace in Harford County voted that Confederates "shall never be permitted to reside within its limits – *whether paroled or not.*" *National American* (Bel Air, MD) 28 Apr 1865.

405   1st Lieutenant Cyrus Irving Ditty (1839-1887), see footnote 302.

Assuming Private Johnson was traveling with an officer of his company, there were four Private Johnsons in Company F: Henry B. Johnson, George Johnson, and two John Johnsons. Driver, *1st & 2nd MD Cavalry,* 246.

406   Rockfish Gap is a wind gap in the Blue Ridge Mountains at Afton, VA, a few miles west of Waynesboro, VA.

Rendezvous,

Where I found a number of our Boys had already assembled. By 10 o'clock the next morning nearly every member of the command was present, when Colonel Dorsey formed us in line and said:

> "General Munford has ordered me to meet him at Salem, Roanoke County, with my Battalion. From there we expect to proceed south and join General Jos. E. Johnston's Army. I want every man to feel that he is at liberty to do as he pleases. Those who are willing to accompany me will ride to the right and form into line."[407]

Ridgely, in the meantime, had fastened our banner to a crude staff, under which every Marylander present rallied, and with Col. Dorsey at the head of the little band we moved forward, passing through Waynesboro, encamping for the night five miles south of the town.

At sunrise the march was resumed, reaching the Valley Pike at Midway, and proceeded southward for three days and a half, passing through Staunton, Lexington and over the Natural Bridge.[408]

We crossed the James River at Buchanan, reaching Cloverdale at noon on April the 29th, 1865. Spring was well advanced, covering the fields with a new crop of grass, upon which our horses fed, but the men had to rely on the generosity of the citizens for subsistence, which proved scant indeed.[409]

Being now near General Munford's home we went into camp, while Colonel Dorsey rode to the General's house, finding him confined to his room by sickness, returning with the following address, which was read to the men by Lieut. Ditty:[410]

---

[407] Salem, VA is an independent city that borders the western side of Roanoke, VA. General Johnston's army was at Greensboro, NC, approximately 100 miles south of Salem. The 1st Maryland Cavalry assembled near Waynesboro, VA the morning of 25 Apr 1865. One day later, General Johnston surrendered the Army of Tennessee, and all remaining Confederate forces still active in North Carolina, South Carolina, Georgia, and Florida, to Union General William T. Sherman at Bennett Place, Durham, NC. Durham was a central location between the two armies respective headquarters of Raleigh and Greensboro, NC. It was the largest surrender of the war, totaling 89,270 soldiers.

[408] The 1st Maryland Cavalry left camp 5 miles south of Staunton, VA the morning of 26 Apr 1865 and traveled almost 90 miles from Waynesboro to Cloverdale, VA in three and a half days.

[409] At Cloverdale, VA the 1st Maryland Cavalry was officially notified by General Munford that their short-lived rally was over: "I have just learned from Captain Emack that your gallant band was moving up the valley in response to my call. I am deeply pained to say that our army cannot be reached, as I have learned it has capitulated" General Thomas Munford to Lieutenant-Colonel Dorsey, 28 Apr 1865. Goldsborough, William Worthington, *The Maryland Line in the Confederate Army, 1861-1865*, (Guggenheimer, Weil & Co., Baltimore, MD), 226.

[410] Cloverdale was located at Tinker's Mill Road near VA 220, or the Roanoke Road, south of Dalesville, VA, about 14 miles north of the company's final destination of Salem, VA. Cloverdale was named for a 3,500-acre 18th century land grant of the same name inherited by Revolutionary War General James Breckinridge (1763-1833). In 1865, the Henry Scarbrooke Langhorne (1790-1854) family owned the land around the village and the Cloverdale grist mill on the Tinker River. The Langhorne wealth came from ownership of the second largest milling firm in Virginia at Lynchburg. The Cloverdale Grist Mill operated continuously for over 100 years, until destroyed by fire in 1968. Nothing re-

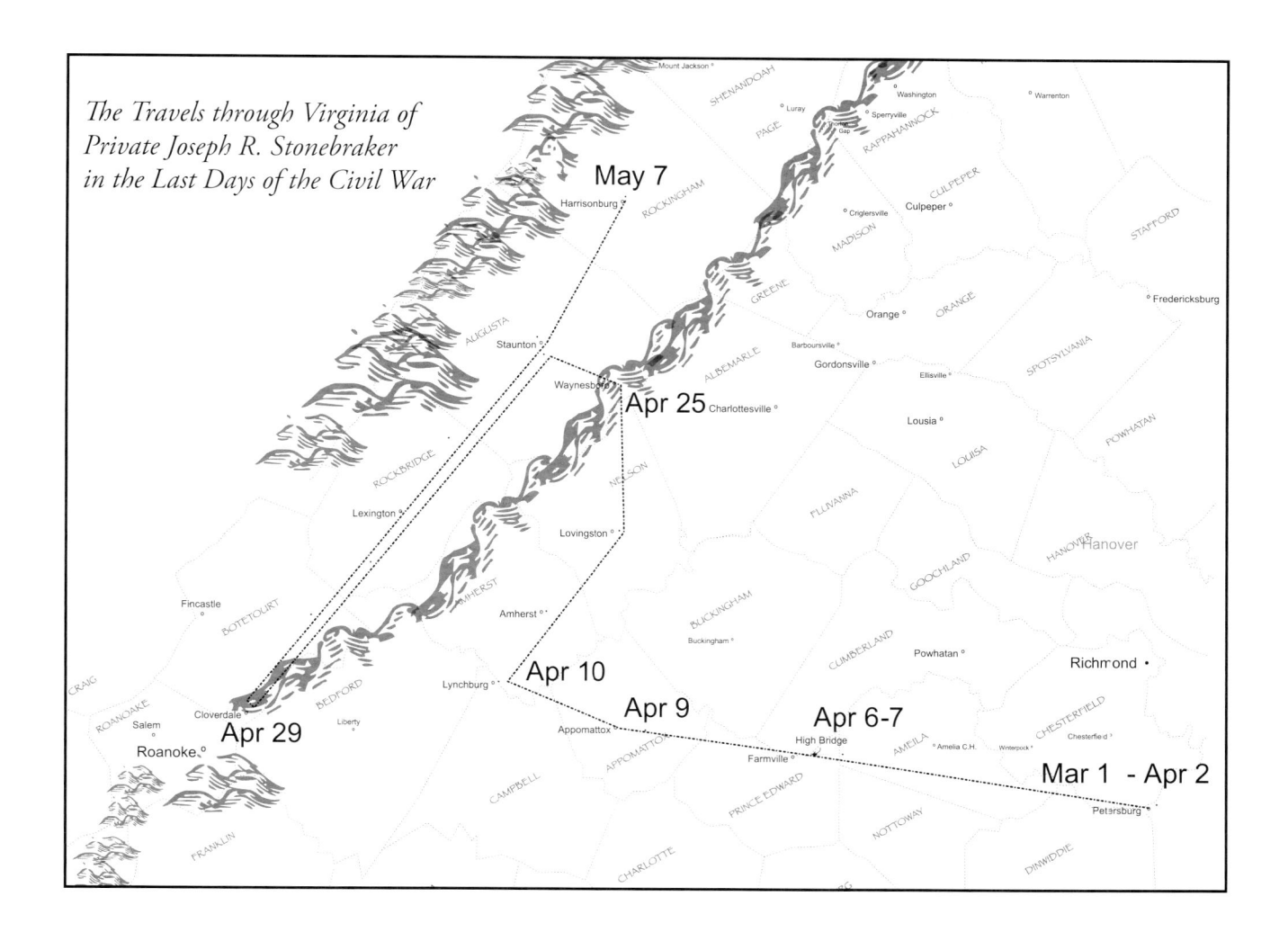

The Travels through Virginia of Private Joseph R. Stonebraker in the Last Days of the Civil War

When the news of General R. E. Lee's surrender reached General Thomas Munford's cavalry, most of the cavalry still mounted did not surrender, but fled to Lynchburg, VA. After resupplying the next morning at Lynchburg, the cavalry was disbanded for 15 days with orders to rendezvous at Waynesboro, VA on April 25, 1865. Why the commanders of the 1st Maryland Cavalry ordered the troops to reassemble 69 miles north when the intent was to travel further south into North Carolina remains a mystery. At Waynesboro the troops were ordered to back down the Shenandoah Valley 90 miles south to Cloverdale, VA. From Cloverdale the troops would have had to trek another 145 miles south to join General Joe Johnston's army in North Carolina. One day after arriving at Cloverdale the troops received word that General Johnston had surrendered at Durham Place, NC.

After releasing the troops at Cloverdale, VA, Joseph Stonebraker, Alexander Norris, Jr., Thomas Grove, and Thomas Shervin traveled north over 100 miles to Harrisonburg, VA where Stonebraker, Norris, and Grove officially surrendered on 7 May 1865.

---

mains today of the Cloverdale district in Botetourt County.

    Stonebraker is mistaken; General Munford did not own a home at Cloverdale. However, General Munford's first wife, Elizabeth Henrietta Tayloe (1833-1864), was the daughter of Mary Elizabeth *Langhorne* Tayloe (1811-1848), the niece of Henry Scarbrooke Langhorne of Cloverdale. General Munford was recuperating at his wife's relatives's home, one of the two Langhorne homes near the Cloverdale Mill. After the war General Munford again married into the Tayloe family when he married Emma Tayloe, the first cousin of his first wife. Tayloe, W. Randolph Breckinridge, *The Tayloes of Virginia and Allied Families*, (Berryville, VA, 1963). Gilmer, Lucy, *Lucy Breckinridge of Grove Hill: The Journal of a Virginia Girl, 1862-1864*, (University of South Carolina Press, 1994). Dorsey, Frank, *Last Days of the First Maryland Cavalry*, Confederate Veteran XXVII (Nashville TN, 1919), 255. Grose, S., *Botetourt County, Virginia Heritage 1770-2000*, (Walsworth Publishing Co., Marceline, MO), 19.

"To the Gallant Band who Claim this Song"

"Soldiers!
I hear the distant thunder hum,
    Maryland, my Maryland
The old line bugle, fife and drum,
    Maryland, my Maryland
She is not dead, nor deaf nor dumb,
Huzza, she spurns the Northern scum,
She breathes, she burns, she'll come, she'll come,
    Maryland, my Maryland.[411]

"You, my veteran friends, who have weathered the storm, may now sing your song with proud hearts. It once could be heard on every lip, but after the Maryland campaign it was discarded, and your gallant little band caught up another air:

"Light hearts we bore to Virginia's land,
The shadows fall o'er us, fast my boys,
We'll drain our cup with a steady hand,
We'll smile what e'er will be our fate, my boys,
Many of us may sleep, beneath Virginia's sod,
Many may go back to our homes, boys,
But the hearts that are true to their Country and God
Will report at the grand reveille, boys.[412]

---

[411] While in Louisiana, English Professor James Ryder Randall was inspired to write "Maryland, My Maryland" after reading of the deadly clash between the Massachusetts troops and the citizens of his native city of Baltimore on 19 Apr 1861. The poem was embraced by pro-Confederate Baltimore and set to the music of an old German Christmas carol "Tannenbaum, O Tannenbaum." Often called "the Marseillaise of the Confederate Cause," the poem refers to President Lincoln as a "despot" and "tyrant," and the last stanza urges Marylanders to "spurn the Northern scum." Adopted as the official Maryland State Song in 1939, numerous unsuccessful attempts have been made by the General Assembly to delete or change the uncomplimentary passages about Lincoln and the citizens of the north. Ravitch, Diane, *The American Reader: Words that Moved a Nation* (HarperCollins Publishers, NY), 252-253.

[412] This poem is a modified version of the poem *"Lines written by an American Officer During the Mexican Campaign."* The entire poem was published in the *Virginia Spectator, Virginia University Magazine,* (Charlottesville, VA, Oct 1875), 85.
    Light hearts we bring to a stranger land,
        Tho' shadow fall o'er them late, my boys,
    We'll drain out cups with a steady hand,
        We'll smile whate'er be our fate, my boys.
    We will some of us sleep 'neath the stranger sod.
        We will some go back o'er the sea, my boys,
    But the hearts that are true to their Country and God,
        Will report at the grand reveille, my boys.

"This had been the spirit of the Maryland Battalion. Three years ago the chivalrous Brown joined my old command with twenty-three men.[413] Yes! twenty-three Maryland volunteers, with light hearts and full of fight. If they had a care, a trouble, or a wish, it was to whip the Yankees. They increased so rapidly that the Captain reminded me of the old woman who lived in her shoe, she had so many children she didn't know what to do, and all she wanted was elbow room.

"As they grew in numbers their reputation and friends increased. They were soon too numerous to remain with me and able to take care of themselves. It was here I learned to admire, to respect and love them for all the qualities which endeared soldiers to their officers. I tell you now, when I see you standing high above all other soldiers and alone, that my heart swells with pride to think that your course, so bright and glorious, was linked in a small degree with my old regiment. Would that I could see the mothers and sisters of every man in this proud old command and tell them how well you have represented your State and our cause.

"But the people of Virginia will not forget you. The fame you have won in after years will be guarded by old Virginia with the pride she feels in her own true sons. You have fought the good fight, and the few remaining members of this old command and of Co."K" might well say:[414]

"When I remember all
The friends so linked together,
I've seen around me fall,
Like leaves in wintry weather,
I feel like one that treads alone,
Some banquet hall deserted,
Whose lights are fled, and garland dead,
And all but me departed.[415]

Confederate Brigadier General Thomas Taylor Munford (1831-19!8). Claiming ill health, Munford wrote, but did personally deliver his farewell speech to the 1st Maryland Cavalry. The speech was read by 1st Lieutenant C. Irving Ditty of Company F.

---

413   The 1st Maryland Cavalry was organized in Nov 1862, with four companies under the command of Major Ridgely Brown (1833-1864). Subsequently they were joined by three other companies. Hollyday, Lamar, *Maryland Troops in the Confederate Service, SHSP, Vol. III*, 130.
414   Before 1861, two cavalry companies formed as the Howard County Dragoons. Both companies were "handsomely uniformed according to United States army regulations, well mounted, and furnished . . with the best cavalry sabres and Colt's revolvers." In Apr 1861 after the Maryland Assembly voted against secession, a significant number of the dragoons enlisted in Company K, 1st Virginia Cavalry. At the end of their one-year enlistment, the Marylanders believed Maryland should have its own cavalry resulting in the formation of the nucleus of Company A, 1st Maryland Cavalry. Hayden, Rev. Horace Edwin, *The First Maryland Cavalry, C.S.A, SHSP, Vol. V*, 251. Driver, *1st & 2nd MD Cavalry*, 6-7.
415   A stanza from the Irish poet Thomas Moore's (1779-1852) *"The Light of Other Days."*

> Cloverdale Botetourt Co Va
> April 29th 1865
> The bearer Private J. R. Stonebreaker
> Co "C" 1st Md Cav having done his duty
> faithfully to the present time is permit-
> ted to go where he pleases until called for
> G Dorsey
> Lt. Col. Comdg 1st Md Cav.

This pass issued to the members of the 1st Maryland Cavalry by Lt. Colonel Gustavus W. Dorsey is an unusual document. It was issued three days after the surrender of General Joe Johnston in North Carolina, yet the wording "until called for" implies the unit was not yet convinced they should surrender. Stonebraker would have these words etched onto his tombstone that stands today in the Loudon Cemetery, Baltimore, MD.

"But it was enough for them to remember:

"The Despot's heel, is on thy shore,
　Maryland, my Maryland,
His touch is at thy temple door,
　Maryland, my Maryland.[416]

"When they fell it was sweet to know they were striking for loved ones at home, and I trust they have gone to a brighter and happier one. It becomes us now to separate, but the ties which so long have bound us together will not be forgotten forever. They will live in memory and in after years will revive amidst our joys and dangers, and whenever we meet we may say this is my old and familiar friend.

"The cause is not dead. I feel sure the great battle is yet to be fought. I have ordered the old brigade to remain at home and be ready, and whenever and wherever we are called I know the gallant Colonel Dorsey and his braves will rally again, and though Virginia and Maryland are now overpowered, we will yet join hands and fling our glorious battle flags to the breeze as the emblems of their majesty and strength.

"In conclusion, let me urge upon you to remain quiet and keep your armor burnished. *You who struck the first blow in Baltimore and the last in Virginia* have done all that could be asked of you.[417]

"Had the rest of our officers and men adhered to our cause with the same devotion, to-day we would have been free from the Yankees. May the God of battles bless you. With many thanks for your generous support and a hearty God bless you, I bid you farewell.

"THOMAS T. MUNFORD,
"Brigadier-General Commanding Division.
"Cloverdale, Botetourt County, Va.,
"April the 29th, 1865."

416　The opening lines of James Ryder Randall's "Maryland, My Maryland" previously noted, footnote 411.

417　General Munford is referring to the 19 Apr 1861 clash between the 6th Massachusetts Militia and the pro-Confederate citizens of Baltimore. The Howard County Dragoons led by Captain George Ridgely Gaither rode into Baltimore to help quell the riots. Driver, *1st & 2nd MD Cavalry*, 7.

A Rebel of '61

Discharge

The Colonel now took each man by the hand, bidding them an affectionate farewell. Hager, Shervin, and I concluded to keep together and headed for Maryland.[418]

When near Fincastle, a gentleman whom we met invited us to accompany him to his home. A shower overtook us, and by the time we reached his home we were thoroughly drenched. Our condition excited his wife's pity, who was exceedingly gracious in her manner, making us feel at home.

He was a large land owner, and as there was a report in circulation that Marylanders would not be allowed to return to their homes he offered to employ several of us about his place until we could ascertain how matters stood. We had faced danger too often to be frightened by rumor, and declined his offer with thanks.[419]

The next morning I gave him my carbine, when we mounted our horses and rode slowly down the pike, halting at the Natural Bridge, viewing that most wonderful freak of nature.

Tradition has it that George Washington, the father of Rebels, in his youth had visited and cut his name high up on the side of the arch. While examining the hundreds of names the thought flashed through my mind, perhaps his feet had rested on the same spot upon which I stood.[420]

JOHN H. HAGER, CO. C, MARYLAND BATTALION

Confederate Corporal Jonathan "Jack" Henry Hager, (1842-1908) was born in Hagerstown, MD and was a descendant of Hagerstown's founder Jonathan Hager. About 1880, Hager moved to Iowa, then Colorado, and later the Dakota Territory where he owned a horse ranch. After an injury, Hager retired to live with his brother in St. Louis, MO, where he died in 1908. Photo from original text.

---

418   Corporal Jonathan Henry Hager (1842-1908) was the son of Hagerstown merchant William H. Hager, a descendant of Hagerstown's founder Jonathan Hager. Hager enlisted 18 Jun 1863, and was promoted to corporal 1 Jun 1864. After the war he returned to Hagerstown where he resumed operations of his father's grist mill on the Antietam Creek. About 1880, he moved to Greene County, IA where he remained until 1898, then moving to Colorado, and later to the Dakota Territory, where he owned a horse ranch. Hager later retired to St. Louis, MO where he died. *CSRV*, microcopy M321, roll 0003. *The Hagerstown Mail,* 14 Aug 1908. *US Federal Census 1880, 1900.*

        Private Thomas Shervin (1837-1920) was the son of Irish immigrant Thomas and Isabella Shervin near Tilghmanton in Washington County, MD. Shervin was one of the original "Company K" Maryland soldiers who enlisted in the 1st Virginia Cavalry. Early in 1864 he transferred to Company K, 1st Maryland Cavalry. After the war he returned to farming in Washington County, MD. By 1870, Shervin was farming in Greene County, IA. In 1880 and 1890 respectively, Shervin is listed as a miner in Lake County, CO, and Carbon County, WY. After 1910 until his death in 1920, Shervin served as county judge for Rio Blanco County, CO. *CSRV*, microcopy M321, roll 0005 and microcopy M324, roll 12. *US Federal Census 1850, 1870-1920. The Herald and Torch Light,* 20 Jun 1866.

419   Fincastle is the county seat of Botetourt County, VA about 8 miles north of Cloverdale. After the assassination of President Lincoln in Washington, DC by John Wilkes Booth of Harford County, MD, Maryland Confederates became extremely cautious about returning to their home state. Attorney General James Speed initially held a moderate view of how the government should deal with the secessionists, but the assassination of the President by a Marylander caused him to develop a less forgiving stance. After the assassination, Speed maintained that "the rebel officers who surrendered to General Grant have no homes within the loyal states and have no right to come to places which were their homes prior to going into rebellion." Several Maryland counties followed suit. The "loyal men" of Havre de Grace in Harford County voted that Confederates "shall never be permitted to reside within its limits – *whether paroled or not.*" *National American* (Bel Air, MD) 28 Apr 1865.

420   Some tour guides claim the initials "G.W." are inscribed on the wall of the bridge about 23

THOS. SHERVIN, CO. K,
MARYLAND BATTALION

Confederate Private Thomas Shervin (1837-1920) was from Tilghmanton, in Washington County, MD. In the 1880s, Shervin was a miner in Colorado and Wyoming. Later he served as county judge for Rio Blanco County, CO. Photo from original text.

The main road passes over the top of the bridge, the arch being almost perfect in shape, and is formed of solid limestone. The center of the arch is over 200 feet from the bed of Cedar Creek, through which it runs emptying into James River several miles below, furnishing power for a Grist Mill which was then operated by a relative of mine and a descendant of the Schäfers.[421]

Night found us at Gibson's Mill, Mr. Henry Locher giving us a hearty welcome.[422] Here we found several other Marylanders, where we all remained for four days. I fished in the James while the boys had a jolly time drinking Apple Jack. The liquor soon gave out, when one of the party scoured the country for more, and traded two barrels of flour for ten gallons of red hot Apple Jack just from the still.[423]

On May the 5th, Hager, Grove, Shervin, Norris and I took up the march for home.[424] Just before we reached Lexington we visited "Stonewall Jackson's" grave.[425] While passing through the town I met Capt. Estell, who informed me that Capt. Stonebraker, after the surrender, left Appomattox for Maryland, going via Richmond.[426]

We encamped along the road seven miles north of Lexington. A Mrs. Gibson gave us our breakfast, and upon reaching Staunton Tom Shervin left the party. Here we learned that the Federals were advancing up the Valley.

We encamped for the night on Col. Harman's place, going to sleep on empty stomachs. We continued on down the Valley, passing through Mount

---

feet above the floor in support of claims that George Washington surveyed the area in 1750 on behalf of Thomas Fairfax, 6th Lord Fairfax of Cameron. Willis, Carrie Hunter and Walker, Etta Belle, *Legends of the Skyline Drive and the Great Valley of Virginia*, (The Deitz Press, Richmond, VA, 1937), 87.

421   Natural Bridge is 215 feet high with a span of 90 feet.
422   The US Federal Census for 1860 and 1870 indicates Henry S. Locher (1823-?), born in Maryland, his wife Lucy (1833-?), and three children resided in District 3 of Rockbridge County, VA.
423   The strong alcoholic beverage of applejack is produced by distilling concentrated apple cider.
424   Private Alexander Norris, Jr., (1835-1904) was the son of Alexander (1785-1872) and Elizabeth Wright Norris (1789-1880) of Harford County, MD. He enlisted in Company K of the 1st Virginia Cavalry in Aug 1862, later transferring to Company C of the 1st Maryland Cavalry. He was captured at Piedmont [Delaplane] Station 15 May 1863, sent to Fort McHenry, MD, transferred to Fort Monroe, VA, and exchanged a few days later. He was paroled at Harrisonburg, VA, 7 May 1865. Norris returned to Harford county, where he lived out his life as a farmer. *CSRV*, microcopy M321, roll 0004. *US Federal Census 1870-1890.*
      Private Thomas H. Grove (1842-?), son of Jacob (1802-1870) and Mary Hite Grove (1806-1877) of Sharpsburg, MD, enlisted in Company C, 1st Maryland Cavalry 18 Jun 1863. Paroled at Harrisonburg, VA, 7 May 1865. *CSRV*, microcopy M321, roll 0002. *US Federal Census 1850 and 1860.*
425   Confederate General Thomas "Stonewall" Jackson (1824-1863) is buried in the Stonewall Jackson Memorial Cemetery, Lexington, VA. His arm that was amputated on 2 May 1863 is buried at *Ellwood*, the home of J. Horace Lacy in the Wilderness of Orange County, VA near the field hospital.
426   Both Captain C. P. Estill and Captain Abraham Stonebraker were ordnance officers under the command of Confederate General John Brown Gordon. Both surrendered at Appomattox. *Paroles of the Army of Northern Virginia, SHSP. Vol. XV,* 212.

Sidney, and reaching Mount Crawford just as the people were going to Church, the ladies looking charming in their newly-starched calicoes—a sight which always causes a soldier's heart to beat quicker.[427]

Just north of the town Mrs. Brown gave us something to eat, the first we had since yesterday morning. We reached Harrisonburg about 4 p.m., and passing a few miles beyond met the advance guard of the Federals, and waiting until the Provost Marshal pitched his tent, when we formally surrendered and received the following evidence of renewed citizenship:[428]

We all rode the McClellan saddle, which had been captured from the Federals.[429] After signing our Parole we were told that we would be expected to leave in camp any Government property that we may have, such as saddles and bridles. The thought of being compelled to ride bare-back for more than a hundred miles before reaching our destination was simply out of the question. We had left our horses outside of the camp while going through the form of surrendering, and on our return we exchanged views and determined to keep our saddles. Fortunately the Federals were busy getting their camp in order, and taking advantage of the bustle we mounted our horses and put off at a brisk gait, expecting every moment to be followed by a squad of soldiers. In our haste we did not notice that Alex. Norris had remained behind, but after being well on the road he overtook us riding bare-back. We were much incensed that he had not done as we did, and refused to allow him to accompany us any further. I am now free to confess that we treated him too harshly. At the time we thought he played the coward, but I have often since thought that he, in complying with the order, saved us from the consequences of our foolhardy act by leading the Federals to believe that he was the only one of the party who had a Government saddle.

THOS. H. GROVE, CO. C, MARYLAND BATTALION

Confederate Private Thomas H. Grove (1842-) of Sharpsburg, Washington County, MD. Photo from original text.

---

427   Confederate Lieutenant Michael Garber Harman (1823-1877) of Augusta County, VA owned and operated a hotel and a stage line in Staunton, VA prior to the war. He entered the Confederacy in Apr 1861 at Staunton, VA as a major and quartermaster. He later served as captain in Company H, 34th Virginia Infantry, then lieutenant colonel of the 52nd Virginia. He briefly acted as General Jackson's Chief quartermaster. After an injury forced him to resign from active fighting, he served as quartermaster until the end of the war. Like so many other Confederates journeying home, Stonebraker and his fellow Marylanders stopped by the quartermaster's home hoping for provisions. Ayers, Edward L., William G. Thomas, and Anne Sarah Rubin, co-editors, *Augusta County, Virginia, Soldiers Records, Valley of the Shadow*, http://valley.vcdh.virginia.edu/govdoc/soldiers_dossier.html.
428   On 7 May 1865 at Harrisonburg, VA, Confederate privates Alexander Norris, Thomas H. Grove, and Joseph R. Stonebraker officially surrendered and received parole. Thomas Shervin did not receive his parole until 13 May 1865. Driver, *1st & 2nd MD Cavalry*, 234, 266, 282, 290.
429   The McClellan saddle was a saddle whose design is credited to Union General George B. McClellan. After touring Europe as the member of a military commission charged with studying the latest developments in engineer and cavalry forces, McClellan proposed a saddle design that was adopted by the Army in 1859. The McClellan saddle was a success and continued in use in various forms until the US Army's last horse cavalry and horse artillery was dismounted in World War II.

A great many Confederate soldiers did not surrender at Appomattox on 9 Apr 1865. Privates Joseph Stonebraker, Alexander Norris, Jr., and Thomas H. Grove surrendered at Harrisonburg, VA on 7 May 1865. Image of parole from original text.

    Soon after leaving Staunton we found much difficulty in getting something to eat, but our horses were literally in clover.

    Hager was the possessor of a ten-dollar gold piece, which had secured us a number of meals on the route, and was still intact.

    A day was assigned to each member of the party as forager. One day I was met by an old lady at her door, and when I made my wants known, she replied promptly, "No, indeed, we are entirely eaten out." When I explained that we were not begging, but would pay her in gold, she agreed to furnish breakfast at fifty cents a head. In due time we were invited in and sat down to a table loaded down with good things. Such a meal as we had not seen for months, and no doubt our famished condition made it appear much better than it really was. I felt as though I would never get satisfied. Hager and I quit, leaving Grove still eating. Finally Hager said, "Tom, will you never get enough?" when the old lady replied, "My boy, just you eat as long as it tastes good to you."

    When I gave her the ten-dollar gold piece her face was a study, as the expression of pleasure and surprise that lit up her countenance soon followed by a shadow of doubt as she said, "I am afraid I can't change this." She went up stairs, remaining quite a time, and from the sound of her movements we concluded she was collecting together sums of money, evidently hidden in various places.

Selfishness is the predominating passion of the human race, and it is needless for me to say we were delighted when she was unable to change our Eagle.

We continued on down the valley, grazing our horses just north of New Market. By the time we reached Mount Jackson it was raining furiously and continued all night to pour in torrents, making the night we spent in the woods south of Edinburg very disagreeable.

The next morning we met a squadron of Federal Cavalry moving up the Valley. We passed through Middletown and grazed our horses on the battle field of Cedar Creek. Night found us in Newtown, remaining over night with "Aunt Mary," noted for her kindness to all soldiers from Maryland.[430]

The next day being May the 10th, and stimulated by the thought of soon being with friends, we were on the move bright and early. We passed the first picket post a short distance beyond the town, having our Paroles examined. Upon reaching Winchester we were surprised at the stir on the business streets and the display of wares everywhere to be seen, presenting a vast difference from Confederate times.

We passed through Brucetown, and Smithfield, and upon reaching Leetown we separated, Hager and Grove going to Colonel Heith's, while I moved towards the Potomac. At Kerneysville Lieut. King from Hagerstown had charge of the Provost Marshal's office, where I was required to register my name.[431] He treated me very courteously, preventing the guard from taking my saddle and asking about the boys from his section. A few miles further

---

[430] Named Stephensburg in 1759 after German immigrant Peter Stephens (1687-1757), the "New Town" on the wagon road south of Winchester, VA holds the distinction as the second oldest town in the Shenandoah Valley. Newtown is today known as Stephen's City, VA.

"Aunt Mary" was the well-known Mary Nicewanger (1806-?), widow of John Nicewanger, Jr. of Newtown, VA. Prior to the war the Nicewangers were employed as inn and tavern keepers along the main street. Today, that inn is the headquarters for the Newtown History Center at 5408 Main Street. In 1863, a year after the death of her husband, Mary purchased the log house that once stood at 5455 Main Street, making it her home. From here Aunt Mary would generously receive and tend weary Confederate soldiers. Mary's log home was the site where Confederate scout Captain John Corbin Blackford (1839-1864) was killed in Jan 1864 (see footnote 163). In 1866 Mary took over the proprietorship of the Rickard's Tavern in New Town after she sold her log house. An image of "The Old Rickard's Tavern, Mary Neiswanger – Proprietor" appears in *The James E. Taylor Sketchbook,* inaccurately crediting that Mary operated Rickard's Tavern during the war years. Other references to Aunt Mary appear in the memoirs of Captain Joseph French Harding (1838-1919) commander of Company F, 31st Virginia Infantry. Thacker, Victor L., *French Harding Civil War Memoirs* (McLain Printing Co., 2000). French, Steve, *Rebel Chronicles, Raiders Scouts, and Train Robbers of the Upper Potomac,* (New Horizons Publishing Company, 2012), 135-139. Taylor, James E., *The James E. Taylor Sketchbook: With Sheridan Up the Shenandoah Valley in 1864: Leaves from a Special Artist's Sketchbook and Diary,* (Morningside Bookshop, Dayton, OH, 1989), 124. Special thanks to curator Bryan C. Smith, Director and Curator of the Newtown History Center, Stephens City, VA for his generous sharing of information on this local legend.

[431] The best candidate for "Lieut. King" is Lieutenant Harrison E. King of Hagerstown, MD. King enlisted as a private in the Union 1st Regiment Potomac Home Brigade 1 Aug 1861. Promoted to corporal of Company D, then 1st lieutenant of Company E in Mar 1865, when he was stationed at Harper's Ferry, WV. Lieutenant King may have been *acting* Provost Marshal in mid-May 1865 when Stonebraker registered. King officially mustered out of the Union Army 29 May 1865.

SOME OF THE BEAUTIES THAT GRACED
THE REUNION PICNIC, SPAW'S SPRING.

Stonebraker does not identify the ladies in the photograph. Unquestionably, one of the young ladies in this early photograph is his future wife, Mary Catherine Bosler of Carlisle, PA. Photo from original text.

took me to my old friend Keplinger just in time to get a good supper, after which I pushed on, arriving in Shepherdstown about sunset, stopping at Uncle Daniel S. Rentch's.[432]

Here I found Captain Stonebraker staying with friends until he could plan for the future, a problem hard to solve, being without a dollar and a wife and three children to support.[433] As he had loaned me the money to purchase my horse I was only too glad to give "Bill" to him, and in a few days he sold him to Mr. Adams, who hitched him to the mail coach that ran between Shepherdstown and Kerneysville, the Captain being $140 better off in this world's goods; as for myself I did not have a cent.

In a few days father and mother came to see me, as the feeling was so bitter against ex-Confederates in Maryland.[434] I arranged to help Uncle about the general store which he was operating. Later on he purchased a store at Kerneysville, when I was sent there as an assistant.

---

432   John Keplinger (1815-1901) and his wife Catherine Hamme Keplinger, 5 daughters, and 2 sons lived on a farm west of Shepherdstown, WV along Route #45 Martinsburg Pike at Billmyer Mill Road. The Keplinger's oldest son, John Frederick Keplinger (1846-1923), enlisted in the 1st Virginia Cavalry 1 Aug 1864 at Shepherdstown and was captured near Shepherdstown 21 days later. He was a prisoner-of-war for the next 10 months at Elmira, NY, released 21 Jun 1865. Civil War Scholars, *http://civilwarscholars.com/people/1st-virginia-cavalry*. *Map of Jefferson County, VA*, Oct 1862, Library of Virginia, Richmond, VA.

       Daniel Shafer Rentch (1821-1918) previously noted footnote 131.

433   Confederate Captain Abraham Stonebraker, the author's uncle, previously cited see footnote 247. Photo page 104. Captain Stonebraker surrendered at Appomattox and likely returned home in mid-Apr 1865 well before Stonebraker.

434   In the summer of 1865, the *Herald and Torch Light* newspaper of Hagerstown, MD reported incidents of former Confederates "treated rather roughly" by former Union soldiers. In nearby Frederick County, MD, the *Banner of Liberty* reported a "Riot at Emmittsburg," when a former Confederate officer offered to shake the hand of a Union citizen, which was refused. The citizen was insulted, at which point another citizen shot the former Confederate. It was reported two "rebels" were killed and seven wounded. *Herald and Torch Light*, [Hagerstown, MD] 5 Jul 1865. *Banner of Liberty*, [Libertytown, MD] 5 Jul 1865.

In the Meshes

In the following month of August the ex-Confederates held a reunion picnic at Spaw's Spring, a few miles from Kerneysville, where a vast crowd had assembled from Jefferson and Berkeley Counties.[435] The Rebels had cast off their faded "Butternut," and were arrayed in store clothes, protected by the linen "duster," the then prevailing fad.[436]

A large platform had been erected, upon which both old and young enjoyed themselves "tripping the light fantastic toe,"[437] to the music made by, as Uncle Remus would say, "some er deze yer ole-time Ferginny fiddlers fum away back yander; one er dem kinder fiddlers w'at can't git the chune down fine, 'less dey pats der foot."[438]

How beautiful and charming the girls looked in their white and delicate colored dresses as they strolled through the woods by the side of the Rebels, whose sun-burned faces were radiant with smiles. Now that

"Grim-Visag'd war hath sooth'd his wrinkled front." [439]

A little Northern girl in a corn colored gown, with a big straw "flat" tied under her chin, making a scoop shape hat, beneath which sparkled a pair of jet black eyes completely captivated me.[440]

---

435   Stonebraker uses the phrase "In the Meshes" as in: to catch in a net, or ensnare. He was captivated, or ensnared by love at first sight of his future wife, Mary Catherine Bosler.

    Within months of the Appomattox surrender, veterans sought out occasions to gather together and relive shared experiences. The Aug 1865 reunion at Spaw's Spring is one of the earliest recorded instance of a Confederate reunion. There are very few references to Spaw's Spring in Berkeley County, WV. In the *History of Berkeley County, West Virginia* (1928) the "Old Spaw's Spring Farm" is noted as adjoining the estate of Revolutionary War General Adam Stephens. General Stephens founded Martinsburg, VA [WV] in 1778 and named the town in honor of Colonel Thomas Bryan Martin, the nephew of Thomas Fairfax, 6th Lord Fairfax of Cameron. Spaw's Spring is listed as the location of an old Indian fort destroyed by the Indians during the French and Indian War. Evans, Willis F., *History of Berkeley County, West Virginia* (Martinsburg, WV, 1928), 254.

436   A summer coat, or duster, is typically made of lightweight linen or canvas worn by horsemen to protect their clothing from road dust. Typically a duster is slit up the back to hip level to drape down both sides of the saddle.

437   Butternut previously cited see footnote 347.

    To "trip the light fantastic toe" is to dance. A line taken from a line from John Milton's 1632 poem *L'Allegro*:
    Com, and trip it as ye go,
    On the light fantastick toe.
    And in thy right hand lead with thee,
    The Mountain Nymph, sweet Liberty;

438   Loosely translated: some of these your old time Virginia fiddlers from way back yonder: one of them kind of fiddlers that can't get the tune down fine, unless they pat their foot. A paraphrase from Joel Chandler Harris "*A Rainy Day with Uncle Remus,*" Chapter IX, *Mr. Benjamin Rams and His Wonderful Fiddle*. As published in *Scribner's Monthly* [serialization] Volume XXII, (NY, Jul 1881), 449.

439   SparksNotes translates the phrase to: "We get to wear easy smiles on our faces rather than the grim expressions of war." From William Shakespeare's Richard III, Act 1, Scene 1 that begins with the familiar phrase "Now is the winter of our discontent." Crowther, John, editor, *No Fear Shakespeare, Richard III*, (Sparks Publishing, NY, 2004).

440   Stonebraker is referring to his future wife, Miss Mary Catherine Bosler (1843-1922), daugh-

This is her picture. Time has frosted her raven locks, but has failed to dim the lustre of her eye or chill her heart. Although a Pennsylvanian by birth, and her home "Bonnie Brook" was within the roar of the guns of the battle of Gettysburg, she is now a member of a Maryland Chapter of the Daughters of the Confederacy.[441]

After their first meeting at Spaw's Spring near Kearneysville, WV, Mary Catherine Bosler would have to wait nine years before she married Joseph Stonebraker. They were married at her parents home near Carlisle, PA on 8 Jan 1874 when they were both almost 30 years old. Photo from original text.

MRS. MARY B. STONEBRAKER

ter of Abraham (1806-1883) and Elizabeth Herman Bosler (1812-1885) of Carlisle, PA. Abraham Bosler's biography notes that he was a produce merchant and for a time was "engaged in merchandising at Hagerstown." It is reasonable that Bosler's daughter, Mary Catherine, would have had social acquaintances among the residents of Washington and Jefferson counties. *History of Cumberland and Adams Counties, Pennsylvania, Part II* (Warner, Beers & Company, Chicago, IL, 1886), 369.

441 The Abraham Bosler farm was south of Carlisle, PA along today's S. Spring Garden Street east of PA State Route 34, the Holly Pike (formerly the Carlisle-Hanover Turnpike) at Letort Springs and Bonnybrook RR Station. The farm was about 30 miles north of Gettysburg, PA. Eschenmann and Barner, *Cumberland County Warrantee Map Atlas, 1872*, Letort District 6 of South Middleton District.

Reconstruction

What Confederate that does not remember with indignation and horror the reconstruction period, "when de bottom rail was on de top?"[442]

During the War when the State of West Virginia was forcibly carved from the Mother of States, Jefferson County became one of its ribs and Shepherdstown was made the County seat.[443]

The most important event of the town in the summer of '65 was the session of the court, held by Judge B _____, which was a travesty on justice.[444]

---

442   Reconstruction began and ended at different times in the rebel states. Reconstruction policies were implemented when a Confederate state came under the control of the US Army. The army conducted new elections in which freed slaves could vote, while whites who had held leading positions under the Confederacy were temporarily denied the right to vote and were not permitted to run for office.

The urban dictionary defines "bottom rail on top," as when one formerly in a position of weakness or subservience gains power or dominance over his former oppressor. Most sources attribute the phrase origin to a former slave describing the status of black Americans after the war, or a comment directed to his former master. One of the earliest appearances is on an 1870 broadside *"The Black Vomit; Or, The Bottom Rail on Top,"* advertising a play in Lynchburg, VA. In 1935, H. James Eckenrode, author of biographies of Jefferson Davis, Nathan Bedford Forrest, Rutherford B. Hayes, and James Longstreet, wrote the novel *Bottom Rail on Top, A Novel of the old South* (Greenburg, NY, 1935) about life in Tennessee before the Civil War and during the reconstruction period. Foner, Eric and Olivia Mahoney, *America's Reconstruction: People and Politics After the Civil War* (HarperCollins Publishers, LSU Press, 1995), 114. http://www.urbandictionary.com/.

443   Less than a month after the Virginia delegates voted to secede from the Union on 17 Apr 1861, a pro-Union convention convened at Wheeling, VA by delegates from the western counties to discuss the formation of a new state loyal to the Union. The two portions of the state were never reconciled as a single state again. Following a Union victory at the Battle of Philippi and the subsequent occupation of northwestern Virginia by General George B. McClellan, a Second Wheeling Convention met in Jun 1861. Delegates formed the Restored, or Reorganized, Government of Virginia, and chose Francis H. Pierpont as governor. President Lincoln recognized the Restored Government as the legitimate government of Virginia. The US Constitution says a new state must gain approval from the original state, which never occurred in the case of West Virginia. Since the Restored Government was considered the legal government of Virginia, it granted permission to itself on 13 May 1862 to form the state of West Virginia.

Berkeley and Jefferson counties, with the consent of the Reorganized Government of Virginia, supposedly voted in favor of annexation to West Virginia in 1863. Many of the counties voters were serving in the Confederate Army when the vote was taken. Upon their return home, they refused to acknowledge the transfer, arguing that Federal troops in the area had affected the outcome of the vote. The Virginia General Assembly repealed the Act of Secession and in 1866 brought suit against West Virginia, asking the court to declare Berkeley and Jefferson counties a part of Virginia. Meanwhile, Congress passed a joint resolution recognizing the transfer on 10 Mar 1866. In 1871, the US Supreme Court decision in Virginia v. West Virginia upheld the secession of West Virginia, including Berkeley and Jefferson counties, from Virginia. Lay, George C. *Interstate Controversies Growing out of the Civil War and the Reconstruction Period, Virginia vs. West Virginia, The Brief: A Quarterly Magazine of the Law, Volume 6,* (New Era Publishing, Lancaster, PA,1906), 98-115.

Even today, the issue of Jefferson County's transfer into West Virginia raises local sentiments. From *"A Brief History of the Jefferson County Court House"* on the Jefferson County Clerk's website: "When West Virginia was formed in 1863, Jefferson County had remained a part of the Commonwealth of Virginia. Shortly after, a highly questionable "election" abducted Jefferson County into the new state." http://jeffersoncountyclerkwv.com/court_house.html.

444   A staunch Unionist during the war, Lewis Penn Witherspoon Balch (1787-1868) of Leetown, VA [WV] was appointed Circuit Court judge for the northeastern counties of West Virginia in Mar 1865. Born in Georgetown, DC, Balch graduated from Princeton in 1806, then studied law with his relative Roger Brooke Taney, later Chief Justice Taney, in Frederick, MD. On 14 Mar 1814, Balch married Elizabeth Wever, and the couple moved to Leesburg, VA, then Leetown, VA [WV], where they operated Balch's Grist Mill. The couple had 12 children, 6 of whom survived to adulthood. The circa 1835 Balch home still stands in Leetown, WV. In 1834, Balch freed his 22 slaves, and, with his

This sketch was made by Col. A. R. Boteler, representing the old Judge going from his boarding house to the Town Hall, which was then used as the Court House.[445] He always took the middle of the street, under the protection of a cotton umbrella—a most comical sight.

Although the picture was intended as a caricature, it was readily recognized by the Judge's wife, who exclaimed, "Why dear, I never saw you in that suit of clothes!" The old man replied, "Why, wife, don't you see I am too big for my breeches!"

I remained in Virginia until fall, then went to my parent's home in Washington County, where I spent the winter, not withstanding the threats of some of my good Union friends, that I would not be permitted to remain, and came to Baltimore, in May 1866.[446]

JUSTICE

Above: Caricature of Judge Balch as drawn by Colonel Alexander R. Boteler, circa 1865. Image from original text. Right: Judge Lewis Penn Witherspoon Balch (1787-1868) of Leetown VA [WV].

young sons, accompanied them on the voyage from Baltimore to an American colony on the west coast of Africa. In 1847 that American colony became the independent nation of Liberia.

Noted as a "slave to popular prejudices, intolerant in his opinions and overbearing in his conduct. . . There is only one man in the country who can do the work which the devil has assigned ex-judge Balch, and that is himself." As Judge Balch presided over the Circuit Court, the volatile issue of *Virginia v. West Virginia* was being debated in higher courts. The Judge's ardent support of the transfer of Jefferson and Berkeley counties to West Virginia, and his outspoken Confederate prejudices combined to make him one of the most hated men in the region. In the *History of Martinsburg and Berkeley County*, Balch is described as "the first judge appointed for the Berkeley circuit after the close of the Civil War and one of the most detested of the 'reconstruction' judges." "This weak-bodied, even weaker-minded old man . . .thrust himself forward . . . to vomit bile which has accumulated upon his dyspeptic mind and disordered nature." He presided as judge from Mar 1865 to Mar 1866, until "even his own party could tolerate him no longer."

Balch's son, Thomas Balch (1821-1877), achieved notability as an American historian best know for his work on the Revolutionary War. The Thomas Balch Library in Leesburg, VA is a history and genealogy library owned and operated by the Town of Leesburg. *Spirit of Jefferson* [Charlestown, VA] 28 Aug 1866. Balch, David R., *The Balch Family of Maryland, The Sixth Generation*, www.balchgenealogy.com/6thGeneration.pdf/2010, 10-14. Aler, F. Vernon, *History of Martinsburg and Berkeley County, West Virginia*, (Hagerstown MD, 1888).

445 Colonel Alexander Robinson Boteler (1815-1892) previously noted, footnote 252.

446 On Christmas Day 1868, President Johnson granted an unconditional pardon to all Civil War participants except high-ranking military and civil officials. In May 1872 the Congressional Amnesty Act gave the right to hold office again to almost all Southern leaders who had been excluded from public office by the 14th Amendment.

A Rebel of '61

The Stonebraker Epilogue

by Sandra Izer

Throughout the Civil War the city of Baltimore had remained staunchly pro-Confederate. Even today, three of the four Civil War monuments in the city are dedicated to the Confederacy: the *Confederate Soldiers and Sailors Monument* (1903), the *Confederate Womens Monument* (1915-1917), and the *Lee and Jackson Monument* (1948). These monuments are a testimony to the thought that "while the state government kept Baltimore officially on the side of the Union, there were many in the city who were clearly, if unofficially, sympathetic to the Southern cause."[447] Only Maryland's official Civil War monument, the *Union Soldiers and Sailors Monument* (1909), pays tribute to the Union. For those Confederate soldiers who found trouble resuming their lives in other parts of post-war Maryland, Baltimore was a sanctuary city.

For the Stonebraker family, the move to Baltimore in the spring of 1866 held great promise for a new beginning. In this busy city they would be one of many ex-Confederate families rebuilding their lives after the war. Former animosity over issues of states rights and slavery were soon replaced by comradery in veterans' groups that focused on battlefield markers, re-burying the dead, and memorial statuary.

Joseph Stonebraker did well for himself in post-war Baltimore. He first worked for his father, then later opened his own liquor business in the downtown warehouse district aptly named "Jos. R. Stonebraker & Co." When his business was producing a steady income sufficient to support a family, Joseph married Miss Mary Bosler of Carlisle, Pennsylvania, the young lady he had admired nine years earlier at the Spaw's Spring veterans reunion near Shepherdstown, West Virginia. In addition to his liquor firm, Joseph was an initial investor and later vice-president of the Fidelity and Deposit Company of Maryland, a bank that is still in business today.

While writing *Rebel of '61* in the years 1897 and 1898, Joseph was in his mid-fifties living comfortably at 1921 Eutaw Place in the Bolton Hill district of Baltimore, a community that was home to a number of other ex-Confederates.[448] More than thirty years had passed since the surrender at Appomat-

The Confederate Soldiers and Sailors Monument along Mount Royal Avenue in Baltimore City. Dedicated in 1903, a wounded soldier is upheld by a laurel-bearing angel. The inscriptions are the Latin phrases, "Gloria Victis" - "Glory to the victor," and "Deo Vindice" - "God vindicates." LOC/P&P. LC-D401-16535.

---

447 Kelly, Cindy, and Edwin H. Remsburg, *Outdoor Sculpture in Baltimore: A Historical Guide to Public Art in the Monumental City*, (Johns Hopkins University Press, Baltimore, MD. 2011), 181.
448 The US Federal Census of 1900 and Stonebraker's obituary list his home address as 1921

Photograph of Joseph Stonebraker's neighborhood on Eutaw Place in the Bolton Hill district of Baltimore. The Stonebraker family lived at 1921 Eutaw Place. Photo circa 1903 by William Henry Jackson (1843-1942). LOC/P&P. LC-DIG-det-4a10716.

tox. He and his beloved wife Mary had three sons and a daughter, three of whom were still living at home. His oldest son, James Bosler, had attended the Virginia Military Institute in class of 1895, and was off trying to strike it rich in the Klondike gold fields of the Yukon. Harry and Joseph Jr., had recently opened their own printing firm in Baltimore, while the youngest child Mary was still in school. Henry Stonebraker, Joseph's father, had been dead for over twenty years, but Angelica, his eighty-three year old mother, was very much alive and glowing with opinions and ideas that she was determined Joseph should include in his book.

Joseph Stonebraker ended *Rebel of '61* with the simple phrase, "came to Baltimore, in May 1866." However, the continued adventures of the Stonebraker clan after their arrival in Baltimore and subsequent generations is a story worthy of remembrance.

HENRY & ANGELICA STONEBRAKER

Unquestionably, one of the more dynamic individuals in the Stonebraker saga is Joseph's father, Henry Stonebraker. After his marriage to Angelica Rentch in 1837, Henry tried his hand as a farmer, a grist mill owner in Missouri, and a hotel-keeper on the Mississippi River. He returned to Maryland and for a time was a machinist, a Funkstown storekeeper, the driver of a mail delivery coach, and a boatman on the Chesapeake & Ohio Canal; he was not particularly successful at any of these vocations.

Henry Stonebraker considered himself an inventor and embraced the early stages of the American industrial revolution. During his brief time as a machinist he invented and patented an improved hydraulic pump that he ex-

Eutaw Place, Baltimore, MD.

hibited at the 1854 Agricultural fair in Baltimore, Maryland.[449] It was an interesting design, but ultimately not profitable for the Stonebraker family.

During his 1857-1860 tenure as a merchant in Funkstown, Henry and his younger brother, Doctor Abraham Stonebraker, began dabbling in the "patent medicine" trade.[450] Abraham had married in 1856, and, by the fall of 1858, was living and practicing medicine in nearby Shepherdstown, Virginia.

It is not clear which brother, Henry or Abraham, first conceived the idea of brewing and bottling medicinal tonics that would eventually lead to the benchmark 1867 lawsuit of *Stonebraker v. Stonebraker* – a case still cited in courts today defending the rights, protection, and ownership of trademarks.[451] In the years just before the Civil War, both Henry and Abraham claimed to have been the original inventor of the noxious formulas they outrageously guaranteed would cure most known diseases.

Stonebraker Medicine's began as a friendly business rivalry between brothers. From his offices in Shepherdstown, Abraham Stonebraker was bottling *Dr. Stonebraker's Celebrated Compounds* that included *Hair Restorative, Healing Balsam, Anodyne Astringent, Magic Nerve and Bone Liniment,* and *Anti-Bilious Pills.* He advertised and shipped his medicines through a network of distributors as far south as Christiansburg, Virginia, and, for a time, arranged deliveries to stores in Peoria County, Illinois.[452] Meanwhile, from the back room of his rented Funkstown store, Henry Stonebraker was brewing a comparable line of remedies and compounds including *Nerve and Bone Liniment, Celebrated Hair Restorative, Balsam or Pain Killer, Dyspepsia Bitters and Liver Invigorator,* and *Vegetable Cough Syrup.* Not content to confine himself to humans, Henry branched out to farmers with his *Horse and Cattle Powders,* and for the household he offered *Bed Bug Exterminator* and *Rat and Roach Exterminator.*

Henry Stonebraker (1815-1877).

---

449 *Baltimore Sun* Newspaper (Baltimore, MD), 6 Oct 1854.
450 Confederate Captain Abraham Stonebraker (1831-1885), the author's uncle, previously cited see footnote 252. Photo page 158.
451 The information on Henry and Abraham Stonebraker's business affairs is taken from: Samuel Stonebraker and Henry K. Hoffman vs. Henry Stonebraker, (Maryland Court of Appeals, April Term 1870, 33 Md., 252) as published in *Reports of Cases Argued and Determined in the Court of Appeals of Maryland, Volume 34* (John Murphy Company, Baltimore, MD, 1872), 444-449. Cassard v. McGlannan et al. (Maryland Court of Appeals, 1898) as published in the *The Atlantic Reporter, Volume 40 Containing all the Decisions of the Supreme Courts of Maine, New Hampshire, Vermont, Rhode Island, Connecticut, and Pennsylvania: Court of Errors and Appeals, Court of Chancery, and Supreme and Prerogative Courts of New Jersey: Court of Errors and Appeals and Court of Chancery of Delaware: and Court of Appeals of Maryland.* (West Publishing Company, St. Paul, MN, 1898), 711-712.
452 Henry and Abraham Stonebraker's sister and brother-in-law, Mary Cornelia Stonebraker (1819-1892) and John Casper Schnebly (1814-1881), had moved to Richwood Township in Peoria County, IL in the mid-1840s. US Federal Census 1850 through 1880. 1873 US Landownership Map for Peoria, IL.

Stonebraker's Internal Painkiller[453]

Painkiller for the cure of diphtheria, croup, sore throat, cramps, colic, cholera, diarrhea, dysentery, and other diseases. It also may be applied externally for cuts bruises and toothache.

To 1 gallon of Alcohol add:
8 ounces Camphor
1 pound Balsam Peru[454]
5 ounces Laudanum[455]
6 ounces Tar Turpentine[456]
8 ounces Tincture Cayenne[457]
1 ounce Olive Oil
8 ounces Tincture Myrrh[458]
4 pounds Sulphur Ether[459]

Dosage: Adults 1/2 a Teaspoon, for children in proportion to age. For an external remedy apply freely, rubbing in well. For croup and sore throat, take a few drops and bathe the neck and chest well. Headache, take a dose, bathe the head, and inhale the fumes.

Stonebraker's External Liniment

Liniment is used to cure rheumatism, ringworm, corns, swellings, rashes, old wounds, bruises, sprains, sweeny,[460] sore throat, pains in the back and limbs, spinal affections, and other diseases requiring an external application.

To 1 ½ Gallons Alcohol add:
2 ¼ pounds Ammonia
¾ gallon Turpentine
10 ounces Linseed Oil
½ pound Origanum[461]
5 ounces Succini[462]
1 ounce Cayenne Pepper
5 ounces Juniper[463]
4 ounces Barbadoes tar[464]
1 ½ ounces Seneca[465]
1 ½ pounds Castile Soap dissolved in water

For corns apply the liniment to raw cotton and bind the corn for 7 or 8 nights, occasionally scraping the corn with a knife. Swelling and sprains take a tablespoon with the hand and rub the parts affected 2 or 3 times a day. Sore throat, pain in the back and limbs, rub well night and morning and on going to bed apply the liniment on flannel and bind the parts affected.

---

453   On 19 Feb 1867 Henry Stonebraker received two patents from the US Patent office. US62297 for his internal painkiller and US62298 his external liniment.

454   Peru Balsam is an aromatic resin extracted from a Central American tree commonly called the Quina or Balsamo tree. It is still used today in diaper rash ointments, hair tonics, anti-dandruff preparations, and feminine hygiene sprays and as a natural fragrance in soaps, detergents, creams, lotions, and perfumes.

455   Laudanum contains almost all of the opium alkaloids, including morphine and codeine. A potent narcotic by virtue of its high morphine concentration, laudanum was historically used to treat a variety of ailments and as a cough suppressant.

456   Turpentine and petroleum distillates such as coal oil and kerosene have been used medicinally since ancient times as topical and sometimes internal home remedies. Topically it has been used for abrasions and wounds, and as a treatment for lice. When mixed with animal fat, it has been used as a chest rub, or inhaler for nasal and throat ailments. Many modern chest rubs, such as the Vicks variety, still contain turpentine in their formulations. Taken internally it was used as a treatment for intestinal parasites because of its alleged antiseptic and diuretic properties, and as a general cure-all.

457   Cayenne tincture is made from dried cayenne peppers.

458   In pharmacy today, myrrh is used as an antiseptic in mouthwashes, gargles, and toothpastes for prevention and treatment of gum disease. Myrrh is currently used in some liniments and healing salves that may be applied to abrasions and other minor skin ailments. Myrrh has also been recommended as an analgesic for toothaches, and can be used in liniment for bruises, aches, and sprains.

459   An ether in which sulfur replaces oxygen. A pleasant-smelling, colorless and highly flammable liquid, ether can be vaporized into a gas that numbs pain but leaves patients conscious.

460   Sweeny is an equine muscular ailment resulting from poor-fitting harness.

461   Also known as oregano. Hippocrates used oregano as an antiseptic, as well as a cure for stomach and respiratory ailments.

462   Succini Acid, historically known as Spirit of amber. Originally obtained from by pulverizing and distilling amber, in the past it was chiefly used externally for rheumatic aches and pains. Succinic acid is used in the food and beverage industry today, primarily as an acidity regulator.

463   Juniper, or Juniper berry, is the female seed cone produced by the various species of the highly aromatic junipers. The Greeks and Romans noted the uses of derivatives of juniper both internally and externally.

464   Webster's 1828 English dictionary describes *Barba'Does Tar* as a mineral fluid, of the nature of the thicker fluid bitumens, of a nauseous bitterish taste, a very strong disagreeable smell, viscid, of a brown, black or reddish color; it easily melts, and burns with much smoke, but is not soluble in ardent spirits. It is recommended in coughs and disorders of the breast and lungs. In 1830, Dr. Richard Reese of London recommended a plaster of Barbadoes tar for the cure of tumors, bunions, and corns. Reese, Richard, *Monthly Gazette of Health or Medical, Dietetic Antiempirical and General Philosophical Journal*, (London, 1830), 418.

465   Most likely Seneca-snakeroot (Polygala senega). This plant got its common name from the Seneca First Nation's use of it as a treatment for snake bite. Other First Nations used the root for respiratory problems, headache, and stomach ache.

Dating to the late 17th century, the patent medicine trade was a profitable business for both doctors and quacks who proclaimed the healing and restorative powers of their wonder-tonics.[466] By the mid-19th century the manufacture and distribution of patent medicines had become a major industry in America. Remedies were available for almost any ailment, including venereal diseases, tuberculosis, hair loss, colic in infants, indigestion or dyspepsia, female discomforts, and even cancer.

Most producers of patent medicines were small family operations bottling vegetable extracts laced with ample doses of alcohol, spiced with opium or cocaine. Just prior to the Civil War, the commercial production and unchecked distribution of the very effective, highly addictive, pain killer *morphine* provided a real punch when added to these over-the-counter tonic remedies.[467] Sadly, many of these concoctions were advertised for and administered to infants and children with tragic results.

Although there were many outspoken critics of these crude and addictive tonics, the industry generated a comfortable income for the producers, and a very generous income for the advertisers of the products. From before the Civil War through the turn-of-the century, newspapers were plastered with columns of outrageous testimonial advertisements paid for by the producers of patent tonics. Not wishing to disrupt a very lucrative enterprise, newspaper editors were cautious to steer away from critical editorials that might interrupt the steady flow of advertising income.

With medical fees too expensive for most Americans to afford except in emergencies, the public turned to these ready-made, over-the-counter remedies. New York entrepreneur Benjamin Brandreth's *Vegetable Universal Pill* became one of the best-selling patent medicines in the United States. A congressional committee in 1849 reported that Brandreth was the nation's largest proprietary advertiser. Between 1862 and 1863, Brandreth's average gross annual income surpassed $600,000.[468]

The patent medicine industry ran virtually unchecked until 1905, when Samuel Hopkins Adams published an exposé in *Collier's Weekly* entitled "The Great American Fraud" that led to the passage of the first Pure Food and Drug Act in 1906.[469] This statute did not ban the alcohol, narcotics, or

Alexandra Gazette (Alexandra, VA) Oct 1865.

---

466 The phrase "patent medicine" comes from the late 17th century marketing of medical elixirs when those who found favor with royalty were issued "letters patent" authorizing the use of the royal endorsement in advertising.
467 Commercial production of morphine began in Darmstadt, Germany in 1827 by the pharmacy that became the pharmaceutical company Merck, with morphine sales being a large part of their early growth. By 1849, Merck advertised the "best quality" morphine available on the commercial market. *Exploring New Horizons - The Merck Group*, Johnson, Barkole A., Editor, *Addiction Medicine: Science and Practice, Volume 1*, (University of VA, Charlottesville, VA, 2011), 822.
468 Atwater, Edward, *An Annotated Catalogue of the Edward C. Atwater Collection of American Popular Medicine and Health Reform, Volume 1*, (Boydell & Brewer, NY, 2004), 117.
469 Adams, Samuel Hopkins, *The Great American Fraud, 4th ed.*, 1907 (American Medical Association, Chicago, IL 1905).

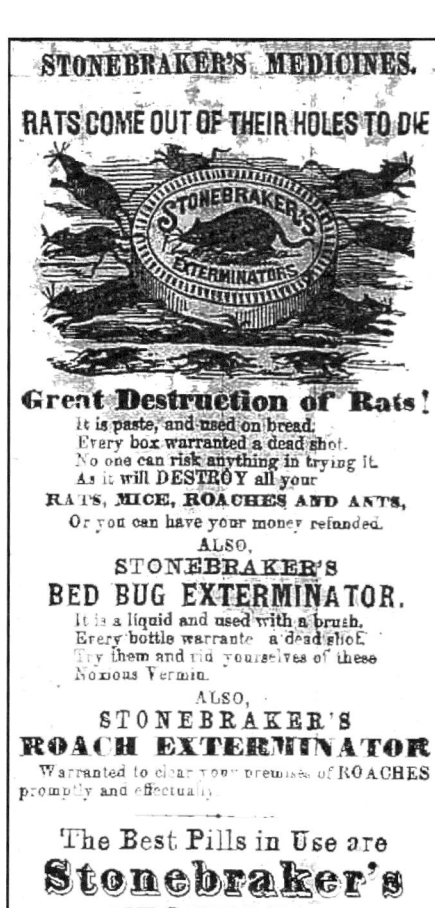

stimulants in the medicines; it only required them to be labeled as such, and curbed some of the more misleading, overstated, or fraudulent claims that appeared on the labels. Not until 1934 were statutes revised that regulated the use of narcotics.[470]

Reasonably, of the two Stonebraker brothers, Abraham Stonebraker with his professional title of "doctor" should have been the more successful of the two brothers; but by late winter of 1860, Abraham Stonebraker's pharmacy and patent medicine business in Shepherdstown, Virginia was failing. In the spring of 1861, one day after Virginia seceded from the Union, 29 year old Abraham enlisted in the 2nd Virginia Infantry Regiment, serving most of the war as quartermaster and doctor.

Meanwhile, Henry Stonebraker, who never claimed to be a doctor and whose life had been a series of failures, finally found a trade in which he excelled. Henry discovered he possessed a real talent for brewing potions and marketing them with outrageous claims in the uncensored newspapers of the 19th century. Touting his tonic as the "Greatest Family Medicine in the World," Henry boldly promised "a sure cure" for almost every known disease or ailment.

During the war Henry found it increasingly difficult to obtain the raw materials needed to produce his tonics. Product shortages, combined with a strained war-time economy, almost put him out of business. Suppliers of laudanum and morphine found more lucrative clients selling to the Union and Confederate armies. Doctors and surgeons in both armies sought to ease the misery of sick and wounded soldiers by issuing what is believed to be millions of doses of morphine. It is estimated that doctors in the Union Army issued more than ten million doses during the war.

While morphine eased the immediate suffering of sick and wounded, the highly-addictive drug also created a generation of addicts among Civil War veterans. A most commonly used term for drug addiction of this period was "The Army Disease." Accurate statistics for the period are hard to come by, but historians believe that as many as 200,000 to 500,000 war veterans left the service addicted to morphine. In some cases, this was an addiction would continue for decades after the war had ended.[471]

As the war trudged into its third year, in June of 1864, when his eldest son Joseph disappeared into the night to "Jine the Cavalry," Henry received a windfall that would irrevocably change the fortunes of the Stonebraker family.[472] Three Baltimore businessmen agreed to invest capital into Henry's

Spirit of Jefferson, (Charlestown, VA) 20 Aug 1867. Despite the fact that Berkeley and Jefferson counties became part of West Virginia in 1863, the Spirit of Jefferson continued to publish as "Charlestown, VA."

---

470   The Uniform State Narcotic Drug Act in 1934 was a revenue-producing act that made the law uniform in the various states with respect to controlling the sale and use of narcotic drugs.
471   Shmoop University, *History of Drugs in America: Shmoop US History Guide.* (Shmoop University, 2010), 19.
472   "Jine the Cavalry!" was among Confederate General J. E. B. Stuart's favorite songs and became the unofficial theme song of his Confederate cavalry corps.

business: Samuel Stonebraker, Henry's uncle; Dr. Henry Fletcher Zollickoffer; and Henry K. Hoffman.[473] Stonebraker and Zollickoffer were formerly from Hagerstown, Maryland, where Zollickoffer had dabbled in the patent medicine trade as early as 1845 offering *Zollickoffer's Worm Remedy* and *Dr. Zollickoffer's Female Health Remedy*.[474] Conflicting testimony at the 1867 trial of *Stonebraker v. Stonebraker* indicates the investment sum was at least $10,000, possibly as high as $30,000. Regardless, Henry and his three Baltimore investors became "jointly interested" in the very profitable business of peddling patent medicines.[475]

The year 1865 was a very good year for Henry Stonebraker. In April of 1865 his son Joseph and brother Abraham returned from the war unscathed, and Henry had finally found a trade that was on course to be a very successful and profitable business. With the infusion of cash money and his Baltimore associates helping to acquire supplies and repair the distribution network, Henry revived his struggling tonic trade with a fervor. By October of 1865, "H. Stonebraker, Funkstown, Md" launched an advertising campaign in the Alexandria, Virginia, newspaper offering *Liniments for Man or Beast, Horse and Cattle Powders,* and *Rat and Bed Bug Extermination*.[476] In his new advertisements Henry unscrupulously guaranteed his liniment to cure "rheumatism, sprains, swelled joints, sore throats, frosted feet, poisons, sores and bruises, fresh cuts, corns, mumps, tetter, pains in the limbs and back, sweeny on man or beast, saddle or collar gall, distemper, scratches, etc." In the later months of 1865 Henry Stonebraker and the Baltimore businessmen officially formed the partnership of "Stonebraker, Hoffman & Company, Proprietors and Manufacturers of Patent Medicines."

Like many other Confederates, Henry's brother, Doctor Abraham Stonebraker, returned home from the war to find no work, no money, and few prospects. Abraham packed his few possessions and small family in a wagon and journeyed over 700 miles to Illinois, optimistic for a new beginning there as a physician.[477] Likewise, young Joseph Stonebraker was also having trouble returning to his old life after Appomattox. Anti-Confederate sentiment still ran strong and deep in Washington County, and, fearing for his safety, Joseph was living with relatives in Shepherdstown.

Henry's Baltimore partners suggested that he consider moving his family from Funkstown to Baltimore. In Baltimore Henry could significantly

---

473 Samuel Stonebraker moved from Washington County to Baltimore in 1839, where he had been a partner in several grain and flour commission businesses. By 1862, Samuel and his partner, Dr. H. Fletcher Zollickoffer, were partners in the business Stonebraker & Company. Scharf, J. Thomas, *History of Western Maryland. Being a history of Frederick, Montgomery, Carroll, Washington, Allegheny, and Garrett counties from the earliest period to the present day; including biographical sketches of their representative men*, (Philadelphia, PA, 1882), 1203.
474 *Herald of Freedom* (Hagerstown, MD), 30 Jul 1845. *Hagerstown News* (Hagerstown, MD), 7 Jan 1846.
475 There is conflicting testimony as to who made the initial proposal. Henry testified that he was approached by the three businessmen for a partnership agreement. Samuel Stonebraker and Henry Hoffman testified that Henry requested a loan of $10,000. *Stonebraker v. Stonebraker.*
476 *Alexandria Gazette* (Alexandra, VA) Oct 1865.
477 There is no documentation where in Illinois the Abraham Stonebraker family moved. It is reasonable he moved near or with his sister's family, John Casper Schnebly and Mary Cornelia Stonebraker Schnebly, who lived north of Peoria, IL.

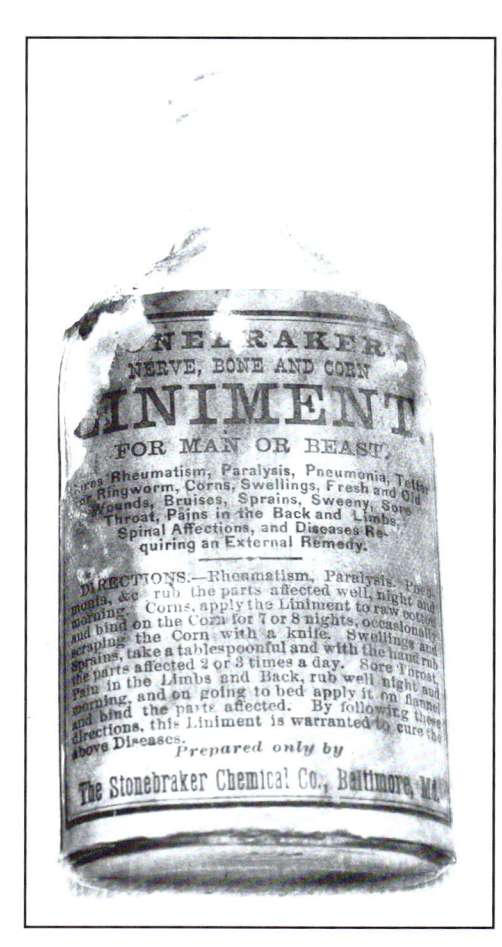

Stonebraker's External Liniment, circa 1870.

expand the business, and the move would also solve the problem of their ex-Confederate son, Joseph. Baltimore was a large, busy city with a strong undercurrent of Southern sympathies where the Stonebrakers could live in peace, just another ex-Confederate family among many.

In May of 1866, Henry and Angelica Stonebraker and their five unmarried children, Joseph, John, Mary Jane, Charles, and Edward, moved from Funkstown into a rented house at 82 S. Paca Street, Baltimore. The three married daughters, Ann Hamilton, Clara Keller, and Ellen Schriver, remained in Washington County with their families.

From a rented warehouse at 84 Camden Street, Henry Stonebraker and his three eldest sons, Joseph, John, and Charles officially adopted the title of "druggist" and set up a facility to produce bottled patent medicines.[478] The partnership business office of Stonebraker, Hoffman & Company was at Samuel Stonebraker's offices at 341 W. Baltimore Street.

The Stonebraker family's future had never looked so optimistic. Henry bragged in a letter to his brother Abraham in Illinois of his successful business arrangement, and of the family's contentment of living in Baltimore. Pleased for his older brother, Abraham replied, "If, at any time, you should want a pharmaceutical or financial clerk, with big pay and little to do, why I am open."[479]

The partnership of Stonebraker, Hoffman & Company that began with much promise lasted less than twenty months. The source of the partners' dispute was the ownership of the formulas. Henry had zealously guarded his recipes and insisted the terms of the partnership did not obligate him to share the recipes with his partners. Legal proceedings ensued, and, after less than two years, the fledgling partnership dissolved on December 10, 1866. Henry's partners were unaware that ten days earlier, determined to retain complete autonomy over his formulas, Henry had applied to the US Patent office for exclusive patents on his liniment and painkiller formulas.[480]

On the surface, the dissolution of the partnership was amicable. The three Baltimore businessmen retained all the ready-to-sell packaged medicines, plus the remaining unused labels that might be used in the case of product returns. They also agreed never again to engage in the patent medicine trade. On his part, Henry agreed not to produce any tonics for a period of three months and not to sell any tonics before six months had passed. In theory, this allowed the Baltimore businessmen time to sell off the remain-

---

478   *Baltimore City Directory*, 1866 and 1867. Within one year Henry and his family moved to 60 N. Greene Street. US Federal Census 1870 lists the male Stonebrakers as having the occupation of druggist.

479   *Stonebraker v. Stonebraker.*

480   Henry applied to the US patent office on 1 Dec 1866. Patents US62297 Internal Pain-Killer and US62298 External Liniment were received on 19 Feb 1867.

ing stock before Henry resumed manufacture as an independent businessman.

In reality, the breakup of the partnership was far from civil. Samuel Stonebraker and Henry Hoffman were not going to relinquish a potential fortune in the patent medicines trade because of a lack of formulas. Testimonial evidence at the later trial suggests that Samuel Stonebraker and Henry Hoffman conspired with three other Baltimore businessmen to outwit Henry Stonebraker by producing a comparable product labeled with the remaining original Stonebraker labels. The new partnership intended to capitalize on the "Stonebraker" trade name that was well-known to the public, and use their well-developed distribution network to supply the local merchants. The only obstacle to their plans was the production of product formulas that closely replicated Henry's original formulas. The solution to Samuel Stonebraker and Henry Hoffman's problem was another Stonebraker family member, now living in Illinois, who knew the ingredients in Henry's formulas.

Offering him a promise of great financial reward, the new partnership contacted Abraham Stonebraker in Illinois and enticed him to return to Maryland. In late 1866, Doctor Abraham Stonebraker and his family moved from Illinois into a house in downtown Baltimore, very near the home of his brother Henry.[481] Unquestionably pleased that his brother Abraham was now living just a few blocks away, Henry was unaware of the ulterior motive for his brother's decision to return to Maryland.

The Stonebraker Civil War broke out on Christmas Day 1866 when Samuel Stonebraker's notice announcing the dissolution of his partnership with Henry Stonebraker appeared in the newspaper. The notice reported that Henry Stonebraker had relinquished all his interest in the Stonebraker patent medicine business to Samuel Stonebraker and Henry Hoffman.[482] Retaining an undisclosed interest, Stonebraker and Hoffman had sold part interest in Stonebraker Medicines to Baltimore chemical merchants *Clotworthy & Company*, a company owned by brothers William P. and Charles A. Clotworthy, and Leonard Passano.[483] Us-

The Greatest Family Medicine in the World,

FOR

Sore Throat, Diptheria, Bronchitis, Cramp Cholic, Cholera Morbus, Cholera, &c.

The attention of the public, and especially the sufferers from that dreadful disease, Diptheria or Sore Throat, is called to the great remedy known as

STONEBRAKER'S BALSAM, OR PAIN KILLER.

As a sure cure for Sore Throat or Diptheria, Croup, Bronchitis, Scarlet Fever, &c., and all other diseases of the throat, and also an infallible remedy for Diarrhœa, Dysentery, Cholera, Cholera Morbus, Sick Headache, Sudden Colds and Coughs, Neuralgia, Phthisic, Old Sores, &c. It is also invaluable for Bruises, Frosted Feet, Swelled Joints, Bites of Poisonous Insects, &c., and a prompt and sure remedy for Cramp Cholic and all Pains in the Stomach and Bowels.

This medicine has been tried in thousands of cases in different parts of the country, and has never failed to cure if used in time, and according to directions. A great amount of suffering might often be saved by having a couple of bottles of this valuable medicine in the house. As an evidence of its great qualities the proprietors warrant every bottle to give entire satisfaction.

Try it and be convinced of its great value.

PRICE 40 CENTS PER BOTTLE.

☞ Agents of Stonebraker's Valuable Family Medicines will be on their guard against the imitation and counterfeiting of them, which is now being done by CLOTWORTHY & CO., Baltimore, and put forth upon the public as the *genuine* articles made by me. A large number of Agents are left under the impression that the undersigned is out of the business, and that CLOTWORTHY & CO. have the sole control of my business, which is not the case. Means, both foul and fair are used to deceive the unwary and the public and to flood the country with spurious articles. A word to the wise may save much trouble.

To my friends and the public I will state that I have re-commenced business at No. 84 Camden Street, Baltimore, where all those who have been selling my medicines, THE ORIGINAL STONEBRAKER'S MEDICINES, will please send their orders, and they will be supplied as before, on the most accommodating terms.

H. STONEBRAKER,
Sole Proprietor and Manufacturer.
No. 84 Camden Street, Baltimore,
Where all orders must be sent for the Genuine Articles.

For sale by
CAMPBELL & MASON,
August 6, 1867—6m. Charlestown, Va.

Spirit of Jefferson, (Charlestown, VA) 20 Aug 1867.

---

481   Abraham Stonebraker appears as a resident of Baltimore City in the 1868 City directory, living at 235 Pennsylvania Avenue. *American and Commercial Advertiser* (Baltimore, MD) 28 Nov 1868.

482   *Baltimore Sun* (Baltimore, MD) 25 Dec 1866. 2.

483   Irish born William Pitt Clotworthy (1829-1902) was the son of immigrant Alexander Clotworthy (1802-1887), a Baltimore furniture merchant. William Clotworthy was a well-known chemical merchant first affiliated with Clotworthy & Flint, then later Clotworthy & Company, Clotworthy Chemical Company, and Smith, Hanway & Company. During his lifetime Clotworthy received several patents, his most notable the special ingredient for baking powder biscuits (US265243a) which was distributed by the Baltimore firm Patapsco Baking Powders. Howard,

> **ANOTHER VERY IMPORTANT NOTICE**
> **TO THE AGENTS OF STONEBRAKER'S MEDICINES.**
>
> HAVING observed in the "Hagerstown Mail," as well as other newspapers, that Messrs. CLOTWORTHY & CO., of Baltimore, a Wholesale Drug House, have published a Card to "Agents of Stonebraker's Medicines," I deem it due to the Agents of these popular Medicines to publish another. The card of CLOTWORTHY & CO., is an *ingenious* affair, and is calculated to be mischievous. They state that I am not authorized to receipt for any money due Stonebraker, Hoffman & Co., leaving the inference that I am doing so, which is not the fact. They also state that "old Agencies will be supplied by wagon as heretofore," and that "applications for Agencies will receive prompt attention." This wording is very ingenious and gives out the impression that Clotworthy & Co. are manufacturing my medicines. This they have no right to do—they can sell off the stock that Stonebraker, Hoffman & Co. had on hand at the time of the dissolution, but they have no right to manufacture, neither have they the *genuine* receipts to do so.— Any attempt to manufacture is a violation of the U. S. Patent Laws, and is *spurious*. Agents are cautioned in reference to this ingenious card, and advised to send their orders to me at 84 Camden street, Baltimore, where I am manufacturing the genuine articles, and where I will be prepared to supply all demands after the 9th day of June next.
> HENRY STONEBRAKER.
> Baltimore, May 23, 1867—3t.

Spirit of Jefferson (Charlestown, VA) 28 May 1867.

ing the formulas provided by Doctor Abraham Stonebraker, Clotworthy & Company quickly produced and bottled their own version of the tonics in their production warehouses and affixed the remaining stock of original Stonebraker labels to the products. Clotworthy & Company notified their merchant distributors that Henry Stonebraker was no longer affiliated with tonic trade and that they would be manufacturing the medicines and would deliver - free of charge - all future shipments. After the supply of original labels was exhausted, Clotworthy & Company produced virtual replicas of the original labels, altering them slightly to read "Dr. Stonebraker's Medicines and Preparations."

An enraged Henry Stonebraker sued them all: Henry Stonebraker v. Abraham Stonebraker; Henry Stonebraker v. Samuel Stonebraker and Henry K. Hoffman; and Henry Stonebraker v. William Clotworthy and Leonard Passano. As the case was deliberated in the Maryland courts from 1867 through 1870, both Henry Stonebraker and Clotworthy & Company continued to produce "Stonebraker Medicines" and wage war in the newspapers. Both parties advertised and guaranteed their product as "genuine" and all others fraudulent imitations.

In a case that continues to be cited today as defending the rights of a patent holder, in April of 1870 the Maryland Courts found in favor of Henry Stonebraker. The courts' opinion was that "one tradesman has no rights to use the trademarks or names previously adopted and used by another, so as to induce purchasers to believe contrary to the fact, that they are buying the articles in which the marks were originally applied."[484]

In the case of Henry Stonebraker v. Abraham Stonebraker, the courts concluded that Abraham Stonebraker was employed by Clotworthy & Company for "no other reason than his name was Stonebraker," and by using that name they could "deceive the public as to the origin of their goods." Furthermore, the courts held that Abraham Stonebraker had no right to "lend or sell his name to perpetrate an injury upon his brother" and thereby fraud the public. Clotworthy & Company was found guilty of the "manufacture of medicines and marked their goods with labels and trade-marks similar to the complainant" and was required to pay Henry all profits obtained from the sale of the fraudulent goods. Interestingly, the courts made no opinion re-

---

George Washington, *The Monumental City: Its Past History and Present Resources*, (Baltimore, MD, 1873), 742. *American and Commercial Daily Advertiser* (Baltimore, MD), 4 Jun 1851, *Baltimore Sun* (Baltimore, MD) 16 Sep 1902.

By 1861, Italian born merchant Leonard Passano (1817-1904) advertised over 25 years experience in selling "Fancy Goods" from 52 Centre Market Space.

484   Hopkins, James Love, *The law of trademarks, tradenames and unfair competition: including trade secrets; goodwill; the Federal Trademark Acts of 1870, 1881 and 1905; the Trademark Registration Acts of the states and territories; and the Canadian Trademark and Design Act; with forms.* (Callaghan and Company, Chicago, IL, 1905).

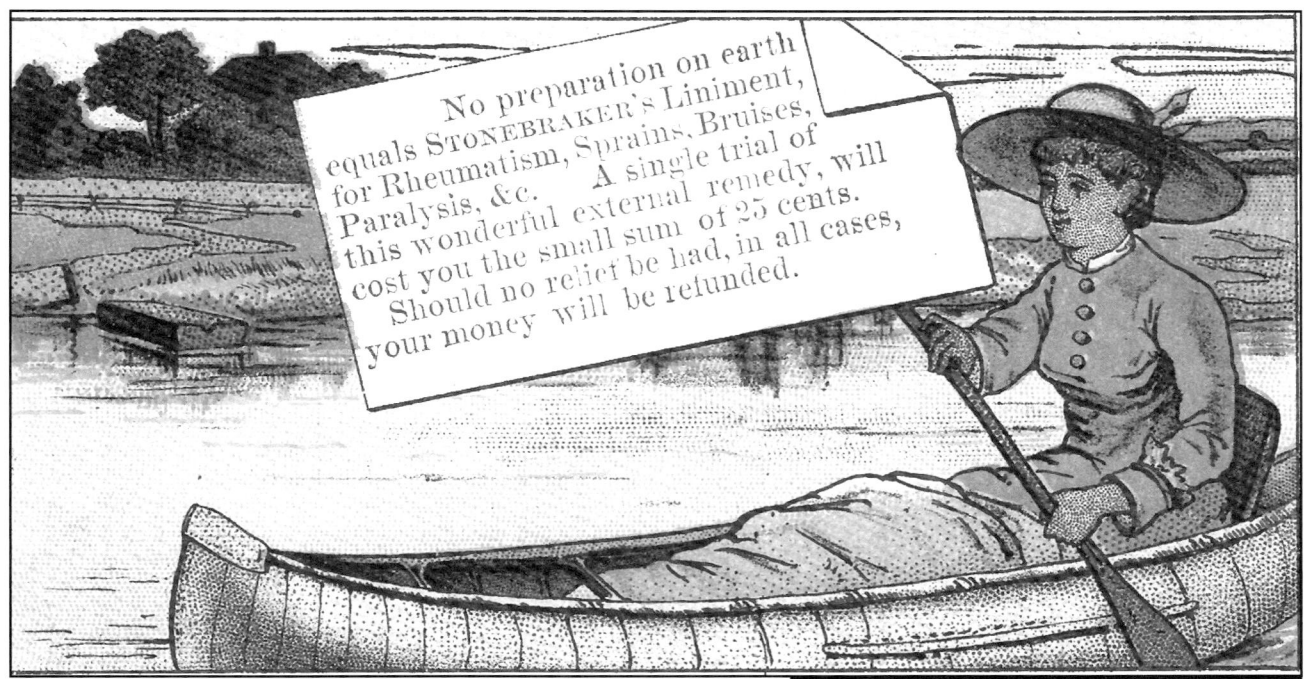

> No preparation on earth equals STONEBRAKER'S Liniment, for Rheumatism, Sprains, Bruises, Paralysis, &c. A single trial of this wonderful external remedy, will cost you the small sum of 25 cents. Should no relief be had, in all cases, your money will be refunded.

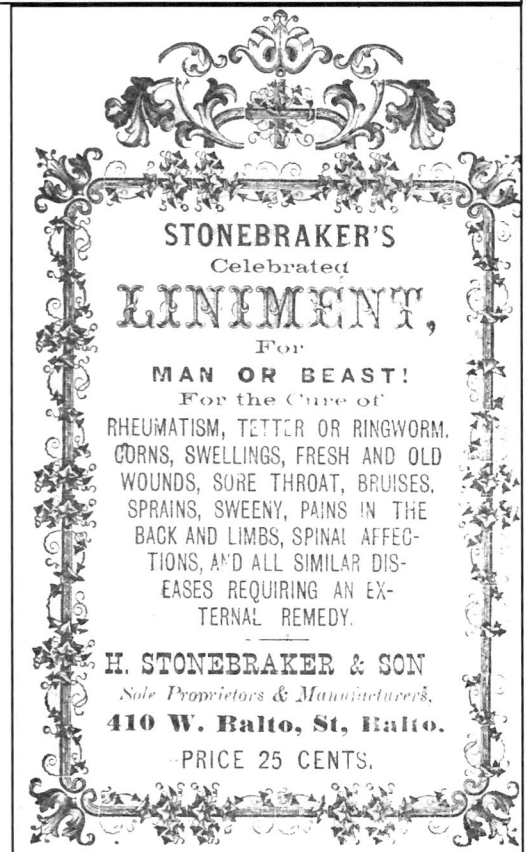

garding Samuel Stonebraker and Henry K. Hoffman, as no proof was presented as to whether they had profited from the scheme.

William Clotworthy, Samuel Stonebraker, Henry K. Hoffman, and Leonard Passano all continued as successful businessmen of Baltimore, the Henry Stonebraker affair only a minor glitch in their many interests, but they never again produced or sold patent medicines. Working as a druggist, Doctor Abraham Stonebraker and his family continued to live in Baltimore City until 1876. For a short time he advertised and sold an "Indian Prophylactic," a preventive medicine and cure for small pox.[485] In 1876, Abraham moved his family to Waco, Texas, where he lived the remainder of his life. It is doubtful he ever reconciled with his older brother. Henry and his sons continued to manufacture and sell *Stonebraker's Medicines and Preparations* from 84 Camden Street, and the patent medicine business continued to be financially successful for the Stonebraker family.[486]

In 1870, Joseph Stonebraker left the family business to open a liquor business. Shortly afterwards, the youngest son, Edward Stonebraker, also left his father's employ to work with Joseph. When Henry Stonebraker died in Febru-

> STONEBRAKER'S
> Celebrated
> LINIMENT,
> For
> MAN OR BEAST!
> For the Cure of
> RHEUMATISM, TETTER OR RINGWORM, CORNS, SWELLINGS, FRESH AND OLD WOUNDS, SORE THROAT, BRUISES, SPRAINS, SWEENY, PAINS IN THE BACK AND LIMBS, SPINAL AFFECTIONS, AND ALL SIMILAR DISEASES REQUIRING AN EXTERNAL REMEDY.
>
> H. STONEBRAKER & SON
> *Sole Proprietors & Manufacturers,*
> 410 W. Balto. St., Balto.
> PRICE 25 CENTS.

Both sides of a rare circa 1870 advertising card for "Stonebraker's Celebrated Liniments."

---

485 Dr. A. S. Stonebraker, occupation druggiest, appears in the *Baltimore City Directory* from 1868 through 1876. In Sep 1869, A.S. Stonebraker purchased 1,476 acres on the Chupaderas Creek 12 miles east of San Antonio for $500. *San Antonio Express* (San Antonio, TX) 2 Sep 1869. The US Federal Census of 1880 shows the Stonebraker family as residents of Waco, TX. Doctor Abraham Stonebraker died in 1885 at age 54 in Waco, TX.

486 *Baltimore Sun* (30 Sep 1870), 4. The Baltimore City 1870 US Federal census lists Henry, Joseph, John, and Edward Stonebraker as druggists living at 60 N. Greene Street.

ary of 1877 at age sixty-one, he willed his recipes, trademarks, and exclusive rights to *Stonebraker's Medicines* to his two sons, John and Charles, who had continued to work in the company with him.

In April of 1881, Charles Stonebraker sold all his interest in the firm to his older brother, John Stonebraker. Four years later in July of 1885, John sold the Stonebraker Medicines business to James J. Lamkin and Gerard Butke, who in turn sold it to Baltimore millionaire Howard Cassard in March of 1892. Although Cassard had many profitable business ventures, he is, unfortunately, remembered most for his "speculator failure" in the creation of an experiential ocean liner 222 feet in length, but only 16 feet wide. In her much publicized debut in November of 1890, instead of revolutionizing trans-oceanic travel, the flounder-shaped ship christened the *Howard Cassard*, keeled over and was later sold for scrap where she lay.[487]

Cassard reorganized the business of *Stonebraker Preparations and Medicines* into the stock corporation of *The Stonebraker Chemical Company,* where it remained a fixture in Baltimore for many years.[488] A fire at the Stonebraker Chemical warehouse in 1894, followed by the passage of the 1906 *Pure Food and Drug Act* targeting the misleading advertisements of patent medicine manufacturers, contributed to the gradual decline of the company.[489] The Stonebraker Chemical Company of Baltimore continued to operate well into the 1930s, but it never again produced products that matched the popularity of their pre-1906 patent medicines.

Henry's widow, Angelica Stonebraker, and daughter Mary Jane continued to live on Arlington Avenue in Baltimore for many years after Henry's death in 1877. In 1882, Mary Jane Stonebraker married Samuel E. Keller. Samuel Keller was the younger brother of Solomon J. Keller, who was married to Mary's older sister Clara Stonebraker. Samuel Keller had moved to Baltimore in the late 1860s where he lived with and worked as a druggist in the Stonebraker family medicine trade.[490] Samuel and Mary Jane Keller had no children and lived the remainder of their lives in the city of Baltimore.

In 1900, Angelica Stonebraker returned to Funkstown to live with her widowed daughter, Ann E. Stonebraker Hamilton, along the main street in Funkstown. Angelica died there in 1906 at age 91. She and Henry are buried together at Rose Hill Cemetery in Hagerstown, Maryland.

---

487   Naulty, Edwin Fairfax, *The Atlantic Ferry, The Era Magazine, An Illustrated Monthly, Volume 11*, (Philadelphia, PA, 1903) 55. *The Pittsburgh Press* (Pittsburgh, PA) 7 Dec 1902.
488   Weiker, Theodore, editor, *Merck's Market Report and Pharmaceutical Journal, Report*, Volume 3 (Merck & Co., NY,1894) 212.
489   *Baltimore Sun* (Baltimore, MD) 28 Aug 1894. Swann, Ph.D., John P., *The 1906 Food and Drugs Act and Its Enforcement*. http://www.fda.gov/AboutFDA/WhatWeDo/History/Origin/ucm054819.htm.
490   US Federal Census 1870 lists Samuel E. Keller, age 26, living in the Stonebraker household, occupation druggist.

The Family of
Henry Stonebraker – Angelica Rentch Stonebraker
(1815-1877)   (1814-1906)

Ann C. Stonebraker (1838-1934)
married Charles Hamilton (1826-1893) in 1857

Grocers on Baltimore St, Funkstown. No surviving children.

Daniel A. Stonebraker (1839-1850)
died young

Ellen Stonebraker (1840-1903)
married Henry Schriver (1833-1903) in 1864

Henry was a school teacher in Leitersburg, later Funkstown. Two daughters survive to adulthood.

Clara Ameila Stonebraker (1842-1902)
married Solomon J. Keller (1840-1899) in 1864

Lived in Funkstown, Purchased a house and lot on Baltimore Street in 1876. US Federal census notes: 1870 no occupation. 1880 works in tobacco house. 1899 obituary lists Keller as a the owner of a general merchandise store and a man of "considerable wealth." One surviving son.

Joseph R. Stonebraker (1844-1903)
married Mary Catherine Bosler (1843-1922) in 1874

Author of *Rebel of '61*. Wholesale Liquor business and Vice-President of a bank in Baltimore. Survived by three sons and one daughter.

John R. Stonebraker (1846-1921)
married Elizabeth M. H. Mackall MacDermott (1839-1894) in 1882

Inherited half-ownership of H. Stonebraker & Sons from his father. Sold business in 1885. Moved to Funkstown 1900. No children.

Mary Jane Stonebraker (1851-1927)
married Samuel E. Keller (1844-1916) in 1882

Samuel E. Keller, younger brother of Solomon J. Keller. Couple lived in Baltimore where Keller was a school teacher. No children.

Charles Henry Stonebraker (1854-1931)
married Martha Jane Valentine (1853-1933) in 1880

Inherited half-ownership of H. Stonebraker & Sons. Sold his interest to brother John in 1881, Worked at Jos. R. Stonebraker Wholesale Liquors until 1916. Survived by one son and one daughter.

Edward L. Stonebraker (1856-1888)
married Elizabeth H. Wicks (1858-) in 1880

Worked for H. Stonebraker & Sons. Clerked for Jos. R. Stonebraker Wholesale Liquor until death by train accident at age 31. No children.

JOHN R. STONEBRAKER (1846-1921)

Henry and Angelica Stonebraker's second son was John R. Stonebraker. Like his older brother Joseph, John was born in Missouri. John's first employment was brewing and bottling patent medicines with his father and brothers. John and his brother Charles continued in their fathers business after his death in 1877. In 1882, John married Elizabeth M. H. Mackall MacDermott (1839-1894) of Baltimore, a wealthy widow seven years his senior who had a 19-year-old son William Mackall MacDermott (1863-1908).

In 1885, John sold the Stonebraker Medicines business to Lamkin and Burke, then he and his step-son transformed the patent medicine production facility at 410 W. Baltimore Street into the wholesale liquor business of *John R. Stonebraker & Son* – a business John operated until 1889.[491] A few years after the death of his wife, John returned to Washington County, where he purchased a seventy-acre farm just east of Funkstown in 1902.[492]

Although too young to have served in the Confederacy, John was a passionate supporter of the southern "lost cause." His outspoken opinions earned him several anonymous warnings from the mysterious "black hands," a turn-of-the-century term first associated with Italian mafia and quickly adopted by vigilantes. On the evening of November 14, 1905, the Washington County "black hands" attempted to torch John's home and barn. The housekeeper was attacked and seriously injured when she surprised the culprits. The farmstead suffered no serious damage.[493]

The attempted arson did not curb John's activities. In January of 1910, he submitted an article to the *Richmond Times-Dispatch* newspaper entitled *Munford's Marylanders Never Surrendered to Foe*, recounting the 1st Maryland Cavalry's daring escape from Appomattox and later attempts to join with General Joe Johnston's army in North Carolina.[494] The article is written as a first-hand account and is taken directly from *Rebel of '61*, his older brother Joseph's book. The article appeared in the *Richmond Times-Dispatch* on February 6, 1910, and was reprinted in the *Southern Historical Society Papers*.[495] Both articles list John R. Stonebraker as the author, few realizing that had he had not served in the Confederacy, and that Joseph R. Stonebraker had been dead for seven years. John continued as a farmer in Funkstown until his death on September 29, 1921, at age seventy-five.

---

491   The *Wood's City Directory for Baltimore* 1885 lists two businesses for John R. Stonebraker at 410 W. Baltimore Street - Henry Stonebraker & Sons Patent Medicines and John R. Stonebraker & Son (William M. McDermott) Wholesale Liquors.
        The John R. Stonebraker & Son Wholesale Liquor operated from 410 W Baltimore (1885-1886), 520 W Baltimore (1887), 230 N Greene (1888-1889).
492   WCLR 116/167-168.
493   *Baltimore American* (Baltimore, MD) 15 Nov 1905, and *The Sun* (Baltimore, MD) 16 Nov 1905.
494   *Richmond Times-Dispatch* (Richmond, VA) 6 Feb 1910, 3.
495   SHSP, Volume 37, 309-312.

```
JOS. R. STONEBRAKER.        ED. L. STONEBRAKER.        CHAS. W. STONEBRAKER.
                JOS. R. STONEBRAKER & CO.
              Wholesale Liquor Merchants
                      No. 16 Light Street,
            Proprietors of                    BALTIMORE, MD.
    Zeigler and Clover Club Pure Rye Whiskies.
```

CHARLES HENRY STONEBRAKER (1854-1931)

Charles Henry Stonebraker was the eighth child and third son of Henry and Angelica Stonebraker. Charles married Martha Jane Valentine in Baltimore in April of 1880. Because Charles and his older brother John remained in the family business with their father until his death in 1877, Henry left each son a half-interest in *H. Stonebraker & Sons,* including all rights to the patents and trademarks. One year later Charles sold his half-interest to John and went to work in the wholesale liquor trade with Joseph. After Joseph's death in 1903, Charles continued to operate the *Jos. R. Stonebraker & Co.* business in Baltimore until 1916. Charles and his wife had three children, two of whom survived to adulthood. Charles and his wife are buried in the Loudon Park Cemetery, Baltimore, Maryland.

EDWARD L. STONEBRAKER (1856-1888)

The youngest member of the Henry Stonebraker family, Edward first worked in his father's business and, like his brother Charles, defected to work with his older brother Joseph in the wholesale liquor trade. Edward married Elizabeth H. Wicks in Baltimore in May of 1880. The couple had no children. In 1888, while on a business trip to Hyattsville, Maryland, Edward was struck and killed by a train when he fell from the platform onto the tracks. He was 31 years old. As a memorial to Edward, his older brother Joseph dedicated a room at the Confederate Soldiers' Home in Pikesville, Maryland, in his memory. It was the only room in the soldiers' home dedicated to a civilian as Edward was only five years old when the war began. Edward is buried in the Loudon Park Cemetery, Baltimore, Maryland.

JOSEPH R. STONEBRAKER (1844-1903)

In May of 1866, the Stonebraker family moved the seventy miles from Funkstown to Baltimore. In addition to their personal and household items, the Stonebrakers had the added burden of carefully moving the equipment used in production of Henry's patent medicines. The family moved into a rented house at 82 S. Paca Street, and Angelica was unquestionably pleased that her husband's manufacturing facility was no longer inside her home, but in a warehouse at 84 Camden Street. From the warehouse Joseph Stonebraker worked alongside his father, three younger brothers, and Samuel E. Keller in the family business of producing patent medicines.

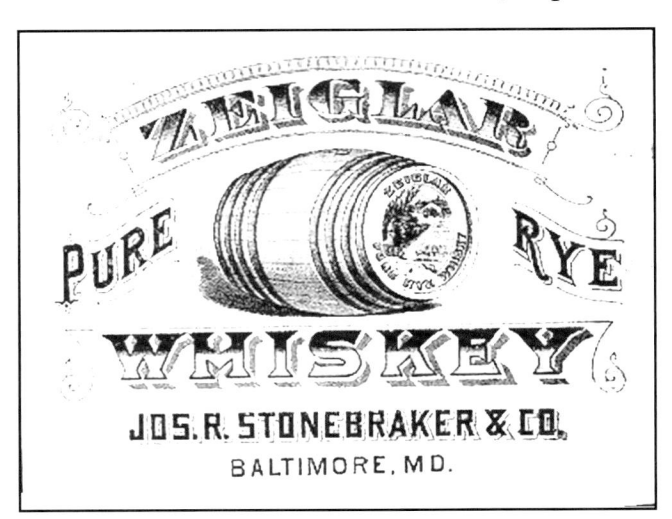

The litigation for the trademark and ownership rights to *Stonebraker Medicines* between his father and uncle Abraham must have been a difficult trial for Joseph. Abraham Stonebraker had been kind and caring to Joseph during his service as a private in the Confederate Army. Numerous times during the war, the Doctor had intervened on Joseph's behalf, providing him with money, horses, food, and shelter.

In 1870, after the *Stonebraker v. Stonebraker* case was settled by the courts, Joseph and a distant cousin from Funkstown, Ellis Emmert, formed a partnership and opened a wholesale liquor business in Baltimore under the name *Emmert & Stonebraker* (1870-1871). By 1873, Joseph had changed partners and was working with Thomas Beall as *Beall & Stonebraker* (1873-1876), and, by 1876, Joseph was on his own with *Jos. R. Stonebraker* (1876-1879), later changing the name to *Jos. R. Stonebraker & Co.* (1880-1916) when he was joined by his brothers Charles and Edward. In 1876, his business was located in a warehouse at No. 89 Camden Street, across the street from his father's warehouse at 84-86 Camden Street.[496]

An early advertising card offering a Rye Whiskey that Joseph and his brothers were producing by "rectification" in their warehouse along Camden Street in Baltimore. Stonebraker later obtained a patent for his Zeiglar Pure Rye.

Although Joseph Stonebraker was labeled as a wholesale liquor dealer, his main industry was as a liquor "rectifier." Rectifying spirits, or rectification, is the process of cutting, blending, mixing, or infusing other ingredients into distilled spirits, causing a reaction that changes the basic character, and often the alcohol content, of the original spirit. The simple mixing of cocktails is not considered rectification. For an industrious individual with the proper equipment and a working knowledge of chemistry, "the profits from this system of blending and mixing [rectifying] must be very great."[497]

The adage "like-father, like-son" is an accurate statement when applied to Henry and Joseph Stonebraker. In essence, Joseph applied the basic chemistry techniques his father used in the production of patent medicines and applied them to the rectification of alcohol. Both men started with a base of neutral grain alcohol purchased from one of the many large distilleries situated around Baltimore. Into the alcohol they blended in various ingredients and cooked well. After some minor distillation and aging, the final product was bottled, labeled with an attractive wrapper, and delivered to one of

---

496   The Baltimore City Directories from 1876 until 1916 list the Jos. R. Stonebraker Wholesale Liquor business at: 89 Camden (1876-1879), 88 Camden (1880-1882), 16 Light (1883-1888), 16 Hanover (1889-1904), 601 W Saratoga (1905), 13-15 E Lombard (1906-1916).

497   Fleischmann, Joseph, *The Art of Blending and Compounding Liquors and Wines*, (Dick & Fitzgerald, NY, 1885) 8.

A Rebel of '61

the many retail merchant distributors in the city. The proximity of two Stonebraker production warehouses suggests that father and son were collaborating their talents, pharmaceutical techniques, equipment, and associations with the local distilleries in the rectifying of their respective products.

The production of beer and alcohol was a time-honored, cherished tradition in Baltimore, and had a significant impact on the economy of the city from the 18th century up to the golden age of Baltimore breweries in the 19th century.[498] Historians have long studied Baltimoreans' love affair with spirit production, especially the late 19th century favorite known as Maryland Rye Whiskey – the product that put little Maryland third in the nation behind giants Kentucky and Pennsylvania in nationwide liquor production.[499] The sophisticated city of Baltimore capitalized on her hometown product with regional descriptors for the Rye Whiskey such as *Maryland Queen, Pikesville, Braddock, Sherbrook,* and *Maryland Club*. Additionally, Baltimore had railroads and a shipping port for nationwide distribution. By the early 20th century, the city of Baltimore lead Maryland in the fight against temperance and was viewed as a "center of resistance to prohibition."[500]

The year 1870 when Joseph Stonebraker entered the liquor trade was a pivotal year for the industry. The Kentucky firm that produced *Old Forester* bourbon revolutionized the industry when they became the first distillery to sell their product in a sealed bottle, packaged with a recognizable label. The sealed bottle safeguarded against product alteration and dilution, while the label served as a product identifier as late 19th century consumers became ever more aware of proprietary names, commercial symbols, and packaging.[501]

After a few years in the trade, Joseph Stonebraker was rectifying, bottling, and labeling his own variations of Maryland Rye Whiskey. Some of Stonebraker's brews included *Oriola Baltimore Rye, Setter Maryland Pure Rye Whiskey, Tarpon Maryland Rye, Wide Awake Maryland Rye, Old Private Stock Fine Rye Whiskey, Zeigler Pure Rye,* and *Swallow Whiskey.*[502]

Joseph R. Stonebraker from his biography in "Monograph of the First Decade 1890-1900, Fidelity and Deposit Company of Maryland." The book was printed by Stonebraker Brothers Printing Company of Baltimore, Joseph's sons.

---

498 O'Prey, Maureen, *Brewing in Baltimore* (Arcadia Publishing, Charleston, SC, 2011).
499 Bready, James H, *Maryland Rye: A Whiskey the Nation Long Fancied—But Now has let Vanish,* Maryland Historical Magazine, (Winter 1990), 359.
500 ibid. O'Prey, *Brewing in Baltimore,* 59.
501 http://www.oldforester.com/1870Society_book.aspx.
 Cowdery, Charles K., *Review: Old Forester Kentucky Straight Bourbon Whiskey, The Bourbon County Reader,* Vol 4, No. 3, (May 1999).
502 Examples of Stonebraker Maryland Rye Whiskey bottles may be seen at the Maryland State Archives, *The James H. Bready Collection of Maryland Rye Whiskey Bottles and Related Ephemera,* Special Collections. MSA SC 5646.
 Joseph R. Stonebraker received a patent for Oriola Baltimore Rye and Wide Awake Maryland Rye on 1 Mar 1899. Charles H. and Joseph R. Stonebraker received a patent for Swallow Whiskey on 26 May 1903. *Annual Report of the Commissioner of Patents for the year 1899.* Serial Set

The following recipes are taken from Joseph Fleishman's 1885, *The Art of Blending and Compounding Liquors and Wines,* a rectifier's guide to producing liquors to be sold to the consumer as rye or bourbon whiskey. The principal ingredient in the lower grade whiskies was neutral grain spirits, a tasteless alcohol.

FACTIOUS WHISKEY

The different grades of whiskeys here given commence with No. 1, the lowest, and increasing in quality with their numbers.

GRADE No. 1.

The lowest grade of whiskey in the market is generally composed of the following ingredients

Spirits, 32 gallons
Water, 16 gallons
Sugar Coloring, 4 ounces
Beading Oil, 1 ounce

The Sugar Coloring, or Caramel, is harmless and can be obtained from any druggist. This grade is about 65% proof, and costs the rectifier 75 cents per gallon. It is sold to the jobbers at 90 cents, and to the saloon proprietors for $1.50. The proof strength of this may be increased to 70°, 80°, or higher, the cost and price being in proportion.

GRADE No. 2.

This quality is generally made by adding to Grade No. 1 either the Oil of Rye, or Oil of Bourbon, making the result Rye Whiskey, or Bourbon, as the case may be. This increases the value five to ten cents on the gallon.

GRADE No. 3.

This is also a cheap article, and consists of:

Spirits, 45 gallons
Prune Juice, ½ gallon
Sugar Coloring, 4 ounces

As the prune juice reduces the proof 2 to 3%, the value will not advance more than five cents per gallon. In all these grades one ounce of Beading Oil is added to the barrel. The reason for it is that, although the rectifier may sell this article at full proof, the jobber may add water, which would otherwise destroy the effect of the Beading Oil. This is important, as these low grades are sold by appearance and without any particular reference to quality.

GRADE No. 4.

Spirits, 45 gallons
Prune Juice, ½ gallon
New England Rum, ½ gallon
Coloring, 4 ounces
Beading Oil, 1 ounce

This grade will cost $1.25 per gallon.

GRADE No. 5.

Spirits, 45 gallons
Prune Juice, ½ gallon
St. John's Bread Extract ½ gallon
New England Rum, ½ gallon
Coloring, 4 ounces
Syrup or Glycerine, 8 ounces
Beading Oil, 1 ounce

This will cost $1.28 per gallon. Glycerine is often used, but it is not advisable to do so. It imports a velvety smoothness at first, more, so, perhaps, than syrup, but it soon turns bitter.

RYE WHISKIES

The common, cheap grades of Rye Whiskey are made of spirits, with coloring, and the addition of Rye Oil and branded "Rye Whiskey." Their preparation is substantially the same as given under Grades Nos. 1, 2, and 3, and need not be repeated here. The following grades have, all of them, less or more genuine whiskey in their composition:

GRADE No. 12.

Spirits, 40 gallons
Hainesville Whiskey, 5 gallons
Tea Extract, ½ gallon
Coloring, 4 ounces
Beading Oil, 1 ounce

This grade will cost $1.30 per gallon.

GRADE No. 13.
Spirits, 35 gallons
Hainesville Whiskey, 5 gallons
Gibson Whiskey, 5 gallons
Tea Extract, ½ gallon
Coloring, 4 ounces
This grade will cost $1.40 per gallon.

GRADE No. 14.
Spirits, 30 gallons
Hainesville Whiskey, 5 gallons
Gibson Whiskey, 5 gallons
Dougherty Whiskey, 5 gallons
Tea Extract, ½ gallon
Coloring, 3 ounces
The increased proportion of genuine whiskeys will raise the cost of this grade to $1.50 per gallon.

GRADE No. 15.
Spirits, 25 gallon
Guckenheimer Whiskey, 10 gallons
Hainesville Whiskey, 10 gallons
Tea Extract, ½ gallon
Coloring, 2 ounce
This makes a very good blend, and costs $1.65 per gallon.

GRADE No. 16.
Spirits, 10 gallons
Guckenheimer Whiskey, 10 gallons
Hainesville Whiskey, 10 gallons
Gibson Whiskey, 15 gallons
Tea Extract, ½ gallon
Coloring, 1 ounce
This contains only a small proportion of spirits and costs $1.80 per gallon.

GRADE No. 17.
Guckenheimer Whiskey, 10 gallons
Hainesville Whiskey, 10 gallons
Monticello, 2 gallons
Tea Extract, ½ gallon
This grade is a very fine article, entirely genuine whiskeys, and judiciously blended. It costs $1.95 per gallon.
It will be readily understood that the combinations of the different brands of whiskeys, with or without the addition of more or less spirits, could be extended almost indefinitely; but the grades already described will actually cover all the varieties in the market.

There is very little difference between the blends of genuine whiskeys, provided that they have been mixed by honest dealers; the Trade, however, have their peculiar fancies for certain brands, deeming them better than others, but there is more imagination than reality in their discrimination, from the fact that different firms will make the same grade of whiskey, arriving at similar results, but not necessarily following the same formula, the main object being to suit the tastes of the consumers, whose preference is usually with blends of pure whiskeys--when they can get it.

FRUIT JUICES AND FLAVORINGS

All newly-distilled liquors and spirits have a rough and pungent taste, which must be remedied before they can be used as beverages. This is done by fruit-juices or flavors, which are mainly alcoholic extracts of fruits and other substances, and are employed in certain proportions to counteract the raw taste of the new spirits.

These extracts may be prepared with very little difficulty, and generally better and cheaper than they can be purchased ready-made, for in these days, articles used only for the purposes of adulteration are themselves largely adulterated and, in the case of fruit extracts especially, often factious.

A very simple apparatus may be made, which will answer every purpose. Procure a barrel of, say, 40 gallons capacity; about four inches from the bottom insert a tightly-fitting false bottom, pierced with a considerable number of holes of about a quarter or a third of an inch in diameter; fit a faucet in firmly, below the false bottom, and the macerating tub is ready for use.

The ingredients to be macerated should be well bruised, and placed in the barrel, and the fluid used poured on then and the whole allowed to macerate together for not less than three days, and as much longer as possible.

A rare surviving bottle of Joseph Stonebraker's Wide Awake Maryland Rye. Photo courtesy John Sullivan, http://minivodkaguy.com/WhiskeyPintsAndHalfPints.html.

Stonebraker was not alone with his efforts to become a nationally recognized brand. The 1877 *Wood's Baltimore City Directory* lists 10 distilleries, 97 wholesale liquor dealers, and 99 retail liquor sales establishments, also known as saloons. By 1885, there were still 10 distilleries, 99 wholesale liquor dealers, but the number of retail establishments had almost tripled to 291.[503] Of Baltimore's 99 wholesale liquor dealers, or rectifiers, almost half were located in the warehouse district near Stonebraker's warehouse.[504]

Whiskey production in Baltimore was an enormously competitive industry where Joseph Stonebraker was merely a bit player. None of his products ever achieved national fame, but there was sufficient business that by 1874 he had earned enough money to marry his long-time sweetheart, Mary Catherine Bosler of Carlisle, Pennsylvania. The couple married in the bride's hometown of Carlisle in January of 1874, and they returned to live in Baltimore at 104 George Street. The marriage produced five children, four that survived to adulthood. Their first child, James Bosler, was born October 11, 1874, followed by a second son, Joseph Rentch, Jr., born in February of 1876. Joseph, Jr. survived only seven months.[505] Another son, Harry, was born to the couple in June of 1877.[506] The Stonebraker's fourth son, also named Joseph Rentch, Jr., was born in December of 1880. Their last child was a daughter, Elizabeth, born to the couple in November of 1884.

Although just a private in the Confederate army, Joseph was proud of his service the Confederacy was very active in the numerous Confederate veterans organizations around Baltimore. *The Society of the Army and Navy of Confederate States in the state of Maryland* was organized in 1871, and, in 1880, General Bradley T. Johnson formed *The Association of the Maryland Line*. All the veterans' organizations seemed to have four common goals: association of comrades; memorials to the dead; aid for the disabled and destitute; and preserving for posterity a "true account of the great struggle."[507]

Volume 3855, 490. *Annual Report of the Commissioner of Patents for the year 1903*, Serial Set Volume 4607, 623.

503   1877 and 1885 *Wood's Baltimore City Directory* (Baltimore MD). Businesses paid to be advertised in the Wood's Directory, suggesting that these numbers, while good indicators, are only a partial listing of the actual number of businesses.

504   ibid, Bready, *Maryland Rye,* MHM, (Winter 1990), 364.

505   Joseph R. Stonebraker, Jr. (1876-1876) is buried in Ashland Cemetery, Carlisle, PA, with the Bosler family members.

506   Harry Stonebraker's tombstone in Loudon Park Cemetery, Baltimore, MD, indicates he was born 9 Jun 1876. This may be in error as Harry lists his birth date as 6 Jun 1877 on his 1900 application for acceptance to Sons of the American Revolution. Ancestry.com *U.S. Sons of the American Revolution Membership Applications, 1889-1970* [database on-line] Provo, UT: Ancestry.com Operations, Inc:, 2011.

507   Booth, Capt. George W, compiler, *Illustrated Souvenir, Maryland Line Confederate Soldiers' Home, Pikesville, Maryland,* (Pikesville, MD, 1894) 11. Hereafter cited as *Souvenir.*

With these goals in mind, in April of 1885, the *Society of the Army and Navy of the Confederate States* hosted a grand, five-day Confederate Bazaar at the Fifth Regiment Armory in mid-town Baltimore to raise money for the continued care of indigent Confederates.[508] They advertised their objective, "although the war is long since over, there are many brave veterans still suffering from its hardships, without pensions – and many almost shelterless."[509]

The response was overwhelming as thousands of Confederate veterans and their families from every nearby state flocked to attend the event. The Friday, April 10th *Baltimore Sun* newspaper reported that over 3,000 people had massed before the building the prior evening seeking admission to the bazaar, and the city police were forced to turn most of them away.[510] The event received coverage in newspapers as far south as South Carolina, Georgia, Louisiana, and west to Kansas City, Missouri.[511] Naturally, the Baltimore newspapers gave their readers daily coverage of all the bazaar's activities. The bazaar raised over $31,000 for the cause.

On the final day, to the amazement of his former comrades, General Bradley T. Johnson presented the 1st Maryland Cavalry Confederate battle flag numbered 42 that he had retrieved from Mrs. Horsely of Nelson County, Va.[512] Joseph and four other members of his former company related the tale of their daring flight from Appomattox and how this flag came to be saved.[513] Joseph vividly brought the past to light for the veterans by read-

The Bolton, Spencer Morton Mansion was the headquarters for the Fifth Regiment Militia in Baltimore, MD, and in 1885, the site for the Confederate Bazaar. Photo circa 1895, estimated to be taken just before demolition of this structure. L.H. Fowler Collection, Baltimore City Life Museum Collection, Maryland Historical Society, MC2130.

---

508   In 1885, the present-day imposing, fortress-style Fifth Regiment National Guard Armory located in midtown Baltimore, MD designed by noted architects Wyatt & Nolting had not yet been built. That structure, now on the National Register of Historic Places, was completed in 1903. The present armory was built on the site of the Bolton, Spencer Morton Mansion.

509   The bazaar was held April 7 through April 11, 1885. *Charleston News and Courier* (Charleston, SC) 28 Feb 1885.

510   *Baltimore Sun* (Baltimore, MD) 10 Apr 1885, 4.

511   *Kansas City Times* (Kansas City, MO) 8 April 1885, *Charleston News and Courier* (Charleston, SC) 28 Feb 1885, 16-20 Mar 1885, *Macon Weekly Telegraph*, (Macon, GA) 20 Mar 1885, *Augusta Chronicle* (Augusta, GA) 31 Mar 1885, *Times-Picayune* (New Orleans, LA) 12 Apr 1885.

512   The 1st Maryland Cavalry battle flag "42" replaced the battle flag that was lost during the raids of Aug 1864. According to Stonebraker's footnote 4, page 162, Confederate General Bradley T. Johnson recovered the flag from Mrs. Florence Horsely of Nelson County, VA sometime after the war. In 1888, the flag was placed on exhibition in a memorial room at the Confederate Soldiers' Home, Pikesville, MD. This battle flag covered the casket of General Johnson in his funeral procession through Baltimore in Oct 1903. The flag is currently housed in the Maryland State Archives, Special Collections, MSA SC 1560-1. *Souvenir*, 21. *Baltimore American* (Baltimore, MD) 8 Oct 1903, 11. Special thanks to Colonel James McGlincy of Baltimore, MD, 1st Maryland Cavalry Battalion CSA for his expertise and this organization's continuing efforts to research and locate the surviving flags and banners of the 1st Maryland Cavalry CSA.

513   See pages 157-161 for Stonebraker's account at Appomattox. See footnote 397, page 162 for an account of the flag.

One of the 22 memorial rooms within the Confederate Soldiers' Home in Pikesville, Maryland. This 1889 photos is of the "Relic Room." Photo courtesy of the Maryland Historical Society. PP159.12.

ing excerpts from his wartime journal. Instead of merely reporting the story of the soldier's escape and trials, the *Baltimore Sun* newspaper reprinted Joseph's complete journal entries that recounted the momentous events of Saturday, April 8, and Sunday, April 9, 1865.[514]

As the century progressed, the plight of the aging, disabled, and indigent Confederate veterans became an issue of increasing priority. It was estimated there were at least a quarter of a million ex-confederate soldiers still alive in 1888, twenty-thousand of them in Maryland.[515] Confederate veterans were ineligible for a Federal pension; therefore, any provision for their support had to be indirect or provided by the state.[516] All eleven secession states, plus the border states of Kentucky, Missouri, and Oklahoma passed legislation awarding state pensions for their Confederate veterans – Maryland was the only border state with organized Confederate regiments that did not offer a pension.[517]

Under the direction of General Bradley T. Johnson, the *Maryland Line Confederate Veterans'* organization continued to raise funds and solicit the Maryland Assembly for the support of Confederate veterans. On February

---

[514] *Baltimore Sun*, (Baltimore, MD), 15 Apr 1885.
[515] Letter from General Bradley T. Johnson on pensions. *Baltimore Sun*, (Baltimore, MD), 3 Feb 1888.
[516] Report on the 50th Congress, first session. *Baltimore Sun*, (Baltimore, MD), 28 Mar 1888, 4.
[517] *Confederate Pension Records,* http://www.archives.gov/research/military/civil-war/confederate/pension.html.

22, 1888, the *Baltimore Sun* newspaper reported that Governor Elihu E. Jackson approved an act dedicating the old government arsenal at Pikesville, Maryland, as a Confederate retirement home with a $5,000 per annum appropriation for the maintenance of the buildings.[518] When the Maryland Line Association took possession of the old arsenal complex in April of 1888, the facility was "little short of that of a ruin."[519] Using the State appropriation, supplemented by generous private contributions and materials, within two months the industrious veterans had sufficiently renovated the complex to open on June 27, 1888 with seven residents and thirty applicants.

With the exception of the *Stonewall Jackson Infirmary*, each of the ten buildings on the arsenal grounds were named after a distinguished Confederate soldier or sailor either born in, or a resident of Maryland. The superintendant's residence was in the *MacKall Building*, christened after Cecil County's Brigadier General William W. MacKall (1817-1891). The surgeon's office and pharmacy were located in the *Elezy Building*, in honor of Maryland-born Major General Arnold Elezy (1816-1871). The remaining buildings housed residents or were multi-purpose. The *Trimble Building* featured a large relic hall displaying Confederate memorabilia, a bathroom, and five residents' rooms.[520] The first floor of the *Archer Building* housed the *Ra-*

The US arsenal in Pikesville, MD was used as the Confederate veterans retirement home from 1888 until 1932. Photo by E. H. Pickering, 1932. LOC/P&P. HABS MD,3-PIKV,1--1

---
518   Governor Elihu Emory Jackson took office 11 Jan 1888. Maryland Laws (1888) 338. Maryland Line Confederate Soldiers' Home, Baltimore American (Baltimore, MD) 28 Jun 1888.
519   *Souvenir*, 14.
520   The Trimble Building was named for Virginia born Major General Isaac R. Trimble (1802-1888). Trimble is frequently noted as "arguably the most famous Maryland resident who fought in the Confederacy." Prior to the war, Trimble lived in Baltimore and worked for the railroad. Trimble is most remembered as one of the three division commanders in Pickett's Charge at Gettysburg. He is buried in Baltimore.

leigh C. Thomas Memorial Reading Room, a wood-paneled, 50' x 27' library with over 1,000 volumes donated by his family, with a store room and servants' quarters on the second floor.[521]

The *Buchanan Building* and *Little Building* housed residents, each room within the building privately appointed for the veteran residents by a local family in memory of their Confederate loved ones. Within the *Buchanan Building* were the *Jenkins, Gill, Brown,* and *Murray* rooms; each of these rooms a memorial to a Maryland Confederate soldier who had been killed in action.[522] The *Little Building* was the largest of the resident buildings, housing nine memorial rooms with more varied themes. The *Virginia Room* was Mrs. Martin B. Brown's memorial to "old Virginia."[523] The *Chantilly Room* was a small bedroom with a single bed and the only memorial room named in honor of an estate.[524] The surviving members of the *Baltimore Light Artillery* furnished a room to honor their deceased comrades. The remaining six memorial rooms, *McKim, Little, Colston, Marshall, Goodwin,* and *Stonebraker* rooms in the *Little Building* were tributes to individuals. The *Stonebraker Room* was furnished by Joseph Stonebraker in honor of his recently deceased brother Edward. About a month after the August 1, 1888, opening of the veterans home, Edward Stonebraker was running to catch a train in Hyattsville, Maryland when he fell onto the tracks and was struck and killed by a train. He was 31 years old. Of the twenty-two memorial rooms in the veterans' home, the *Stonebraker Room* was the only room dedicated to a civilian, as Edward did not serve in the Confederate Army, being just eight years old when Joseph enlisted in the Confederacy.[525]

By October of 1898 the center housed over 100 veterans. A brochure described the facility as providing the veterans "a haven of rest . . . to which they may retire and find refuge, and, at the same time, lose none of their self-respect, nor suffer in the estimation of those whose experience in life is more

Mrs. Ridgely Brown of Montgomery County, MD, memorialized her husband with a room in the Confederate Soldiers Home. Lieutenant Colonel Ridgely Brown, Co. A, 1st Maryland Cavalry, was killed in action 1 Jun 1864, at So. Anna, VA. Photograph of Mrs. Brown in her widow's weeds holding an 11-star Confederate flag. LOC/P&P. LC-DIG-ppmsca-38065.

---

521   The Archer Building was named for Brigadier General James J. Archer (1817-1864) from near Havre De Grace, MD. The Raleigh C. Thomas Reading Room was a memorial to Private Raleigh Colston Thomas (1844-1887), a private in Company C, 1st Maryland Cavalry. Thomas was the great-great-great grandson of John Hanson, first President of the Continental Congress, an old and affluent family of Baltimore.

522   John Carroll Jenkins, Baltimore, Maryland Guard, 21st Virginia Infantry, KIA 11 Oct 1861.
      Corporal Sommerville Pinkney Gill, Annapolis, MD, Company A, 2nd Maryland Infantry, KIA Pegrams Farm, VA.
      Lieutenant Colonel Ridgely Brown, Montgomery County, MD, 1st Maryland Cavalry, KIA 1 Jun 1864, So. Anna, VA.
      Captain William H. Murray, Anne Arundel County, MD, Captain Company A of the 1st/2nd Maryland Battalion under General George H. Steuart. KIA Culp's Hill, Gettysburg PA.

523   *Baltimore Sun,* (Baltimore, MD) 28 Jun 1888, supplement, 1.

524   In the fall of 1861 into 1862, the 1st Maryland Infantry camped at the plantation *Chantilly,* then owned and occupied by Corneila Lee Turberville Stuart (1797-1883), the widow of Charles Calvert Stuart (1794-1846). In February 1863 Federal troops burned the circa 1817 mansion house. It is generally considered that the town of Chantilly, VA takes its name from the plantation. *Northern Virginia History Notes,* http://www.novahistory.org/Chantilly.html.

525   Based on Goldsborough's description of the 10 buildings and 22 furnished memorial rooms in *The Maryland Line in the Confederate Army, 1861-1865,* 349-371.

fortunate."⁵²⁶ The facility quietly closed in 1932 after homes were found for the last two veterans.

As his wholesale liquor business continued to prosper, Joseph continued as an advocate for Confederate veterans affairs. In January of 1890, Joseph and James R. Wheeler of Company E, appeared at the Capitol in Washington, DC, inviting prominent ex-confederates to attend the annual banquet of the *Confederate Society of Maryland*.⁵²⁷

In 1890, Joseph and several other Baltimore businessmen collaborated to open a new bank in Baltimore called the Fidelity and Deposit Company of Maryland. Joseph persuaded his brother-in-law, wealthy businessman John Herman Bosler of Carlisle, Pennsylvania, to make a significant investment in the new bank, an action that virtually guaranteed the success of the new firm.⁵²⁸ As one of the founders and incorporators of the company, Joseph Stonebraker was named a vice-president of the company two years later.

Joseph had always loved to fish. Now in his late 40s and moderately successful, he frequently vacationed along the east coast for recreational sport fishing. While vacationing at Sarasota Pass, Florida, in March of

The executives of the Fidelity and Deposit Company of Maryland. Top row left to right: Seymour Mandelbaum, George Warfield, Thomas A. Whelan, John H. Wight. Seated left to right: President Edwin Warfield, General Clinton P. Paine, H. Crawford Black, Joseph R. Stonebraker, General Robert Ober. Photo from Monograph of the First Decade of the Fidelity and Deposit Company of Maryland 1890-1900 *(Stonebraker Brothers Printing, Baltimore, MD 1900).*

---

526   ibid, Goldsborough, William Worthington, *The Maryland Line*, 346.
527   *Evening Star* (Washington DC) 14 Jan 1890, 6.
528   John Herman Bosler (1830-1897) of Carlisle, PA had many diversified financial interests. He had made a fortune in land speculation of western lands near Omaha, NE, was owner of the Carlisle [PA] Manufacturing Company, president of the Carlisle Shoe Factory, a director of the Carlisle Deposit Bank, the Merchants' National Bank, the Carlisle Gas & Water Company, the Cumberland Valley Railroad Company, and president of the Carlisle Land & Improvement Company, an enterprise that built a large addition to the town of Carlisle, PA. *History of Cumberland and Adams Counties Pennsylvania, Part II* (Chicago, IL, 1886) 369-370.

Giant Jew Fish of approximately the same size as the fish caught by Stonebraker in 1890. This 1909 California Jew fish is so large a child is seated in its mouth. This species of grouper is considered endangered today and protected in the United States and Caribbean. LOC/P&P. LC-USZ62-88722.

1890, he snagged a monstrous 450 pound, 6'10" Jew Fish.[529] Dragging the fish carcass home to Baltimore, Joseph had the giant stuffed and mounted, and proudly exhibited in the storefront of Mr. E. A. Maull, a tobacconist at Baltimore and Calvert Streets.[530] Two years later, Joseph shipped his mounted fish to General Scott Shipp at the Virginia Military Institute in Lexington, Virginia, for permanent exhibition. Joseph's son, James Bosler Stonebraker, was a student there at the time.[531] Joseph was extraordinarily proud that his Jew fish weighed 450 pounds, while the Jew Fish on display at the Smithsonian Institution in Washington, DC., was a mere 300 pounds.[532] Time and early taxidermy processing must have taken it's toll, as today, the Virginia Military Institute is unable to locate the whereabouts of Joseph Stonebraker's gigantic mounted fish.

As excerpts from his civil war journal appeared in the Baltimore Sun newspaper, Joseph received encouragement from his fellow Confederate veterans and family to transform his handwritten journals into a published work. Now aged 53, Joseph worked on his book project from his home at 1921 Eutaw Street from 1897 through 1899.[533] His mother, Angelica Stonebraker, who lived nearby, provided the details of the Stonebraker family's short residency in Missouri, while his second cousin, Anne Rosina Locher Johnson of Berkeley Springs, West Virginia, helped with genealogical information.

Joseph liberally supplemented his memoirs with both personal and borrowed photos, and enlisted the talent of fellow ex-Confederate and renowned artist Allen Christian Redwood for two commissioned illustrations. The illustrations Redwood provided were *Maryland Battalion on the Warpath* [1898], depicting the 1st Maryland Cavalry trudging through a December 1864 winter storm, and the *Last Charge – Maryland Battalion at Appomattox* [1899]. In the "Last Charge" illustration, there is little doubt that the mounted Confederate private in the foreground is Joseph Stonebraker himself mounted on "Bill." By 1898, Redwood had just returned from Cuba, covering the ten-week Spanish American War for *Harper's Weekly*. In addi-

---

[529] The Atlantic goliath grouper or itajara (*Epinephelus itajara*), is commonly referred to as the jewfish. The world record for a hook and line-captured specimen is 680 pounds caught off Fernandina Beach, Florida, in 1961.

[530] *Baltimore Sun* (Baltimore, MD) 10 Apr 1890, 4.

[531] Joseph's oldest son, James Bosler Stonebraker, attended VMI from 1890 until 1892. VMI records indicate he resigned 12 Sep 1892 when he "failed for 3rd class."

[532] *Baltimore Sun* (Baltimore, MD) 20 Sep 1892, 8.

[533] The publication date of the book is noted as 1899 on the title page. The preface is dated April 2, 1897. The Redwood illustrations are dated 1898 and 1899.

tion to his paintings and illustrations, Redwood was also publishing articles and reminiscences of his war adventures such as *Jackson's Foot Cavalry at Second Bull Run* and *Stonewall: Memories from the Ranks and Other Places.*

In 1899, Joseph Stonebraker's completed memoirs were published by the New York firm of Wynkoop, Hallenbeck, Crawford Company. The mid-1880s through the early 1900s were an explosive time for veterans from both sides of the war to publish and strive to impress upon the public their memories of the war for posterity. Probably the first to publish his recollections was Baltimore Confederate Colonel Harry Gilmor with *Four Years in the Saddle* in 1866. As the century progressed, General William T. Sherman published his memoirs in 1875. General Ulysses S. Grant, then former-President Grant, wrote the *Personal Memoirs of U.S. Grant* in 1885. General Robert E. Lee published the *Memoirs of Robert E. Lee, His Military and Personal History* in 1886.[534] In 1893, under the direction of the Secretary of War, Daniel S. Lamont, the United States Government published *War of the Rebellion, A Compilation of the Official Records of the Union and Confederate Armies in 128 volumes.* As hundreds of veterans read the published works, they also came forward and published, offering the public their recounting, or corrections, of events as they had occurred in the tumultuous years from 1861 until 1865.

By 1903, two of Joseph and Mary Stonebrakers' sons were engaged to be married. Harry Stonebraker was set to marry Edith Dushane Hynson of Baltimore on October 1, 1903, and, in July of 1903, the Stonebrakers announced the engagement of their youngest son, Joseph, Jr., to Baltimore socialite and heiress Constance Whitely Stilwell, the daughter of William Tecumseh Stilwell. Their wedding was set for October of 1904.[535]

On October 25, 1903, Joseph R. Stonebraker died at his home after a brief illness. In addition to the eloquent obituaries and death notices, the Sunday, November 1, 1903, article in the Baltimore Sun newspaper reported his passing with the headline: *Ardent Fisherman Gone–the Late Joseph R. Stonebraker had a Love for Tarpon Catching.*

At probate a few months later, the Joseph Stonebraker estate was valuated at over $65,000. The majority of his wealth came from his shares in the Fidelity and Deposit Company of Maryland, and a lesser amount was interest in the firm of Joseph R. Stonebraker wholesale liquors.[536]

Allen Christian Redwood (1844-1922) of the 55th Virginia, Company C, and later the 1st Maryland Cavalry, Company C. Redwood lived his final years with his brother Henry in Asheville, NC.

---

534 Gilmor, Colonel Harry, *Four Years in the Saddle* (Harper & Brothers, NY, 1866), Sherman, William T., *Memoirs of General William R. Sherman, by Himself,* in 2 volumes (S. Appleton & Company, NY, 1875), Mrs. U. S. Grant posthumously published the *Personal Memoirs of U.S. Grant* (Charles L. Webster & Co., New York, 1894), Long, A. L. *Memoirs of Robert E. Lee, His Military and Personal History* (London, 1886). U.S. War Department, *War of the Rebellion, A Compilation of the Official Records of the Union and Confederate Armies.*
535 *Baltimore Sun,* 5 Jul 1903.
536 *Baltimore Sun* 26 Oct 1904, 7.

The will and codicil made few bequests. His widow Mary received ⅓ of the estate, while his four children divided ⅔ of the estate. Among the specific bequests, Joseph gave his portrait of himself in his Confederate uniform, along with his rifle and pistol, to his namesake and youngest son Joseph, Jr. The eldest son James received his diamond ring, while Henry received a diamond stud. Elizabeth received an oil painting entitled "the Welcome Kiss."[537]

Mary Bosler Stonebraker moved to Ridge Road in Hill Top Park, Mt. Washington in Baltimore, where she remained until her death in 1922.

Joseph Stonebraker's tombstone in Loudon Park Cemetery, Baltimore, Maryland, is a strikingly beautiful, approximately fifteen-foot tall obelisk of granite. The words inscribed on the tombstone are a poignant double entendre of his last orders from the Confederate Army:

Joseph Stonebraker died on 25 Oct 1903 after a short illness on. He is buried in Loudon Park Cemetery in Baltimore, MD.

CLOVERDALE, BOTETOURT Co. Va. APRIL 29, 1865
THE BEARER JOS. R. STONEBRAKER, Co. C. 1st MARYLAND CAVALRY HAVING DONE HIS DUTY FAITHFULLY TO THE PRESENT TIME, IS PERMITTED TO GO WHERE HE PLEASES UNTIL CALLED FOR.

G. W. DORSEY
LT. COL. COM. 1st. Md. CAVALRY C. S. A.

Joseph Rentch Stonebraker

Obituary of Joseph Rentch Stonebraker. The Daily Mail (Hagerstown, MD) 26 Oct 1903.

Joseph R. Stonebraker, vice-president of the Fidelity and Deposit Company, and head of the firm of Joseph R. Stonebraker & Co., Baltimore, died suddenly Sunday morning at 10 o'clock at his residence, 1921 Eutaw Place, of Bright's disease and heart failure.[538] The end came very unexpectedly, as Mr. Stonebraker had been ill only since last Wednesday.

Sunday morning at 8 o'clock he appeared to be much improved and expressed himself as feeling better. A personal friend called to see him shortly before 10 o'clock. They talked for a while, and Mr. Stonebraker jokingly referred to his having to remain indoors and said he expected to be up and out again very soon. Almost without warning he rolled over on his side and closed his eyes in death. Those in the room at the time were wholly unprepared for such an outcome and suffered a great shock.

The deceased was born at La Grange, Lewis County, Mo., February 1, 1844. His father, Henry Stonebraker, had emigrated to that place in 1840 from Washington County. His maternal grandfather was one of the religious refugees from the Rhine Palatinate, and arrived in New York in 1710. His great-great-grandfather, John Schaffer, located at Roxbury in 1772.

Mr. Stonebraker came to Maryland with his parents from Missouri when a child. He received a public school education, and when the Civil War broke out he, then in his teens, sided with the South and joined the Confederate forces as a private. In 1862 he was arrested in Baltimore by the Federal authorities and confined in Fort McHenry for several months. Finally he was exchanged, and then joined a company of Confederate cavalry, serving until the close of the war. He was present at Appomattox Courthouse on April 9, 1865, and participated in the last charge made by the Maryland battalion at that historical spot. In 1866 he returned to Baltimore and engaged in the mercantile business. He was one of the incorporators of the Fidelity and Deposit Company, and for the last eight years he has been its vice-president.

Mr. Stonebraker is survived by a widow, who was Miss Mary Bosler, of Carlisle, one daughter, Miss Eliza Stonebraker, and three sons—Messrs. Joseph B., Harry, and Joseph R. Stonebraker, Jr. His mother, who is 90 years old, also survives. She resides at Funkstown.

---

537   Baltimore American 6 Nov 1903, 13.
538   Bright's disease is a historical classification of kidney diseases that would be described in modern medicine as acute or chronic nephritis.

A Rebel of '61

The Family of
Joseph Rentch Stonebraker – Mary Catherine Bosler Stonebraker
(1844-1903) (1843-1922)

James Bosler Stonebraker (1874-1950)
married Cora Cator Cunningham (1875-1971) in Dec 1906

Born in Baltimore, MD. Graduated Virginia Military Institute in 1895. Resident of Baltimore City where he worked with his brothers Harry and Joseph in Stonebraker Brother Printing Company until the business was destroyed by fire in 1904. Continued as a salesman in Baltimore until 1925 when he moved for a short time to Bridgeport, CT. From 1930 until his death in 1950, he and Cora lived in Queens, NY. James and Cora Stonebraker are buried in Loudon Park Cemetery, Baltimore, MD. No children.

Joseph Rentch Stonebraker, Jr. (1876-1876)
Survived only 7 months.

Harry B. Stonebraker (1877-1910)
married Edith Dushane Hynson (1876-1937) in Oct 1903
    daughter Anna Stonebraker (1876-1937)
    son Harry W. Stonebraker (1906-1907)
    son Henry W. Stonebraker (1908-2001)

Born in Baltimore, MD. Worked with his brother James and Joseph in the firm of Stonebraker Brothers Printing Company until the business was destroyed by fire in 1904. Worked as an insurance salesman until his death at age 34 from heart failure. He is buried in Loudon Park Cemetery, Baltimore, MD. By 1920, Edith and her children had moved to Los Angles, CA.

Joseph Rentch Stonebraker, Jr. (1880-1972)
married Constance Whitely Stilwell (1879-1952) in Oct 1904
    son William Stilwell Stonebraker (1908-?)
    daughter Nancy Katherine Stonebraker (1911-1983)
married Helen P. Applebee (1895-1982) in 1944

Born in Baltimore, MD. Worked with his brothers James and Harry in the firm of Stonebraker Brothers Printing until the business was destroyed by fire in 1904. After his marriage to an heiress socialite in 1904, the couple briefly lived with his mother and his brothers in Baltimore. By 1907 the couple lived in New York City with his father-in-law as Joseph tried numerous occupations. The couple had two children. In 1914 Joseph divorced his wife, alleging infidelity. Although the courts awarded Joseph custody of his children, they remained with their mother and adopted her new husband's last name of Cornelius. Joseph remained in New York living in Brooklyn working in the insurance business, a salesman of liquor, and in printing firms. In 1944 he married Helen P. Applebee and moved to her hometown of Brookfield, CN, where he died in 1972. He is buried in Danbury, CN. There is no evidence he ever reconciled with his children.

Elizabeth B. Stonebraker (1884-1979)
Born in Baltimore, MD, Elizabeth remained in her mother's home until about 1924. From 1930 until her death in 1979 she lived in Brooklyn and Queens, NY, where she worked in hospitals. Elizabeth never married.

JAMES BOSLER STONEBRAKER (1874-1950)

Joseph and Mary Stonebrakers oldest son, James Bosler Stonebraker, attended the Virginia Military Institute from 1890 through 1892. Returning home to Baltimore, he worked at his father's bank for a few years. In August of 1898, 23 year old James, in the company of two other young Baltimore gentlemen, set out to make his fortune in the gold fields of Dawson City in the Yukon Territory of Canada where gold had been discovered earlier that year. James wrote home of his adventures:

> "We reached here the 1st of November had a rough trip, full of excitement and hardships. . . Men blow in their money here as fast as they make it. I saw a man lose $2200 in one night. Think of it– a fortune. . .I often watch the miners blow in their money on the girls and gambling tables. It costs $1 for each dance with a girl, the drinks for the two included. Last winter a miner sold his claim for $30,000 and by spring his dance bill was $2,800."[539]

After James returned from the gold fields sometime in 1899, presumably richer, the three Stonebraker brothers James, Harry, and Joseph, Jr., opened the printing firm of *Stonebraker Brothers Printing Company*. One of the brother's first printing commission was to print a history of their father's bank entitled, *"Monograph of the First Decade of the Fidelity and Deposit Company of Maryland 1890-1900."* The publication included biographies and photographs of all the company's executives, including the second-vice president, their father Joseph R. Stonebraker.[540] Interestingly in 1901, the Stonebraker Brother's firm published a calendar featuring a color half-tone print of the *Last Charge of the Maryland Battalion*, by Allen C. Redwood. This suggests that the Stonebraker family was in possession of the original work of art by Redwood.[541]

In 1903, Stonebraker Brothers Printing Company landed the contract to publish the 1904 yearbook for the Baltimore College of Dental Surgery, a fairly important publication formerly published by the larger, more established firm of Williams & Wilkins Printing Company of Baltimore.[542] When finally printed, the 1904-5 yearbook reported their book was delayed, "owing to the fact that the establishment of Stonebraker Bros., and also that of the Acme Engraving Co., were destroyed in the recent fire. . ."[543]

---

539   *Baltimore Sun*, 1 Mar 1898, 2.
540   *Monograph of the First Decade of the Fidelity and Deposit Company of Maryland 1890-1900* (Baltimore MD, 1900).
541   *The Inland Printer, A Technical Journal Devoted to the Art of Printing.* Volume 26, (Chicago IL, Mar 1901), 983.
542   Williams & Wilkins Co. of Baltimore, MD, printed the college yearbook in 1902, 1903, and 1906. Stonebraker Brothers Co. printed the yearbook in 1904 and 1905. Williams & Wilkins Co. would later merge with the Philadelphia firm of J. B. Lippincott Company, ultimately forming Lippincott, Williams & Wilkins in 1998. They are still in business today printing scientific, technical, and medical textbooks and reference works.
543   *The Baltimore College of Dental Surgery, The College Annual* (Baltimore, 1905) 141. Printed

A Rebel of '61

On Sunday, February 7, 1904, the central city warehouse district of Baltimore caught fire and continued to rage throughout the following day. Over 1,500 buildings covering almost 140 acres were destroyed. The 1904 Baltimore fire is rated by historians as the third worst fire to affect an American city, surpassed only by the 1871 Great Chicago fire, and the 1906 San Francisco earthquake fire.

One reason for the fire's long duration was the lack of national standards in fire-fighting equipment. Although fire engines from nearby cities such as Philadelphia and Washington, D.C., responded with horse-drawn pumpers, wagons and other equipment carried by the railroad on flat cars and box cars, as well as units from New York City, Virginia, Wilmington, and Atlantic City, many could not help because their hose couplings did not fit Baltimore's fire hydrants. Among the buildings damaged or destroyed included No. 16 Hanover Street, the business of Joseph R. Stonebraker & Company Wholesale Liquor, and the Stonebraker Brothers Printing Company at 217 E. Baltimore Street.

Determined to rebuild their printing business, the three Stonebraker brothers borrowed a large sum of money from the bank, supplemented with a loan from their mother, and purchased new everything necessary to re-open as a full-line printing plant. They bought two of the latest Miehle cylinder presses from Chicago, Illinois, four regular job presses, two complete monotype typesetting machines, type cabinets, binding machinery, cutters, and all manner of the latest office fixtures – an investment of more than $25,000. The newly furnished business opened at 403-405 E. Oliver Street in Baltimore and survived for one year. In April of 1905, Stonebraker Brothers Printing Company declared bankruptcy, and the company was placed in receivership.[544] Mary was forced to sue her sons for her $3,700 investment. On October 4, 1905, the assets of Stonebraker Brothers Printing Company were sold at auction. The auction advertisement noted that "the entire plant is practically new, as everything was purchased new subsequent to the Baltimore fire in February, 1904."[545]

James married Cora Cator Cunningham in December of 1906. The couple had no children. James sold insurance and later managed a toy factory. In about 1925 they moved to Bridgeport, Connecticut, later settling in Queens, New York, where James was likely again in the printing trade with his youngest brother Joseph. James died in New York on May 28, 1950, at age 75. He and his wife Cora are buried along with the other members of the Stonebraker family in the Loudon Park Cemetery in Baltimore, Maryland.

The Joseph R. Stonebraker Wholesale Liquor business at 16 Hanover Street in Baltimore, MD, was damaged, but not destroyed on 7 Feb 1904 in the great Baltimore fire that destroyed most of the warehouse district. Photo courtesy Enoch Pratt Free Library.

---

by Stonebraker Brothers Printing Company.
544   *Baltimore American Newspaper*, (Baltimore, MD) 26 Apr 1905. Johnson, Henry Lewis (editor) *The Printing Art*, Volume V, Mar 1905 – Aug 1905 (Cambridge, MA) 355.
545   *The Baltimore Sun*, (Baltimore, MD) Sep 1905.

HARRY STONEBRAKER (1876-1910)

Harry Stonebraker married Edith Dushane Hynson (1876-1937) of Baltimore in October of 1903, at the Brown Memorial Presbyterian Church in Baltimore, Maryland.[546] The couple had three children, two of whom survived to adulthood; Anna (1904-1991) and Henry W. Stonebraker (1908-2001). Harry was a partner with his brother James and Joseph, Jr. in the printing firm of Stonebraker Brothers until 1905 when the company folded. Like his older brother James, Harry sold insurance for a time.[547] Harry died at age 34 in 1910 of heart failure and is buried in Loudon Park Cemetery. By 1920, his widow Edith and the two children had moved to Los Angles, California, where Edith died in 1937.

JOSEPH RENTCH STONEBRAKER, JR. (1880-1972)

In his Baltimore society wedding in October of 1904, Joseph Rentch Stonebraker, Jr would have been resplendent in a formal black frock coat with silk lapels, cashmere trousers, and Ascot-knotted cravat. His bride, Nancy Katherine Constance Whitely Stilwell, wore white satin covered with French lace and adorned with flowers.

Of the three sons of Joseph and Mary Catherine Bosler Stonebraker, the youngest son Joseph R. Stonebraker, Jr., had by far the most memorable life. Raised in the relative comfort of his father's prosperity, young Joseph was handsome and charming. By 1900, he became partners with his brothers in the Stonebraker Brothers Printing Company. Active among the young fashionable gents of Baltimore, in July of 1903, Joseph proposed to Miss Nancy Katherine Constance Stilwell, an heiress and socialite, who divided her time between Baltimore and New York. Miss Stilwell, known as Constance, was the only child of William Tecumseh Stilwell, president of the Mapos Central Sugar Company, with offices in Cuba, New York, and Baltimore.

Reported in the newspapers of Baltimore and New York as "a marriage of much interest," on Wednesday, October 12th, 1904, at 8 pm, Joseph Rentch Stonebraker, Jr., married Constance Stilwell. The elegant, formal wedding took place at the Arundel Apartments building on North Charles Street in Baltimore City, where the bride had an apartment.[548] Constance's gown was described as "an imported gown of white selencieux over white satin, trimmed with rose point lace. Her only ornament was an antique brooch, worn by her grandmother upon the fiftieth anniversary of her wedding." Following the ceremony was a wedding supper for over 100 guests with music by a stringed orchestra. There were guests from New

---

546 *Baltimore American Newspaper*, (Baltimore, MD) 2 Oct 1903.
547 US Federal Census, 1910.
548 *Evening Star Newspaper* (Washington, DC) 26 Sep 1904, 5.

York, Washington, DC, Alabama, New Jersey, and Delaware. The couple's wedding gifts were described as "silver, cut glass, onyx, rare china, and bric-a-brac." After the wedding, the newlyweds honeymooned on a multi-city tour of New York, Atlantic City, Philadelphia, and Washington.[549] Thirteen days after his marriage, Joseph Stonebraker, Jr., received his inheritance from his father's estate. While the Stonebraker men were moderately successful merchants of Baltimore, Joseph Jr.'s marriage to the prominent Miss Stilwell was quite a step up on the social ladder for the son of an ex-Confederate liquor merchant.

After the honeymoon, the newlyweds returned to Baltimore and took up residence in 2104 St. Paul's Street – the home of Joseph's mother Mary, his sister Elizabeth, brother James and his wife Cora, brother Harry and his wife Edith and their small child. The Stonebraker home was a fine brick, three-story city row house with a good address in Baltimore, but life with her mother-in-law and extended family was decidedly not the style of living to which the pampered daughter of a sugar baron was accustomed. Constance's mother-in-law, Mary Bosler Stonebraker, generally confined her activities to her son's livelihood and her work for the Confederate Veterans Association in honor of her husband.

Like his older brothers James and Harry, Joseph's livelihood was destroyed when the Great Baltimore fire burned their printing firm in February of 1904. Although they tried to revive the business, a few months later the Stonebraker Brother's printing business filed for bankruptcy, and Joseph was unemployed and significantly in debt. By 1907, Joseph and Constance had moved to New York City, presumably to be near her father who kept an apartment in the Walbert building, and to seek suitable employment for Joseph.

Two children were born to the Stonebrakers' while living in New York city; a son William Stilwell Stonebraker in 1908, then a daughter Nancy Katherine Stonebraker in 1911. In New York, Joseph changed jobs numerous times, first working with his father-in-law, then in the insurance trade, and later the banking business. But none of his jobs generated an income sufficient to accommodate his high-maintenance, socially prominent wife.

After a tumultuous ten-year marriage, in February of 1914, Joseph did the unthinkable – he filed for divorce from his socialite wife in a divorce suit that was sensationalized in newspapers nationwide. One newspaper of the time noted that Joseph R. Stonebraker was a "record breaker" in that his divorce suit named an unprecedented twelve "corespondents" or co-respondents as having had affairs with his wife.[550] Newspapers of the day re-

One of the many photos of Constance W. Stilwell Stonebraker that appeared in newspapers across the county in their highly publicized 1914 divorce.

---
549   *Baltimore American Newspaper* (Baltimore MD) 13 Oct 1904.
550   The term co-respondent is derived from the British Matrimonial Causes Act 1857. In a petition for divorce on the ground of adultery, a co-respondent is a person charged with misconduct

Divorce Bill Hits Men in High Places

Pittsburg, March 8.—Men in high places are numbered among the 13 co-respondents named by J. R. Stonebraker, insurance man in his divorce suit against his wife, Constance S. Stonebraker. Alexander R. Peacock, Pittsburg steel millionaire; "Big Bill" Edwards, Princeton football hero, and recently street commissioner of New York, and B. Clifford Kline, brother of former Mayor Kline of New York are named.

Mrs. Stonebraker

As publicity about the divorce suit continued throughout 1914, the newspaper photos of Constance W. Stilwell Stonebraker became increasingly unflattering. Daily Illinois State Journal (Springfield, IL) 4 Mar 1914.

ported that the list of Mrs. Stonebraker's alleged lovers read like a who's-who list of New York society and included such notable figures as: millionaire Alexander R. Peacock, first vice-president of Carnegie Steel; B. Clifford Kline, the younger brother of former New York Mayor Adolph Lodges Kline; William Hanford "Big Bill" Edwards, a former Princeton football player and New York's Street cleaning commissioner; Louis E. Lambert of Baltimore, Maryland, president of the Lambert Automobile Company; Pittsburg millionaire Merrill Downs of Flushing, Long Island; James P. Gougs of Nutley, New Jersey; Albert Silverberg of New York; Lester Orr of Brooklyn; Nat M. Perry of Washington, DC; Perry House of Newport, Rhode Island; Morton Woolman of New York City; and handsome pharmacist Frederick Alfred Cornelius, the son of a Manhattan piano maker.[551]

Adding more fuel to an already inflamed story, Joseph Stonebraker petitioned the New York courts to impose an injunction on the co-respondents to "restrain them from continuing their alleged improper attentions" on Mrs. Stonebraker until the divorce was settled. Stonebraker continued that the co-respondents would "surreptitiously and clandestinely" continue in their improper attentions unless they were restrained.[552] Constance's lawyers argued against the injunction, citing it was "without precedent in New York court, if not any American court."[553] The requested injunction was the spark that ignited media and public attention coast-to-coast. Here was a beguiling socialite so beautiful that twelve of New York's most prominent men had to be forcibly restrained from seeking her affections.

The front page of the *Cincinnati Enquirer's* headline simply read "Constance." The *Schenectady Gazette* reported the juicy details of the co-respondents' names and listed the dates and the locations of their alleged assignations with Constance in the finest apartments and hotels in New York City.

"It is all bosh," Constance defended herself in an interview. When asked about her relationship with "Big Bill" Edwards, Constance said "At one time people said we were engaged…But, then, you know Southern girls

---

with the petitioner's spouse.
  Stonebraker was noted as a record-breaker by the *Jackson Citizen Patriot* Newspaper (Jackson MI) 26 Feb 1914.
551 *Schenectady Gazette* (Schenectady, NY) 25 Feb 1914, 1. The front page article further noted the exact dates and locations where Mrs. Stonebraker met her alleged lovers.
552 *Chicago Daily Tribune* (Chicago IL) 25 Feb 1914, 1.
553 *Santa Cruz Evening News* (Santa Cruz, CA) 11 Mar 1914.

are usually engaged three times before the right man comes along. I knew "Big Bill" as a football player in Princeton, and I have always regarded him as a close friend." Constance's reference to herself as a "southern" girl was ironic in that she was born in Canada and raised in New York City. Of the other eleven gentlemen, Constance continued, "they are all stanch, loyal friends. Why, I have been bothered to death all morning answering their telephone calls. Every last one of them have volunteered to stand by me, and I know they will." Constance vowed that when she was through "Joe won't have a leg to stand on."

When Joseph was asked about rumors of a reconciliation, "There'll be nothing like that [Constance] in my family," he replied. "There are 18 men who could be called in the case to testify, but I've only got evidence against 12, and, in the case of the 12, the proof is positive."[554] Reportedly Joseph brought a separate law suit against "Big Bill" Edwards for $50,000 for "alienation of affections" from Constance.

The divorce proceedings began on March 2, 1914, and much to the reporter's and public's disappointment, only one of the accused testified and the public was denied the juicy details. The courts exonerated "Big Bill" Edwards and Alexander R. Peacock. Joseph was granted a divorce from Constance and awarded custody of the two children.[555]

Just prior to the announcement of the divorce, on August 19, 1913, Constance's mother, Mrs. Katherine Stilwell, committed suicide at her residence in Baltimore by gas inhalation. When her will was probated a few months later, the family once again made headlines when it was reported that after her death Mrs. Stilwell wished an electric needle be used to puncture her heart, and that her body be cremated and her ashes be thrown into the ocean.[556]

In May of 1915, from a hotel in Newark, New Jersey, Constance sent a note to *The Sun* newspaper in Baltimore announcing her marriage to the pharmacist Frederick Alfred Cornelius of New York City, and their intention to make their home on the fashionable upper west side of New York on Riverside Drive. Now considered yesterday's news, Constance's announcement of her second marriage rated only a mention on the inner pages of the reporting newspapers, "Wed 1 of 12 Accused" reported the *Washington Post* on page three.[557]

Although Joseph Stonebraker had been awarded custody of his two children, William and Nancy Katherine, now ages six and three, within the year the children were living with Constance and her new husband in New Rochelle, West Chester County, New York, and were now called William and Nancy Katherine Cornelius.[558]

Constance's marriage to Frederick Cornelius was as unsettled as her first marriage. By 1917, Constance was living with her father in Cos Cub in

---

554 *The Cincinnati Enquirer* (Cincinnati, OH) 14 Feb 1914, 1.
555 *The New York Times*, (New York, NY) 10 Mar 1914.
556 *The News* (Frederick, MD) 1 Sep 1914.
557 *Washington Post* (Washington, DC) 14 May 1915, 3.
558 US Federal Census 1920.

WEDNESDAY, NOVEMBER 20, 1929.

COLOR PICTURES GAVE THIS PRETTY RED-HEAD HER FIRST "BREAK"

BY DAN THOMAS
NEA Service Writer

HOLLYWOOD, Calif. — The new vogue of natural color pictures is proving a boon to some of Hollywood's red-heads.

There is, for instance, Miss Nancy Cornelius.

Nancy has a shock of striking reddish-blond hair. Until very recently, it never got her anything but a lot of admiring glances and the nickname "Red." But when Dennis King's new picture, "The Vagabond King," was being filmed, it provided just the break Nancy wanted.

This film was being made in technicolor. Along with 100 other girls, Nancy had a small part in it. When the first films were run off for the executives, Nancy's flaming hair stood out in all its beauty—and Nancy promptly was lifted out of the ranks of the extras and given an important bit in the show. Studio casting directors, incidentally, have issued a warning to all movie aspirants pointing out that not all red-heads can be used in the movies. Some red hair looks nice in color films and some doesn't.

But, anyway, it worked for Miss Nancy Cornelius.

* * *

A whole lot of New York girls have gone to Hollywood to try for jobs in the movies. Lucille Williams, however, was about the first to reverse the process. She went from Hollywood to New York to break into the film game.

Lucille lived in Los Angeles. She had ambitions for a movie career, but she didn't try to crash the gates here in Hollywood. Instead she went to New York to study singing and dancing. Then, after a couple of years of that kind of training, she went to the Pathe studio in New York and won a job in George LeMaire's comedies.

Hardly had she got established when she received a telegram telling her that her mother was seriously ill and asking her to return home. She obeyed; but when her mother recovered, Lucille went straight back to the movies. This time she didn't have to go back to New York, though; the contacts she had made in the movie world enabled her to land something at the Hollywood studios.

She had a good part in "Half Way to Heaven," with Buddy Rogers and Jean Arthur. Now Pathe has signed her to a long-term contract, and big things are expected of her.

Nancy Cornelius

Miss Nancy Katherine [Stonebraker] Cornelius, 1929. Nancy was the daughter of Constance W. Stilwell and Joseph Rentch Stonebraker, Jr.

Greenwich, Connecticut.[559] After her father's death, Constance returned to New York City, presumably living off her inheritance, and for a short time was reunited with Frederick Cornelius.

Constance was delighted to realize her red-haired daughter was blossoming into a beautiful young lady. Nancy Katherine Cornelius auditioned for and was accepted in the Ziegfeld Follies, the glory of 1920s jazz age of New York City. As a Ziegfeld Girl, Nancy would have been on stage with performance greats such as W. C. Fields and Will Rogers, and future movie stars Paulette Goddard and Joan Blondell.

In the mid-1920s, Constance left Frederick behind in New York City and moved her budding movie star daughter to Los Angles, California. The perky redhead first gained public attention in April 1927 when she garnered more than 200,000 votes to be crowned "Miss Adohr Milk" in a agricultural merchants' exhibit fair.[560] In addition to her crown, young Nancy was dubbed "Queen of Hollywood," and signed to a movie contract with Hollywood movie producer Mack Sennett.[561] Sennett included Nancy in his bevy of starlets known as the "Sennett Bathing Beauties."

Nancy Cornelius had some minor roles in several Hollywood movie productions from 1927 until 1933. Her first screen appearance was in the 1927 silent film "Gold Digger of Weepah," where she and Carole Lombard portrayed dance hall girls. In 1933, the 22 year old aspiring actress married 39 year old Jerome Saffron, a movie executive for Columbia Pictures.[562] By 1940, the Saffrons' were living in a mansion on Roxbury Drive in Beverly Hills. In the 1950s, Roxbury Drive was known as "the street of the stars," and the home address to celebrities Jimmy Stewart, Lucille Ball, Jack Benny, and other well-known personalities. In 1934, the Saffrons' had twin daughters, but by 1947, the couple had divorced and remarried different partners.

---

559 *The Sun* (Baltimore, MD) 25 Apr 1914, 14. Obituary of William Tecumseh Stilwell at age 66. The Obituary notes he was "survived by his daughter, with whom he made his home."
560 The Adohr Milk farm was located at the intersection of Ventura Boulevard and Lindley Avenue in Los Angeles CA. It was once noted as having the largest herd of Guernsey milk cows in the world. The farm was sold during the depression. *Los Angeles Times* (Los Angeles, CA) 29 May 1997.
561 *The Van Nuyes News* (Van Nuyes, CA) 29 Apr 1927.
   Once dubbed "The King of Comedy," in his early career producer and director Mack Sennett (1880-1960) promoted early notables such as Charlie Chaplin, Gloria Swanson, and Fatty Arbuckle. By the late 1920s, Sennett's formula for movie production was proving out-dated and he was struggling to maintain his edge over rising studios such as Paramount and Warner Brothers.
562 On 10 Jun 1929, 19 year old Nancy Cornelius first married insurance salesman, Lawrence Eric Smith (1903-). In 1933, newspapers reported "Film Executive Weds an Actress in Yuma. Hollywood, Cal., Sept 30 - A few hours after Jerome Safron, 38, movie business executive, received a Mexican "mail order" divorce from the former Rose Winson, stage actress, he flew to Yuma, Ariz., with Nancy Cornelius, 22, movie actress, and married her today." *The Bakersfield Californian* (Bakersfield, CA) 2 Oct 1933.

Constance Stilwell Stonebraker Cornelius continued to live in Los Angeles, her last known occupation as a hostess in a Turkish bath in 1930.[563] She died in 1952.

Joseph Stonebraker, Jr., remained in Brooklyn, New York, most of his adult life, where he owned a small printing business, later selling wine and liquor. In 1944 at age 64, he married a second time to Helen Applebee and moved to Brookfield, Connecticut, where Helen had inherited property. Joseph died there in 1972, and is buried in Danbury, Connecticut. There is no evidence he ever reconciled with his children.

Mack Sennett Bathing Beauties Kathryn Stanley, Leota Winters, Madeline Hurlock, Carole Lombard, Marie Pergain, and Nancy Cornelius. Circa 1930.

ELIZABETH B. STONEBRAKER (1884-1979)

The youngest child of Joseph R. and Mary Bosler Stonebraker was a daughter, Elizabeth B. Stonebraker. Elizabeth stayed with her mother in Baltimore until Mary's death in 1922. She then moved to Queens, New York, presumably to be near her brother Joseph. She never married and died in New York at age 94.

---

563   US Federal Census 1930.

Legend of Funkstown

George Alfred Twonsend seated with his friends, author Samuel L. Clemens (Mark Twain), and David Gray editor of the Buffalo Courier *newspaper. LOC/P&P. LC-DIG-cwpbh-04761.*

Clemens wrote a review for Townsend's Tales of the Chesapeake:
"I read it more than half through the first evening, picking out the plums, such as 'The Big Idiot,' and greatly enjoyed the entertainment."
–S.L. Clemens (Mark Twain)

The humorous poem *Legend of Funkstown* was one of twenty-five short stories and poems written by George Alfred Townsend in his book *Tales of the Chesapeake* as published in 1880. Townsend was a contemporary and friend of great American authors such as Samuel L. Clemens, Oliver Wendell Holmes, and Henry Wadsworth Longfellow: all three of whom wrote glowing reviews of Townsend's *Tales of Chesapeake* that were printed in the preface of the book.

The *Legend of Funkstown* centers around elderly Nick Hammer, a tavernkeeper in Civil War era Funkstown, who spent much of his time observing the town from the front porch of the tavern. Hammer often contemplates why no members of the Funk family live in Funkstown.

One summer day in June of 1859, as Hammer was again dwelling on the missing Funks of Funkstown, he observes two wagons roll into town driven by a bearded man and his sons. One wagon is filled with wooden fork handles, the other wagon is loaded with wooden boxes. Hammer arrives at the erroneous conclusion that this bearded old man is none other than the missing founder of Funkstown, Jacob Funk. Noting the contents of the wagons, Hammer surmises that Jacob Funk has returned to Washington County to secretly mine gold ore from the local mountains. He concludes the wooden fork handles are actually divining rods, while the other wagon contains crucibles needed to melt the ore. Nick Hammer has just mistaken the abolitionist John Brown for Jacob Funk.

Years after the Civil War, and long after John Brown and his sons have been convicted and hanged in nearby Charles Town, Nick Hammer remains confident that he alone guessed the truth: the grizzled old man who drove into Funkstown that day in 1859 was not John Brown, but Jacob Funk. He postulates that since John Brown is Jacob Funk, then Jacob Funk is responsible for the Civil War.

Joseph Stonebraker identifies the fictitious Nick Hammer as Funkstown resident Thomas South (1781-1873). The South family operated a tavern in a stone home along Funkstown's main street; the same stone residence built by the town's founder, Jacob Funk in the 1769 (see photo page 36).

218   *A Rebel of '61*

I Nick Hammer sat in Funkstown
Before his tavern door—
The same old blue-stone tavern
The wagoners knew of yore,
When the Conestoga Schooners
Came staggering under their load,
And the lines of slow pack-horses
Stamped over the National Road.

Nick Hammer and son together,
Both blowing pipe-smoke there,
Like a pair of stolid limekilns,
In the blue South Mountain air;
And the mills of the Antietam,
Grinding the Dunker's wheat.
So oldly and so slowly,
Groaned up the deserted street.

"What think'st thou, Nick, my father?
Said Nick the old man's twin,
"This whole year thou art silent,
Let a little speech begin.
Thou think'st the bar draws little;
That the stables are empty yet,
And the growing pride of Hagerstown,
Thou can'st not that forget."

"Thou lie'st Nick my boy;
For Hager's bells I hear
Like the bells of olden travel,
Forget upon mine ear,
In a wonderful thing once asked him
Thy dear old daddy is sunk—
I have sot here a year and wondered
Who the devil was Mr. Funk!

II A year ago I was smoking,
When a stranger, a young fellow came by.
He was taking notes on paper,
And the rum in his'n was *rye*.
Says he: I'm a writin' a hist'ry—
'Twas then I thought he was drunk—
And I want to see your graveyard,
And the tomb of your founder, Funk!'
"I think if he'd sot there, sonny,
I'd looked at him a week;
But he vanished tow'rd the graveyard,
Before your daddy could speak.
Directly back he tumbled,
Before I had quit my stare,
And he says: I'm disappointed!
No Funk is buried there.'

"'The Funks is all up-country'—
That's all I could think to say,
'There never was Funks in Funkstown,
And there ain't any Funks to-day.'
'Why man,' he says, 'the city
That stands on Potomac's shores
Was settled by Funk, the elder,
Who afterwards settled yours!

'The Carrols, they bust him yonder;
Old Hager, he bust him here;
But my heart will bust till I find him,
And make a sketch of his bier.
Oh shame on the Funkstown spirit
That in Maryland does dwell!
He wouldn't consent to be buried,
Where you can keep a hotel.'"

III "There's old John Stockslager, daddy,"
Said young Nick, thinking much;
"A hundred years he's settled
Amongst the mountain Dutch.
Ask *him!*" Said young Nick Hammer,
You young fellows run too fast:
I shall set out here a thinking,
And maybe Funk'll go past!"

IV He drank and smoked and pondered,
And deep in the mystery sunk;
And the more Nick Hammer wondered
The duller he grew about Funk.
The wagoners talked it over,
And a new idea to trace
Enlivened the dead old village
Like a new house built in the place.

V One day in June two wagons
Came over Antietam bridge
And a tall old man behind them
Strode up the turnpike ridge.
His beard was long and grizzled,

His face was gnarled and long,
His voice was keen and nasal,
And his mouth and eye were strong.

One wagon was full of boxes
And the other full of poles,
As the weaver's wife discovered,
While the weaver took the tolls.
Two young men drove the horses,
And neither the people knew;
But young Nick asked a question
And the old man looked him through.

A little feed they purchased,
And their teams drank in the creek,
And two and fro they travelled
As silently for a week—
Went southward laden heavy,
And northward always light,
And the gnarled old man aye with them,
With the long beard flowing white.

From Sharpsburg up to Cavetown
The story slowly rolled—
That old man knew the mountains
Were filled with ore and gold.
The boxes held his crucibles;
'Twas haunted where he trod;
And every shafted pole he brought
Was a divining rod!

And none knew whence he came there,
Nor they his course who took,
Down the road to Harper's Ferry,
In a shaggy mountain nook;
But Nick the Sire grew certain,
While from his eye he shrunk,
That old man was none other
Than, the missing Mr. Funk:

The famous city-builder
Who once had pitched upon
The sunny ledge of Funkstown,
And the site of Washington.
Again he was returning
To the Potomac side,
To found a temple in the hills

Before he failed and died!
And Nick laughed gently daily,
That he alone had guessed
The mystery of the elder Funk
That had puzzled all the rest.
And younger Nick thought gently:
"Since that chap asked for Funk.
There's been commotion in this town,
And daddy's always drunk."

VI But once the ring of rapid hoofs
    Came sudden in the night,
And on the Blue Ridge summits flashed
The camp-fire's baleful light.
Young Nick was in the saddle,
With half the Valley men,
To find the old man's fighting sons
Who kept the ferry glen.

And like the golden ore that grew
To his divining rod,
The shining, armed soldiery
Swarmed o'er the clover sod;
O'er Crampton's Gap the columns fought,
And by Antietam fords,
Till all the world, Nick Hammer thought,
At Funkstown had drawn swords.

VII Together as in the quiet days,
    Before the battle's roar,
Nick Hammer and his one-legged son
Smoked by the tavern door.
The dead who slept on Sharpsburg Heights,
Were not more still than they;
They leaned together like the hills,
But nothing had to say;

Save once, as at his wooden stump
The younger man looked awhile,
And damned the man who made that war—
He saw Nick Hammer smile.
"My little boy," the old man said,
"Think long as I have thunk—
You'll find the war rests on the head
Of that 'air Mister Funk!"

The Battle of Funks–town

by Sandra D. Izer

ST. PATRICK'S DAY IN FUNKSTOWN

Growing up in the village of Funkstown, Joseph Stonebraker had often heard the elders of the town speak of the 1823 St. Patrick's Day riot. He also heard that Thomas Kennedy (1776-1832), a local legislator and part-time poet, had memorialized the incident in a poem. Yet seventy-five years later as Stonebraker was writing *Rebel of '61*, he was unable to find a copy of the poem in any library, personal or public. The fact that Stonebraker refers to the work as a "short" poem confirms that he never saw the original twenty-seven page work – a rather lengthy poem even for the verbose Kennedy.

If Stonebraker had not mentioned the poem in his memoirs, it is doubtful that anyone would have identified Thomas Kennedy as the author, as the poem is signed "Mr. York, PA," and was published in Chambersburg, Pennsylvania. Only recently was a copy of Kennedy's rare work located in the American Antiquarian Society Library in Worcester, Massachusetts, and is reprinted here for the first time in nearly two hundred years.

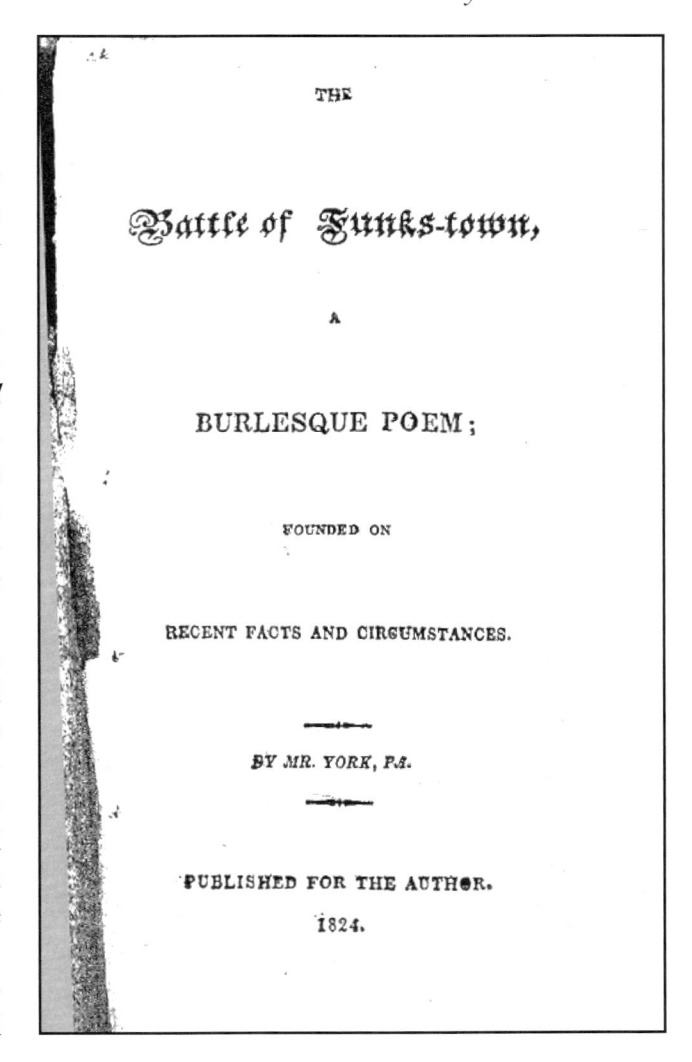

A burlesque work is a comic imitation of a serious work in which serious subjects are treated lightly, and the frivolous treated seriously. Examples of burlesque poem can be found in almost every period of history: early Greek literature; Chaucer's medieval works; and Kennedy's contemporaries such as Robert Burns' *Burlesque Lament for Wm. Creech's Absence*, and later Robert Browning's 1845 *Flight of the Duchess*. An amusing example is from Henry Cary's 1734 "most tragical tragedy" *Chrononhotonthologos,*

The cover of Thomas Kennedy's poem immortalizing the 1823 Irish riot in Funkstown, MD.

> Go call a coach, and let a coach be called;
> And let the man who calls it be the caller;
> And in his calling, let him nothing call,
> But coach! coach! coach! Oh! for a coach,
> ye gods!

In *The Battle of Funks-Town* all are equally satirized by Kennedy's pen. The Irish are riotous, drunken "Shamrocks," while the German-born Funk-

Painting by 20th century artist Carl Rakeman, The First MacAdam Road 1823, *showing a group of workers breaking stones along the Boonsborgh Turnpike, the first macadam road surface in the United States. John Loudon McAdam's principle directed that after side ditches were dug, large rocks were broken with a hammer "so as not to exceed 6 ounces in weight or to pass a two-inch ring." Today the road is Alternate US Route 40. (Courtesy of the Federal Highway Administration)*

stown residents are "son of crouts."[564] The local ladies are humorously mocked as they "scampered up and down" the streets with bonnets and lacy ruffles flapping, shouting for the local magistrate to restore order.

The St. Patrick's Day fiasco began on Sunday evening, March 16, 1823, at a tavern along the National Pike near Funkstown when an instigator hung a "Paddy" on the hotel sign post. A Paddy was a life-sized, straw-stuffed figure decorated with anti-Irish symbolism. Paddies usually had ape-like features, and were decorated with strings of potatoes, mackerel, and liquor bottles; the entire caricature designed to annoy the Irish. This particular Paddy had been fashioned with "dye sticks" for arms, reported to have been provided by an employee of the Funkstown woolen factory.

In 1823, a community of approximately 200-300 transient Irish workers lived in a make-shift village south of Funkstown known locally as "Cork."[565] The workers had been hired to complete the National Turnpike from Boonsboro to Hagerstown.[566] Named for County Cork, Ireland, Stonebraker identifies Cork as "just east of where the National pike makes a turn, and the

---

[564] According to the *Oxford English Dictionary* (Third Edition 2010, online version November 2010) this disparaging use of the word "crout" for Germans is almost 100 years earlier then most other references.

[565] All reports of the 1823 riot at Funkstown estimate the Irish mob at 150 turnpike workers. As many of the workers were living with their families, that could easily double the estimated population at Cork.

[566] Advertising for workers for the "Boonsborough Turnpike Road" between Hagerstown and Boonsboro, Maryland began in 1822. This turnpike is considered the first macadam surface in the United States as the construction specifications were designed by John Loudon McAdam, a Scottish immigrant.

A Rebel of '61

houses along the road which leads to Beaver Creek."[567] This description places the village of Cork somewhere along present day Cool Hollow Road.[568] Today there is no evidence that the village of Cork ever existed. Stonebraker's 1890s photo of a "Shanty in Cork" that appeared in *Rebel of '61* is the only known photo of a dwelling in that village.[569]

In the early 1820s, Funkstown was a small village in rural Washington County occupied by about 500-600 residents of predominantly German and English heritage; all industrious, hard-working solid Lutherans, Episcopalians, and Methodists.[570] The economic and social impact of 200-300 Irish migrant turnpike workers living in temporary housing just three miles south of town cannot be overstated. These were not gentle, aristocratic Irish farmers such as Charles Carroll, signer of the Declaration of Independence. These Catholic Irish were tough, hard-working, hard-drinking, unskilled laborers, who had fled even harsher times in Ireland. They were like nothing the local population had ever encountered, especially in such a large quantity.[571]

Advertising for contractors and laborers to build the federally and state funded Boonsboro Turnpike began in 1822, with offered wages of one dollar per day.[572] These wages were slightly above average at a time when wages for unskilled labor in nearby Baltimore City were about 75 cents or less per day.[573] In addition to enticements of good wages and steady work, the workers were promised cheap or free housing for their families. The broadsides for laborers advertised "the climate is healthy, provisions cheap and plenty, and firewood and house-rent will cost them nothing," and "Men who have families, can live very cheap; provisions being plenty, and house-rent comparatively nothing."[574] In reality, the shanty village of Cork was far from idyllic or healthy, the work was back-breaking, and the locals disapproving of migrant workers they considered to be of the lowest social class.

The Paddy dangling from the tavern post south of Funkstown had the predictable effect on the Irishmen of Cork. According to Stonebraker, the Irish were "so enraged. . .that they refused to go to work, but formed in a body. . .and marched through town, caught several of its citizens, which they nearly beat to death, and threatened to destroy the village." Kennedy likened the turnpikers, armed with clubs and homemade weapons, as yelling

---

567 See Stonebraker's original text, page 42.
568 Matching Stonebraker's description, Cool Hollow Road begins at a sharp bend on the Old National Pike and leads directly to the village of Beaver Creek.
569 See photograph of a Cork shanty on page 42.
570 There are no exact population records for Funkstown in 1820. The 1850 census was the first enumeration to list household members and differentiate between town residents and rural residents. In 1850, Funkstown was estimated to have had a total population of 793. 1850 US Federal Census.
571 Irish immigration grew dramatically in the 1820s and 1830s and reached its peak after the Irish potato famine of the late 1840s. It is estimated that more than 1.5 million Irish came to the United States during and after the famine. Bates, Christopher G., editor, *The Early Republic and Antebellum America* (Routledge, London, UK. 2010) 197.
572 Williams, T. J. C. and Folger McKinsey, *History of Frederick County, Maryland, Volume 1*, (Genealogical Publishing Company, Inc. Baltimore, MD), 172.
    Wages of one dollar per day were advertised for turnpike workers on the Great Western Turnpike in Allegany County in 1814. *Allegany Freeman* (Cumberland, MD) 8 Jan 1814.
573 Wage estimates taken from a letter criticizing Baltimore City Mayor John Montgomery's (1764-1828) reduction of wages paid to city laborers. *The Poor Man's Oppressor, Baltimore Patriot* (Baltimore, MD) 21 Aug 1822.
574 *Allegany Freeman* (Cumberland, MD) 8 Jan 1814.

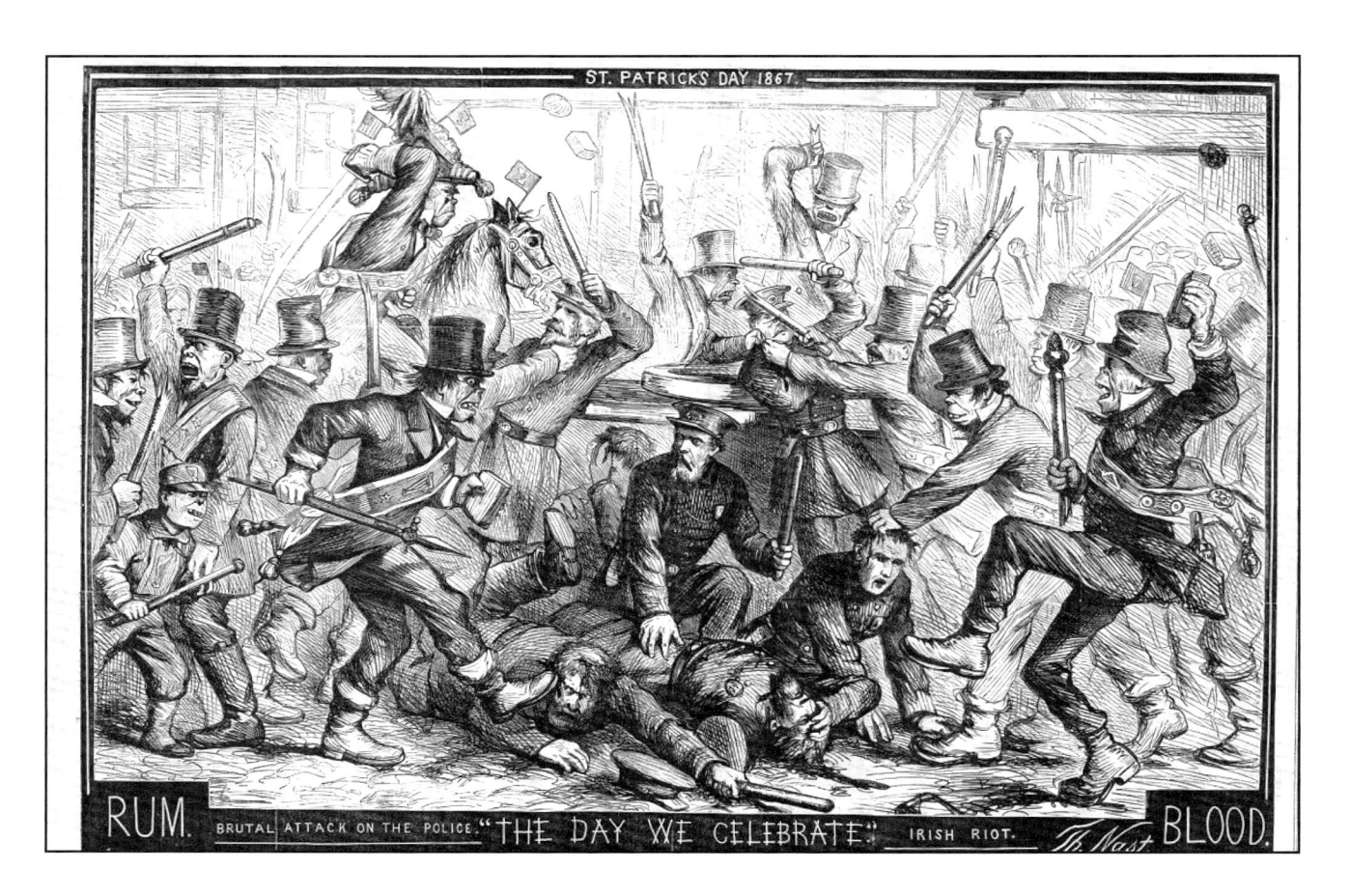

An illustration by caricaturist and editorial cartoonist Thomas Nast (1840-1902) for Harper's Weekly entitled "St. Patrick's Day 1867, Rum, Blood, The Day we Celebrate." *Harper's Weekly 6 Apr 1867.*

and shouting like "rabble dogs on the scent of a fox." Most reports indicate the destination of the Irish mob was the woolen factory they believed had provided the dye-stick arms for the Paddy; their intention was to "tear the building from its foundation."

In Kennedy's poem, the townsfolk lapsed into complete chaos when they "saw and heard afar, the terrors of the coming war" of the approaching Irish. Those members of the Yager Funkstown Rifle Corp who valiantly formed in the street to halt the aggressors were, "tumbled down, And wallowed in the mire and mud, begging for quarters. . ."

Stonebraker's account of the battle (the recollections of the elder citizens of Funkstown) gives a much better accounting of the Yager riflemen's actions. In this version the riflemen barricade themselves in the factory with men stationed at each window, ready to defend the property with their lives. The truth is probably a mixture of both versions and depended on who was telling the story.

Kennedy continued his humorous version of the tale with the town magistrate (likely Michael Isenminger) making a valiant attempt to bully the Irish into submission. "Vat for de tevil you com'd here," he shouted, "I'll send you puggers to de jail," and he read them the "riot act," and warned of the consequences of a civil disturbance.

The Irish stared blankly at the roaring magistrate, unable to understand his words spoken in his thick German accent. Enraged by the mob's obvious disregard for his authority, the frustrated magistrate launched into a tirade of curses. Finally, here were some words the Irish could comprehend, and they knocked the magistrate off his soapbox and down into the mud. For good measure, his honor received a whack on the head and a kick in the "breech." The fallen magistrate wisely chose to remain prostrate until reenforcements arrive. Delighted with their victory, the Irish continued their march through town cheering "huzzas," and swearing vengeance on every "whore's and mother's son of the black-hearted country born."

Meanwhile, a lone rider raced Paul Revere-like through Hagerstown, shouting that Funkstown was being invaded. Unfortunately, the rider failed to make clear the cause of the threat, and the result was pandemonium. Many Hagerstown residents, believing the town was on fire, come charging out with ladders and buckets. Others interpreted the alarm as a slave insurrection, or possibly even an Indian attack, and readied their firearms, prepared to defend their homes.

The Hagerstown folks quickly recovered from their confusion, and soon members of the "American Blues" Light Dragoon cavalry troop under the command of Captain Jacob Barr, reinforced by local militia, charge to the rescue of Funkstown.[575]

The Irish rebels may have had no problem routing a few armed locals, but they were not a match for mounted, trained cavalrymen eager for a fight. After some skirmishing, and "parleying," the militia forces secured "the high ground" in the town, disbursed the mob, and restored order. The ring leaders of the mob were carted off to jail in Hagerstown, and the militia remained on guard for the remainder of the night, but no further disturbances were reported.[576]

Two days later, on March 19, 1823, the five ringleaders of the Irish rebels appeared before the judge of the Circuit Court in Hagerstown. David Clagett and William Bishop brought charges of assault and battery against Ganett O'Donnell, Francis McAllion [M'Callion], Terence Saacy [Seacey], Patrick Rourk, and Thomas Crogan.[577] While the records are not clear as to the ruling of the court, the *Torch Light* reported that the accused were found guilty and fined five dollars each, plus the cost of prosecution.[578]

Kennedy ends his *Battle of Funks-Town* poem blaming a "Negro Wench" as the maker of the Paddy, and the "cause of all the war, A woman and a man of straw." He wisely concluded that "'Tis better to adjust and settle, Disputes, before than after the battle."

Troop Orders.

IN compliance with Brigade Orders, the *American Blues* will parade at Clear Spring, on Saturday the 10th—at Sharpsburg on Saturday the 17th, and in Hagerstown on Saturday the 24th day of September, in complete order, with six rounds of blank cartridge at each parade.
THOS. E. TILGHMAN,
1st Lieut. Commanding.
September 6.   45—3w.

The local militia took great pride in their appearance and military skills. Announcements for assemblies and parades were published in the local newspaper. Torch Light & Public Advertiser *(Hagerstown, MD) 6 Sep 1825.*

---

575   On page 43 Stonebraker mistakenly notes the commander of the American Blues as Captain George W. Barr. Jacob Barr was captain of the American Blues horse troop as early as 1814 during the battle at Bladensburg, MD. Williams, T. J. C, *A History of Washington County, Maryland Volume 1, Part 1*, 182,186. Also see *Torch Light & Public Advertiser* (Hagerstown, MD) 22 May 1821: At an election at Thomas Johnson's tavern, on Saturday the 18th inst. the following gentlemen were elected officers of the troops of horse called the American Blues, heretofore commanded by Capt. Barr: Jacob Barr, Captain, Benjamin Kershner, 1st Lieut, John Silmer, 2nd Lieut, Joseph Newcomer, Cornet.
576   *Torch Light & Public Advertiser* (Hagerstown, MD) 25 Mar 1823.
577   Washington County Court, Docket and Minutes 1801-1850, March Court 1823. Maryland Archives, MSA C3004.
578   *Torch Light & Public Advertiser* (Hagerstown, MD) 8 Apr 1823.

The Tuesday, March 25th edition of the *Torch Light & Public Advertiser* reported on "occurrences of rather a disagreeable character," under the headline *"Funks-Town Campaign."* The article reported that the Funks-Town Rifle Corp, reinforced by troopers from the Hagerstown American Blues, and other local militia, had admirably stood their ground against Irish turnpike workers who became annoyed by the appearance of a Paddy. The *Torch Light* article amusingly concluded with: "None killed, one wounded by the kick of a horse, some a little and some a good deal frightened, a few made prisoner– and the insurrection quashed!" The article reported the incident as a potentially volatile situation quickly brought under control by the decisive actions of the local militia.[579]

Within the week of the St. Patrick's Day affair, Thomas Kennedy wrote and distributed a short poem describing the days events in less complimentary, more humorous terms. At a town meeting in Funkstown on the 5th of April, magistrate Michael Isenminger caustically alluded to Kennedy's version citing "a certain great man has said little things to the contrary." Although he does not identify him by name, there is little doubt Iseminger is referring to Kennedy, and found no humor in the Scotsman's literary skills. Iseminger praised the Hagerstown militia for their "prompt assistance in quelling the disturbance," and called the conduct of the troops orderly and highly praiseworthy."[580]

The St. Patrick's Day events in Funkstown made national news. The *Torch Light* article of the Irish insurrection had the charming appeal of amusement, dashing dragoons, and a happy ending, so much so that the story was repeated word-for-word in many large newspapers including the *Baltimore Patriot*, the *Pittsburgh Weekly Gazette*, and the New York *Evening Post*, to name a few.[581] The citizens of Funkstown never imagined their little riot would have received so much national attention. The editor of the *Torch Light* later wrote that the Funkstown campaign "seems to have attracted as much attention. . .as had the anticipated war between France & Spain."[582]

The one important newspaper that did not carry the *Torch Light* version of the incident was the *Niles Register* of Baltimore, Maryland. The same day as the town meeting in Funkstown, the story in the April 5th edition of the *Niles Register* article called the Irish "warm-hearted, but hot-headed," and thought it insensitive for someone local to have created an offensive Paddy with intent to "trifle thus with the feelings of any people." On the other hand, the Irish should not become hostile at what was meant as a "piece of fun."[583]

Considered to have had the largest circulation of any American newspaper of its time, from 1811 until 1849, the *Niles Register* carried the latest in world events, political, commercial, agricultural, and industrial news. It was virtually unprecedented for the *Register* to report on a local event such as the Funkstown riot.

---

579   *Torch Light & Public Advertiser* (Hagerstown, MD) 25 Mar 1823.
580   *Torch Light & Public Advertiser* (Hagerstown, MD) 8 Apr 1823.
581   *Baltimore Patriot* (Baltimore, MD) 29 Mar 1823, *Pittsburg Weekly Gazette* (Pittsburgh, PA) 4 Apr 1823, *Evening Post*, (New York, NY) 31 Mar 1823.
582   *Torch Light & Public Advertiser* (Hagerstown, MD) 8 Apr 1823.
583   *Niles Register* (Baltimore, MD) 5 Apr 1823, 71-72.

In his next edition of the *Torch Light,* editor William D. Bell fired back at the *Niles Register.* He pointed out that Hezekiah Niles was wrong in "taking for granted" the Paddy had been made by someone from Funkstown. Bell suggested the possibility that the Irish created the Paddy themselves as an excuse to create mayhem. He continued that "after an impartial and full examination into the facts of the case" by the judge of the Circuit Court, the Irish rebels were found guilty and fined.[584]

THE BATTLE OF FUNKS-TOWN POEM

Kennedy's final twenty-seven page version of the *Battle of Funks-town* was not published until June of 1824, over a year after the event.[585] Nowhere in this poem is Thomas Kennedy's name mentioned. The author is listed as "Mr. York, PA." This version of the poem opens with an amusing paragraph by the printer, George Kenton Harper, hinting that he might *possibly* know the author, and apologizes for the author calling the Germans "Crouts." Harper was the editor and printer of the *Franklin Repository* newspaper in Chambersburg, Pennsylvania.

Only the beginning and end of this lengthy poem relate to the events of March 17, 1823. The main body of Kennedy's work is a treatise on the anti-professional and anti-government sentiments that were rapidly changing the face of American politics. Kennedy's world was evolving from the post-War of 1812 "era of the good feeling," into the Jacksonian "era of the common man." This version of the *Battle of Funks-town* is in part a humorous poem about local events, but a much longer political statement lambasting the educated classes whom Kennedy felt were manipulating politics and politicians for financial gain.

In his politics, Kennedy was an anti-Federalist Republican who believed an American aristocracy was emerging from the "business community and eastern elites."[586] The anti-Federalist saw the Federal government bloating out of control and the wealthy attempting to manipulate the succession of the Presidency. These sentiments would reach a zenith in late 1824, when John Quincy Adams was selected President of the United States over Andrew Jackson by the House of Representatives.[587]

---

584   *Torch Light & Public Advertiser* (Hagerstown, MD) 8 Apr 1823.
585   The first advertisement for the *Battle of Funks-Town* appeared in the *Torch Light and Public Advertiser* (Hagerstown, MD) on 1 Jun 1824 at a cost of 12 ½ cents.
586   By 21 Aug 1821 Kennedy had signed and published 15 letters to the *Baltimore Federalist* newspaper with the pen name "Republican in the country to a Federalist in Baltimore." *Torch Light & Public Advertiser* (Hagerstown, MD) 21 Aug 1821.
587   Four men vied for the office of Presidency in 1824, including President Monroe's heir apparent, John Quincy Adams. After the votes were cast, the coarse, uneducated, but immensely popular war hero Andrew Jackson easily won the popular vote, but failed to secure sufficient electoral votes to claim the office as dictated by the provisions of the Twelfth Amendment to the United States Constitution. For the next four years Jackson would promote the idea that the eastern elitists had stolen the election away from the common voter. In the presidential election of 1828, Jackson easily won the office and became the first president born west of the Appalachians, and the first President who had been born poor.

The Battle of Funks-Town opens with a few stanzas on the events in Funkstown, then Kennedy, in his own words, "digresses." He digresses through the next eleven pages with biting examples of foolishness and corruption of those he considers the educated upper class. He rails on politicians, incompetent doctors, and misguided scientists. He focuses, almost spitefully, against any vocation that requires a college certification, including preachers, lawyers, and scientists, and all of those who "Must first be made Academicians." He admonishes the current higher-education system that produces ""Diploma'd" quacks too brainless ever to be taught."

Throughout his narrative, Kennedy often interjects his admiration for the common man, "The boy, who can a basket make, The woman who can spin and bake, is of more value to a nation, than scores, who prate of derivation." He defends men of healing with no formal education or degree, but blessed with "Deep skills in Therapeutic arts."

Kennedy seems particularly fond of ridiculing Pennsylvania politicians. He begins with the Representative who attempted to fine women for their fashion choices, and flows to the newly elected Pennsylvania Governor who vetoed a bill authorizing the issuance of a state medical license.[588] Kennedy believed the Governor was protecting college professors who issued medical licenses for a large fee in addition to the cost of tuition, thereby "by legislative tricks like these, The rich secure monopolies."[589] He scoffs at the scientist who postulate that the earth was hollow with entry holes at both poles, and thought doctors with their foolish remedies were "doomed to quackery and crime." In general, he laid the problems of the country at the feet of the wealthy, educated classes.

KENNEDY AND THE JEW BILL

The months from March of 1823 until the *Battle of Funks-town* was published in June of 1824, were particularly trying times for Kennedy. An elected delegate representing Washington County in the Maryland Assembly since 1817, Kennedy was the author and champion of the controversial "Jew Bill." Until the Maryland Constitution was amended in 1826, only Christians were permitted to hold any elected office. Kennedy's proposed "Act to extend to the sect of people professing the Jewish religion the same rights and privileges that are enjoyed by Christians," had been introduced and defeated a number of times in both the House and Senate.[590] His outspoken support of equality for Jews set off a political fire-storm in Maryland of which Kennedy became a casualty. In the fall of 1823, incumbent Thomas Kennedy lost the election and his seat in the Maryland House.

---

588   Alexander Ogle (1766-1832) of Somerset, a member of the PA House of Representatives.
589   Kennedy accused Governor Shulze of Pennsylvania of protecting the practice of college teachers charging students a large additional fee for a medical license at the conclusion of their studies.
590   Kennedy was first elected to the Maryland House in 1817. In 1818 he was appointed to a House committee to consider removing the "political disability of the Jews." That bill was first introduced and defeated in January of 1819.

Elections for the four Maryland House Representatives were held annually in mid-October. In the late summer or early fall interested gentlemen would publicly declare their candidacy. For the next several weeks until the election, the newspapers were filled with letters from the candidates promoting their qualifications and positions on current issues. There were also plenty of letters from prominent citizens with glowing endorsements for their candidate, and unsigned letters with stinging allegations of misconduct and every imaginable sin. After the elections, in late December or early January, the elected assemblymen would travel to Annapolis and take their seats to represent the county.

Although Thomas Kennedy had been promoting his bill for religious tolerance as early as 1819, his hometown troubles began with the 1822 fall election. In September of 1822, the *Torch Light* newspaper listed four candidates for the 1822-3 Assembly: Thomas Kennedy, William Yates, Colin Cook, and Thomas Kellar. By the 1st of October the field had swelled to twelve candidates, including the last minute addition of 72-year old Colonel Elie Williams. Colonel Williams was the younger brother of General Otho Holland Williams of Revolutionary War fame. Elie Williams had also served in the Revolutionary War and was a well-known and respected resident of Hagerstown.

During the fall campaign of 1822, the editor of the *Torch Light,* William D. Bell, left little doubt that he was not a Thomas Kennedy fan. Although some Kennedy endorsements were printed, the majority of the published letters were anti-Jew Bill and anti-Thomas Kennedy. One of the more vitriolic slurs Bell published was, ironically, a poem:

> How the Kennedy Tom
> Old Scotland from,
> Late appear'd in newspapers,
> Cutting High Capers,
> Like unto Sky Scrapers:
> By which he expects,
> To command the respects,
> Of all true Democrats,
> Who, must pull off their Hats,
> When he passes by,
> And each trustily cry!
> Oh! the Great KENNEDY!

Despite the negative press, Kennedy received the highest number of votes. Also elected to represent Washington County for the 1822-3 term were Ignatius Drury, Thomas Kellar, and Elie Williams.

> "Religious liberty does not exist in Maryland, for religious liberty cannot be said to exist under any government where men are not permitted to worship God in the manner most agreeable to the dictates of their own consciences, or what is the same thing, denied the enjoyment of civil rights, and rendered incapable of holding any office, civil, military or judicial, except they acknowledge their belief in a particular system of religion."

From Thomas Kennedy's report Religious Liberty, delivered to the Legislature of Maryland, 18 Dec 1822. Reprinted in the Niles Register 28 Dec 1822.

The Maryland Assembly opened on Monday, December 2, 1822, with delegates Drury and Kellar in attendance. Kennedy chose to forgo the opening day ceremonies, and Elie Williams was too ill to travel to Annapolis. The following day Kennedy motioned for permission to introduce his bill "An act to extend to the citizens of Maryland, the same civil rights and religious privileges that are enjoyed under the constitution of the United States."[591] Newly elected delegate Elie Williams never took his seat in Annapolis. On the 29th of December 1822, he died at Georgetown, DC.

Back in Washington County, the campaign for the vacant seat of Elie Williams quickly gathered momentum. Four candidates offered themselves: Colonel Henry Fouke, who had finished fifth in the recent elections, Colin Cook, David Brookhart, and 70 year old Benjamin Galloway.

Once again, William Bell used his position as editor of the *Torch Light* to promote his Whig politics. Endorsements for Galloway appeared in large, bold typeface, and twice as often as for any other candidate. One unsigned endorsement suggested that Galloway, the "old Revolutionary whig," should be elected instead of "young fry of unfledged, new-fangled, would-be patriots."[592]

The election for the vacancy of Williams was held January 15, 1823, with very low voter turnout. In the previous fall election almost 8,300 votes were cast for eight candidates. In the January election only 1,565 votes were cast, with Galloway receiving almost 50% of the votes.[593] One week later Benjamin Galloway took his seat in Annapolis.[594]

---

591   It is noteworthy that the bill presented by Kennedy on 3 Dec 1822 was different from the bills he had previously introduced. Kennedy's earlier bills recommended political equality for "people professing the Jewish religion." The 1822-3 session bill was a universal version extending the same constitutional rights and privileges to *all* citizens of Maryland. Many delegates objected to this version more than the Jew-specific bill, citing it allowed atheists or Muslims to hold office. *Votes and Proceedings of the House of Delegates* (Maryland), MSA, SC N 12329, 699.

    Col. Elie Williams has not yet arrived [in Annapolis], but we expect him soon after New Year. *Torch Light & Public Advertiser* (Hagerstown, MD) 24 Dec 1822.

592   *Torch Light & Public Advertiser* (Hagerstown, MD) 17 Jan 1823.

593   Galloway 755, Gouke, 413, Brookhart 371, Cooke 26. *Torch Light & Public Advertiser* (Hagerstown, MD) 21 Jan 1823.

594   Wednesday 22 Jan 1823, Ben Galloway took his seat in the assembly. *Easton Gazette*.

Election Results fall 1822 for the 1822-3 Session, Thomas Kennedy received the highest number of votes.

OFFICIAL STATEMENT OF THE WASHINGTON COUNTY POLLS.

DISTRICTS.	M. C. Sprigg	John Lee	T.C. Worthington	C. W. Wever	Wm. Gabby	G. Nourse	Tho. Kennedy	Ignatius Drury	Elie Williams	Thomas Kellar	Henry Fouke	O. H. W. Stull	Ezra Slifer	D. Brookhart	D. Newcomer	Wm. Webb	Wm. Yates	John McClain
Sharpsburg	00	267	59	24	1	2	89	93	274	73	9	252	83	17	66	2	54	1
Williams-Port	78	49	124	38	8	00	214	211	151	70	94	27	25	11	19	9	59	57
Hagers-town	363	57	88	93	102	00	540	314	276	432	376	161	153	33	106	49	50	15
Clear Spring	153	5	57	25	11	00	155	96	61	102	153	32	52	3	27	8	81	78
Hancock	35	1	51	42	2	00	89	54	59	58	10	40	9	17	19	1	95	2
Boonsborough	44	134	177	78	9	00	220	163	127	107	19	120	203	297	79	6	23	3
Cave-town	53	36	11	60	196	00	169	196	124	154	106	55	57	39	83	219	13	5
TOTALS	726	549	567	360	329	2	1476	1127	1072	996	767	687	522	417	399	294	375	166

A Rebel of '61

Candidate	Andrew Kershner	Joseph Gabby	James H. Bowles	Joseph I. Merrick	Thomas Kennedy	Ignatius Drury	T.B. Hall	Thomas Kellar	Benjamin Galloway
Affiliation	*No Jew-Bill*	*No Jew-Bill*	*No Jew-Bill*	*No Jew-Bill*	*Jew-Bill*	*Jew-Bill*	*Jew-Bill*	*Jew-Bill*	*No Jew-Bill*
Results	*1252*	*1213*	*1159*	*974*	*739*	*640*	*620*	*560*	*196*

From the moment he arrived, Benjamin Galloway's singular goal as a politician seemed to be the annihilation of "Kennedy's Jew Baby."[595] Despite Galloway's acrimonious outspoken testimonies against anything non-Christian, Kennedy's bill passed in the House with a vote of 40 to 33. Galloway was the only delegate from Washington County to vote against the bill.

The legislative session closed on February 24, 1823, after having passed Kennedy's bill in both the House and Senate.[596] Kennedy and his fellow delegates returned home to Washington County, arriving just in time for St. Patrick's Day and the Funkstown fiasco.

As the fervor over the Irish riot slowly subsided, the next exciting occurrence in Washington County in 1823 was the fall campaign for the seats in the Maryland House. Benjamin Galloway set the tone for the campaign with an early announcement that, contrary to his original intention to serve only one term, he could not "desert the cause" and allow Thomas Kennedy to continue to undermine Christianity with his hated "Jew Bill."[597] Galloway identified himself as a three-score and ten unwilling candidate who preferred ". . .Christianity to Judaism, Deism, Unitarianism, or any other sort of ISM."[598] Galloway was once again aided in his campaign by *Torch Light* editor William D. Bell. In the weeks leading up to the election, every issue of the *Torch Light* carried a disproportionate number of inflammatory letters and heavy-handed editorials lambasting Kennedy and the other pro-Jew Bill candidates as the "enemy of Christianity."

Regardless that there were other equally important campaign issues, in this election the nine candidates became labeled as either a "No Jew Bill," or "Jew Bill" candidate. Andrew Kershner, Joseph Gabby, James H. Bowles, Joseph I. Merrick, and Benjamin Galloway identified themselves as No Jew Bill, Constitution, or Christian candidates. While T. B Hall, and incumbents Thomas Kennedy, Ignatius Drury, and Thomas Kellar, were classified as Jew Bill candidates.

By election day Washington County voters clearly had had their fill of this vitriolic campaign. With 1,200 fewer votes cast than the previous year, four "No Jew Bill" candidates won the four seats in the assembly. Thom-

Election Results fall 1823 for the 1823-4 Session, Thomas Kennedy lost his seat finishing in fifth place. Benjamin Galloway finished last.

(Easton, MD) 1 Feb 1823.
595   Eitches, Edward, *Maryland's "Jew Bill," American Jewish Historical Quarterly* Volume LX, Sep 1970-Jun 1971, 276.
596   To become law, a bill had to pass both the House and Senate in two successive legislative sessions. The Jew bill was defeated by the House in the 1824 session. It finally passed in the 1825 and 1826 sessions and become law on 5 Jan 1826.
597   Galloway, Benjamin, *"To the Christian Voters residing in Washington County, Maryland." Maryland Herald* (Hagerstown, MD), 19 Aug 1823.
598   *Torch Light & Public Advertiser* (Hagerstown, MD) 26 Aug 1823.

as Kennedy finished in fifth place. The most surprising result of the day was Galloway's last place finish. Of the over 7,000 votes cast, only 196 were cast for Galloway.[599] Washington County voters may not have been ready to place non-Christians on an equal footing, but they liked Benjamin Galloway's over-the-top tactics even less.

After three months of defensive campaigning, for Kennedy to lose this election was a devastating blow. Therefore, in the winter of 1823 into the new year of 1824, Thomas Kennedy found himself sitting home in Hagerstown writing rules for the Potomac Company's proposed canal, and venting his political rage in his expanded version of *The Battle of Funks-Town* – a poem that would sell very few copies, virtually none that survived.

Thomas Kennedy ran again for House delegate in the fall of 1824 and was once again defeated.[600] But, more importantly, during his absence in the 1824-5 session of the Assembly, his bill on religious equality was re-introduced.[601] This time it passed easily in the Senate, while in the House, the bill passed by a narrow margin of 26 to 25 on the last day, with 29 members absent.

Kennedy ran for office again in the fall of 1825, this time regaining his House seat. He was in Annapolis in January of 1826 when the bill was presented to the Assembly for the second time, this time passing, and became part of the laws of Maryland.

Emigrating to the United States from Scotland in 1796, Kennedy tried and failed in several businesses before becoming a lawyer and politician.[602] A prodigious writer, in 1816, Kennedy self-published a small volume of his best works in a book simply entitled "Poems" that contains some charming poems such as his "Ode to a Mammoth Cheese," a tribute to the 1,230 pound wheel of cheese presented to President Jefferson in 1801.[603] The *Battle of Funks-town* is not an undiscovered literary masterpiece. Tediously long and layered with ambiguous references, it is almost painful to read unless one is exceptionally well-versed in early 19th century politics and events. His reasons for writing this poem were complex: disappointment at his constituents who failed to support him in the election; annoyance with wealthy politicians who used their office for financial gain; combined with his passion to defend the oppressed, whether Jewish, or in this particular case, the Irish:

> Hence 'tis that I a luckless wight,
> Tho' doomed in poverty, to write
> The history of this great battle,
> And save a sprig of Irish mettle.

---

599   *Torch Light & Public Advertiser* (Hagerstown, MD) 14 Oct 1823. James H. Bowles, Joseph Gabby, Andrew Kershner, and Joseph I. Merrick were elected delegates for 1823-4.
600   *Torch Light & Public Advertiser* (Hagerstown, MD) 5 Oct 1824. James H. Bowles, Henry Fouke, Joseph I. Merrick, and Isaac S. White were elected delegates for 1824-5
601   The bill that was introduced and subsequently passed was Kennedy's original Jewish equality version. The broader version Kennedy introduced in 1822 allowing equality for all citizens was set aside with the argument that it allowed the election of Muslims, atheists, and non-believers.
602   Kennedy emigrated from Scotland to Georgetown, MD in 1796 at age 19. By 1798 he was living in Williamsport, MD. In 1805 he purchased a business and lots in Williamsport with a mortgage of over 600£. In 1807 he declared bankruptcy, but vowed he would settle every claim. *Federal Gazette* (Baltimore, MD) 11 Sep 1807.
603   Kennedy, Thomas, *Poems* (Washington City, 1816).

The Battle of Funks-town,
A BURLESQUE POEM:

FOUNDED ON
RECENT FACTS AND CIRCUMSTANCES
BY MR. YORK, PA.
PUBLISHED FOR THE AUTHOR
1824.
ADVERTISEMENT.

IF this little poem, now presented to the public, possess any literary merit, the writer has it by the most indefatigable industry, or by intuition; for we believe we know the author; and if we are right in our conjectures he is not a literary man. In its praise we are permitted to say nothing, save that we have read it with pleasure. Some may incline to suppose him a son of Bacchus;[604] we can assure the reader however, this is not the case, for we do know enough about the history of this orphan of muses, to justify us in saying he is rigidly temperate. – The Battle of Funks-town, be it known, was not found in "a secret drawer of my deceased Grand-father" –"translated from an old Hindoo manuscript"– "found on a old Book-stall in Grub Street,"[605] or "among the ruins of Herculaneum,"[606] but was written by a "poor wight" (as he styles himself) on the southern precincts of a neighboring state.[607] The digression may perhaps be thought too long: for our own parts we are satisfied with the authors reason for its length; and as he has not permitted us to sleep in his excursion, he has certainly been less unfortunate than many brethren of the quill, whose education, at least should entitle them to some literary notice. The Germans (some of them) may perhaps take umbrage at the word "Crout";[608] it should be remembered however, that the whole was a ludicrous affair, and the writer has treated it as such. - From the playful good humor manifested in his narration, we should judge there is no ill will intended to any body – inclined to laugh himself he is anxious that others should laugh also. Had he wined about the hardness of the times he might possibly have struck a string more in union (at this time) with popular feeling.

THE PUBLISHER.

Hagers-town, March 20, 1824.

---

604 Fond of wine and spirits.
605 According to Dr. Samuel Johnson's Dictionary, Grub Street was "originally the name of a street in Moorfields in London much inhabited by writers of small histories, dictionaries, and temporary poems; whence any mean production is called grubstreet."
606 Herculaneum is an ancient Roman town that was located in the shadow of Mount Vesuvius.
607 The phrase "poor wight" appears in Chaucer's *The Canterbury Tales, The Wife of Bath's Tale,* as a reflection on poverty and gentility. During Kennedy's lifetime, "poor wight" appears in numerous Scottish poems synonymous with a poor devil, poor wretch, ragamuffin, luckless wight, or sorry wight.
608 According to the Oxford English Dictionary (Second Edition, 1989) This potentially derogatory use of "Crout" for those of German heritage is almost 100 years earlier any other references. Most sources cite 1918 as the date "Kraut" appears as a derogatory term for a German, identifying them with Sauerkraut, or Sourcrout. By World War II, a Kraut was slang for a German soldier.

The BATTLE of FUNKS-TOWN

That bravery might have its glory,
'Tis said that fame invented story.

Once on a time as story say,
A Funks-town, on St. Patrick's day
Happened a most heroic feat,
In which the valiant saint was beat;
The potent saint that chas'd the frogs
And toads and snakes from Irish bogs.[609]
This mighty saint (by history proven,
Could heat with snow a baker's oven,[610]
And for the good of church and state
Do other miracles as great,
By heretics was overcome)
By dint of musquetry and drum.[611]

So much by way of introduction,
To deeds of valour and destruction;
Of mangled limbs and broken bones,
Appalling shrieks and dying groans,
Such as were heard at mount St. John
'Twixt Bonaparte and Wellington.[612]

Some turnpike-men of Irish blood
With good St. Patrick at the head,
On famous Funks-town made a sally
Arm'd with Hibernian shilela –[613]
Mattocks, pickaxes, hoes and shovels
(You'd think they were as many devils)
For priming each had ta'n a gill
Warm from the worm-pipe of the still,[614]

To teach the native cudgel-law
And lay in courage for the war.
– Thus arm'd the shamrocks came in view,
But not as soldiers two and two,
Or indian file as riflemen
With dangling arms along the plain,
But scatter'd like a flock of rooks
Or rabble dogs on scent of fox,[615]
With yells as num'rous as the rabble
Of the builders of the tow'r of babel.[616]

Poor Funks-town saw and heard afar
The terrors of the coming war,
Flew to their arms and beat the drum
To save their "firesides and their home"
And send the knaves 'to kingdom come.'

Arranged our heroes firmly stood
The threat'ning charge of death or blood.

Next say we how the women fared,
How much the lovely sex was scared
And how they scampered up and down
From one to 'tother end of town–
How bonnets, caps and ruffles flew,
Some lost a shawl and some a shoe
Mid mortar mingled snow and mud,
While mute as statues others stood,
Some roared aloud for justice Bog[617]
And call'd him good for nothing hog.
The air resounds with mingled cries
A hideous and terrific noise
Of frightened cats and howling dogs,
Of scared or hungry squalling hogs.

To see the proud reason disconcerted.
Poor lowly instinct felt deserted,

---

[609] St. Patrick did not have a difficult time driving snakes from Ireland as none lived there. Due to the glacial development of Ireland and Britain, the climate was not hospitable for the cold-blooded reptiles.
[610] In another legend, while traveling with friends, a chilled St. Patrick breathed onto a snow mound, and it caught fire.
[611] This phrase seems to imply St. Patrick was martyred for performing miracles in the name of Christ. Most sources indicate that, after approximately forty years of preaching the gospel to the pagan Irish, St. Patrick died from natural causes in the year 493.
[612] Kennedy is comically comparing the events at Funks-town with the battle of Waterloo where Napoleon Bonaparte was defeated by the Duke of Wellington. Mount St. John is a farm and orchard at Waterloo in present day Belgium.
[613] Hibernia is the classical Latin name for the island of Ireland. A shilela, or shillelagh, is a wooden walking stick that doubles as a club. Typically it is made from stout knotty wood with a large knob at the top.
[614] Ta'n is a contraction for "taken." A gill is an antiqued measurement term for a quarter of a pint used in the production of alcoholic spirits. The worm pipe is the circular coils inside a still used in the distillation of alcohol.
[615] The Rook, or "Church Parson" is a member of the crow family and is common to Ireland. Rooks tend to roost together in colonies in tall trees called rookeries.
[616] A reference to the biblical story in the Book of Genesis explaining the origin of different languages.
[617] The most probable suspect for "Justice Bog" is Michael Isenminger. A few days after the battle a public meeting was held in which Michael Isenminger presided. Williams, Thomas J. C. *A History of Washington County, Maryland"* (Chambersburg, PA, 1906), 155.

As though his majesty the sun,
Had hid himself behind the moon.

Now justice Bog had heard the noise
And sallied forth among the boys,
With pipe and cudgel fiercely armed
With whiskey law and tansy warmed,
And braved the shamrocks face to face
As guardian of the public peace;
To whom the squire began oration
Or as some say expostulation:
"Vat for de tevil you com'd here
"Mid your tam cudgel as for war?
"I'll send ye puggers to de jail
"Dere try your gargases awhile!"
Thus having eloquently spoke
He gravely opened his book
And read aloud the riot act,[618]
But in so strange a dialect
The shamrock's could not comprehend him,
Had they desired to understand him.
So finding he could not disperse 'em,
Flew in a rage and 'gan to curse 'em–
Next laying down his pipe and hat,
Bantered their best man out to fight;
Though little understanding Dutch,
An Irish woman's skill was such,
She judged his motions spoke of war
More plainly than his words of law;
So hit him lounder in the lug[619]
And down fell Mr. Justice Bog,
Then smack'd her fists and d–d his eyes
And bid the lying rascal rise;
But justice having tasted wattle,[620]
Had rather lay, than rise to battle–
Chose rather to be daubed with mud
Than ornament his brows with blood;
Since honor cannot patch a head
And of small worth is to the dead.
Venturing howe'er to mutter "bitch,"

She kicked his honour in the breech, [621]
And following up with tooth and claw
Was mangling sore the man of law,
Until his friends beheld his plight
And bore his honor from the fight.
Loud laughing Shamrocks cheer'd huzzas,
The distant echoes sung applause;
While helter skelter here they ran,
Erin's proud saint was marching on
Swearing dire vengeance to the town
Of every "whore's and mother's son
Of the black-hearted country born."

Loud beat the drum, prepare! prepare!
To nerve each arm. But not a cheer
Poor Funks-town gave, but quaked with fear.
The foe arrived, they all engaged,
From left to right the battle raged;
Shilelas, shovels, mattock's flew,
(Arms always to the battle true)–
Concussive flint and steel miss fire
And baulk the heroes ardent ire,
But when shilela give a lounder,
It lays the foe as flat's as flounder –
So here 'twas verified and shewn,
The Funks-town heroes tumbled down.
And wallowed in the mire and mud,
Begging for quarters others stood–
Yet dead to mercy pat laid on
(While down his beard the claret run)
'Till all were tumbled down or kill'd
Or scared ignobly from the field.
Victorious shamrocks rais'd the shout
Of triumph o'er the sons of crout,
And threw their hats up high in air,
To thank his grace the God of war,
And curs'd in most opprobious strain,[622]
The dead and wounded on the plain;
But whether there were any dead,
Or merely prostrate in the mud,
The surgeons have not made report,
So venture not ourselves to do it,
Who write for history forsooth
And therefore nothing but the truth!

---

[618] The 1714 Riot Act was an act of the Parliament of Great Britain that authorised local authorities to declare any group of twelve or more people to be unlawfully assembled, and thus have to disperse or face punitive action.
[619] To lounder is to beat with heavy strokes.
[620] Likely a reference to wattle and daub which is a antiquated composite building material of thin branches "wattle," held together with the composite "daub" that could be made from clay, lime, chalk dust, or limestone dust.

[621] British variant of honor.
[622] A misspelling of the word *opprobrious* meaning to express with scorn or criticism.

But from experience, we trust
Not many veterans lick'd the dust,
(Or rather sirs perhaps we should
Have said, been slain and lick'd the mud,)
Since kindly nature maketh thick
The skull whene'er the brains are weak.

But ah! the treacherous God betray
And we pursue the tragic lay,
The memoirs of this bloody fray.
It seems the first appearance shewn,
Of battle that was coming on,
A crafty coward Funks-town wight
To Hagerstown had ta'en his flight,
Loud bawling to the sons of crout:
"Funks-town's invaded! out! turn out!
"A numerous herd of turnpike-men,
"Arm'd with shilelas stout and green,
"Picks, forks, and every tool of tillage
"Threat'ning destruction to our village,
"To plunder and to burn our houses,
"Ravish our maidens and our spouses,
"If they, too much for Funks-town mettle
"Should overcome them in the battle,
"And though for the reverse I've prayed,
"Who knoweth what hath been decreed!"

The uproar 'mong the Hagers flew,
But whence it sprang, few people knew:
All were alarm'd and all confused,
Some bellowed Fire! and some abused
The negroes for a hellish plot,
Made fast the doors and windows shut;
Many sought refuge in the jail,
(*Sans* constable or seeking bail;)
Alarm bells rang. Here beat the drum,
Some ran with ladders, buckets some;
All ranks partook of agitation,
All felt the dearth of information;
The Burgess and the Council met,
In solemn cogitation sat;
Feeling as those of former days
When murderous Potowatamies[623]
Threatened with tomahawk and knife

To scalp the settler, bairns and wife,[624]
To burn or pillage cot or cabin,
To leave nor clap-board nor a slab on.

It may seem strange, yet so it was,
None of the Hager-higher-powers,
Had heard the Funk-man's proclamation,
That rais'd this fearful consternation.
But this it seems is no strange matter,
On this "enlightened side o' the water;"
For had our big folks ought expected,
What even scavengers predicted;
At Washington the red-coat rabble,
Had feasted not at Sammy's table;
The City topsy turvy turned,
The books and public buildings burned,
But 'stead of Madisonian beef,[625]
Had dined on blood and supped in grief;
Mad Ross had found *quietus* there,[626]
(The laurel won at Baltimore,)
There he had drawn his final ration
And Cockburn talk'd of "demonstration;"[627]
For so the English when they're beat,
Wipe off the odium of defeat.
Then Jackson had not lived to see,
His famous Orleans victory;
Of Indian fame had been content,
Nor sighed to be the President.[628]

---

623   Indians, also spelled Potawatomi, Potowamies, Pouteat-amies, Poutewatemis, Puttawattimes, Puttewatamies, Puttewattamies.

624   Bairn is a Scottish word for a child.
625   On August 24th, 1814 British troops arrived at a nearly deserted Washington, DC and entered the White House where they found the dining room laid out for a dinner party. After enjoying President Madison's "beef," the British then burned the mansion.
       "Sammy," or Major General Samuel Smith, was commander of the defenses of Baltimore during the Battle of Baltimore and Fort McHenry on September 11-13th of 1814. The victory at Baltimore is largely attributed to General Smith's preparedness in the defenses of Baltimore.
626   British General Robert Ross was killed at the Battle of North Point.
627   Vice Admiral Sir Alexander Cochrane was the British commander-in-chief during the attacks on Washington and Baltimore. Cochrane wrote to London that the attack on Baltimore was not a lost battle, but rather a "demonstration" of British naval power. Kennedy has mistakenly attributed the quote to Cochrane's subordinate, Rear Admiral George Cockburn. Lord, Walter, *The Dawn's Early Light*, (W. W. Norton & Company, 1972), 299.
628   Kennedy wrote this poem in 1824 as four candidates were vying for the presidency: John Quincy Adams, Andrew Jackson, William H. Crawford, and Henry Clay. Although Jackson garnered the highest number of electoral votes the number was insufficient to constitute a majority, and the selection for President fell to the House of Representatives, who voted for John Quincy Adams.

But fate by either whang or tether,
Ties hard and fast events together,
And one draws after it another;
Hence 'tis our nacky editors can so,
Unsay what's said a month ago.

(Pardon dear Sirs this short digression,
The warriors must take a ration;
To keep the vet'ran on the field,
The paunch should now and then be filled;
Hence 'tis for fight we feed the brave,
To rule him hence, we starve the slave—
So leave we them to take "their bite,"
And lay in courage for the fight,
While farther we indulged our flight.)
Hence 'twas in some eventful struggle,
Nature squeezed out her darling Ogle,
To swell and to illume debate,
And patch the morals of the State!
Him bless'd with happiest of ken,
Could see of women or of men,
At once their interest and their sin,
The bless'd descendants of old Penn;
(As shrewdest tinkers skilled in metals,
Can shew the cracks of worn-out kettles,)
His huge sagacity can trace,
The good or evil of our dress:
And then so modest. If the fair,
Would tempting leg or bosom bare,
Or let them peep through flimsy veil,
He'd blush from elbows to the tail.
If petticoats were long enough,
Or made of too transparent stuff,
His mammoth talents could perceive,
And curative prescriptions give*;[629]
Could with the magic of his wand,
Hurl vice and quackery from the land.

Hence Shulze the friend of purge and pill,
Takes a year's nap upon the bill,
To fasten Gag upon the quacks,
And hinder them from going snacks
With richer knaves, who've heard a lecture,
And come out dubb'd a 'learned Doctor!"[630]

By legislative tricks like these,
The rich secure monopolies.

Prate of their dignified profession,
And feed the sages of the nation;
As learned Anatomist we know,
Our Senators have stomachs too,
And these we craftily assail,
When other arts of Logic fail:
For brains or belly spread the net,
Till round majorities are caught.
Tinkers methinks will shortly want,
And pray a legislative grant,
For power to punish common men,
Who dare to patch their pot or pan;
And next the cross-legged Knight of stitches,
The saving dog who darns his breeches;
The busy dog who makes the news,
And either side of quarrel shews –
The noisy heroes of the type,
For cash or quarrel ever ripe –
Staunch advocates of truth or lies,
As interest may cast the dies!
Call Tory, Democrat, or Fed,
Patent Republican, or Quid,
Whatever black-guard name or names
May suit the torrent of the times.
Sow-Gelder's too shall have an act,[631]
Their trade and profits to protect.
This policy prevents intrusion,
And give quietus to confusion;
As soldiers soon we'll know our ranks,

---

629 Original text: **See proceeding of the Legislature of Pennsylvania 1811-12, and 1823-24**.
  Alexander Ogle (1766-1832) was born in Frederick County, MD and moved to Somerset, PA in 1795. He served in either the House or Senate almost continually from 1803 until 1828. In February of 1812, Ogle proposed a resolution to the Pennsylvania legislature to "restrain the ladies from dressing in the present fashionable state of nudity." He proposed a $100 fine for each offense. The resolution was met with "peals of laughter from the members." *Tickler* Newspaper (Philadelphia, PA) 12 Feb 1812.

630 The Pennsylvania state legislature passed a medical practice statute in 1824 for the issuance of a state issued medical licence for qualified doctors. Governor John Andrew Shulze vetoed the statue citing both constitutional concerns and general policy objections. Shulze, John Andrew, *"To the Assembly Vetoing 'An Act to Regulate the Practice of Physics and Surgery Within this Commonwealth,'"* Papers of the Governors in PA Archives 4th Series (1900) 542-543.

631 One who spays sows. An occupation probably not associated with the higher levels of society.

All give the Legislature thanks.
Os. Coccygas the puny stump, [632]
By nature made to form the rump,
Will keep its place nor sign to lead,
Or lord it o'er the lordly head.

We do indeed despise the dog,
Dosing credulity with drug;
In nothing read, save almanacs,
Sunday, and missionary tract:
Watching, if signs be up or down,
As well the changes of the moon,
To guide him or cup and bleed,
(Both which, his every patient need.)
In charms, professing wondrous skill,
Of amulets, can wonders tell;
And though has never been to College,
Display a deal of saving knowledge.

We too esteem the man of parts,
Deep skills in Therapeutic arts:
And many such we know there be,
Who, ne'er solicited M.D.

What then? Among our learned folks,
We know there are "Diploma'd" quacks
Too brainless ever to be taught,
Sages, whose only merit lie,
In bawling Quack and charging high.

In medicine, we have our sects,
Our authodox and heretics.[633]
And some there are in pray a Pope,
To build and prop the temple up.

In learning some places such reliance,
They set dame nature to defiance.
"Our Colleges," say they, " with ease,
"Make of whatever stuff we please;
"Of any booby, knave or ass on,
"As Doctor, Lawyer, or a Parson.
"As sculptors, blocks or marble can,
"Turn into either horse, or man.
"For those in Greek and Latin read,

"Can prove that black is white or red;
"Their balderdash is shrewdest sense,
"Their sophistry, true eloquence,
"Whate'er they preach, we vulgar folks,
"Call Physic, Law, and orthodox.

In such ironic stuff they rail,
(Rightly we call them infidel.)
Their paunches long for loaves and fishes,
Destined by fate to other dishes.

Schools, surely shew that fools may speak,
In Cherokee, Hindoo, or Greek;
And that by homespun English, we
May converse with Philosophy.
Hydraulics, Optics, Mathematics,
Astronomy and Hydrostatics,
Metaphysics and Pneumatics,
Naval and military tactics,
Chemistry and Aereology,
Electricity, and Astrology,
Mechanics, and Geography,
Agriculture and History,
A navy, state or army wield,
May govern men, or have them kill'd.
Every science, every art,
Our homely language may impart,
But Preachers, Lawyers and Physicians,
Must first be made Academicians.
Yet after all to gain diploma,
(From the *Os Calcis* to the *vomer*,)[634]
From modern Chapman back to Homer;[635]
Though one of the lore of learning chime,
He's doomed to quackery and crime;
Should he deny as orthodox,
Opinions of the ruling folks.*[636]

632 A small triangular bone at the base of the spinal column commonly called the tailbone.
633 Authodox is assumed to be a amusing variation of orthodox by the author.
634 From the heel bone to the tip of one's nose.
635 Nathaniel Chapman (1780-1853) of Philadelphia was a well-known American physician and the founding president of the American Medical Association in 1847.
636 **Original footnote - See the case of Dr. Whilldon a candidate for the degree of D.M. at the Medical University of Philadelphia.**
     Dr. Whilldon, is John Galloway Whilldin (1797-1824). Today the name is more commonly known as Wheldon. In 1819, Whilldin completed his studies at the Medical University of Pennsylvania and submitted his thesis necessary to obtain a medical degree. Entitled *"An essay on the Nature and Treatment of that State of Disorder generally called Dropsy,"* Whilldin's thesis included several paragraphs the reviewing professors found objectional, citing "strange and unheard-of measures." Whilldin was notified

While very little learning need,
The booby knave of supple creed,
So he but signs their *ipse dixit*, [637]
Their learn'd professionships can fix it.
This done, the fees of college paid,
All's right. The law is satisfied.
He may now bleed, give wine or brandy,
And prate of *"modus operandi."*[638]
Look grave, prescribe *"quantum sufficit,"*[639]
And charge an eagle for his "visit."[640]
This in a goodly *"repitandum,"*
Coward in that, or *"desperandum."*[641]

(Now what are words, but signs of things?
To ideas what are words, but wings?
In whatsoever tongue we speak,
Plain English, Latin, Dutch or Greek.)
The Grecian bards have wisely sung,
And that too in the Grecian tongue.
Did Horace Sirs: who sung so sleek,
Know aught of Hebrew or of Greek?–
–The boy, who can a basket make,
The woman, who can spin and bake,
Is of more value to a nation,
Than scores, who prate of derivation.
Skill'd but in etymologies, [642]
A man's a drone among the bees.
He pines in idleness to eat,
The honey which industry get.
Grave as an owl, set up for critic,
The goggles mount, a stern Dogmatic.

Yet of our vulgar staring's spite,
Nature in truth asserts her right:
(Since when she means to make a fool;
He laughs contemptuous at the school.)
She through the passions warps the will,
She long hath ruled and ruleth still.
–Hence Banks, by legislative wand,
Were strew'd as rapeseed o'er the land,
To fill with money every hand.
To change our Gold, for paper dreams;
Fill us, with money making schemes.
But e'er our riches scarce were felt,
Our palaces and barns were built;
Stern discount and depreciation,
Alarm's the dupes of speculation.
As well they might. A sheriff's sale,
Winds up the visionary tale.

Sage history in vain doth preach,
Where avarice presumes to teach.
Now if rain wets the folks of China,
'Twill surely wet in Pennsylvania.
All men can retrospect a law,
Assembly-men should see before.

'Tis right majorities should rule us,
Though sometimes they perchance may fool us.
We shall minorities prefer,
When once convinced, they never err!

---

that his medical degree would be withheld unless the offending paragraphs were deleted from the thesis. Whilldin complied, obtained his degree, then retaliated by publishing his original entire thesis including a preface that related the events that Whilldin believed were unfair.

Under normal circumstances, Whilldin's mediocre thesis would not have merited publication, and especially not in the widely read *American Medical Recorder, of original papers and intelligence in medicine and surgery*. The editors reprinted Whilldin's thesis and his difficulty in obtaining his medical degree in its entirety. In their review, the editors found no fault with Whilldin's thesis, applauded his "valuable observations," and questioned whether the university faculty had the right to censure a student's work and withhold a degree because the student presented alternative theories. Additionally, the editors questioned the customary practise of the professors charging each student an additional $100 to review each thesis. In an average year university professors regularly reviewed 50 to 60 theses at a cost of $100 each, significantly supplementing their annual income of $8,000-$10,000 for four months work. The editors argued that this practice "if not checked by the interference of the regents of the establishments, will, in a very short time, lower the character of the institution, and destroy the reputation of her diplomas."

After practicing for a few years, John Galloway Whilldin, M.D., died in 1824 at the age of 27 on the island of St. Thomas in the West Indies.

Whilldin, John G., *An Essay on the Nature and Treatment of that state of Disorder Generally called Dropsy, Printed for the Author by William Fry*, (Philadelphia, PA. 1820). Eberle, John, M.D., editor, *The American Medical Recorder of Original Papers and Intelligence in Medicine and Surgery, Volume 3*, (Philadelphia, PA. 1820) 590-605.

637   Ipse Dixit. [Latin, He himself said it.] An unsupported statement that rests solely on the authority of the individual who makes it.
638   Modus operandi is a Latin phrase, approximately translated as "method of operation".
639   Quantum sufficit a Latin phrase, a sufficient quantity.
640   The eagle is a base-unit of denomination issued only for gold coinage by the United States Mint based on the original values designated by the Coinage Act of 1792. It has been obsolete as a circulating denomination since 1933.
641   Latin for despair.

642   The study of the origin of words and the way in which their meanings have changed throughout history.

Hence men are fit for all things made,
Each occupation, art and trade.
A Newton given to walk the skies, [643]
And send aloft his wondering eyes;
Till he forgot the humble earth,
That gave his mammoth genius birth.

A Symmes, was destined to the pole,[644]
To find an aperture or hole;
In which first venturing to peep,
Courageous grown, would inward creep,
To find out if the inet be so,
The world is big with young or no.
Another wight (from Yankee town,)
Would make a world at Washington;
For sickly fools to find their health in,
Or spend a little surplus wealth in,
Matters for which our thousands roam,
May then be gatherer nigher home.
Our convalescent patients there,
May chose what food, breathe any air,
Their "Learned Physicians" may direct,
Without a fear of being wrecked.
May laugh at Boreas' wild commotion, [645]
Nor tremble at the boisterous ocean.
(For thousands running from disease,
Grim death has nabb'd upon the seas.)[646]
Or if a voyage must be taken,
To save a puny patients bacon;
He may a trip to India take,
Or longer one to China make,
Select Siberian air to cough in,
The mild Italian breeze to laugh in.
Drink Ballstown, Bath, or Seltzer waters,[647]
Madeira wine, or London porters.

Cull from whatever latitude,
He pleases, articles of food.
Season with any spice his dish,
Of vegetable, flesh or fish.

Oh, what a darling place 'twill be,
What feasting for Philosophy.
Her pendulums of lead and twine,
May be suspended on the line;
Or hung up over Symmes' hole,
Or if she please the other pole,
And from the difference of vibrations,
Confirm her learned calculations.
Here, she will shortly learn no doubt,
Why Etna's fuel's not burned out, [648]
How earthquakes, clouds, and thunder's made,
Why the mid-sea's not emptied;
Or rather, why not overflow,
Exhaled, or oozing out below.
Whether the moon 'tis makes the tide,
Or rocked the seas from side to side.
Whether the sun is cold or hot,
Composed of earth, or fire or what;
And why at times he looks so spotted,
Their number and their areas noted.
Whether the comets feed the sun,
With Caloric as with a spoon, [649]
Of what composed their gaudy trail,
Electric, or Phosphoric tail.
Whether they carry war or peace,
Or what their wondrous business is.
What forms the belt of Jupiter,
And what the rings of Saturn are.
If Georgium Sidus be so cold, [650]
Merc'ry so hot, as we are told,
And if so, how do folks contrive,
The means by which to toil and live.
These, get their ice, to cool their gruel.

---

[643] Sir Isaac Newton, an English physicist and mathematician.
[644] In 1818, John Cleves Symmes, Jr. (1779-1829) was the most famous of the early "Hollow Earth" proponents. Symmes suggested that Earth was a hollow shell with openings at both poles and proposed making an expedition to the North Pole hole. President John Quincy Adams indicated he would approve the expedition, but he left office before this could occur. The new President, Andrew Jackson, halted the attempt.
[645] Boreas was the purple-winged god of the north wind, one of the four directional Anemoi (wind-gods).
[646] 18th and 19th physicians often recommended ocean voyages to islands for patients to cure or relieve rheumatic, skin, or repository diseases.
[647] Ballstown Spa in Saratoga, NY, the town of Bath in England, and Selter, or Seltzer (Lahn) in Germany are all famous for their natural mineral springs waters.

[648] Mount Etna is an active stratovolcano on the east coast of Sicily, Italy. It is the tallest active volcano on the European continent.
[649] In the late 18th and early 19th centuries, Caloric was a hypothetical fluid substance thought to be responsible for the phenomena of heat.
[650] The planet Uranus was first known as "The Georgium Sidus" (the Georgian Planet) in honor of King George III of England. The name "Uranus" was first proposed by German astronomer Johann Elert Bode to conform with the other classical mythology planetary names. Uranus is the ancient Greek deity of the Heavens, the earliest supreme god. The name did not achieve common use until 1850.

Those, were to warm it, get the fuel.
How men are made of every colour,
The white, the black, the red, the yellow,
Whether if made with tails or no,
And perhaps when they lost them too. [651]
Whether a land or water creature,
Or whether of amphibious nature.
If instinct be another name,
For Reason, in the pig and lamb,
Their difference what? in what, the same.
If Mores' history be true, [652]
The world when made, or old or new.
Or whether it was drown'd or not,
There probably will be found out.
And there too many schemes sagacious,
Will probably turn out fallacious.
Here we may climb proud Teneriffe, [653]
Or cross the ocean in a skiff.
Here mounted on the snowy scalps
Of Andes, view the distant Alps.
And from our far famed Niagara,
See the dear heights of Tipperary.[654]
Trace the mad course of Alexander, [655]
The nobler of the French commander,
And when at last th' alliance catch'd him,
The rock, on which, they chain'd & watch'd him.[656]

When finished, what a fine place this,
For making new discoveries.
Chemist, by crucible and still,
May analyze whate'er they will;
And tell us the component matter,
Of earth, fire, metal, earth or water.
What in the lungs 'tis, change the blood,
So rapidly from black to red;
Or oxygen or other matter,
Or what the process is of nature.
There by their Hydrogenian ray.[657]
Turn winter's night, to Summer's day.
There, form a second paradise,
There give us more than Eden bliss,
In plenteous nitrous oxyd Gas.[658]

Our Doctors too, may find out there,
The long desired panacea;[659]
To break the skulls of gout and pain,
(For which the ancients sought in vain.)
The long sought Hypocratean key, [660]
That holds the life or sets it free,
And here an end to their disputes,
Relating or to men or brutes.
How so much misery is endured,
Or how of their diseases cured.
Do veins absorb disease or not,
Or if by sympathy driven out,
Or whether by the stomach taken,
In water, gruel, mush or bacon.
Whether this organ grinds the food,
To pumice ready for the blood,
Or whether 'tis fermented there,
And manufactured into beer;
Whether or not the lacteals sup,[661]
The spirit, or the low wines up;
Whether, of wisdom to select,
Or whatsoever please reject,
Or whether like a pump hydraulic,
Whate'er the guts presents to haul up.

The sources of corporeal heat,
So partial why to ninety-eight,
Why we are chill'd or why we sweat.

---

[651] In a folktale, Saoras of Orissa of India determined men originally had long tails. This was fine as long as there were not too many people around.
[652] Probably a reference to Sir Thomas More (1478-1535) and his writing of *Utopia* about an island nation.
[653] Mount Teneriffe is a mountain in central Australia.
[654] **Tipperary is a town in County Tipperary, Ireland.**
[655] Alexander III of Macedonia, or Alexander the Great, spent most of his ruling years on an unprecedented military campaign through Asia and northeast Africa.
[656] Napoleon Bonaparte was twice exiled to an island. The first time was in 1814 to the island of Elba, In 1815, he escaped from Elba and returned to power for roughly 100 days, but was finally defeated at the Battle of Waterloo. He spent the last six years of his life in confinement by the British on the remote island of Saint Helena.
[657] In the 1820s, Sir Goldsworthy Gurney's (1793-1875) experiments with hydrogen led to the development of the oxy-hydrogen blowpipe, as a form of illumination. This lead to the invention of limelight once used in the illumination of theaters and dance halls.
[658] Nitrous oxide, more commonly known as laughing gas, was first synthesized by English natural philosopher Joseph Priestly in 1772. In 1800, Humphry Davy published his research on the uses of the gas as an analgesic in his book *Researches, Chemical and Philosophical: Chiefly Concerning Nitrous Oxide, Or Dephlogisticated Nitrous Air, and Its Respiration* (London, 1800).
[659] Panacea is a solution of remedy for all difficulties or diseases.
[660] A reference to the Hippocratic oath taken by physicians to uphold a specific ethical standard.
[661] A lacteal is a lymphatic capillary that absorbs dietary fats in the villi of the small intestine.

Our surly or our laughing mood,
Occasioned's by Galvani's fluid,[662]
Creeping or galloping amain,
Along the nerves or in the brain,
To give us pleasure, ease or pain.
Or has the moon or other planet,
In friendship or in malice done it.
A thousand other things disputed,
Orthodox now, and then refuted,
Relating to the economy,
Of animal machinery,
Will be so clearly understood,
That muscles, tendons, bones and blood;
Will be by common fellows made,
And patching men, as shoes, a trade.
What then will signify our act?
Our "learn'd profession" to protect.
Then with our medicated candy,
Away goes lancets, Brown and brandy.[663]
Away goes Bolus, draught and pill,[664]
Our darling main-stay calomel.[665]
Away the humoral dietetic,[666]
Away too goes the sympathetic.
The plaster, liniment and blister,
Sialagogue, anodyne and clyster.[667]
Rabbits and dogs, no more are slaughtered,
Or horses, cats, or monkies tortured.

To leave unsettled the disputes,
Of learned phisiologic brutes.

There avarice too may learn the trade,
How 'tis that gold and silver's made;
And so by dint of transmutation,
Make us all rich. Enrich the nation,
And paying debts be all the fashion.

Thus 'tis that we may not be sad.
Fate turns events to make us glad.
(At least whoever deigns to use them,
And not ungratefully refuse them.)
Hence 'tis that I a luckless wight,
Tho' doomed in poverty, to write
The history of this great battle,
And save a sprig of Irish mettle,
That otherwise had surely slunk,
Into oblivious huge trunk;
With millions there to lay and rot,
And mingle with the mass forgot.
Hence 'tis, that I can laugh at folly,
Which make so many melancholy.
Though nabobs round me count their sums,[668]
And with good eating treat their gums;
For whom, both Indies pour their treasures,
Zealous which most can aid their pleasures;
Though destined scanty meals to take,
On dodgers, mush, or jonny-cake;
Though lean, and lank, find joys abound me,
While fatter fools are sighing round me.
Thanks to my stars. Or thanks to fate,
Whose every joint is made to fit,
(As baby's mouth and mamma's tit.)
By whom, my stomach staunch and good,
Is fitted to my humble food.
While others guzzle down Madeira,
Cold water from the fountain cheer me;
Or now and then perhaps made frisky,
By wholesome stimulus of whiskey;
Whose merits, these our wiser days,
Are given sorely to dispraise;
Then blessed Lethe of the poor,[669]
Then fittest us for peace or war;

---

662 Luigi Aloisio Galvani (1737 – 1798) was an Italian physician, physicist and philosopher who lived and died in Bologna. In 1780, he discovered that the muscles of dead frog's legs twitched when struck by an electrical spark. He believed the twitch was activated by an electrical fluid that is carried to the muscles by the nerves.
663 John Brown (1735-1788) was a Scottish physician. Brown's lectures contained attacks on the preceding systems of medicines of the times.
664 In medicine, a bolus (from Latin bolus, ball) is the administration of a discrete amount of medication, drug or other compound in order to raise its concentration in blood to an effective level.
665 Medical uses for calomel, or mercury chloride, were common well into the 19th century. It acted as a purgative, killed bacteria, and also did irreversible damage to their human hosts. The three physicians attending George Washington's final hours administered calomel to the dying President.
666 Humeral as in relating to the body fluids, especially with regard to immune responses. Humeral dietetic relates to the theory that a proper diet of fresh foods was believed to ensure humeral balance. Shprintsen, Adam D., *The Vegetarian Crusade: The Rise of an American Reform Movement, 1817-1921* (University of North Carolina Press, 2013).
667 Sialagogue is a drug or substance that increase the flow rate of saliva. Anodyne was a drug believed to relieve or sooth pain by lessening the sensitivity of the brain or nervous system. Clyster is an enema.

---

668 A nabob is a person of conspicuous wealth or high status.
669 In Greek mytholgy, Lethe was one of the five rivers of Hades. All who drank from it experienced complete forgetfulness.

If haggard sickness makes us droop,
Thy kindly aid doth lift us up;
Then sweetly teach us to forget,
At once our creditors and debt;
Disarms the jail of all its terrors,
Dry up the current of our sorrows.
If we are visited by pain,
Thou fetch us back our ease again;
Hence, Doctors to despise thee feign,
Yet love thee, trust me in the main.
Without thee, how were juleps made?
Thou pith and backbone of their trade,
Shouldst thou desert their stinking shops,
They'd find small merit in their drops.
Ungrateful Dogs! The praise is thine,
Of every cure, of every wine;
And when as oft' it hap' they kill,
'Tis lack of whiskey in the pill;
Though learned be their nomenclature,
They dare not rob thee of thy nature;
Though fain would plunder thee of fame,
By calling thee outlandish name.
As Alcohol, thou'rt whiskey still,
Soul of their bolus, draught or pill;
'Twere better if persuaded they,
Would throw their other truck away,
Metallic calxes, powders, weeds,[670]
Gums, berries, oils and foreign seeds;
Their asafoetida and castor,[671]
And things, if possible far nastier;
Things fitted but to make us sick,
To aid the money-making trick,
The epidemic of the times,
Which all have catched, save men of rhymes,
Who drink no medicated teas,
Or laugh too much to catch disease,
Were all like us, the pots and jugs,
Of Doctors, and their filthy drugs,
Would soon be tumbled to the gutters,
To rot with other offall matters;
Their every bottle jar or jug,
Instead of boasting fly and bug,
Would hold thee, blushing as the rose,

Pure as the chrystal fount that flows.[672]
Then touch'd with thy all-healing wand,
Pale sickness would desert the land;
And every foreign fool of wealth,
Be running hence to seek his health,
Or buy thee, dear of native quack,
Disguised with Cam or other truck;
(For thus the learning of the schools,
Is made to pluck and plunder fools.)
But we they further praise pursue,
The knaves in time will get their due;
When sober fools are wiser grown,
And they high supremacy own.
Thou renovat'st our every part,
Fill with new energies the heart,
Thou giv'st the blood a livelier flow,
More than this far-famed opium do;
To whom, I learned thou'rt near akin'd,
But of the two our better friend.
Since he alone on riches wait,
Cringe to, and fawning on the great,
Thou curest men of every state.
And then he's such a dirty creature,
Thou first must purify his nature;
And make him descent to be drank,
Perform the cure, and get no thank.
The worthless alien. Tory, knave!
Why condescend to be his slave?
The filthy animal to wash?
To be the vehicle of trash?
And one who boasts the credit too,
Of doing, what alone you do.
Fye whiskey! leave him after this,
They'll find out what the rascal is;
Were his demerits understood,
He's even filthier than mud.
Vile infidel! ungracious Turk!
Forbidden, yet devouring pork.
He, nastiest onions eat, and leeks,
And then he's murdering the Greeks.[673]
Rise, precious staple of the nation,

---

670   Calxes are the crumbly residues left after a mineral or metal has been roasted.
671   Asafoetida is the dried latex exuded from the root of an herb often used to treat digestive ailments.
672   Crystal fountains.
673   Most Turks are muslins and forbidden to eat pork. The relations between the Greek and the Turkish states have been marked by alternating periods of mutual hostility and reconciliation ever since Greece won its independence from the Ottoman Empire in 1821. Since then the two countries have faced each other in four major wars beginning with the Greco-Turkish War in 1897.

Assert thy claim to estimation;
Thou, givest zest to every dinner,
From the proud Bishop to the sinner;
And ingrate dogs, who slander most,
Pay thee due homage at the feast;
At thy commanding sceptre kneel,
To thank thee for the joys they feel.
Does war present to us a foe?
Thou nerv'st each arm, direct'st each blow;
Each drummer, when of thee he's full,
Feels big as any General.
Statesmen, who never spoke before,
Feeling thy impulse, take the floor;
Astounding speak. The admiring crowd,
The benches thwack in plaudits loud.
Thou tumblest all distinction down,
(Betwixt the beggar and the crown)
Down to the level of a man,
Thou'rt truly a Republican.
And when we feel thee in our heads,
We hear no more of Tories, Feds,
Loyalists, Democrats or Quids.[674]
Such are thy honours powers of Rye,
Such is thy noble quality;
And though not halt thy praise be sung,
Think not I slight or mean thee wrong;
But take my tribute choicest spirit,
Though far beneath thy sterling merit;
Since what I may in language lack,
By good intention is made up.
But hold, we ramble long and far,
And must again return to war;
Where last we left the council sitting,
In quandary deliberating;
And there awhile we'll let them sit,
Themselves can publish their debate.
We must our bloody tale pursue,
And stick by those of brighter view;
Since, for the turnpike-men, forsooth,
Too many folks had learned the truth.
The roads were lined with men of crout,
On horse-back some and some afoot;

To win the day, and like brave fellows,
Send the poor Shamrocks "to the gallows"
While some, more devilish or less civil,
Would hurl them headlong "to the devil."
The air resounds with Hager spunk,
To save the chop-fallen folk of Funk;
Each bosom burned with vengeance dire,
And all besmeared with mud and mire,
The foremost of the throng came there,
The Shamrock's victory shouts to hear;
At which the folk of Funkstown rally;
Determined on another sally;
With Hagers men to join their forces,
In hopes to make up for the losses,
In hope, in turn the foe to beat,
Wipe off the stain of their defeat.
The Hager folks being mostly mounted,
Look'd much like Cavalry disjointed;
In little squads of eight or ten,
Some thirty, some of forty men;
Making in all a goodly number,
Of rude, and heterogenious lumber;[675]
And while the infantry were forming,
It seemed all Hagerstown were coming;
On every side, and flank and rear,
Thick, and more thick, the throng appear.

Charge! charge! some desperate warrior said,
Let loose the rein, and spurred the steed;
Which was no sooner said and done,
All galloped 'mongst the turnpike men,
Who fiercely met the struggling blow,
As sturdy veteran warriors do;
Their sledges plied to Hager bones,
As if on turnpike breaking stones.

Down many a noble Hager fell,
And many a turnpike man as well;
With crow-bar some made desperate plunges,
All fought most nobly in the fray,
And not a Shamrock ran away,
But struggled manfully in blood,
Or tumbled headlong in the mud;
All valiantly kept on the field,
Although at last compelled to yield.
The bravest oft' are overpowered,

---

[674] The *tertium quids*, sometimes shortened to quids, refers to various factions of the American Democratic-Republican Party during the period 1804–1812. In Latin, tertium quid means "a third something." Quid was a disparaging term that referred to cross-party coalitions of Federalists and moderate Democratic-Republicans.

[675] Heterogeneous, diverse in character or content.

And so our Shamrock heroes fared;
As so it fared with Nap we know,
In far-famed fight of Waterloo.[676]

Though beaten bravery is praised,
While coward victors are disgraced;
As proven at the Grecian pass,
By Xerxes and Leonidas.[677]

As Persians were the Hagers so?
By no means says my tale, no, no;
The combatants all acted well,
As many a deep wrought scar shall tell,
When bloody noses are forgotten,
And knowing sceptics would be doubting;[678]
When eyes, or purple, black, or blue,
Shall have regained their wonted hue;
They deep impress'd shall tell of Glory,
Confirm my bloody brilliant story.

But now the din of battle's o'er,
And wounds are wiped to bleed no more,
Though skulls, and back, and bones are sore,
Each side appoints commissioners,
To learn if possible the cause;
Why they had been involved in battle?
Why urged to try each others mettle?
As nations wise are wont to do it,
When both occasion have to rue it.

Now it appeared, the wondrous cause,
Of all this bloody doing was,
Some Negro Wench had made a paddy,
And dress'd for him a Shela lady.
Hence the great cause of all the war,
A woman, and a man of straw.

Now what can poetry avail?
Unless some moral's in the tale.

From this our shrewd folks may discern,
(And learned nations too many learn,)
'Tis better to adjust and settle
Disputes, before than after the battle.

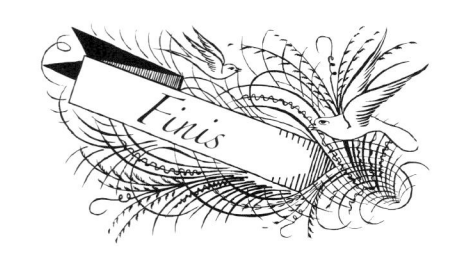

---

676   A reference to Napoleon.
677   At the Battle of Thermopyale, King Leonidas of Sparta met Xerxes I of Persia during the second Persian invasion of Greece. Xerxes was defeated but Leonidas was killed. The Battle of Thermopylae as an example of the power of a patriotic army defending its native soil.
678   Variation of skeptic.

Note: Thomas Kennedy makes frequent use of the grammatical bracket }symbol. According to Lindley Murray's *English Grammar Adapted to the Different Classes of Learners. With an Appendix, Containing Rules and Observations, for Assisting the More Advanced Students to Write with Perspicuity and Accuracy* (Collins and Perkins, NY, 1809) 271, Murray notes "A Brace } is used in poetry at the end of a triplet or three lines, which have the same rhyme."

Index

Page number in ***italics*** indicates photo.
Estates and plantations names in *italics*.

1st/2nd Maryland Battalion 204
1st Cavalry Division 126
1st Division of the Cavalry Corp 119, 136
1st Jameson's Regiment 23
1st Kentucky Brigade 104
1st Maryland Cavalry, CSA 121, 122, 127, 129, 130, 131, 132, 137, 141, 145, 149, 158, 159, 162, 163, 166, 169, 171, 172, 194, 201, 204, 206
1st Maryland Cavalry, US 100
1st Maryland Infantry 129, 204
1st North Carolina Artillery 86
1st New Jersey Infantry 119
1st Regiment Potomac Home Brigade 175
1st Rhode Island battery 88
1st Virginia Cavalry 122, 127, 130, 146, 152, 169, 171, 172, 176
1st Virginia Rockbridge Light Artillery Battery 68
2nd Division of the Army of Tennessee 151
2nd Maryland Infantry 204
2nd Regiment, Schucht's 23
2nd Regiment Wise Legion 143
2nd South Carolina Volunteer Infantry Regiment 108
2nd US Dragoons 87
2nd Virginia Cavalry 153
2nd Virginia Infantry Regiment 104, 160, 186
2nd Virginia Stonewall Brigade 109
3rd and 4th USS Artillery Regiment 120
3rd Kanawha Regiment 102
3rd Local Defense Troop of Richmond 141
3rd New York Battery 88
3rd Stembel's Regiment 23
3rd US Cavalry 155
4th Massachusetts Cavalry 151, 152, 153
4th Virginia Cavalry 90
5th North Carolina Cavalry Brigade 84
5th Corp, US 157
6th Massachusetts Militia 170
6th Texas Cavalry 138
7th Virginia Cavalry 79, 85, 159
8th Illinois Cavalry 87
8th US Cavalry 87

9th Virginia Cavalry 84
10th North Carolina Militia 120
10th North Carolina State Troops 86
11th Georgia Regiment 85, 91, 93
11th Virginia Cavalry 84
12th Illinois Infantry 152
12th Virginia Cavalry 153, 158
12th Virginia Cavalry, Laurel Brigade 79
13th Virginia Infantry 94
13th Virginia Cavalry 84
14th Corp, US 157
14th North Carolina State Troops 158
18th Georgia 91
19th Virginia 153
21st Virginia Infantry Regiment 131, 204
24th Virginia Infantry 102
26th battalion 129
30th Virginia 155
31st Virginia Infantry 175
34th Virginia Cavalry 84
34th Virginia Infantry 173
35th Virginia Cavalry 153
36th Ohio Volunteer Infantry 118
45th Virginia Infantry 117
50th North Carolina Cavalry 84
50th Regiment Armory, Baltimore MD 201
52nd Virginia Infantry 173
54th Pennsylvania Infantry 151
59th Virginia Infantry 143
123rd Ohio Infantry 151
1850 Fugitive Slave Act 17
1854 Agricultural Fair, Baltimore, MD 183
1906 Pure Food and Drug Act 192

A

Adams, John Quincy 228
Adams, Samuel Hopkins 185
Addition to Good Luck [land tract] 35
Afton, VA 165
Alexandria and Manassas Railroad 127

246 *A Rebel of '61*

Allen, Col. 115
Ambler's Bridge, VA 141
Ambler, William Marshall 141
Amelia Court House, VA 19, 148, 149
Amelia Springs, VA., battle of 149
American Antiquarian Society Library 223
American Blues Light Dragoon Cavalry 226-227
American Party [political] 24
Amherst, VA 163
Amherst Court House, VA 163
Anderson, George "Tige" Thomas 85, 86, 88, 128
Annapolis, MD 35, 72
Anne Arundel County, MD 44
Antietam, MD., battle of 7, 9, 10, 76, 82, 95, 108, 128, 149
Antietam Canal Company 37
Antietam Creek 14, 22, 34, 35, 36, 37, 38, 39, 49, 50, 51, 53, 80, 86, 95, 103, 128, 171
Antietam Woolen Manufacturing Company 36, 224
Antietam woolen mill 14, 37, 224-225
Applebee, Helen P. 209, 217
Appomattox, VA 87, 94, 102, 105, 117, 119, 127, 143, 144, 146-152, 154, 155, 157–163, 167, 172, 174, 176, 187, 194, 201, 208
Appomattox Campaign 144, 146, 150
Appomattox Court House, VA 149, 155, 157, 158, 160
Appomattox River 143, 146, 148, 149, 150, 151, 154
Archer, James J. 204
Arlington National Cemetery, VA 115
Army Disease 186
Army of the James 151, 152
Arundel Apartments building, Baltimore, MD 212
Ashby, John William 158
Ashby's Gap, VA 126
Ashby, Thomas 126
assassination of President Lincoln 165
Association of the Maryland Line 200
Augusta Stone Church, Fort Defiance, VA 112, 113
Averell, General William Woods 102, 105

B

Bai Yuka 152
Baker,
    Lavinia Thomas 88
    Samuel 88
Bakersville, MD 27, 28, 29, 48, 68, 69, 70, 95, 96

Bakersville Cemetery 48
Bakersville Road 26
Balch,
    Elizabeth Wever 179
    Lewis Penn Witherspoon 179, 180
    Thomas 180
Balch's Grist Mill 179
balloon ascension 71
Baltimore (City), MD 10, 11, 13, 18, 19, 30, 36, 38, 43, 47, 57, 61, 63, 68, 69, 72–79, 93, 100, 102, 104, 105, 109, 122, 127, 129, 138, 141, 153, 159, 160, 162, 166, 168, 170, 180–183, 186–197, 200–217, 225
Baltimore and Ohio Railroad 102
Baltimore Central Police Station 72
Baltimore County, MD 17, 162
Baltimore fire 1904 211, 212
Baltimore Light Artillery 204
Baltimore College of Dental Surgery 210
Bankard, Henry Nicholas 79
Banks,
    Harriett 48
    Jesse Dallas 48
Barboursville, VA 140
Barr, George W. 43, 226
Barr, Jacob 226
Barrot/Barrett Family 141
Barleycorn, John 48
Battle of Funks-Town, The [poem] 43, 223, 227-229, 232-245
Beachley,
    Daniel 66
    Jacob Hanson 66
Beall & Stonebraker 196
Beall, Thomas 196
bear fighting 50
Beaty, Elie 59
Beaver Creek, MD 42, 46, 78, 86, 88, 95, 224
Beaver Dam, VA 127
Bedford 106, 107
Bedford, PA 54, 60
Belcher, Lieutenant 151
Belle Grove 116
Bell, John 63, 65
Bell, William D. 228, 230-231
Benevola, MD 67
Bennett Place, Durham, NC 166
Berkeley County, WV 45, 79, 96

247

Berkley, MA 38
Berryville, VA 108
Bethlehem Iron Company 77
Bethlehem Steel 77
Betts/Betz
    Alfred 64
    George 64
    Hotel, Funkstown, MD 66, 92
    John H. 64, 92
    Mary E 64
    Robert 64
    Rose 64
    Thomas 64
big slack water 70
Billmyer Mill Road, Shepherdstown, WV 176
Bishop, Wiliam 226
black hands 194
Black, Erin *(Photographer)* 25-27, 36, 47
Black, H. Crawford 205
Black Horse Cavalry 145
Black Republicans 17
Black Rock, MD 34, 49
Blackford,
    Helena 76
    John Corbin 76, 79, 175
Blackford's Ford, MD/WV 79 Bladensburg, MD 23
Bladensburg, battle of 29
Blondell, Joan 216
Bloody Lane 128
Bloomfield, VA 127
Bluemont, VA 126
Blue Ridge Mountains 112, 113, 124, 126, 136, 163–165
Boerstler,
    Christian 39, 47, 50
    Daniel 39
    George W. 47
Boliver, MD 67
Bolton Hill district, Baltimore MD 181, 182, 201
Bonnie Brook 178
Bonnybrook RR Station, PA 178
Bonwill, C. E. H. 97
Boonsboro, MD 29, 46, 67, 80, 81-83, 87, 95, 96, 98, 100, 224
Boonsborough Turnpike 224-225
Booth, John Wilkes 163, 165
Borglum, Gutzon 119
B. & O. R. R 78

Bosler,
    Abraham 178
    Elizabeth Herman 178
    John Herman 205
    Mary Catherine 177, 178, 181, 193, 200, 209
Botany Bay 78
Boteler,
    Alexander Robinson 105, 107, 180
    Edward L. 91
    George W. 91
    Rebecca Chaney 91
    Robert H. E. 91
Botetourt County, VA 166
Boucicault, Dion 70
Bowling Green 159
Bowles, James H. 231-232
Bowman, Reverend Francis Henry 113
Bowman's Ford, VA 117
Bowman's mill, VA 117
Boydton Plank Road, VA 146, 147
Braddock, General Edward 35, 103
Braddon, Mary Elizabeth 143
Brady, Mathew 65
Brandreth, Benjamin 185
Brandy Station, VA 122
Brandy Station, VA., battle of 152
Breathed, James 152–154
Breathesville, MD 154
Breckenridge, John Cabell 26, 63–65, 104, 120, 147
Breckenridge's Division 119
Breckinridge, James 167
Brendle, A. S. 22
Bridgeport, CN 211
British Parliament 1
Brook, John 128
Brookhart, David 230
Brown,
    Barzillai 112
    Benajah 112
    Benjamin 111, 112
    Bernard 112
    Bernis 112
    Bezaleel 112
    Brightberry 112
Brown, John 17, 58, 61, 107, 220
Brown, Ridgely 127, 169, 204
Brown Memorial Presbyterian Church, Balto., MD 212

Brown, Mrs. 173
Brown, Mrs. Martin B. 204
Brown's Gap, VA 111
Browning, Robert 223
Brucetown, VA 175
Brussels carpets 36
Bryan, Goode 85, 86
Buchanan, VA 166
Buchanan, President James 26, 65, 106
Buford, John 81, 85, 87, 119, 136, 134
Buford's Cavalry 96
Bull Run, [First], battle of 67, 108
Bull Run [Second], VA., battle of 82, 156
Bunker Hill, VA 104
Burns, Robert 223
Burner's Ford, VA 122
Burnside, General Ambrose Everett 66
Butke, Gerard 192
Butternut uniforms 142, 177
Byers, George Newton 68
Byron, George Gordon (Noel) 103

C

Caldwell, Captain 151
Caldwell, John C. 128
Caldwell's brigade 128
Camp Maryland [see *Redlands*] 162
camp shoe 138
Carlisle, PA 17, 22
Carroll, Charles 225
Carroll, Mary 129
Carter,
    Margaret Smith 162
    Robert Hill 162
Cartersville, VA 142
Cary, Henry 223
Cassard, Howard 192
Cass, Lewis 63
Cattle Scales Road, Augusta County, VA 162
Cavetown, MD 86, 223
Cedar Creek 112, 116, 119, 120, 172
Cedar Creek, VA., battle of 10, 118, 120
Centerville, VA 23
Central Police Station, Baltimore, MD 73
Chambersburg, PA 43, 102, 105, 223
Chambliss, John R. 81, 83

Chancellorsville, VA., battle of 152
Chaney House, Funkstown, MD 91, 93
Chaney,
    Elias 91
    Joseph Penn 91, 93
    Mary 91
    Sarah Eastburn 91
Chantilly, VA 204
Chapman,
    Ann O. 131
    Edmund G. 131
    George H. 108
    William Henry 131
Charleston, SC 63
Charles Town, WV 62, 105, 106
Charlottesville, VA 113
Charlottesville Road, VA 163
Chesapeake and Ohio Canal 9, 58, 68, 70, 182
Chew, Roger Preston 86, 153
Chewsville, MD 83, 86
Chicago, IL 57, 62
chinaberry dye 142
Cholera 57, 58
Christiana Riot 17
Christiansburg, VA 183
Civil War monuments, Baltimore, MD 181
Clagett
    Elizabeth Ann 47
    Davey/David 42, 43, 50, 226
    Dr. 58
    Hezekiah 50
    John 43
    Sarah 44
Clagett's mill dam 53
Clay, Henry 24, 26
Clear Spring, MD 67
Clemens, Samuel L. 220
Clotworthy,
    Alexander 189
    Charles A. 189
    William Pitt 189–191
Clotworthy & Company 189, 190
Cloverdale, VA 162, 166, 167, 170, 171
Cloverdale Grist Mill 167
Clover Hill Plantation 147–148
Clover Hill Railroad, VA 148
Cloyd's Mountain, battle of 81

cock fighting 49
Cole, Henry Alexander 100
Coleman family 139
Cole's Cavalry 100
Confederate Cemetery at Appomattox, VA 158
Confederate Congress (Second), Richmond, VA 140
Confederate Society of Maryland 205
Confederate Soldier's Home, Pikesville, MD 162, 195, 201–204
Confederate veterans bazaar 160, 201
Conococheague, MD 67
Conococheague Creek 37, 94
Conococheague Manor 24
Conrad, W. B. 153
Cook,
    Colin 229-230
    David 24
Cooley,
    Benjamin C. 116
    John W. 116
Cooly House 116
Corelli, Marie 62
Cork, village of near Funkstown 42, 224-225
Cork, Ireland 57, 224
Cornelius,
    Constance Stilwell [Stonebraker] 209, 212–217
    Frederick Alfred 214–216
    Nancy Katherine [Stonebraker] 215–217
    William Stilwell [Stonebraker] 215
Corn & Flour Exchange, Baltimore, MD 78
County Cork, Ireland 42
Cox,
    Catherine Virginia 148
    Henry 148
    James 148
    John 148
    James Henry 148
    Joseph Edwin 148
    Martha Reid 148
Craig, Reverend John 113
Crampton's Gap, MD 224
Crawford, Sarah 58
Criglersville 131, 132
Crogan, Thomas 227
Croll, Reverend Phillip Columbus 20, 21
Crook, General George 102, 118, 119
Crook's Corps 119

Crystal Caverns, VA 116
Cumberland, MD 18, 30, 58, 118
Cumberland Road 42
Cumberland Valley 23
Cumberland Valley Railroad and Depot, Hagerstown, MD 73
Cunningham, Cora Cator 209, 211
Curtis,
    Ann L. 40
    Thomas 40
Custer, George Armstrong 113, 114

D

Dabney's Ferry, VA 158
Dalesville, VA 167
Dall, Horatio McPherson 131, 139
Dam #4, Potomac River, MD 9, 70, 94
Danville, VA 46
Darkesville, WV 103, 104
Davidson, Henry Brevard 127, 129
Davies, Henry E. 149
Davis,
    Angela Kirkham 66
    Jefferson Finis 96, 98, 143
    Joseph F. 66
    Lieutenant 151
Dawson City, Yukon Territory, Canada 210
Dayton, VA 114
Dearing, James 152
Deep Bottom (Second), battle of 81
Deep Creek, VA 149
Deep Gully, VA 164
Delaplane, VA [*see Piedmont*] 127
Democratic Party 24, 26, 64
Democratic-Republican Party 26
Devin, Thomas Casimer 87
De Young Museum, San Francisco, CA 141
Dickey, Paula Stoner 27
Dickinson College, PA 17
distillery 31, 48
Ditty,
    Cyrus Irving 127, 165, 166, 169
    George T. 127
    Harriet Winterson 127
Dorsey,
    Margaret D. Owens 130

Frederick 44
John Clagett 44
Gustavus Warfield 130, 162, 166, 170
Douglas,
Helena Blackford 77, 79
Henry Kyd 76
Robert 53, 76, 77, 79
Stephen Arnold. 17, 63, 65, 106
Downs,
Charles 94
Merrill 214
Downsville, MD 25, 28, 30, 68, 84, 92, 94
Downsville Pike, MD 92
Doyle, Arthur Conan 48
Doyle's River, VA 112
Drury, Ignatius 230-233
Dublin, Ireland 57
Durham, NC 166
Duval, John C. 60

E

Eakle, William H. 31
Early, Jubal Anderson 10, 102–104, 108, 110, 112, 115, 116, 118, 188, 119, 120, 122
Edge Hill 147
Edinburg, VA 175
Edwards, William Hanford "Big Bill" 214, 215
Egerton,
Abraham Dubois 76
Adeline L. P. McRea 76
Eisenminger family 41
Elezy, Major General Arnold 203
Elgar, Sir Edward 128
Ellen Rench canal boat 70
Ellisville, VA 139, 141
Ellwood 172
Elmira, NY 176
Emack, Captain 166
Emerson, Ralph Waldo 159
Emmerson,
Frank 96
Warner 96
Emmert,
Ellis 196
Mary Newcomer 100
Samuel 100

Emmert & Stonebraker 196
Emmitsburg, MD 81
Engle, Anna 21
English Chapel 40
English Church 41
Enoch, Charles 40
Episcopal Chapel 40
Establishment 36
Estill, Captain C. P. 115, 172
Eutaw Place, Baltimore, MD 182
Evans, Augusta Jane 140
Ewell, General Richard Stoddert 94, 96
Eyerly Farm 94
Eyerly, Henry 92

F

Fairfax, Thomas 171, 177
Fairfield County, PA 47
Fairfield Gap, PA 84
Fairplay, MD 24, 25, 27, 95
Falling Waters, WV 44, 94, 95, 96, 98
Farmville, VA 151, 153, 154, 155
Faukler, Michael 29
Faulkner, Charles James 106
Federalist Party 26, 228
Felker, Hester 91
Fellows, George H. 101
Ferguson, Milton Jameson 81
Ferry Hill Plantation 53, 76, 77, 79
Fidelity and Deposit Company of Maryland 181, 205, 207, 208, 213
Fielding, Henry 165
Fields, W. C. 216
Fifth Regiment Armory, Baltimore MD 201
Fincastle VA 171
First Confederate Congress 81
Fisher's Hill, battle of 10, 115, 119
Fisher's Hill, VA 108, 110, 111, 115, 116, 119, 120, 122, 130
Fisherville, VA 112
Five Forks 144, 146, 147
Flat Creek, VA 149
Fleming,
Clorinda Chaney 91
James 58
Jenrous K. 91, 93

Fogerty Rifle Company 158
Forbes, Edwin 112
Ford Depot, VA 147
Forsyth, James W. 126
Fort Defiance, VA 112, 113
Fort Duquesne, PA 35
Fort Gregg, VA 144, 145
Fort Lee, VA 145
Fort McHenry, MD 10, 72, 73, 74, 76, 78, 80, 101, 172, 208
Fort Monroe, VA 172
Fort Mountain, VA 121
Fort Stedman, VA 144, 145
Fort Sumter, SC 64
Fort Valley, VA 98, 100, 101, 102, 104, 105, 107, 108, 110, 111, 112, 113, 114, 115, 116, 120, 121, 124, 126, 127, 131
Fouke, Henry 230-232
Fountain Rock 105, 106, 107
Fox, Charles James 1
Fox Deceived 86, 89
Franklin County, PA 23
Fraser, John 41
Frederick, MD 67
Frederick County, MD 22
Fredericksburg, battle of 82, 130
French & Indian War 1, 35
Frick, George 51
Frick's foundry, Waynesbsoro PA 51
Front Royal, VA 122, 123
Frye, Dennis E. 12
Fugitive Slave Act 1850 17
Funk, Jacob 35, 36, 40, 61, 116, 220
Funk's Court House, Funkstown, MD 38
Funk's mill, Funkstown, MD 36
Funkstown 5, 6, 9, 10, 12, 24, 30, 31, 35–38, 40, 42–44, 46, 47, 49, 50, 58–62, 64, 66, 67, 70, 72, 76, 80, 82, 85–89, 91–95, 100, 101, 103, 116, 187, 188, 192–195, 220, 221, 223-225
Funkstown, MD, 1863 battle of 10, 12
Funkstown, MD, 1823 battle of 42,43, 223-229
Funkstown Library, Funkstown, MD 40
Funkstown Manufacturing Company, MD 38

G

Gabby, Joseph 231-232
Gaither, George Ridgely 170
Galloway, Benjamin 230-232
Gamble, William 87
Gardner, Alexander 145
General Order No. 76..96
Georgetown, DC 68, 69, 70
George Washington National Forest, VA 110
Georgia Tech University, Atlanta, GA 92
German Reformed Church 22, 40
Gettysburg, PA, battle of 10, 35, 81, 82, 83, 84, 85, 86, 87, 88, 91, 95, 108, 114, 143, 152, 178
Gibson, Mrs. 172
Gibson's Mill, VA 172
Gilbert,
    John 86
    Susan 86
Gilbert's Field, Funkstown, MD 89
Gill, Sommerville Pinkney 204
Gilmor, Harry 207
Goddard, John D. B. 151, 152
Goddard, Paulette 216
Godwin, Archibald 108
Goldsborough, William W. 158
Goldsmith, Oliver 165
Goode's Bridge, VA 149
Good Luck 35
Goose Creek, VA 126
Gordon 117
Gordon,
    James Bryon 84
    John Brown 116, 120, 145, 149, 157, 172
    Nathaniel 134
Gordon's Division 119
Gordonsville, VA 134, 135, 136, 139, 140
Gorsuch, Edward 17
Gougs, James P. 214
Grant 123
Grant, Lewis Addison 88
    Ulysses S 102, 107, 108, 113, 114, 124, 126, 157, 158, 161, 207
Great Falls, VA 37
Greenawalt, Philip Lorenz 21
Gregg,
    David McMurtrie 146
    John Irvin 155

252

A Rebel of '61

Grimes,
> Sarah Rentch 96
> William Henry 95, 96

Grime's Mill 96
grist mill 31, 39, 48, 50, 51, 68, 96, 167, 171, 172, 182
Grosh, Frederick 95
Grove,
> Jacob 172
> Mary Hite 172
> Thomas H. 15, 172–175

H

Hager,
> Jonathan 35
> Jonathan "Jack" Henry 15, 68, 171, 172, 174, 175
> William H. 68, 171

Hagerstown, MD 7, 9, 17, 22, 29, 30, 32, 35, 38, 40, 41, 43, 44–86, 89, 91, 92, 94, 95, 96, 100, 102, 103, 109, 122, 226
Hagerstown-Boonsboro Turnpike 95
Hagerstown Evening Globe, Hagerstown, MD 7
Hainesville, WV 96
Hall, T. B. 231-232
Hamilton, Alexander 26
Hamilton,
> Ann E. (Stonebraker) 188, 192
> Charles T. 101, 193

Hammer, Nick 58, 61, 62, 220, 221, 224
Hampton Roads Conference, Newport News, VA 140
Hancock, MD 67, 85, 105, 154
Handy, Levin 65
Hanover Dragoons 140
Hanson, John 204
Harbaugh's Valley, Frederick Co., MD 81
Harding, Joseph French 175
Hare's Hill, Petersburg, VA 145
Harman, Michael Garber 172
Harn, William A. 88
Harper,
> Ann Rebecca Shawen 100
> George Kenton 43, 228
> William 100

Harper's Ferry 61, 64, 76, 102, 111, 175, 223
Harrisburg, PA 22, 73
Harris, Joel Chandler 177
Harris Mill, Woods Mills, VA 163

Harris Mill, above Dam #4, VA 70
Harrisonburg, VA 11, 113, 114, 163, 172, 173, 174
Harrison's Landing, above Dam #4, VA 70
Hatcher's Run, VA 146, 147
Hatleberg, Dr. Steven 7
Hauck,
> Dennis William 143
> Jacob 86, 89
> Sabina Brewer 86

Heidelberg, PA 22
Heidelberg Township, PA 21
Heimiller, Herman 15, 159
Heith, Colonel 175
Hess,
> Elizabeth 23
> Jacob 23
> Polly 41

Hicks, Thomas 65
High Bridge, VA., battle of 150, 151, 153, 154, 156
Hill,
> Ambrose Powell 81, 94, 96
> Ira 38

Hite, Isaac 116
Hodges,
> William Townsend 151, 153
> George Foster 153

Hoffman,
> Clara Jane Knode 59
> Henry 189
> Henry K. 183, 187, 189, 190, 191
> John Calvin 59

Hoffman's Men's Wear, Hagerstown, MD 59
Hogmire, Conrad 86
Hollingsworth, Howard 17
Holmes, Oliver Wendell 220
Horsely,
> Florence Massie Tunstall 163, 201
> John Dunscombe 162, 63

hot-air balloon 9
House, Perry 214
Howard County Dragoons, MD 169, 170
Hundley, George Jefferson 151–153, 155
Hunter,
> Andrew 106, 107
> David 102, 106, 107
> Elizabeth Rowland 66

Hunter Hill, Charles Town, WV 107

253

Hunter, Ranney 66
Hunter's field 66
Huntingdon, PA 54
Hupp, George F. 116
Hupp's Cavern, Va 116 *see also Crystal Cavern*
Hupp's Hill, VA 116, 117
Hurlock, Madeline 217
Huyette,
    Daniel 47
    Peter Lewis 47
Hyattsville, MD 195
Hynson, Edith Dushane 207, 209, 212

I

Imboden, John Daniel 81, 82, 84
Indian, American 38, 41, 52
Indian Springs, MD 67
Inloes,
    Charles E. 129
    Joshua S. 129
Inwood, WV 104
Irish immigrants 42
Irish Road, Nelson Co., VA 164
Irvington, Baltimore, MD 127
Isenminger, Michael 225, 227
Iverson, Alfred 83
Izer,
    Jean 7
    Sandra 7, 181, 223

J

Jackson, Andrew 46, 228-229
Jackson, William Lowther 137
Jackson, General Alfred Eugene 137
Jackson, Elihu E. 203
Jackson, Thomas J. "Stonewall" 10, 86, 105, 110, 137, 149, 172
Jacksonville, IL 65
Jackson, William Henry 182
Jack's Shop, VA 134
Jameson's 1st Regiment 23
James River, VA 97, 142, 166, 172
Jarman, William 112
Jarrett's Station, Petersburg, VA 143
Jasper, John 22

Jefferson County, KY 35, 36
Jefferson County, IA 47
Jefferson County,, WV 79
Jeffersonian Republican–Democrat 26
Jeffersonian Republican Party 26
Jefferson, Thomas 26
Jenkins,
    Albert Gallatin 81
    John Carroll 204
    Lieutenant Colonel 151
Jerusalem, MD 35 *see also Funkstown, MD*
Jetersville, VA 149
Jew Bill 229-232
Jew Fish 205
John Marchmont's Legacy [novel] 143
Johnson, Anne Rosina Locher 14, 44, 45, 206
Johnson,
    Bradley Tyler 12, 14, 19, 105, 162, 200, 201, 202
    George 165
    Hard Times 45
    Henry B. 165
    James 44, 45
    John 165
    Andrew 102, 180
Johnson's Island, Sandusky Bay, OH 91
Johnston, General Joseph E. 144, 146, 162, 166, 194
Jones,
    Pembroke 132
    Albert 132
    William Edmondson "Grumble" 82, 83
    Harriet Margaret Smith 132
    John Beauchamp 60
    Sarah Ann South 95
    William 95, 96
Jones Landing, VA 97

K

Kailor, Margaret 40
Kansas-Nebraska bill 63
Kearneysville, WV 175–178
Kearns, Leon O. 31
Keedy, John 23
Keedysville, MD 23
Keedysville Road, MD 35
Keene, Laura 70
Kellar, Thomas 229-232

Keller,
- C. Harry 72
- Clara 188
- Elizabeth Newcomer 72, 91, 93
- John 91
- John Henry 72
- Mary Jane 192
- Mrs. 10
- Samuel E. 192, 193, 196
- Solomon J. 14, 72, 73, 75, 77, 78, 80, 93
- William N. 91

Keller House 91, 93
Kemp,
- Andrew 86
- David 86
- George 86

Kennedy,
- James 17
- Thomas 43, 57, 223, 225, 227-232

Kentucky Riflemen 47
Keplinger,
- Catherine Hamme 176
- John 176
- John Frederick 176

Kerfoot, Richard 66
Kernstown [Second], battle of 102, 118
Kershaw, Joseph Brevard 108, 112, 116, 117, 120
Kershner,
- Andrew 231-232
- Benjamin 226

Key, Francis Scott 73
Kilpatrick, Hugh Judson 81, 85, 96
Kilpatrick's Cavalry 81
King George III 1
King, HarrisonE. 175
King Solomon 38
King, William Rufus DeVane 52
Kline, B. Clifford 214
Kline, Adolph Lodges 214
Klondike gold fields, AK 182
Knode,
- Anne 66
- Hester Anne Stonebraker 69
- John 91
- John Eckert 68-70
- Simon 66, 92

L

Lacy, J. Horace 172
Lacy's Springs, VA 113
La Grange, Lewis County, MO 33
Lambert Automobile Company, Baltimore, MD 214
Lambert, Louis E. 214
Lamkin, James J. 192
Lamont, Daniel S. 207
Lancaster County, PA 17, 21, 22, 24
Landis,
- Anna 29
- Nancy 29

Langhorne,
- Henry Scarbrooke 167
- Mary Elizabeth 167

Lappan, Alexander H. 96
Lappan's Crossroads 24, 96
laudanum 186
Lebanon County, PA 21
Lebanon Valley, PA 20
Lee,
- Edmund Jennings II 106, 107
- Fitzhugh 83, 84, 88, 90, 108, 138, 140, 145, 151, 154, 155, 157, 159, 160, 161, 162
- Robert Edward 35, 61, 81, 83, 86, 96, 98, 102, 106, 107, 108, 114, 115, 119, 144–149, 157, 158, 159, 160, 161, 207
- Henrietta Bedinger 107

Leesburg, VA 102
Leetown, WV 105, 175, 179
Legend of Funkstown (poem) 58, 61, 220
Leitersburg, MD 81, 82, 193
Lesler, Thomas 29
Letort Springs, PA 178
Lexington, KY 26
Lexington, VA 166, 172
Liberty Mills, VA 134, 137
Lieber, Francis 101
Light, John A. 50, 71
Lilly, Samuel 29
Limerick, Ireland 57
Limited Express train 31
Lincoln, Abraham 62–65. 95, 143, 108, 163, 165, 168, 179
Little Antietam Creek, Washington County, MD 23
Little, Colonel Francis H. 91
Little Fort Valley, VA 114

255

Little Washington, VA 124, 128, 136
Liverpool, England 57
Lloyd, James 103
Locher,
    Ann Rosina 206
    George 44
    Henry S. 172
    Lucy 172
Locofoco Party 24
Locust Grove plantation 110
Logan, Catherine Virginia Cox 148
Lomax, Major General Lunsford Lindsay 84, 135, 137
Lombard, Carole 216, 217
Longfellow, Henry Wadsworth 220
Longstreet, General 85, 86, 96, 141, 147, 151, 153
Longstreet's Corp 157
Lord Baltimore 24
Los Angeles CA 216, 127
Lotteries 22
lottery ticket 21
Loudon Park Cemetery, Baltimore, MD 195, 200, 209, 211, 212
Loudon Valley, VA 126
Louisa Court House, VA 139, 141
Lovingston, VA 163
Luffman, Lieutenant Colonel William 91
Luray-Front Royal Turnpike, VA 122
Lurman, Gustav William 87
Luray Valley, VA 114, 121
Lutheran Church 40
Lydia, (St James) MD 92
Lynchburg, VA 102, 120, 135, 144, 157, 158, 159, 160, 162, 163, 167, 179
Lynchburg Road , VA 157, 158, 159

M

Macaria, Alters of Sacrifice (novel) 140
MacDermott,
    Elizabeth M. H. Mackall 193, 194
    William Mackall 194
Macgill,
    Charles Griffith Worthington 109, 111, 122
    David 122
    James 122
    William D. 122

MacKall,
    William W. 203
    Elizabeth M. H. 193
Madison Court House, VA 132, 136, 137
Madison, James 26
Manassas [First], VA., battle of 117, 143 *see also Bull Run*
Manassas [Second], VA., battle of 143 *see also Bull Run*
Manassas Gap Railroad, VA 127
Mandelbaum, Seymour 205
Manly, Basil "Baz" Charles 86, 90
Mapos Central Sugar Company 212
Marshall,
    John 85
    Thomas 85
Marsh Run, near Bakersville, MD 14, 48, 96
Marshton 96
Martin, Thomas Bryan 177
Martinsburg, WV 85, 86, 101, 103, 104, 106, 108, 177
Maryland Chapter of the Daughters of the Confederacy 178
Maryland Gazette (newspaper) 41
Maryland Line 105
Maryland Line Confederate Veterans 202
Maryland Rye Whiskey 197, 200
Maryland Steel 77
Mason and Dixon line 18, 67, 81
Mason,
    Elizabeth Ann Armistead Thomson 137
    John Thomson 72, 73, 77, 78
Massanutten Mountain, VA 110, 120, 121, 122
Massie, Florence 163
Maull, E. A. 206
Mauve, Anton 53
Maynard, Dr. Edward 164
Maynard rifle 164
McAdam, John Loudon 224
McAllion/M'Callion, Francis 227
McCausland, General John 102, 105 135, 137
McClellan, George B. 66, 128, 173, 179
McClintock, Professor John 17
McClintock Riots 17
McDaniel, Henry Dickerson 91–93
McIlhenny,
    Edmund 57
    John 57
McIntosh, John B. 108
McKinley, President William 117

McLaughlin, John 57
McLean house, Appomattox, VA 151
McLean, Wilmer 158
McMahon's Mill, near Williamsport, MD 70
McNeill, Captain John Hanson 110
MD 18, 23, 24, 44, 72, 118, 200, 201, 203, 209
Meade, George Gordon 35, 38, 95, 96
Meagher, Thomas Francis 128
Meagher's Irish Brigade 128
Meigs,
    John Rodgers 114, 115
    Montgomery Cunningham 114, 115
Melville, Herman 119
Merrick, Joseph I. 231-232
Merritt, Wesley 87, 113, 126, 127
Mexican-American War 52
Middleburg, PA 23
Middlekauff, Leonard 29
Middletown, MD 67
Middletown, VA 116, 117, 118, 119, 123, 175
Midway, VA 166
Milam's Gap, VA 131
Milford, (Overall) VA 122, 123
Milford, VA., battle of 122
Miller,
    Catharine 23
    Geo. S. 59
    John 57
Miller Park, Lynchburg, VA 162
Miller's tavern, South Mountain, MD 46
Millstone Point, MD 67
Mississippi River 33, 182
Missouri 30–33
Mitchell, Nancy 91
Moffett, William 57
Monocacy River 37
Monocacy, battle of 102, 104
Monterey Pass, PA 81, 82, 84
Montgomery, General Richard 1
Montpelier, near Clear Spring, MD 72, 137
Montpelier, Sperryville, VA 124
Montreal, Canada 57
Moorefield, WV 105
Moore, Thomas 169
Morgan Grove Park, Shepherdstown, WV 107
morphine 185, 186
Morris, William Walton 74, 77, 78

Mosby, John Singleton 124–127, 131
Mosby's Raiders/Rangers 124
Mount Crawford, VA 173
Mount Jackson, VA 110, 111, 113, 115, 175
mount moriah 14, 25
Mount Moriah 26–28, 30, 33, 48
Mount Moriah Church 26, 27
Mount Sidney, VA 173
Moyer, Daniel 40
Mudwall Jackson 137
Munford, Thomas Taylor 122, 145, 149, 154, 155, 160–162, 166, 167, 169, 170
Murray, William H. 204
Museum of the Confederacy, Richmond, VA 141
My Confederate Girlhood (novel) 148
Myers, Frank M. 153
Maryland, my Maryland (song) 168, 170

N

Nast, Thomas 226
Natural Bridge, VA 166, 171, 172
Nelson Court House, VA 163
Newcomer, Benjamin Franklin 77, 78
Newcomer,
    Catherine 78
    John 78
    Joseph 226
New Market, VA 113, 115, 175
New Market, VA., battle of 114
Newtown, VA 123, 175
Newtown History Center, Newtown, VA 175
Newtown (Stephens City) VA 79
New York City, NY 211–217
Nicewagner,/Nisewanger,
    John 175
    Mary 175
Niles, Hezekiah 228
Nolan, Nicholas Merritt 85
Norris,
    Alexander 172
    Alexander 172–174
    Elizabeth Wright 172
North Anna River, VA 139, 141
Northern Central Railroad Company 78
Northern Democratic Party 65
North Mountain, VA/WV 34, 113, 117

257

O

Oakland, MD 18
Ober, Robert 205
O'Donnell, Ganett 226
Ohio River 30, 46
Ohio State Medical Association 47
Old National Pike 30, 39, 42, 46, 49, 62, 66, 86, 87, 89, 92, 95, 103
Ogle, Alexander 229
Opequon, battle of 108, 110, 120
Orange & Alexandria Railroad (O&ARR) 127
Orange Court House, VA 135, 139
Orange Plank Road, VA 139
Orange Springs, VA 139
Orange Turnpike,vA 139
Ord, Edward Otho Cresap 151
Orndorff, Margaret 23
Orr, Lester 214
O'Sullivan, Timothy H. 139, 157
Overall, VA 122 *see also Milford*
Over,
    David 60
    David J. 60
    Elizabeth 60
    Miller 60
    Newcomer 60
    Sally 60
Owens, Margaret D. 130

P

paddy, (Irish) 42, 223-225, 227
Paine, General Clinton P. 205
Paine's Brigade of Cavalry 145
Palmetto flag, SC 64
Panic of 1857 59
Paris, France 57
Passage Creek, VA 121
Passano, Leonard 189, 190, 191
patent medicines 183, 184, 185–188, 192, 194, 195, 196
Patton, George S. 108
Payne, William Henry Fitzhugh 145
Peacock, Alexander R. 214, 215
Peale, Charles Willson 105
Pearre,
    Catherine E. 122, 123
    Catherine Marian Springer 122
    Sarah Ellen 123
    William 122, 123
Pennsylvania Railroad Station 73
Pennsylvania Steel Company 77
pensions, veterans 202
Peoria County, IL 183, 187
Pergain, Marie 217
Perry, Nat M. 214
persimmon seed buttons 142
Peterburg Fair Ground, VA 144
Petersburg, VA 139, 141, 142, 143, 144, 145, 146, 147, 150
Petersburg Courthouse, VA 144, 146
Philadelphia, PA 21, 57
Philadelphia & Reading Depot 73
Philippi, battle of 179
Physic Hill Plantation 143, 148
pickaninnies 55
Pickett, George 147
Pickett's Charge 203
Piedmont Station, VA 127, 172 *see also Delaplane, VA*
Piedmont, VA., battle of 82
Pierce, Franklin 52, 98
Pierpont, Francis H. 179
Pikesville, MD 162, 201
pitch pine sticks 144
Pleasanton, Alfred 87
Point Lookout, MD 18
polkberry juice 52
Pollard's Farm, VA 158
pontoon bridge 97
Poor House, Petersburg, VA 146
Port Republic, VA 111, 112
Potomac Company 37
Potomac River 37, 58, 68, 70, 95, 97, 100, 102, 103
powder mill 47, 50
Powell, Lewis 165
Price,
    Samuel J. 72
    William C. 158
Protzman,
    David R. 72
    Sarah Sanger 72
Pumunkey River, VA 158
Pure Food and Drug Act in 1906 185
Putnam, General Israel 26

Q

Quebec, Canada 57
Quebec, battle of 1
Queens, NY 211, 217

R

Ramsburg,
> Barbara 101
> Ezra 101
> Harriett Anne 101
> Margaret Jane Waggoner 101

Ramseur, Stephen Dodson 120
Ramseur's Division 119
Randall, James Ryder 168, 170
Rapidan River, VA 134
Rappahannock, VA 124, 131
Rakeman, Carl 224
Rawl, Major 148
Read,
> Theodore 151, *152*, 153
> Thomas Buchanan 119

reconstruction 179, 180
rectification of liquor 196–200
Rectortown, VA 128
Redlands 162, 163
Redwood,
> Allen Christian 15, 128, 133, 141, 156, 161, 206, 207, 210
> Henry 141
> James William H. "Willie" 15, 141, 143

Reel, Henry 76
Reformed Church 22, 26
Rench/Rentch,
> Andrew 96
> Angelica E. 30, 182
> Catharine 14, 24–26, 28, 33, 48, 68
> Daniel Shafer 68, 79, 139, 176
> Eleanor "Ellen" Barbary 68
> Eleanor Margaret 68
> John 26, 28, 48, 68
> Julia 93
> Sarah 96

Republican party 26, 62
Revolutionary War 1, 21, 29, 50
Rhode's Division 119
Richmond, VA 84, 108, 112, 123, 130, 136, 140-149, 155, 162, 171, 172, 176
Rickard's Tavern, New Town, VA 175
Ridgely,
> John 15, 162, 159, 160, 163, 166
> John T. 159

Ringgold, MD 72
Ringgold Manor 27
Ritchie, Sergeant Ivy 158
Roach, Elisha James 91
Roanoke, VA 166
Robertson, Beverly Holcombe 82
Robinson River, VA 131
Rochelle, VA 134
Rock Creek, Georgetown, DC 58
Rockfish Gap, VA 165
Rodes, Robert Emmet 108, 120
Rodgers, Commodore John 114
Rogers, Will 216
Rosser, Thomas Lafayette "Tex" 117, 120, 149, 151, 153, 154, 161, 162
Rourk, Patrick 227
Roxbury 22, 208
Royal Blue Train 31
Rude,
> Anders Rudolph 110
> William Steenbergen 111

Rude's Hill, VA 110, 115
Russell, David A. 108

S

Saacy, Terence *see also Seacey* 227
Safe Deposit & Trust Company, Baltimore, MD 78
Saffron, Jerome 216
Sager, Mrs. 59
Saint James School, St. James, MD 92, 95, 152, 154
Salem, VA 166, 167
Salem Village [Danvers], MA 26
Sandusky Bay, OH 91
saw mill 48, 96
Saxe, Comte Hermann Maurice de 159
Saylor's Creek, VA., battle of 108, 155
Schaeffer/Schäfer/Schäffer/Shafer/Shaffer,
> Anna Maria 23
> Alexander 14, 20, 21, 22, 23
> Barbara 23

259

Catharina 23
Catherine 26, 48
Catherine Miller 26
Elizabeth 44
family 172
Frederick 21
George 23, 36
Henry 23, 35, 36, 37, 39
Henry I. 36, 47
Henry Johan Heinrich 21, 38
John 14, 22, 23, 26, 33, 208
John Henry 22, 39, 36, 44
John George 22
John John 22–24
John Leonard 22
Johan Nicholas 21
Jonathan 19, 23, 24, 26, 35
Leonard 23
Maria Elizabeth 23
Michael 21
Rev. F. D. 22
Samuel 14, 48
Schaefferstown, PA 20, 21, 22, 23
Schleigh, John 57
Schnebly,
    John Casper 183, 187
    Mary Cornelia Stonebraker 187
Schoharie Valley, NY 21
Schooley,
    David 7
    Patricia 7
Schriver,
    Ellen 188
    Henry 193
Scott, Winfield 52
Scruggs,
    Abram E. T. 153
    Albea E. 153
    Calvin Scott 153
    Francis Parks Shepherd 153
    James Egington 153
    Joseph A 153
    Joseph C 153
    Samuel M 153
    William P. 153
Seacey, Terence, *see also Saacy* 227
Second Confederate Congress. Richmond, VA 140

Sedgwick, John 88
Semmes,
    Albert Gallatin 85
    Paul Jones 85, 86
    Raphael 85
Seneca Creek, MD 37
Sennett, Mack 216, 217
Seward, William Henry 165
Shafer, *see Schaeffer/Schäfer/Schäffer*
Sharpsburg, MD 34, 53, 76, 77 92, 94, 96, 98, 102, 223
Sharp, William 153
Shelby County, MO 30, 31
Shelby County Historical Society, Shelbina, MO 31
Shenandoah National Forest, VA 112
Shenandoah River 37, 100–102, 104, 105, 107, 108, 110–114, 116, 117, 119, 121–124, 126
Shenandoah Valley, VA 7, 11, 56, 100, 101, 102, 104, 105, 107, 108, 110–114, 124
Shepherd, Francis Parks 153
Shepherdstown, WV 27, 68, 76, 79, 102, 105–107, 123, 139, 176, 179, 181, 183, 186, 187
Sheridan, General Sheridan, Philip Henry 10, 84, 108, 110, 113–116, 118, 119, 120, 122, 123, 126, 147, 157
Sherman, William T. 166, 207
Shervin,
    Isabella 171
    Thomas 15, 171–173
shillalah 43
Shilling, Jonathan H. 58
Shipp, General Scott 206
Shulze, John Andrew 229
Signal Knob, VA 110
Silmer, John 226
Silverberg, Albert 214
Smith, Bryan C. 175
Smithburg, MD 81, 86
Smith, Dill Armor 80
Smith family 41
Smithfield, VA 175
Smith, General Samuel 162
Smith,
    John 62, 63
    John Spears 162
    Lawrence Eric 216
Smithsonian Institution, Washington, DC 206
Snider, Mrs. Daniel 57
Snickers, Edward 126

Snickers Gap, VA 126
Snickersville,VA 126
Snider, Henry 35
Snow Hill, MD 18
Society of the Army and Navy of Confederate States in the State of Maryland 200, 201
Soldiers' Relief Association 76
South,
    Barbara 42, 58
    Benjamin 61
    David 58
    John 58
    Thomas 42, 58, 61, 62, 220
Southern Aid Society 76
Southern Democrats 26, 65
Southern Relief Association 76
South Mountain, MD 34, 46, 49, 58, 66, 81, 82, 84, 101, 102, 112
South's Hotel, Funkstown, MD 61
Southside Railroad 143, 147, 151
South West Mountain, VA 135
Spangler's mill, Cedar Creek, VA 118
Spanish American War 141, 206
Sparrow, Thomas 77
Sparrows Point Steel Works, Baltimore, MD 77
spatterdashes 138
Spaw's Spring 176–178, 181
spectator spat boots 138
Speed, Attorney General James 163
Spencer carbine 158
Spencer Morton Mansion, Baltimore, MD 201
Spencer repeating rifle 158
Sperryville, VA 124, 131
Spielman Road, near Bakersville, MD 25, 26
Spotswood Hotel, Richmond, VA 145
Spotsylvania Court House, VA., battle of 88, 152
Squatter Sovereignty 63
Stanley, Kathryn 217
Stannardsville Road 132, 134
Staunton, VA 81, 112, 113, 143, 162, 166, 172, 173, 174
St. Clement's Isle, MD 18
Steele's Tavern, VA 166
Steenbergen, Elizabeth 110
Stembel's 3rd Regiment 23
Stephen, General Adam 177
Stephensburg, VA 175 *see also Newtown, VA*
Stephen's City, VA 175

Stephens, Peter 175
Stilwell,
    Constance Whitely 207, 209, 212, 213, 214, 216
    Katherine 215
    William Tecumseh 207, 212, 216
Stinson, Merry 7
St. James College, St. James, MD 92, 95, 152, 154
St. Joseph, MO 47
St. Lawrence River 57
St. Louis, MO 30
St. Mary's County, MD 18
Stockslager,
    Conrad 88
    George 92, 94
    John 222
    Peter 88
    Rebecca Laudenslager 88
    Sarah Carnes 88
Stonebraker,
    Abraham S. 10, 14, 104 113, 115, 122, 140, 141, 143, 147–149, 172, 176, 183, 186–191, 196
    Angelica E. (Rentch) 14, 28, 31, 182, 188, 192, 193, 195, 206, 208
    Anna 209, 212
    Ann C. 193
    Ann E. 101, 192
    Barbara Ann 76
    Catherine Elizabeth 47
    Catherine E. Pearre 123
    Charles 188, 192
    Charles H 200
    Charles Henry 193, 195
    Clara Ameila 31, 72, 192, 193
    Constance Whitely Stilwell 213, 214
    Cora 211, 213
    Daniel A. 193
    Edith 213
    Edward 188, 191, 193, 195, 204
    Elizabeth B. 200, 208, 209, 213, 217
    Ellen 31, 193
    Gerard/ Gerrard/Garrott/Gerhart 29, 86
    Harry 182, 200, 207, 208, 210, 212, 213
    Harry B. 209
    Harry W. 209
    Henry 14, 28, 29, 30, 31, 32, 33, 58, 59, 67, 70, 92, 100, 104, 181–196, 208
    Henry W. 209, 212

Hester Anne 68
James Bosler 182, 200, 208–213
John 100, 188, 192, 195
John R. 33, 193, 194
John W. 86, 89
Joseph Rentch 7, 9, 14, 15, 27, 29, 30, 59, 78, 80, 93, 103, 121, 160, 161, 173, 174, 178, 181, 187, 188, 191, 193–197, 200,–213, 216, 217, 220, 223-225
Joseph 207
Joseph B 208
Joseph Rentch, Jr. 182, 200, 207, 208,210, 214, 215
Mary Catherine Bosler 15, 178, 182, 207–213, 217
Mary Cornelia 183, 187
Mary Jane 188, 192, 193
Michael 14, 29, 68, 69
Samuel 183, 187, 189, 190, 191
Savilla 68, 79
William Stilwell 209, 213, 215
Stonebraker's Medicine's 183
Stonebraker Brothers Printing Company 209–213
Stonebraker Chemical Company 192
Stonebraker v. Stonebraker 183, 187, 188, 190, 196
Stonehenge, Wiltshire, England 29
Stonewall Brigade 104, 122
Stouffer/Stover
    John W. 92, 94
    Samuel 86, 87, 89
    Sarah Schneider 87, 89
Stover's woods 87
Strasburg, VA 105, 110, 111, 115, 116, 117
Stuart 130, 186
Stuart,
    Charles Calvert 204
    Corneila Lee Turberville 204
Stuart, James Ewell Brown Jeb 81–85, 92, 105, 134, 145, 152, 153
Stuart's Horse Artillery 86
Suabian Hills, Schaefferstown, PA 21
Sullivan, Franklin 75, 76
Susquehanna River, PA 21
Switzer, Jerome 29

T

Tabasco Sauce ™ 57
Taney, Roger Brooke 179

Tayloe,
    Elizabeth Henriette 167
    Emma 167
    Mary Elizabeth Langhorne 167
Taylor,
    Walter Herron 119
    President Zachary 140
Terry, William 108
Thomas, Raleigh Colston 203, 204
Thompson, Lieutenant 151
Thoreau, Henry David 56
Thornton, Colonel Francis III 124
Thornton's Gap, VA 124
Thornton's Gap Turnpike Company, VA 124
Three Top Mountain, VA 110, 117
Thulstrup, Thure de 118
Tidball, John Caldwell 87, 90
Tidball's Light Horse Artillery 87
Tilghman, Frisby 24, 39
Tinker River, VA 167
Tommytown Road, near Bakersville, MD 69
Tom's Brook, VA 110
Torbert, Alfred Thomas Archimedes 119, 136
Townsend, George Alfred 58, 61, 220
Trimble, Isaac R. 203
Tritch, William 57
Troutman, Angelica 23
Tucker, Luther 55
Tulpehocken Creek, Lebanon County, PA 21
Tunstall,
    Florence Massie 163
    John L. 163
Turnbull, William 147
Turner's Gap, MD 66

U

Union Church 40, 44, 46
Union Reformed Church 40
United Daughters of the Confederacy 163
United States arsenal, Harper's Ferry, WV 61
United States Hotel, Harrisburg, PA 73
Upperville, VA 126
Upton, Brigadier Generals Emory 108
Urz/Urtz/Utz
    Harriet Margaret Smith Jones 132
    Fielding Fisher 132

George 132
Gustavas 132
Julius 132
Michael 132
Valentia 50
Valentine, Martha Jane 193, 195
Vermont Brigade 88
Virginia Historical Society, Richmond, VA 141
Virginia Military Institute, Lexington, VA 206, 209, 210
Virginia v. West Virginia 179, 180

W

Wade, Captain 69, 70
Waggoner, Margaret Jane 101
Walden, Gregory R. 137
Walke,
    John Robertson 143
    John Wistar 143
Warfield,
    Edwin 205
    George 205
War of 1812 24
Washburn, Colonel Francis 151, 152
Washington, DC 31, 57, 58, 124
Washington, George 1, 22, 41, 124, 171
Washington Hotel, Hagerstown, MD 61, 63
Washington Riflemen 47
Waterman, Richard 88
Watters, Lieutenant James D. 121, 122
Watts,
    Lydia 95
    Thomas B. 94, 95
    William 95
Waynesboro, PA 51, 162, 163, 165, 166
Waynesboro, VA 112
Webb Family 142
Wenger, Diane 20
Western Maryland Railroad 73
West Greenwich, CT 26
Wever, Elizabeth 179
Wharton,
    Elizabeth Ann Armistead Thomson Mason 137
    Gabriel Colvin 117
    John "Jack" Thomson Mason Wharton 138
    John Overton 137
    William Fitzhugh 15, 108, 116, 137–139
Wharton's Cavalry 138
Wheeler, James R. 205
Wheeling, WV 30, 32, 46, 179
Whelan, Thomas A. 205
Whig Party 52, 230-231
White,
    Abraham 59
    Caroline 59
    Isaac S. 232
    William Wilkinson 85, 86, 88
White House, VA 145
Whittingham, Bishop William 92
Whyte, Governor William Pinkney 73
Wickham, Williams Carter 140, 153
Wickham's Brigade 140
Wicks, Elizabeth H. 193, 195
Wight, John H. 205
Wilderness Campaign 82
Williams,
    Catherine 72, 80
    Elie 229-231
    Ella 80
    Ellen 72
    Josiah E. 14, 72, 75, 78, 80
    Mary 72
    Otho Holland 230
Williamson, Jacob 70
Williamsport, MD 24, 43, 58, 81, 83, 84, 85, 92, 94, 95, 96, 97, 98, 103
Williams, Roger 88
Willis Family 140
Wilson, James H. 122
Wiltshire, England 29
Winchester, VA 102, 104, 108, 109, 112, 118, 119, 120, 136, 175
Winchester (Third), VA., battle of 138
Winchester, battle of 108, 119
Winchester Repeating Arms Company 158
Winson, Rose 216
Winterpock, Chesterfield Co., VA 148
Winters, Leota 217
Witcher, Vincent Addison 84, 87
Witkowski, Karl 56
Woburn Manor, south of Downsville, MD 68
Wolfsville, MD 101
Wolftown, VA 132, 134

263

Wood, Frederick 77
Wood, Nancy 138
Woodlands, (The), Amelia County, VA 19
Woods Mill, Nelson County, VA 163, 164
Woodstock, VA 110, 113, 115
Woody, William E. 79
Wooldridge, Lieutenant Colonel William B. 90
woolen factory, Funkstown, MD 47
Wool, Major General John Ellis 75, 78
Woolman, Morton 214
Worchester County, MD 18
Wroe, Doctor John Absolom 91

Y

Yager riflemen 43, 225, 227
Yanceyville, VA 141
Yates, William 229
Yellow Tavern, VA., battle of 84, 130, 152
York River, VA 145
Young, James Sterling 23

Z

Wood
    Nancy 138
    Zach 138
Zeiglar Pure Rye 196
Ziegfeld Follies, NY 216
Zion Church 81
Zollickoffer, Dr. Henry Fletcher 187